Introduction to C++

Introduction to C++

Steve Heller
Chrysalis Software Corporation

ACADEMIC PRESS

San Diego   London   Boston   New York   Sydney   Tokyo   Toronto

Copyright © 1997 by Academic Press
Copyright © 1997 by Chrysalis Software Corporation

ACADEMIC PRESS
525 B Street, Suite 1900, San Diego, CA 92101-4495, USA
1300 Boylston Street, Chestnut Hill, MA 02167, USA
http://www.apnet.com

ACADEMIC PRESS LIMITED
24–28 Oval Road, London NW1 7DX, UK
http://www.hbuk.co.uk/ap/

Library of Congress Cataloging-in-Publication Data

Heller, Steve, 1949 Apr. 17–
    Introduction to C++ / Steve Heller.
      p. cm.
    Includes bibliographical references and index.
    ISBN 0-12-339099-0 (alk. paper)
    1. C++ (Computer program language) I. Title.
QA76.73.C15H46 1997
  005.13′3—dc21   97-10071
                                             CIP

Printed in the United States of America
97 98 99 00 01 IC 9 8 7 6 5 4 3 2 1

Contents

Chapter 5: Functional Literacy   113

Chapter 8: Down the Garden Path 261

Chapter 9: Stocking Up 323

Figures

xvii

xxii

This book is dedicated to Susan Patricia Caffee, the light of my life.
Without her, this book would not be what it is; even more important,
I would not be what I am: a happy man.

Acknowledgements

I'd like to thank Andrew Morrow for his help with arcane details of formatting in Sprint, the word processor used to produce this manuscript.

My students at the University of Texas at Dallas and Collin County Community College have contributed valuable comments that have helped me refine the discussion in this book.

Chuck Glaser, my editor at Academic Press, has been everything that a technical author could hope for (and most don't get).

Finally, I'd like to thank all of the managers who convinced me that there had to be a better way to make a living than commercial software development.

Preface

Is this book for you? If you're a programmer in a language other than C++ and want to upgrade your skills, then the answer is yes. But what if you have no previous programming experience? In that case, here's a little quiz that may help you decide:

1. Do you want to know how the programs in your computer work and how to write some of your own?
2. Are you willing to exert yourself mentally to learn a complex technical subject?
3. Do you have a sense of humor?

If you've answered yes to these questions and follow through with the effort required, then you will get a lot out of this book.

The common wisdom states that programming is a difficult subject that should be reserved for a small number of specialists. One of the main reasons that I have written this book is that I believe this attitude is wrong; it is possible, and even desirable, for you to learn how programs work and how to write them. Those who don't understand how computers perform their seemingly magical feats are at an increasing disadvantage in a society ever more dependent on these extraordinary machines.

Regardless of the topic, I can see no valid reason for a textbook to be stuffy and dry, and I've done everything possible to make this one approachable. However, don't let the casual tone fool you into thinking that the subject is easy; there is no "royal road" to programming, any more than there is to geometry. Especially if you have no prior experience in programming, this book will stretch your mind more than virtually any other subject you could study.

While we're on the topic of your studying, this would be a good time to tell you how to get updates and help with any errors you might find in the book or any other questions you might have. The best way is to visit my WWW page:

http://ourworld.compuserve.com/homepages/steve_heller.

If you don't have WWW access, you can write to me care of my publishers at the following address:

Steve Heller
c/o Academic Press
1300 Boylston Street
Chestnut Hill, MA 02167

Now that those preliminaries are out of the way, let's proceed.

About the Author

Steve Heller had always been fascinated by writing. In his childhood days in the 1950s and 1960s, he often stayed up far past his bedtime reading science fiction. Even in adulthood, if you came across him in his off-hours, he was more likely to be found reading a book than doing virtually anything else.

After college, Steve got into programming more or less by accident; he was working at an actuarial consulting firm and was selected to take charge of programming on their time-sharing terminal, because he was making much less than most of the other employees. Finding the programming itself to be more interesting than the actuarial calculations, he decided to become a professional programmer.

Until 1984, Steve remained on the consuming side of the writing craft. Then one day he was reading a magazine article on some programming-related topic and said to himself, "I could do better than that". With encouragement from his wife of the time, he decided to try his hand at technical writing. Steve's first article submission — to the late lamented *Computer Language Magazine* — was published, as were a dozen more over the next ten years.

But although writing magazine articles is an interesting pastime, writing a book is something entirely different. Steve got his chance at this new level of commitment when Harry Helms, then an editor for Academic Press, read one of his articles in *Dr. Dobb's Journal* and wrote him a letter asking whether he would be interested in writing a book for AP. He answered, "Sure, why not?", not having the faintest idea of how much work he was letting himself in for.

The resulting book, *Large Problems, Small Machines* received favorable reviews for its careful explanation of a number of facets of program optimization, and sold a total of about 20,000 copies within a year after publication of the second edition, entitled *Efficient C/C++ Programming*.

By that time, Steve was hard at work on his next book, *Who's Afraid of C++*, intended to make object-oriented programming intelligible to anyone from the sheerest novice to the programmer with years of experience in languages other than C++. To make sure that his exposition was clear enough for the novice, he posted a message on CompuServe requesting the help of someone new to programming. The responses included one from a woman named Susan Spino, who ended up contributing a great deal to the book. Her contribution was wonderful, but not completely unexpected.

What *was* unexpected was that Steve and Susan would fall in love during the course of this project, but that's what happened. Since she lived in Texas and he lived in New York, this posed some logistic difficulties. The success of his previous book now became extremely important, as it was the key to Steve's becoming a full-time writer. Writers have been "telecommuting" since before the invention of the telephone, so his conversion from "programmer who writes" to "writer" made it possible for him to relocate to her area, which he promptly did.

Steve and Susan plan to be married in June of 1997.

Introduction to C++

Chapter 1

Prologue

Introduction to Programming

"Begin at the beginning, and go on till you come to the end: then stop." This method of telling a story is as good today as it was when the King of Hearts prescribed it to the White Rabbit in *Alice in Wonderland*. In this book, we must begin with you, the reader, since my job is to explain a technical subject to you. It might appear that I'm at a severe disadvantage; after all, I've never met you.

Nevertheless, I can make some pretty good guesses about you. You almost certainly own a computer and know how to use its most common application, word processing. If you use the computer in business, you probably also have an acquaintance with spreadsheets and perhaps some database experience as well. Now you have decided to learn how to program the computer yourself rather than relying completely on programs written by others. On the other hand, you might be a student using this book as a text in an introductory course on programming. In that case, you'll be happy to know that this book isn't written in the dry, overly academic style employed by many textbook writers. I hope that you will enjoy reading it as much as my "test readers" have.

Whether you are using this book on your own or in school, there are many good reasons to learn how to program. You may have a problem that hasn't been solved by commercial software; you may want a better understanding of how commercial programs function so you can figure out how to get around their shortcomings and peculiarities; or perhaps you're just curious about how computers perform their seemingly magical feats. Whatever the initial reason, I hope you come to appreciate the great creative possibilities opened up by this most ubiquitous of modern inventions.

Of course, it's also possible that you already know how to program in another language and are using this book to learn how to do so in C++. If so, you'll have a head start; I hope that you'll learn enough to make it worth your while to wade through some material you already know. In any event, before we begin, we should agree on definitions for some fundamental words in the computing field.

Why start with words? Because knowing the correct meaning of the words you're reading is really important, even more so than you might suspect. If you don't understand words as they are used in a subject, you'll get lost very quickly and decide that the subject is "hard" or "not for you", when all along the problem may be just the words that you don't know. We'll start with some definitions of technical words that you'll need to know; however, if at any time you run across a word that you're not sure you understand, take the time to find a definition, understand it, and use the word in sentences until you're sure you have it.

Many of the technical words used in this book are in the Glossary at the end of the book; it is also very helpful to have a good technical dictionary of computer terms. You should also be aware that the word giving you trouble is not necessarily a technical word; it can be a very simple word in plain English. In any case, you should not pass by a word you don't understand; you'll just get confused later. Make sure you understand what you're reading, and you'll have an easier time learning.

Of course, you may not be able to remember all of these technical definitions the first time through. If you can't recall the exact meaning of one of these terms, just look up the word or phrase in the index; it will direct you to the page where the definition is stated. You could also look in the Glossary at the end of the book, which lists key technical terms in alphabetical order.

To give you some idea of what to expect while you're reading, I have provided a list of objectives at the beginning of each chapter after this one. For the moment, let's start with definitions of some programming terms.

Definitions

Hardware refers to the physical components of a computer, the ones you can touch. Examples include the keyboard, the monitor, and the printer.

Software refers to the other, nonphysical components of a computer, the ones you cannot touch. If you can install it on your hard disk, it's software. Examples include a spreadsheet, a word processor, and a database program.

An **algorithm** is a set of precisely defined steps to calculate an answer to a problem or set of problems, which is guaranteed to arrive at such an answer eventually. As this implies, a set of steps that might never end is *not* an algorithm.

Programming is the art and science of solving problems by the following procedure:

1.   Find or invent a general solution to a class of problems.
2.   Express this solution as an algorithm or set of algorithms.
3.   Translate the algorithm(s) into terms so simple that a stupid machine like a computer can follow them to calculate the specific answer for any specific problem in the class.

An **application program** is a program that actually accomplishes some useful or interesting tasks. Examples include inventory control, payroll, and game programs.

`Problem`
`Algorithms`
`C++`
`Executable`
`Hardware`

Data are the pieces of information that are operated on by programs. The singular of "data" is "datum"; however, the word "data" is commonly used as both singular and plural.

Source code is a program in a form suitable for reading and writing by a human being.

An **executable program** (or just an *executable*, for short) is a program in a form suitable for running on a computer.

Object code is a program in a form suitable for incorporation into an executable program.

Compilation is the process of translating source code into object code. Almost all of the software on your computer was created by this process.

A **compiler** is a program that performs compilation as defined above.

Compile time means "while the compiler is compiling the source code of a program".

How to Write a Program

Now you have a definition of programming. Unfortunately, however, this doesn't tell you how to write a program. The process of solving a problem by programming in C++ follows these steps:[1]

Problem: After discussions between the user and the programmer, the programmer defines the problem precisely.

Algorithms: The programmer finds or creates algorithms that will solve the problem.

C++:   The programmer implements these algorithms as source code in C++.

Executable: The programmer runs the C++ compiler, which must already be present on the programmer's machine, to translate the source code into an executable program.

```
Problem
Algorithms
C++
Executable
Hardware
```

Hardware: The user runs the resulting executable program on a computer.

These steps advance from the most abstract to the most concrete, which is perfectly appropriate for an experienced C++ programmer. However, if you're using this book to learn how to program in C++, obviously you're not an experienced C++ programmer, so before you can follow this path to solving a problem you're going to need a fairly thorough grounding in all of these steps. It's not really feasible to discuss each step exhaustively before going to the next one,[2] so I've created a little "step indicator", which you'll see on each page of the text, with the currently active step shown in bold. For example, when we're discussing algorithms, the indicator will display **Algorithms** in bold.

The five steps of this indicator correspond to the five steps in problem solving just defined. I hope this device will make it easier

---

1. This description is actually a bit oversimplified. We'll examine another step in the process of making an executable program, called *linking*, in a later chapter.

2. The steps don't actually occur in such an exact progression anyway. In real life most programs are written in an incremental process as assumptions are changed and errors are found and corrected.

for you to follow the sometimes tortuous path to programming knowledge.

The steps for solving a problem via programming might sound reasonable in the abstract, but that doesn't mean that you can follow them easily without practice. Assuming that you already have a pretty good idea of what the problem is that you're trying to solve, the Algorithms step is likely to be the biggest stumbling block. Therefore, it might be very helpful to go into that step in a bit more detail.

Baby Steps

If we already understand the problem we're going to solve, the next step is to figure out a plan of attack, which we will then break down into small enough steps to be expressed in C++. This is called **stepwise refinement**, since we start out with a "coarse" solution and refine it until the steps are within the capability of the C++ language. For a complex problem, this may take several intermediate steps, but let's start out with a simple example. Say that we want to know how much older one person is than another. We might start with the following general outline:

Problem
Algorithms
C++
Executable
Hardware

1. Get ages from user.
2. Calculate difference of ages.
3. Print the result.

This can in turn be broken down further as follows:

1. Get ages from user.
   a. Ask user for first age.
   b. Ask user for second age.
2. Subtract second age from first age.
3. Print result.

This looks okay, except that if the first person is younger than the second one, then the result will be negative. That may be acceptable. If so, we're just about done, since these steps are simple enough for us to translate them into C++ fairly directly. Otherwise, we'll have to modify our program to do something different depending on which age is higher. For example,

1. Get ages from user.

       a.   Ask user for first age.
       b.   Ask user for second age.
2.   Compute difference of ages.
       a.   If first age is greater than second, subtract second age from first age.
       b.   Otherwise, subtract first age from second age.
3.   Print result.

You've probably noticed that this is a much more detailed description than would be needed to tell a human being what you want to do. That's because the computer is extremely stupid and literal: it does only what you tell it to do, not what you meant to tell it to do. Unfortunately, it's very easy to get one of the steps wrong, especially in a complex program. In that case, the computer will do something ridiculous, and you'll have to figure out what you did wrong. This "debugging", as it's called, is one of the hardest parts of programming. Actually, it shouldn't be too difficult to understand why that is the case. After all, you're looking for a mistake you've made yourself. If you knew exactly what you were doing, you wouldn't have made the mistake in the first place.

```
Problem
Algorithms
C++
Executable
Hardware
```

I hope that this brief discussion has made the process of programming a little less mysterious. In the final analysis, it's basically just logical thinking.[3]

On with the Show

Now that you have some idea how programming works, it's time to see exactly how the computer actually performs the steps in a program, which is the topic of Chapter 2.

---

3. Of course, the word *just* in this sentence is a bit misleading; taking logical thinking for granted is a sure recipe for trouble.

Chapter 2

Hardware Fundamentals

Getting Started

Like any complex tool, the computer can be understood on several levels. For example, it's entirely possible to learn to drive an automobile without having the slightest idea of how it works. The analogy with computers is that it's relatively easy to learn how to use a word processor without having any notion of how such programs work. On the other hand, programming is much more closely analogous to designing an automobile than it is to driving one. Therefore, we're going to have to go into some detail about the internal workings of a computer, not at the level of electronic components, but at the lowest level accessible to a programmer.

This is a book on learning to program in C++, not on how a computer works.[1] Given that goal, it might seem better to start with the C++ language and eliminate this detour into the hardware, and indeed many (perhaps most) books on C++ do exactly that. However, in working out in detail how I'm going to explain C++ to you, I've come to the conclusion that it would be virtually impossible to explain *why* certain features of the language exist and how they actually work without your understanding *how* they relate to the underlying computer hardware.

I haven't come to this position by pure logical deduction, either. In fact, I've worked backward from the concepts that you will need to know to program in C++ to the specific underlying information that you will have to understand first. I'm thinking in particular of one

---

1. While some people believe that you should learn C before you learn C++, obviously I'm not one of those people. For that matter, neither is the inventor of C++, Bjarne Stroustrup. On page 169 of his book, *The Design and Evolution of C++*, he says, "Learn C++ first. The C subset is easier to learn for C/C++ novices and easier to use than C itself."

specific concept that is supposed to be extremely difficult for a beginning programmer in C++ to grasp. With the approach we're taking, you shouldn't have much trouble understanding this concept by the time you get to it in Chapter 7; it's noted as such in the discussion there. I'd be interested to know how you find my explanation there, given the background that you'll have by that point; don't hesitate to e-mail me about this topic (or any other, for that matter).[2]

On the other hand, if you're an experienced programmer, a lot of this will be just review for you. Nonetheless, it can't hurt to go over the basics one more time before diving into the ideas and techniques that make C++ different from other languages.

Now let's begin with some definitions and objectives for this chapter.

Definitions

```
Problem
Algorithms
C++
Executable
Hardware
```

A **digit** is one of the characters used in any positional numbering system to represent all numbers starting at 0 and ending at one less than the base of the numbering system. In the decimal system, there are ten digits, 0 through 9, and in the hexadecimal system there are sixteen digits, 0 through 9 and a through f.

A **binary** number system is one that uses only two digits, 0 and 1.

A **hexadecimal** number system is one that uses 16 digits, 0–9 and a–f.

A **cache** is a small amount of fast memory where frequently used data is stored temporarily.

Objectives of This Chapter

By the end of this chapter, you should

1. Understand the programmer's view of the most important pieces of hardware in your computer.

---

2. The concept I'm referring to is the *pointer*, in case you want to make a note of it here.

2.   Understand the programmer's view of the most important pieces of software in your computer.
3.   Be able to solve simple problems using both the binary and hexadecimal number systems.
4.   Understand how whole numbers are stored in the computer.

Behind the Curtain

First we'll need to expand on the definition of *hardware*. As noted earlier, *hardware* means the physical components of a computer, the ones you can touch.[3] Examples are the monitor (which displays your document while you're working on it), the keyboard, the printer, and all of the interesting electronic and electromechanical components inside the case of your computer.

Right now, we're concerned with the programmer's view of the hardware. The hardware components of a computer with which you'll be primarily concerned are the disk, RAM (short for Random Access Memory), and last but certainly not least, the CPU (short for Central Processing Unit). We'll take up each of these topics in turn.

Problem
Algorithms
C++
Executable
Hardware

Disk

When you sit down at your computer in the morning, before you turn it on, where are the programs you're going to run? To make this more specific, suppose you're going to use a word processor to revise a letter you wrote yesterday before you turned the computer off. Where is the letter, and where is the word processing program?

You probably know the answer to this question; they are stored on a hard disk inside the case of your computer. Disks use magnetic recording media, much like the material used to record speech and music on cassette tapes, to store information in a way that will not be lost when the power is turned off. How exactly is this information (which may be either executable programs or data such as word processing documents) stored?

We don't have to go into excruciating detail on the storage mechanism, but it is important to understand some of its characteristics. A disk consists of one or more circular *platters*,

---

3. Whenever I refer to a *computer*, I mean a modern microcomputer capable of running MS-DOS; such computers are commonly referred to as *PCs*. Most of the fundamental concepts are the same in other kinds of computers, but the details differ.

which are extremely flat and smooth pieces of metal or glass covered with a material that can be very rapidly and accurately magnetized in either of two directions, "north" and "south". To store large amounts of data, each platter is divided into many millions of small regions, each of which can be magnetized in either direction independent of the other regions. The magnetization is detected and modified by *recording heads*, similar in principle to those used in tape cassette decks. However, in contrast to the cassette heads, which make contact with the tape while they are recording or playing back music or speech, the disk heads "fly" a few millionths of an inch away from the platters, which rotate at very high velocity.

The separately magnetizable regions used to store information are arranged in groups called *sectors*, which are in turn arranged in concentric circles called *tracks*. All tracks on one side of a given platter (a *recording surface*) can be accessed by a recording head dedicated to that recording surface; each sector is used to store some number of *bytes* of the data, generally a few hundred to a few thousand. "Byte" is a coined word meaning a group of 8 *bi*nary dig*its*, or *bits* for short.[4] You may wonder why the data isn't stored in the more familiar decimal system, which of course uses the digits from 0 through 9. This is not an arbitrary decision; on the contrary, there are a couple of very good reasons that data on a disk is stored using the binary system, in which each digit has only two possible states, 0 and 1. One of these reasons is that it's a lot easier to determine reliably whether a particular area on a disk is magnetized "north" or "south" than it is to determine 1 of 10 possible levels of magnetization. Another reason is that the binary system is also the natural system for data storage using electronic circuitry, which is used to store data in the rest of the computer.

While magnetic storage devices have been around in one form or another since the very early days of computing, the advances in technology just in the last 10 years have been staggering. To comprehend just how large these advances have been, we need to define the term used to describe storage capacities: the megabyte. The standard engineering meaning of *mega* is "multiply by 1 million", which would make a megabyte equal to 1 million (1,000,000) bytes. As we have just seen, however, the natural number system in the computer field is binary. Therefore, "one megabyte" is often used instead to specify the nearest "round"

Problem
Algorithms
C++
Executable
Hardware

---

4. In some old machines, bytes sometimes contained more or less than 8 bits, but the 8-bit byte is virtually universal today.

number in the binary system, which is 2^20 (2 to the 20th power), or 1,048,576 bytes.[5]

1985, a Space Odyssey

With that detail out of the way, we can see just how far we've come in a short period of time. In 1985, I purchased a 20 megabyte disk for $900 ($45 per megabyte); its **access time**, which measures how long it takes to retrieve data, was approximately 100 milliseconds (milli = 1/1000, so a millisecond is one thousandth of a second). In January 1997, a 5100 megabyte disk cost as little as $470, or approximately 9 *cents* per megabyte; in addition to this almost 500-fold decrease in cost, its access time was 10 milliseconds, which is approximately 10 times as fast as the old disk. Of course, this significantly understates the amount of progress in technology in both economic and technical terms. For one thing, a 1997 dollar is worth considerably less than a 1985 dollar. In addition, the new drive is superior in every other measure as well: it is much smaller, more reliable, and energy-efficient than the old one.

This tremendous increase in performance and decrease in price has prevented the long-predicted demise of disk drives in favor of new technology. However, the inherent speed limitations of disks still require us to restrict their role to the storage and retrieval of data for which we can afford to wait a relatively long time.

You see, while 10 milliseconds isn't very long by human standards, it is a long time indeed to a modern computer. This will become more evident as we examine the next essential component of the computer, the *RAM*.

```
Problem
Algorithms
C++
Executable
Hardware
```

RAM

The working storage of the computer, where data and programs are stored while we're using them, is called **RAM**, an acronym for Random Access Memory.[6] For example, your word processor is

---

5. In case you're not familiar with the ^ notation, the number on its right indicates how many copies of the number to the left have to be multiplied together to produce the final result. For example, 2^5 = 2 * 2 * 2 * 2 * 2, whereas 4^3 = 4 * 4 * 4. Of course, I've just introduced another symbol you might not be familiar with: the * is used to indicate multiplication in programming.

6. *RAM* is sometimes called "internal storage", as opposed to "external storage", that is, the disk.

stored in RAM while you're using it. The document you're working on is likely to be there as well unless it's too large to fit all at once, in which case parts of it will be retrieved from the disk as needed. Since we have already seen that both the word processor and the document are stored on the disk in the first place, why not leave them there and use them in place, rather than copying them into RAM?

The answer, in a word, is *speed*. RAM is physically composed of millions of microscopic switches on a small piece of silicon known as a *chip*: a 4-megabit RAM chip has approximately 4 million of them.[7] Each of these switches can be either on or off; we consider a switch that is "on" to be storing a 1 and a switch that is "off " to be storing a 0. Just as in storing information on a disk, where it was easier to magnetize a region in either of two directions, it's a lot easier to make a switch that can be turned on or off reliably and quickly than one that can be set to any value from 0 to 9 reliably and quickly. This is particularly important when you're manufacturing millions of them on a silicon chip the size of your fingernail.

A main difference between disk and RAM is what steps are needed to access different areas of storage. In the case of the disk, the head has to be moved to the right track (an operation known as a *seek*), and then we have to wait for the platter to spin so that the region we want to access is under the head (called *rotational delay*). On the other hand, with RAM, the entire process is electronic; we can read or write any byte immediately as long as we know which byte we want. To specify a given byte, we have to supply a unique number called its **memory address**, or just **address** for short.

`Problem`
`Algorithms`
`C++`
`Executable`
`Hardware`

Return to Sender, Address Unknown

In case the notion of an address of a byte of memory on a piece of silicon is too abstract, it might help to think of an address as a set of directions as to how to find the byte being addressed, much like directions to someone's house. For example, "Go three streets down, then turn left. It's the second house on the right". With such directions, the house number wouldn't need to be written on the house. Similarly, the memory storage areas in RAM are addressed by position; you can think of the address as telling the hardware which street and house you want, by giving directions similar in concept to

---

7. Each switch is made of several transistors. Unfortunately, an explanation of how a transistor works would take us too far afield. Consult any good encyclopedia, such as the *Encyclopedia Britannica*, for this explanation.

the preceding example. Therefore, it's not necessary to encode the addresses into the RAM explicitly.

Since it has no moving parts, storing and retrieving data in RAM is much faster than waiting for the mechanical motion of a disk platter turning.[8] As we've just seen, disk access times are measured in milliseconds, or thousandths of a second. However, RAM access times are measured in **nanoseconds** (abbreviated *ns*); *nano* means one billionth. In early 1997, a typical speed for RAM was 70 ns, which means that it is possible to read a given data item from RAM about 150,000 times as quickly as from a disk. In that case, why not use disks only for permanent storage and read everything into RAM in the morning when we turn on the machine?

The reason is cost. In early 1997, the cost of 64 megabytes of RAM was approximately $285. For that same amount of money, you could have bought a disk with a capacity of about 2500 megabytes! Therefore, we must reserve RAM for tasks where speed is all-important, such as running your word processing program and holding a letter while you're working on it. Also, since RAM is an electronic storage medium (rather than a magnetic one), it does not maintain its contents when the power is turned off. This means that if you had a power failure while working with data only in RAM, you would lose everything you had been doing. This is not merely a theoretical problem, by the way; if you don't remember to save what you're doing in your word processor once in a while, you might lose a whole day's work from a power outage of a few seconds.[9]

Problem
Algorithms
C++
Executable
Hardware

Before we get to how a program actually works, we need to develop a better picture of how RAM is used. As I've mentioned before, you can think of RAM as consisting of a large number of bytes, each of which has a unique identifier called an *address*. This address can be used to specify which byte we mean, so the program might specify that it wants to read the value in byte 148257, or change the value in byte 66666.

This is all very well, but it doesn't answer the question of how the program actually uses or changes values in RAM, or performs

---

8. There's also another kind of electronic storage, called **ROM**, for Read-Only Memory; as its name indicates, you can read from it, but you can't write to it. This is used for storing permanent information, such as the program that allows your computer to read a small program from your *boot disk*; that program, in turn, reads in the rest of the data and programs needed to start up the computer. This process, as you probably know, is called *booting* the computer. In case you're wondering where that term came from, it's short for *bootstrapping*, a reference to the notion of pulling yourself up by your bootstraps.

9. Most modern word processors can automatically save your work once in a while, for this very reason as well as to protect you against system crashes. I heartily recommend using this facility; it's saved my bacon more than once.

arithmetic and other operations; that's the job of the CPU, which we will take up next.

The CPU

The **CPU** (Central Processing Unit) is the "active" component in the computer. Like RAM, it is physically composed of millions of microscopic transistors on a chip; however, the organization of these transistors in a CPU is much more complex than on a RAM chip, as the latter's functions are limited to the storage and retrieval of data. The CPU, on the other hand, is capable of performing dozens or hundreds of different fundamental operations called *machine instructions*, or just *instructions* for short. While each instruction performs a very simple function, the tremendous power of the computer lies in the fact that the CPU can perform (or *execute*) tens or hundreds of millions of these instructions per second.[10]

Problem
Algorithms
C++
Executable
Hardware

These instructions fall into a number of categories: instructions that perform arithmetic operations such as adding, subtracting, multiplying, and dividing; instructions that move information from one place to another in RAM; instructions that compare two quantities to help make a determination as to which instructions need to be executed next; instructions that implement that decision; and other, more specialized types of instructions.

Of course, adding two numbers together (for example) requires that the numbers be available for use. Possibly the most straightforward way of making them available is to store them in and retrieve them from RAM whenever they are needed, and indeed this is done sometimes. However, as fast as RAM is compared to disk drives (not to mention human beings), it's still pretty slow compared to modern CPUs. For example, the computer on which I started to write this book had a 66 megahertz (abbreviated MHz) CPU, which can execute up to 66 million instructions per second (abbreviated MIPS),[11] or one instruction approximately every 16 ns.[12]

---

10. Each type of CPU has a different set of instructions, so that programs compiled for one CPU cannot in general be run on a different CPU. Some CPUs, such as the very popular 80x86 ones from Intel, fall into a "family" of CPUs in which each new CPU can execute all of the instructions of the previous family members. This allows upgrading to a new CPU without having to throw out all of your old programs, but correspondingly limits the ways in which the new CPU can be improved without affecting this "family compatibility".

11. You shouldn't get the idea from the coincidence of the megahertz and MIPS numbers that 1 MIPS means the same as 1 MHz. It so happens that, for the 486, the fastest instructions take one clock cycle, and only one instruction can finish executing in each clock cycle. Therefore, if most of the instructions your program executes are one-cycle instructions, you

To see why RAM is a bottleneck, let's calculate how long it would take to execute an instruction if all the data had to come from and go back to RAM. A typical instruction would have to read some data from RAM and write its result back there; first, though, the instruction itself has to be loaded (or *fetched*) into the CPU before it can be executed. Let's suppose we have an instruction in RAM, reading one data item also in RAM, and writing the result back to RAM. Then the minimum timing to do such an instruction could be calculated as in Figure 2.1.

```
Time         Function

  70 ns      Read instruction from RAM
  70 ns      Read data from RAM
  16 ns      Execute instruction
  70 ns      Write result back to RAM
------
 226 ns      Total instruction execution time
```

Figure 2.1: RAM vs. CPU speeds

To compute the effective MIPS of a CPU, we divide 1 second by the time it takes to execute one instruction. Given the assumptions in this example, the CPU could execute only about 4.5 million instructions per second, which is a far cry from the peak performance of 66 MIPS claimed by the manufacturer.[13] If the manufacturer's claims have any relation to reality, there must be a better way.

In fact, there is. As a result of a lot of research and development, both in academia and in the semiconductor industry, it is possible to approach the rated performance of fast CPUs, as you will see later, in Figure 2.12. Some of these techniques have been around as long as we've had computers; others have fairly recently "trickled down" from supercomputers to microcomputer CPUs. One of the most important of these techniques is the use of a number of different kinds of storage devices having different performance characteristics; the arrangement of these devices is called the **memory hierarchy**.

```
Problem
Algorithms
C++
Executable
Hardware
```

---

can approach 66 MIPS on a 66 MHz 486. This relationship doesn't hold in general; for example, the Pentium™ machines can execute two instructions simultaneously in some cases, and therefore a 90 MHz Pentium can run at up to 180 MIPS in the ideal case.

12. In the case of MHz, *mega* really means "million" (that is, 1,000,000), in contrast to its use in describing storage capacities. I'm sorry if this is confusing, but it can't be helped.

13. 1 second/226 ns per instruction = 4,424,788 instructions per second.

Figure 2.2 illustrates the memory hierarchy on my home machine at the time I started writing this book.

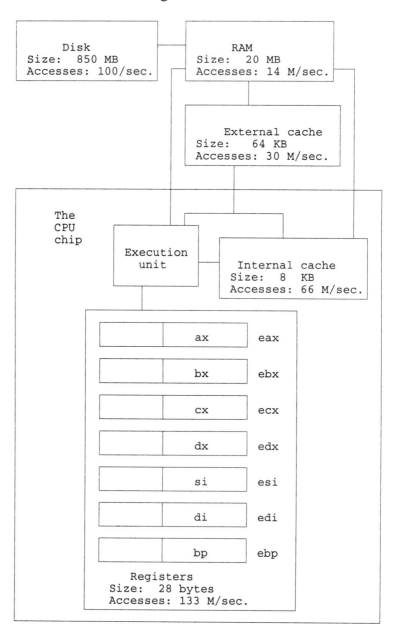

Problem
Algorithms
C++
Executable
Hardware

Figure 2.2: The memory hierarchy

We've already seen that the disk is necessary to store data and programs when the machine is turned off, while RAM is needed for its higher speed in accessing data and programs we're currently using.[14] But why do we need the *external cache*?

Actually, we've been around this track before, when we questioned why everything isn't loaded into RAM rather than being read from the disk as needed; we're trading speed for cost. To have a cost-effective computer with good performance requires the designer to choose the correct amount of each storage medium.

So just as with the disk vs. RAM trade-off before, the reason that we use the external cache is to improve performance. While RAM can be accessed about 14 million times per second, the external cache is made from a faster type of memory chips, which can be accessed about 30 million times per second. While not as extreme as the speed differential between disk and RAM, this difference is still significant. However, we can't afford to use external cache exclusively instead of RAM, because it would be too expensive to do so. In early 1997, the cost of 1 MB of external cache was in the neighborhood of $100. For about the same amount of money, you could have bought 24 MB of RAM. Therefore, we must reserve external cache for tasks where speed is all-important, such as supplying frequently used data or programs to the CPU.[15]

The same analysis applies to the trade-off between the external cache and the *internal cache*. The internal cache's characteristics are similar to those of the the external cache, but to a greater degree; it's even smaller and faster, allowing access at the rated speed of the CPU. Both characteristics have to do with its privileged position on the same chip as the CPU; this reduces the delays in communication between the internal cache and the CPU but means that chip area devoted to the cache has to compete with area for the CPU, as long as the total chip size is held constant.

```
Problem
Algorithms
C++
Executable
Hardware
```

---

14. According to the diagram, RAM functions more or less as a cache for the disk; after all, we have to copy data from a slow disk into fast RAM before we can use it for anything. While this is a valid analogy, I should point out that the situations aren't quite parallel. Our programs usually read data from disk into RAM explicitly; that is, we're aware of whether it's on the disk or in RAM, and we have to issue commands to transfer it from one place to the other. On the other hand, caches are "automatic" in their functioning. We don't have to worry about them, and our programs work in exactly the same way with them as without them, except faster. Whether or not you think of RAM as a cache for the disk, the interaction of these two types of storage explains why the speed of the disk is also illustrated in the memory hierarchy.

15. There are other reasons to limit the size of an external cache. For one thing, it uses a lot of power and thus produces a lot of heat; this isn't good for electronic components.

Unfortunately, we can't just increase the size of the chip to accommodate more internal cache because of the expense of doing so. Larger chips are more difficult to make, which reduces their *yield*, or the percentage of good chips. In addition, fewer of them fit on one *wafer*, which is the unit of manufacturing. Both of these attributes make larger chips more expensive to make.

Caching In

To oversimplify a bit, here's how caching reduces the effects of slow RAM. Whenever a data item is requested by the CPU, there are three possibilities:

1. It is already in the internal cache. In this case, the value is sent to the CPU without referring to RAM at all.
2. It is in the external cache. In this case, it will be "promoted" to the internal cache and sent to the CPU at the same time.
3. It is not in either the internal or external cache. In this case, it has to be entered into a location in the internal cache. If there is nothing in that cache location, the new item is simply added to the cache. However, if there is a data item already in that cache location, then the old item is displaced to the external cache, and the new item is written in its place. If the external cache location is empty, that ends the activity; if it is not empty, then the item previously in that location is written out to RAM and its slot is used for the one displaced from the internal cache.[16]

```
Problem
Algorithms
C++
Executable
Hardware
```

Please Register Here

Another way to improve performance that has been employed for many years is to create a small number of private storage areas, called **registers**, that are on the same chip as the CPU itself. Programs use these registers to hold data items that are actively in use; data in registers can be accessed within the time allocated to instruction execution (16 ns in our example), rather than the much

---

16. This is fairly close to the actual way caches are used to reduce the time it takes to get frequently used data from RAM (known as *caching reads*); reducing the time needed to write changed values back to RAM (*caching writes*) is more complicated.

longer times needed to access data in RAM.[17] This means that the time needed to access data in registers is predictable, unlike data that may have been displaced from the internal cache by more recent arrivals and thus must be reloaded from the external cache or even from RAM. Most CPUs have some **dedicated registers**, which aren't available to application programmers (that's us), but are reserved for the operating system (e.g., DOS, Unix, OS/2) or have special functions dictated by the hardware design. However, we will be concerned primarily with the **general registers**, which are available for our use.[18]

The general registers are used to hold working copies of data items called **variables**, which otherwise reside in RAM during the execution of the program. These variables represent specific items of data that we wish to keep track of in our programs, such as weights and numbers of items.[19]

You can put something in a variable, and it will stay there until you store something else there; you can also look at it to find out what's in it. As you might expect, several types of variables are used to hold different kinds of data; the first ones we will look at are variables representing whole numbers (the so-called **integer variables**), which are a subset of the category called **numeric variables**. As this suggests, there are also variables that represent numbers that can have fractional parts. We'll look at these so-called floating-point variables briefly in a later chapter.

Problem
Algorithms
C++
Executable
Hardware

Different types of variables require different amounts of RAM to store them, depending on the amount of data they contain; a very common type of numeric variable, known as a short, requires 16 bits (that is, 2 bytes) of RAM to hold any of 65536 different values, from −32768 to 32767, including 0. As we will see shortly, these odd-looking numbers are the result of using the binary system.

---

17. In case you're wondering how a small number of registers can help the speed of a large program, I should point out that no matter how large a program is, the vast majority of instructions and data items in the program are inactive at any given moment. In fact, less than a dozen instructions are in various stages of execution at any given time even in the most advanced microcomputer CPU available in 1997. The computer's apparent ability to run several distinct programs simultaneously is an illusion produced by the extremely high rate of execution of instructions.

18. All of the registers are physically similar, being just a collection of circuits in the CPU used to hold a value. As indicated here, some registers are dedicated to certain uses by the design of the CPU, whereas others are generally usable. In the case of the general registers, which are all functionally similar or identical, a compiler often uses them in a conventional way; this stylized usage simplifies the compiler writer's job.

19. Since RAM doesn't maintain its contents when power is turned off, anything that a program needs to keep around for a long time, such as inventory data to be used later, should be saved on the disk. We'll see how that is accomplished in a future chapter.

By no coincidence at all, the early Intel CPUs such as the 8086 had general registers that contained 16 bits each; these registers were named ax, bx, cx, dx, si, di, and bp. Why does it matter how many bits each register holds? Because the number (and size) of instructions it takes to process a variable is much less if the variable fits in a register; therefore, most programming languages, C++ included, relate the size of a variable to the size of the registers available to hold it. A short is exactly the right size to fit into a 16-bit register and therefore can be processed efficiently by the early Intel machines, whereas longer variables had to be handled in pieces, causing a great decline in efficiency of the program.

Progress marches on: more recent Intel CPUs, starting with the 80386, have 32-bit general registers; these registers are called eax, ebx, ecx, edx, esi, edi, and ebp. You may have noticed that these names are simply the names of the old 16-bit registers with an e tacked onto the front. Intel changed the names because when the registers were extended to 32 bits with the advent of the 80386, it didn't want to change the behavior of existing programs that (of course) used the old names for the 16-bit registers. So the old names, as illustrated in Figure 2.2, now refer to the bottom halves of the "real" (that is, 32-bit) registers; instructions using these old names behave exactly as though they were accessing the 16-bit registers on earlier machines. To refer to the 32-bit registers, you use the new names eax, ebx, and so on, for "extended" ax, "extended" bx, and so forth.

Problem
Algorithms
C++
Executable
Hardware

What does it mean to say that instructions using the 16-bit register names "behave exactly as though they were accessing the 16-bit registers on earlier machines"? Before I can explain this, you'll have to understand the binary number system, on which all modern computers are based. To make this number system more intelligible, I have written the following little fable.

Odometer Trouble

Once upon a time, the Acme company had a factory that made golf carts. One day, Bob, the president of Acme, decided to add an odometer to the carts, so that the purchaser of the cart could estimate when to recharge the battery. To save money, Bob decided to buy the little numbered wheels for the odometers and have his employees put the odometers together. The minimum order was a thousand odometer wheels, which was more than he needed for his initial run of 50 odometers. When he got the wheels, however, he noticed that they were defective. Instead of the numbers 0–9, each wheel had only two numbers, 0 and 1. Of course, he was quite irritated by this error and attempted to contact the company from which he had purchased the wheels, but it had closed down for a month for summer vacation. What was he to do until it reopened?

While he was fretting about this problem, Jim, one of his employees, who was in charge of putting the wheels together to make an odometer, came into his office and said, "Bob, I have an idea. Since we have lots of orders for these odometer-equipped carts, maybe we can make an odometer with these funny wheels and tell the customers how to read the numbers on the odometer."

Bob was taken aback by this idea. "What do you mean, Jim? How can anyone read those screwy odometers?"

Jim had given this some thought. "Let's take a look at what one of these odometers, say with five wheels, can display. Obviously, it would start out reading 00000, just like a normal odometer. After one mile has elapsed, the rightmost wheel turns to 1, so the whole display is 00001; again, this is no different from a normal odometer.

"Now we come to the tricky part. The rightmost wheel goes back to 0, not having any more numbers to display, and pushes the 'tens' wheel to 1; the whole number now reads 00010. Obviously, one more mile makes it 00011, which gives us the situation shown in Figure 2.3."

Problem
Algorithms
C++
Executable
Hardware

```
Normal odometer    Funny odometer
   00000               00000
   00001               00001
   00002               00010
   00003               00011
```

Figure 2.3: The first few numbers

Jim continued, "What's next? This time, the rightmost wheel turns over again to 0, triggering the second wheel to its next position. However, this time, the second wheel is already at its highest value, 1; therefore, it also turns over to 0 and increments the third wheel. It's not hard to follow this for a few more miles, as illustrated in Figure 2.4."

```
Normal odometer    Funny odometer
   00004               00100
   00005               00101
   00006               00110
   00007               00111
```

Figure 2.4: The next few numbers

Bob said, "I get it. It's just like counting normally, except that you skip all the numbers that have anything but 0s or 1s in them."

"That's right, Bob. So I suppose we could make up a list of the 'real' numbers and give it to the customers to use until we can replace these odometers with normal ones."

"Okay, Jim, if you think they'll buy it. Let's get a few of the customers we know the best and ask them if they'll try it; we won't charge them for the odometers until we have the real ones, but maybe they'll stick with us until then."

Jim went to work, making some odometers out of the defective wheels; however, he soon figured out that he had to use more than five wheels, because that allowed only numbers from 0 to 31. How did he know this?

Each wheel has two numbers, 0 and 1. So with one wheel, we have a total of two combinations. Two wheels can have either a 0 or a 1 for the first number, and the same for the second number, for a total of four combinations. With three wheels, the same analysis holds: 2 numbers for the first wheel * 2 for the second wheel * 2 for the third wheel = 8 possibilities in all; actually, they are the same 8 possibilities we saw in Figures 2.3 and 2.4.

Problem
Algorithms
C++
Executable
Hardware

A pattern is beginning to develop: for each added wheel, we get twice as many possible combinations. Figure 2.5 shows the first few numbers in the sequence of combinations vs. number of wheels.

Number of wheels	Number of combinations[20]
1	2
2	4
3	8
4	16
5	32
6	64
7	128
8	256
9	512
10	1024
11	2048
12	4096
13	8192
14	16384
15	32768
16	65536

Figure 2.5: How many combinations?

20. If you think that last number looks familiar, you're right. It's the number of different values that can be stored in a type of numeric variable called a short. This is no coincidence; read on for the detailed explanation.

Jim decided that 14 wheels would do the job, since the lifespan of the golf cart probably wouldn't exceed 16,383 miles, and so he made up the odometers. The selected customers turned out to be agreeable and soon found that having even a weird odometer was better than none, especially since they didn't have to pay for it. However, one customer did have a complaint: the numbers on the wheels didn't seem to make sense when translated with the chart supplied by Acme. The customer estimated that he had driven the cart about 9 miles, but the odometer displayed the following number,

11111111110111

which, according to his translation chart, was 16,375 miles. What could have gone wrong?

Jim decided to have the cart brought in for a checkup, and what he discovered was that the odometer cable had been hooked up backward. That is, instead of turning the wheels forward, they were going backward. That was part of the solution, but why was the value 16,375?

Just like a car odometer, in which 99,999 (or 999,999, if you have a 6-wheel odometer) is followed by 0, going backward from 0 reverses that progression. Similarly, the number 11111111111111 on the funny odometers would be followed by 00000000000000, since the "carry" off the leftmost digit is lost. Therefore, if you start out at 0 and go backward 1 mile, you'll get

Problem
Algorithms
C++
Executable
Hardware

11111111111111

The next mile will turn the last digit back to 0, producing

11111111111110

What happens next? The last wheel turns back to 1 and triggers the second wheel to switch as well:

11111111111101

The next few "backward" numbers look like this:

11111111111100
11111111111011
11111111111010
11111111111001

11111111111000
11111111110111

and so on. If you look at the right-hand end of these numbers, you'll
see that the progression is just the opposite of the "forward" numbers.

As for the customer's actual mileage, the last one of these is the
number the customer saw on his backward odometer. Apparently, he
was right about the distance driven, since this is the ninth "backward"
number. So Jim fixed the backward odometer cable and reset the
value to the correct number, 00000000001001, or 9 miles.

Eventually, Acme got the right odometer wheels with 0–9 on
them, replaced the peculiar ones, and everyone lived happily ever
after.

THE END

Back to the Future

Problem
Algorithms
C++
Executable
Hardware

Of course, the wheels that made up the funny odometers contain only
two digits, 0 and 1, so the odometers use the binary system for
counting. Now it should be obvious why we will see numbers like
65536 and 32768 in our discussions of the number of possible
different values that a variable can hold: variables are stored in RAM
as collections of bytes, each of which contains 8 bits. As the list of
combinations indicates, 8 bits (1 byte) provide 256 different
combinations, while 16 bits (2 bytes) can represent 65536 different
possible values.

But what about the "backward" numbers with a lot of 1s on the
left? As the fable suggests, they correspond to "negative" numbers.
That is, if moving 2 miles forward from 0 registers as
00000000000010, and moving 2 miles backward from 0 registers as
11111111111110, then the latter number is in some sense equivalent
to –2 miles. This in fact is the way that negative integers are stored in
the computer; integer variables that can store either positive or
negative values are called signed *variables*. If we don't specify
whether we want to be able to store either positive or negative values
in a given variable, the C++ language assumes that we want that
ability and provides it for us by default.

However, adding the ability to represent negative numbers has a
drawback; namely, you can't represent as many positive numbers.
This should be fairly obvious, since if we interpret some of the
possible patterns as negative, they can't also be used for positive

values. In some situations (such as keeping track of the number of employees in a company) we don't have to worry about negative numbers. In such cases we can specify that we want to use unsigned *variables*, which will always be interpreted as positive (or 0) values. An example is an unsigned short variable, which uses 16 bits (that is, 2 bytes) to hold any number from 0 to 65535, which totals 65536 different values. This capacity can be calculated as follows: since each byte is 8 bits, 2 bytes contain a total of 16 bits, and 2^16 is 65536.

It's important to understand that the difference between a short (that is, a signed short) and an unsigned short is exactly which 65536 values each can hold. An unsigned short can hold any whole number from 0 to 65535, whereas a short can hold any value from −32768 to +32767.

Over-Hexed

You may have noticed that it's tedious and error prone to represent numbers in binary; a long string of 0s and 1s is hard to remember or to copy. For this reason, the pure binary system is hardly ever used to specify numbers in computing. However, we have already seen that binary is much more "natural" for computers than the more familiar decimal system. Is there a number system that we humans can use a little more easily than binary while retaining the advantages of binary for describing internal events in the computer?

Problem
Algorithms
C++
Executable
Hardware

As it happens, there is. It's called **hexadecimal**, which means "base 16". As a rule, the term *hexadecimal* is abbreviated to *hex*. Since there are 16 possible combinations of 4 bits (2*2*2*2), hexadecimal notation allows 4 bits of a binary number to be represented by one hex digit. Unfortunately, however, there are only 10 "normal" digits, 0–9. To represent a number in any base, you need as many different digit values as the base, so that any number less than the base can be represented by one digit. For example, in base 2, you need only two digits, 0 and 1. In base 8 (*octal*), you need eight digits, 0–7.[21] So far, so good. But what about base 16? To use this base, we need 16 digits. Since only 10 numeric digits are available, hex notation needs a source for the other six digits. Because letters of

---

21. In the early days of computing, base 8 was sometimes used instead of base 16, especially on machines that used 12-bit and 36-bit registers; however, it has fallen into disuse because almost all modern machines have 32-bit registers.

the alphabet are available and familiar, the first six letters, a–f, were adopted for this service.[22]

The correspondence between hex digits and groups of four bits is illustrated in Figure 2.6.

```
4-bit value   1-hexit value

0000            0
0001            1
0010            2
0011            3
0100            4
0101            5
0110            6
0111            7
1000            8
1001            9
1010            a
1011            b
1100            c
1101            d
1110            e
1111            f
```

```
Problem
Algorithms
C++
Executable
Hardware
```

Figure 2.6: Binary to hex conversion table

As indicated in the figure, an 8-bit number, such as

0101 1011

can be translated directly into a hex value, like this:

5   b

For this reason, binary is almost never used. Instead, we use hex as a shortcut to eliminate the necessity of reading, writing, and remembering long strings of bits.

Here's an exercise you can use to improve your understanding of this topic: invent a random string of four binary digits and see where it is in Figure 2.6. I guarantee it'll be there somewhere! Then look at the "hex" column and see what "digit" it corresponds to. There's nothing really mysterious about hex; since we have run out of digits

---

22. Either upper- or lower-case letters are acceptable to most programs (and programmers). I'll use lowercase because such letters are easier to distinguish than uppercase ones; besides, I find them less irritating to look at.

after 9, we have to use letters to represent the numbers 'ten', 'eleven', 'twelve', 'thirteen', 'fourteen', and 'fifteen'.

Figure 2.7 shows the correspondence between some decimal, hex, and binary numbers, with the values of each digit position in each number base indicated and the calculation of the total of all of the bit values in the binary representation.

Decimal place values 10 1	Hexadecimal place values 16 1	Binary place values 16 8 4 2 1		Sum of binary digit values
0	0 0	0 0 0 0 0	=	0 + 0 + 0 + 0 + 0
1	0 1	0 0 0 0 1	=	0 + 0 + 0 + 0 + 1
2	0 2	0 0 0 1 0	=	0 + 0 + 0 + 2 + 0
3	0 3	0 0 0 1 1	=	0 + 0 + 0 + 2 + 1
4	0 4	0 0 1 0 0	=	0 + 0 + 4 + 0 + 0
5	0 5	0 0 1 0 1	=	0 + 0 + 4 + 0 + 1
6	0 6	0 0 1 1 0	=	0 + 0 + 4 + 2 + 0
7	0 7	0 0 1 1 1	=	0 + 0 + 4 + 2 + 1
8	0 8	0 1 0 0 0	=	0 + 8 + 0 + 0 + 0
9	0 9	0 1 0 0 1	=	0 + 8 + 0 + 0 + 1
1 0	0 a	0 1 0 1 0	=	0 + 8 + 0 + 2 + 0
1 1	0 b	0 1 0 1 1	=	0 + 8 + 0 + 2 + 1
1 2	0 c	0 1 1 0 0	=	0 + 8 + 4 + 0 + 0
1 3	0 d	0 1 1 0 1	=	0 + 8 + 4 + 0 + 1
1 4	0 e	0 1 1 1 0	=	0 + 8 + 4 + 2 + 0
1 5	0 f	0 1 1 1 1	=	0 + 8 + 4 + 2 + 1
1 6	1 0	1 0 0 0 0	=	16 + 0 + 0 + 0 + 0
1 7	1 1	1 0 0 0 1	=	16 + 0 + 0 + 0 + 1
1 8	1 2	1 0 0 1 0	=	16 + 0 + 0 + 2 + 0
1 9	1 3	1 0 0 1 1	=	16 + 0 + 0 + 2 + 1

Problem
Algorithms
C++
Executable
Hardware

Figure 2.7: Different representations of the same numbers

Another reason to use hex rather than decimal is that byte values expressed as hex digits can be combined directly to produce larger values, which is not true with decimal digits. In case this isn't obvious, let's go over it in more detail. Since each hex digit (0–f) represents exactly 4 bits, two of them (00–ff) represent 8 bits, or one byte. Similarly, 4 hex digits (0000–ffff) represent 16 bits, or a short value; the first two digits represent the first byte of the 2-byte value, and the last two digits represent the second byte. This can be extended to any number of bytes. On the other hand, representing 4 bits requires two decimal digits, as the values range from 00–15, whereas it takes three digits (000–255) to represent one byte. A 2-byte value requires five decimal digits, since the value can be from 00000 to 65535. As you can see, there's no simple relationship between the decimal digits representing each byte and the decimal representation of a 2-byte value.

Exercises

Here are some exercises that you can use to check your understanding of the binary and hexadecimal number systems.[23] I've limited the examples to addition and subtraction, as that is all that you're ever likely to have to do in these number systems. These operations are exactly like their equivalents in the decimal system, except that, as we have already seen, the hexadecimal system has six extra digits after 9: a, b, c, d, e, and f. We have to take these into account in our calculations: for example, adding 9 and 5, rather than producing 14, produces e.

1. Using the hexadecimal system, answer these problems:
    a.   1a + 2e = ?
    b.   12 + 18 = ?
    c.   50 − 12 = ?
2. Using the binary system, answer these problems:
    a.   101 + 110 = ?
    b.   111 + 1001 = ?
    c.   1010 − 11 = ?

```
Problem
Algorithms
C++
Executable
Hardware
```

Consider the two types of numeric variables we've encountered so far, short and unsigned short. Let's suppose that x is a short and y is an unsigned short, both of them currently holding the value 32767, or 7fff in hex.

3. What is the result of adding 1 to y, in both decimal and hex?
4. What is the result of adding 1 to x, in both decimal and hex?

Answers to the preceding exercises can be found at the end of the chapter.

5. A certain soft drink manufacturer offers a number of different versions of their best-selling product. It can be purchased with or without caffeine, with or without sugar, with or without added cherry flavor, and in "old" and "new" flavors. Assuming that they make a version of their product with every possible combination of these attributes, how many variations do they make in all, and why?

---

23. Please note that the ability to do binary or hexadecimal arithmetic is **not** essential to further reading in this book.

Registering Relief

Before we took this detour into the binary and hexadecimal number systems, I promised to explain what it means to say that the instructions using the 16-bit register names "behave exactly as though they were accessing the 16-bit registers on earlier machines". After a bit more preparation, we'll be ready for that explanation. Let's start by looking at some more definitions that we'll need to discuss this topic.

More Definitions

A **machine instruction** is one of the fundamental operations that a CPU can perform. Some examples of these operations are addition, subtraction, or other arithmetic operations. Other possibilities include operations that control what instruction will be executed next. All C++ programs must be converted into machine instructions by a *compiler* before they can be executed by the CPU.

An **assembly language** program is the human-readable representation of a set of *machine instruction*s; each assembly language statement corresponds to one machine instruction. By contrast, a C++ program consists of much higher-level operations that cannot be directly translated one-for-one into machine instructions.

Problem
Algorithms
C++
Executable
Hardware

Some Assembly Required

First, let's take a look at some characteristics of the human-readable version of machine instructions: assembly language instructions. The **assembly language** instructions we will look at have a fairly simple format.[24] The name of the operation is given first, followed by one or more spaces. The next element is the "destination", which is the register or RAM location that will be affected by the instruction's execution. The last element in an instruction is the "source", which represents another register, a RAM location, or a constant value to be used in the calculation. The source and destination are separated by a

---

24. I'm simplifying here. There are instructions that follow other formats, but we'll stick with the simple ones for the time being.

comma.[25] Here's an example of a simple assembly language instruction:

add ax,1

In this instruction, add is the operation, ax is the destination, and the constant value 1 is the source. Thus, add ax,1 means to add 1 to the contents of ax, replacing the old contents of ax with the result.

Now we're finally ready to see what the statement about using the 16-bit register names on a 32-bit machine means. Suppose we have the register contents shown in Figure 2.8 (indicated in hexadecimal).

32-bit register	32-bit contents	16-bit register	16-bit contents
eax	1235ffff	ax	ffff

Figure 2.8: 32- and 16-bit registers, before add ax,1

If we were to add 1 to register ax by executing the instruction add ax,1, the result would be as shown in Figure 2.9.

Problem
Algorithms
C++
Executable
Hardware

32-bit register	32-bit contents	16-bit register	16-bit contents
eax	12350000	ax	0000

Figure 2.9: 32- and 16-bit registers, after add ax,1

In case this makes no sense, consider what happens when you add 1 to 9999 on a four-digit counter such as an odometer. It "turns over" to 0000, doesn't it? The same applies here: ffff is the largest number that can be represented as four hex digits, so if you add 1 to a register that has only four (hex) digits of storage available, the result is 0000.

As this illustrates, instructions that refer to ax have no effect whatever on the upper part of eax; they behave exactly as though the

---

25. Of course, the actual machine instructions being executed in the CPU don't have commas, register names, or any other human-readable form; they consist of fixed-format sequences of bits stored in RAM. The CPU actually executes machine language instructions rather than assembly language ones; a program called an **assembler** takes care of translating the assembly language instructions into machine instructions. However, we can usually ignore this step, because each assembly language instruction corresponds to one machine instruction. This correspondence is quite unlike the relationship between C++ statements and machine instructions, which is far more complex.

upper part of eax did not exist. However, if we were to execute the instruction add eax,1 instead of add ax,1, the result would look like Figure 2.10.

32-bit register	32-bit contents	16-bit register	16-bit contents
eax	12360000	ax	0000

Figure 2.10: 32- and 16-bit registers, after add eax,1

In this case, eax is treated as a whole. Similar results apply to the other 32-bit registers and their 16-bit counterparts.

On a RAMpage

Unfortunately, it isn't possible to use only registers and avoid references to RAM entirely, if only because we'll run out of registers sooner or later. This is a good time to look back at the diagram of the "memory hierarchy" (Figure 2.2) and examine the relative speed and size of each different kind of memory.

Problem
Algorithms
C++
Executable
Hardware

The "size" attribute of the disk and RAM are specified in megabytes, whereas the size of an external cache is generally in the range from 64 kilobytes to 1 megabyte. As I mentioned before, the internal cache is considerably smaller, usually in the 8 to 16 kilobyte range. The registers, however, provide a total of 28 *bytes* of storage; this should make clear that they are the scarcest memory resource. To try to clarify why the registers are so important to the performance of programs, I've listed the "speed" attribute in number of accesses per second, rather than in milliseconds, nanoseconds, and so forth. In the case of the disk, this is about 100 accesses per second. RAM can be accessed about 14 million times per second. The clear winners, though, are the internal cache and the registers, which can be accessed 66 million times per second and 133 million times per second, respectively.

Registering Bewilderment

In a way, the latter figure (133 million accesses per second for registers) overstates the advantages of registers relative to the cache. You see, any given register can be accessed only 66 million times per second; however, many instructions refer to two registers and still execute in one CPU cycle. Therefore, the maximum number of references per second is more than the number of instructions per second.

However, this leads to another question: Why not have instructions that can refer to more than one memory address (known as *memory-to-memory* instructions) and still execute in one CPU cycle? In that case, we wouldn't have to worry about registers; since there's (relatively) a lot of cache and very few registers, it would seem to make more sense to eliminate the middleman and simply refer to data in the cache.[26] Of course, there is a good reason for the provision of both registers and cache. The main drawback of registers is that there are so few of them; on the other hand, one of their main advantages is also that there are so few of them. Why is this?

The main reason to use registers is that they make instructions shorter: since there are only a few registers, we don't have to use up a lot of bits specifying which register(s) to use. That is, with 8 registers, we only need 3 bits to specify which register we need. In fact, there are standardized 3-bit codes that might be thought of as "register addresses", which are used to specify each register when it is used to hold a variable. Figure 2.11 is the table of these register codes.[27]

Problem
Algorithms
C++
Executable
Hardware

Register address	16-bit register	32-bit register
000	ax	eax
001	cx	ecx
010	dx	edx
011	bx	ebx
100	sp	esp
101	bp	ebp
110	si	esi
111	di	edi

Figure 2.11: 32- and 16-bit register codes

---

26. Perhaps I should remind you that the programmer doesn't explicitly refer to the cache; you can just use normal RAM addresses and let the hardware take care of making sure that the most frequently referenced data ends up in the cache.

27. Don't blame me for the seemingly scrambled order of the codes; that's the way Intel's CPU architects assigned them to registers when they designed the 8086, and it's much too late to change them now. Luckily, we almost never have to worry about their values, because the assembler takes care of the translation of register names to register addresses.

By contrast, a "memory-to-memory" instruction would need at least 2 bytes for the source address and 2 bytes for the destination address.[28] Adding 1 byte to specify the type of instruction would make the minimum instruction size 5 bytes; by contrast, instructions that use only registers can be as short as 1 byte. This makes a big difference in performance because the caches are quite limited in size; big programs don't fit in the caches and therefore require a larger number of RAM accesses than those that do fit. As a result, they execute much more slowly than small programs.

This explains why we want our programs to be smaller. However, it may not be obvious why using registers reduces the size of instructions, so here's an explanation.

Most of the data in use by a program is stored in RAM. When using a 32-bit CPU, it is theoretically possible to have over 4 billion bytes of memory (2^{32} is the exact number). Therefore, that many distinct addresses for a given byte of data are possible; to specify any of these requires 32 bits. Since there are only a few registers, specifying which one you want to use takes only a few bits; therefore, programs use register addresses instead of memory addresses wherever possible, to reduce the number of bits in each instruction required to specify addresses.

Problem
Algorithms
C++
Executable
Hardware

A Fetching Tale

Another way of reducing overhead is to read instructions from RAM in chunks, rather than one at a time, and feed them into the CPU as it needs them; this is called *prefetching*. This mechanism operates in parallel with instruction execution, loading instructions from RAM into special dedicated registers in the CPU before they're actually needed. These registers are known collectively as the *prefetch queue*. Since the prefetching is done by a separate unit in the CPU, the time to do the prefetching doesn't increase the time needed for instruction execution. When the CPU is ready to execute another instruction, it can get it from the prefetch queue almost instantly, rather than having to wait for the slow RAM to provide each instruction. Of course, it does take a small amount of time to retrieve the next instruction from the prefetch queue, but that amount of time is included in the normal instruction execution time.

---

28. If we want to be able to access more than 64 kilobytes worth of data, as required in most modern programs, we'll need even more room to store addresses.

The effect of combining the use of registers and prefetching the instructions can be very significant. In our example, if we use an instruction that has already been loaded, which reads data from and writes data only to registers, the timing reduces to that shown in Figure 2.12.

```
Time          Function
0  ns         Read instruction from RAM[29]
0  ns         Read data from register[30]
16 ns         Execute instruction
0  ns         Write result back to register[31]
- - - - -
16 ns         Total instruction execution time (as advertised)
```

Figure 2.12: Instruction execution time, using registers and prefetching

As I indicated near the beginning of this chapter, the CPU manufacturers aren't lying to us; if we design our programs to take advantage of these (and other similar) efficiency measures taken by the manufacturer, we can often approach the maximum theoretical performance figures.

You've just been subjected to a barrage of information on how a computer works. Let's go over it again before continuing.

Problem
Algorithms
C++
Executable
Hardware

Review

Three main components of the computer are of most significance to programmers: disk, RAM, and the CPU; the first two of these store programs and data that are used by the CPU.

Computers represent pieces of information (or data) as binary digits, universally referred to as *bits*. Each bit can have the value 0 or 1. The binary system is used instead of the more familiar decimal system because it is much easier to make devices that can store and retrieve 1 of 2 values than 1 of 10. Bits are grouped into sets of 8, called *bytes*.

The disk uses magnetic recording heads to store and retrieve groups of a few hundred bytes on rapidly spinning platters in a few milliseconds. The contents of the disk are not lost when the power is

---

29. Since the instruction is already in the prefetch queue, this step doesn't count against the execution time. Hence the 0 in the time column.

30. This time is included under "Execute instruction".

31. This time is included under "Execute instruction".

turned off, so it is suitable for more or less permanent storage of programs and data.

RAM, which is an acronym for Random Access Memory, is used to hold programs and data while they're in use. It is made of millions of microscopic transistors on a piece of silicon called a *chip*. Each bit is stored using a few of these transistors. RAM does not retain its contents when power is removed, so it is not good for permanent storage. However, any byte in a RAM chip can be accessed in about 70 nanoseconds (billionths of a second), which is hundreds of thousands of times as fast as accessing a disk. Each byte in a RAM chip can be independently stored and retrieved without affecting other bytes, by providing the unique memory address belonging to the byte you want to access.

The CPU (also called the *processor*) is the active component in the computer. It is also made of millions of microscopic transistors on a chip. The CPU executes programs consisting of instructions stored in RAM, using data also stored in RAM. However, the CPU is so fast that even the typical RAM access time of 70 nanoseconds is a bottleneck. Therefore, computer manufacturers have added both *external cache* and *internal cache*, which are faster types of memory used to reduce the amount of time that the CPU has to wait. The internal cache resides on the same chip as the CPU and can be accessed without delay. The external cache sits between the CPU and the regular RAM; it's faster than the latter, but not as fast as the internal cache. Finally, a very small part of the on-chip memory is organized as *registers*, which can be accessed within the normal cycle time of the CPU, thus allowing the fastest possible processing.

Problem
Algorithms
C++
Executable
Hardware

Conclusion

In this chapter, we've covered a lot of material on how a computer actually works. As you'll see, this background is essential if you're going to understand what really happens inside a program. In the next chapter, we'll get to the "real thing": how to write a program to make all this hardware do something useful.

Answers to Selected Exercises

1. Hexadecimal arithmetic
    a.   48
    b.   2a
    c.   3e

2. Binary arithmetic
    a.   1011
    b.   10000
    c.   111

3. 32768 decimal, or 8000 in hex

4. −32768, or 8000 in hex

    Why is the same hex value rendered here as −32768, while it was 32768 in Exercise 3? The only difference between short and unsigned short variables is how their values are interpreted. In particular, short variables having values from 8000h to ffffh are considered negative, while unsigned short values in that range are positive. That's why the range of short values is −32768 to +32767, whereas unsigned short variables can range from 0 to 65535.

Problem
Algorithms
C++
Executable
Hardware

Chapter 3

Basics of Programming

Creative Programming?

After that necessary detour into the workings of the hardware, we can now resume our regularly scheduled explanation of the creative possibilities of computers. It may sound odd to describe computers as providing grand scope for creative activities; aren't they monotonous, dull, unintelligent, and extremely limited? Yes, they are. However, they have two redeeming virtues that make them ideal as the canvas of invention: They are extraordinarily fast and spectacularly reliable. These characteristics allow the creator of a program to weave intricate chains of thought and have a fantastic number of steps carried out without fail. We'll begin to explore how this is possible after we go over some definitions and objectives for this chapter.

Definitions

An **identifier** is a user-defined name; variable names are identifiers. Identifiers must not conflict with keywords such as if and while; for example, you cannot create a variable with the name while.

A **keyword** is a word defined in the C++ language, such as if and while. It is illegal to define an identifier such as a variable name that conflicts with a keyword.

Objectives of This Chapter

By the end of this chapter, you should

1. Understand what a program is and have some idea how a program works.
2. Understand how to get information into and out of a program.
3. Understand how to use if and while to control the execution of a program.[1]
4. Understand how a portion of a program can be marked off so that it will be treated as one unit.
5. Be able to read and understand a simple program I've written in C++.

Speed Demon

Problem
Algorithms
C++
Executable
Hardware

The most impressive attribute of modern computers, of course, is their speed; as we have already seen, this is measured in MIPS (millions of instructions per second).

Of course, raw speed is not very valuable if we can't rely on the results we get. ENIAC, one of the first electronic computers, had a failure every few hours, on the average. Since the problems it was used to solve took about that much time to run, the likelihood that the results were correct wasn't very high. Particularly critical calculations were often run several times, and if the users got the same answer twice, they figured it was probably correct. By contrast, modern computers are almost incomprehensibly reliable. With almost any other machine, a failure rate of one in every million operations would be considered phenomenally low, but a computer with such a failure rate would make dozens of errors per second.

Blaming It on the Computer

On the other hand, if computers are so reliable, why are they blamed for so much that goes wrong with modern life? Who among us has not been the victim of an erroneous credit report, a bill sent to the wrong address, or a long wait on the phone because "the computer is

---

1. Please note that capitalization counts in C++, so IF and WHILE are not the same as if and while. You have to use the latter versions.

down"? The answer is fairly simple: It's almost certainly not the computer's fault. More precisely, it's very unlikely that the CPU was at fault; it may be the software, other equipment such as telephone lines, tape or disk drives, or any of the myriad "peripheral devices" that the computer uses to store and retrieve information and interact with the outside world. Usually, it's the software; when customer service representatives tell you that they can't do something obviously reasonable, you can count on its being the software. For example, I once belonged to a 401K plan whose administrators provided statements only every three months, about three months after the end of the quarter. In other words, in July I found out how much my account had been worth at the end of March. The only way to estimate how much I had in the meantime was to look up the share values in the newspaper and multiply by the number of shares. Of course, the mutual fund that issued the shares could tell its shareholders their account balances at any time of the day or night. However, the company that administered the 401K plan didn't bother to provide such a service, as it would have required doing some work. Needless to say, whenever I hear that "the computer can't do that" as an excuse for such poor service, I reply, "Then you need some different programmers."

Problem
Algorithms
C++
Executable
Hardware

That Does Not Compute

All of this emphasis on computation, however, should not blind us to the fact that computers are not solely arithmetic engines. The most common application for which PCs are used is word processing, which is hardly a hotbed of arithmetical calculation. While we have so far considered only numeric data, this is a good illustration of the fact that computers also deal with another kind of information, which is commonly referred to by the imaginative term **nonnumeric variables**. Numeric variables are those suited for use in calculations, such as in totaling a set of weights. On the other hand, nonnumeric variables are items that are not used in calculations like adding, multiplying, or subtracting: Examples are names, addresses, telephone numbers, Social Security numbers, bank account numbers, or drivers license numbers. Note that just because something is called a *number*, or even is composed entirely of the digits 0–9, does not make it numeric data by our standards. The question is how the item is used. No one adds, multiplies, or subtracts drivers license numbers, for example; they serve solely as identifiers and could just as easily have letters in them, as indeed some do.

For the present, though, let's stick with numeric variables. Now that we have defined a couple of types of these variables, short and unsigned short, what can we do with them? To do anything with them, we have to write a C++ program, which consists primarily of a list of operations to be performed by the computer along with directions that influence how these operations are to be translated into machine instructions.

This raises an interesting point: Why does our C++ program have to be translated into machine instructions? Isn't the computer's job to execute (or *run*) our program?

Lost in Translation

Yes, but it can't run a C++ program. The only kind of program any computer can run is one made of machine instructions; this is called a **machine language** program, for obvious reasons. Therefore, to get our C++ program to run, we have to translate it into a machine language program. Don't worry, you won't have to do it yourself; that's why we have a program called a *compiler*. The most basic tasks that the compiler performs are the following:

Problem
Algorithms
C++
Executable
Hardware

1. Assigning memory addresses to variables. This allows us to use names for variables, rather than having to keep track of the address of each variable ourselves.
2. Translating arithmetic and other operations (such as +, −, etc.) into the equivalent machine instructions, including the addresses of variables assigned in the previous step.

This is probably a bit too abstract to be easily grasped, so let's look at an example as soon as we have defined some terms. Each complete operation understood by the compiler is called a **statement**. Each statement ends with a semicolon (;). Figure 3.1 shows some sample statements that do arithmetic calculations.[2]

By the way, to enter such statements in the first place, you can use any text editor that generates "plain" text files, such as the EDIT program that comes with DOS or Windows' Notepad. Whichever text editor you use, make sure that it produces files that contain only what you type; stay away from programs like Windows Write™ or

---

2. The // marks the beginning of a *comment*, which is a note to you or another programmer; it is ignored by the compiler. For those of you with BASIC experience, this is just like REM (the "remark" keyword in that language); anything after it on a line is ignored.

Word for Windows™, as they add some of their own information to indicate fonts, type sizes, and the like to your file, which will foul up the compiler.

```
short i;
short j;
short k;
short m;

i = 5;
j = i * 3;            // j is now 15
k = j - i;            // k is now 10
m = (k + j) / 5;      // m is now 5
i = i + 1;            // i is now 6
```

Figure 3.1: A little numeric calculation

Once we have entered the statements for our program, we use the compiler, as indicated, to translate the programs we write into a form that the computer can perform. As defined in Chapter 1, the form we create is called *source code*, since it is the source of the program logic, while the form of our program that the computer can execute is called an *executable program*, or just an *executable* for short.

As I've mentioned before, there are several types of variables, the short being only one of these types. Therefore, the compiler needs some explanatory material so that it can tell what types of variables you're using; that's what the first four lines of our little sample program fragment are for. Each line tells the compiler that the type of the variable i, j, k, or m is short; that is, it can contain values from −32768 to +32767.[3]

After this introductory material, we move into the list of operations to be performed. This is called the *executable* portion of the program, as it actually causes the computer to do something when the program is executed. The operations to be performed, as mentioned above, are called **statements**. The first one, i = 5;, sets the variable i to the value 5. A value such as 5, which doesn't have a name but represents itself in a literal manner, is called (appropriately enough) a **literal** value.

This is as good a time as any for me to mention something that experienced C programmers take for granted but has a tendency to confuse novices: the choice of the = sign to indicate the operation of setting a variable to a value, which is known technically as **assignment**. As far as I'm concerned, an assignment operation would

Problem
Algorithms
C++
Executable
Hardware

---

3. Other kinds of variables can hold larger (and smaller) values; we'll go over them in some detail in future chapters.

be more properly indicated by some symbol suggesting movement of data, such as 5 => i;, meaning "store the value 5 into variable i". Unfortunately, it's too late to change the notation for the **assignment statement**, as such a statement is called, so you'll just have to get used to it. The = means "set the variable on the left to the value on the right".

Now that I've warned you about that possible confusion, let's continue looking at the operations in the program. The next one, j = i * 3;, specifies that the variable j is to be set to the result of multiplying the current value of i by the literal value 3. The one after that, k = j − i;, tells the computer to set k to the amount by which j is greater than i; that is, j − i. The most complicated line in our little program fragment, m = (k + j) / 5;, calculates m as the sum of adding k and j and dividing the result by the literal value 5. Finally, the line i = i + 1; sets i to the value of i plus the literal value 1.

This last may be somewhat puzzling; how can i be equal to i + 1? The answer is that an assignment statement is *not* an algebraic equality, no matter how much it may resemble one. It is a command telling the computer to assign a value to a variable. Therefore, what i = i + 1; actually means is "take the current value of i, add 1 to it, and store the result back into i." In other words, a C++ variable is a place to store a value. The variable i can take on any number of values, but only one at a time; any former value is lost when a new one is assigned.

Now let's look at exactly what an assignment statement does. If the value of i before the statement i = i + 1; is 5 (for example), then that statement will cause the CPU to perform the following steps:

1. Take the current value of i (5).
2. Add one to that value (6).
3. Store the result back into i.

After the execution of this statement, i will have the value 6.

Problem
Algorithms
C++
Executable
Hardware

What's Going on Underneath?

In a moment we're going to dive a little deeper into how the the CPU accomplishes its task of manipulating data, such as we are doing here with our arithmetic program. First, though, it's time for a little pep talk for those of you who might be wondering exactly why this apparent digression is necessary.

If you don't understand what is going on under the surface, you won't be able to get past the "Sunday driver" stage of programming in C++. In some languages it's neither necessary or perhaps even possible to find out what the computer actually does to execute your program, but C++ isn't one of them. A good C++ programmer needs an intimate acquaintance with the internal workings of the language, for reasons that will become very apparent when we get to Chapter 7. For the moment, you'll just have to take my word that working through these intricacies is essential; the payoff for a thorough grounding in these fundamental concepts of computing will be worth the struggle.

Now let's get to the task of exploring how the CPU actually stores and manipulates data in memory. As we saw previously, each memory location in RAM has a unique *memory address*; *machine instructions* that refer to RAM use this address to specify which *byte* or bytes of memory they wish to retrieve or modify. This is fairly straightforward in the case of a 1-byte variable, where the instruction merely specifies the byte that corresponds to the variable. On the other hand, the situation isn't quite as simple in the case of a variable that occupies more than 1 byte. Of course, no law of nature says that an instruction couldn't contain a number of addresses, one for each byte of the variable. However, this solution is never adopted in practice, as it would make instructions much longer than they need to be. Instead, the address in such an instruction specifies the first byte of RAM occupied by the variable, and the other bytes are assumed to follow immediately after the first one. For example, in the case of a short variable, which as we have seen occupies 2 bytes of RAM, the instruction would specify the address of the first byte of the area of RAM in which the variable is stored.

Problem
Algorithms
C++
Executable
Hardware

However, there's one point that I haven't brought up yet: how the data for a given variable is actually arranged in memory. For example, suppose that the contents of a small section of RAM (specified as two hex digits per byte) look like Figure 3.2.

```
Address    Hex byte value

1000       41
1001       42
1002       43
1003       44
1004       00
```

Figure 3.2: A small section of RAM

Also suppose that a short variable i is stored starting at address 1000. To do much with a variable, we're going to have to load it into a *general register*, one of the small number of named data storage locations in the CPU intended for general use by the programmer. This proximity allows the CPU to operate on data in the registers at maximum speed. You may recall that there are seven general registers in the 386 CPU (and its successors); they're named eax, ebx, ecx, edx, esi, edi, and ebp.[4]

Unfortunately, there's another complication here: These registers are designed to operate on 4-byte quantities, while our variable i, being of type short, is only two bytes long. Are we out of luck? No, but we do have to specify how long the variable is that we want to load. This problem is not unique to Intel CPUs, since any CPU has to have the ability to load different-sized variables into registers. Different CPUs use different methods of specifying this important piece of information; in the Intel CPUs, one way to do this is to alter the register name. As we saw in the discussion of the development of Intel machines, we can remove the leading e from the register name to specify that we're dealing with 2-byte values; the resulting name refers to the lower two bytes of the 4-byte register. Therefore, if we wanted to load the value of i into register ax (that is, the lower half of register eax), the instruction could be written as follows:[5]

Problem
Algorithms
C++
Executable
Hardware

    mov ax,[1000][6]

Who's on First?

Now I have a question for you. After we execute the assembly language statement mov ax,[1000] to load the value of i into ax, what's in register ax? That may seem like a silly question; the answer is obviously the value of i. Yes, but what is that value exactly? The first byte of i, at location 1000, has the value 41 hexadecimal (abbreviated 41h), and the second byte, at location 1001, has the value 42h. But

---

4. Besides these general registers, a dedicated register called esp plays an important role in the execution of real programs. We'll see how it does this in Chapter 5.

5. It's also possible to load a 2-byte value into a 32-bit (i.e., 4-byte) register such as eax and have the high part of that register set to 0 in one instruction by using an instruction designed specifically for that purpose. This approach has the advantage that further processing can be done with the 32-bit registers.

6. The number inside the brackets [ ] represents a memory address.

the value of i is 2 bytes long; is it 4142h or 4241h? These are clearly not the same!

That was a trick question; there's no way for you to deduce the answer with only the information I've given you so far. The answer happens to be 4241h because Intel decided to store the low part of the value in the byte of RAM where the variable starts. Some other CPUs do it the opposite way, where the high part of the value is stored in the byte of RAM where the variable starts; this is called *big-endian*, since the big end of the value is first, while the Intel way is correspondingly called *little-endian*. And some machines, such as the Power PC, can use either of these methods according to how they are started up. This makes it easier for them to run software written for either of these memory orientations.

As you might have surmised, the same system applies to 4-byte values. Therefore, when we write the instruction mov eax,[1000] on a little-endian machine it loads the eax register with the value 44434241h; that is, the four bytes 41, 42, 43, and 44 (hex) would be loaded into the eax register, with the byte having the lowest address loaded into the low end of the register.

Here's another example. A little-endian system would represent the number 1234 (hex) stored at address 5000 as in Figure 3.3.

Problem
Algorithms
C++
Executable
Hardware

Address	Value
5000	34
5001	12

Figure 3.3: One little-endian

A big-endian system would represent the same value 1234 (hex) as illustrated in Figure 3.4.

Address	Value
5000	12
5001	34

Figure 3.4: A big-endian example

This really isn't much of a problem as long as we don't try to move data from one type of machine to another. However, when such data transportation is necessary, dealing with mixed endianness can be a real nuisance!

Before going on, let's practice a bit with this notion of how data is stored in memory.

Exercises, First Set

1. Assume that a short variable named z starts at location 1001 in a little-endian machine. Using Figure 3.5 for the contents of memory, what is the value of z, in hex?

```
Address    Hex byte value

1000       3a
1001       43
1002       3c
1003       99
1004       00
```

Figure 3.5: Exercise 1

The answer to this exercise can be found at the end of the chapter.

Underware?

```
Problem
Algorithms
C++
Executable
Hardware
```

I can almost hear the wailing and tooth gnashing out there. Do I expect you to deal with all of these instructions and addresses by yourself? You'll undoubtedly be happy to learn that this isn't necessary, as the compiler takes care of these details. However, if you don't have some idea of how a compiler works, you'll be at a disadvantage when you're trying to figure out how to make it do what you want. Therefore, we're going to spend the next few pages "playing compiler"; that is, I'll examine each statement and indicate what action the compiler might take as a result. I'll simplify the statements a bit to make the explanation simpler; you should still get the idea (I hope). Figure 3.6 illustrates the set of statements that I'll compile. In case you were wondering, blank lines are ignored by the compiler; you can put them in freely to improve readability.

```
short i;
short j;

i = 5;
j = i + 3;
```

Figure 3.6: A really little numeric calculation

Compiler's Eye View

Here are the rules of this game:

1. All numbers in the C++ program are decimal; all addresses and numbers in the machine instructions are hexadecimal.[7]
2. All addresses are 2 bytes long.[8]
3. Variables are stored at addresses starting at 1000.
4. Machine instructions are stored at addresses starting at 2000.[9]
5. A number *not* enclosed in [ ] is a literal value, which represents itself. For example, the instruction mov ax,1000 means to move the value 1000 into the ax register.
6. A number enclosed in [ ] is an address, which specifies where data is to be stored or retrieved. For example, the instruction mov ax,[1000] means to move 2 bytes of data starting at location 1000, *not* the value 1000 itself, into the ax register.

Now, let's start compiling. The first statement, short i;, tells me to allocate storage for a 2-byte variable called i that will be treated as signed (because that's the default). Since no value has been assigned to this variable yet, the resulting "memory map" looks like Figure 3.7.

Problem
Algorithms
C++
Executable
Hardware

```
Address      Variable name

1000         i
```

Figure 3.7: Compiling, part 1

The second statement, short j;, tells me to allocate storage for a 2-byte variable called j that will be treated as signed (because that's the default). Since no value has been assigned to this variable yet, the resulting "memory map" looks like Figure 3.8.

---

7. However, I've cheated here by using small enough numbers in the C++ program that they are the same in hex as in decimal.

8. The real compiler on the CD-ROM actually uses 4-byte addresses, but this doesn't change any of the concepts involved.

9. These addresses are arbitrary; a real compiler will assign addresses to variables and machine instructions by its own rules.

```
Address    Variable name

1000       i
1002       j
```

Figure 3.8: Compiling, part 2

The next line is blank, so we skip it. This brings us to the statement i = 5;, which is an executable statement, so we need to generate one or more machine instructions to execute it. We have already assigned address 1000 to i, so we have to generate instructions that will set the 2 bytes at address 1000 to the value that represents 5. One way to do this is to start by setting ax to 5, by the instruction mov ax,5, then storing the contents of ax (5, of course) into the location where the value of i is kept, namely 1000, via the instruction mov [1000],ax.[10]

Figure 3.9 shows what our "memory map" looks like so far.

Problem
Algorithms
C++
Executable
Hardware

```
Address    Variable Name

1000       i
1002       j

Address    Machine Instruction        Assembly Language
                                       Equivalent

2000     ┌──────────────────┐
         │   b8 05 00       │          mov ax,5
         └──────────────────┘
2003     ┌──────────────────┐
         │   a9 00 10       │          mov [1000],ax
         └──────────────────┘
```

Figure 3.9: Compiling, part 3

The last statement, j = i + 3;, is the most complicated statement in our program, and it's not that complicated. As with the previous statement, it's executable, which means we need to generate machine instructions to execute it. Because we haven't changed ax since we used it to initialize the variable i with the value 5, it still has that value. Therefore, to calculate the value of j, we can just add 3 to the value in ax by executing the instruction add ax,3. After the execution of this instruction, ax will contain i + 3. Now all we have to do is to store that value in j. As indicated in the translation of the statement

---

10. The first byte of each instruction is the "operation code", or "op code" for short, which tells the CPU what kind of instruction to execute. In the case of the instruction mov ax,5, b8 specifies a "load register ax with a literal value" instruction. The literal value is the next 2 bytes, which represent the value 5 in little-endian notation; therefore, the full translation of the instruction is "load ax with the literal value 5".

short j;, the address used to hold the value of j is 1002. Therefore, we can set j to the value in ax by executing the instruction mov [1002],ax.

Figure 3.10 shows what the "memory map" looks like now.

```
Address      Variable Name

1000            i
1002            j

Address      Machine Instruction        Assembly Language
                                         Equivalent

2000         ┌─────────────────┐         mov ax,5
             │   b8  05  00    │
             ├─────────────────┤
2003         │   a9  00  10    │         mov [1000],ax
             ├─────────────────┤
2006         │   05  03  00    │         add ax,3
             ├─────────────────┤
2009         │   a9  02  10    │         mov [1002],ax
             └─────────────────┘
```

Figure 3.10: Compiling, part 4

By the way, don't be misled by this example into thinking that all machine language instructions are 3 bytes in length. It's just a coincidence that all of the ones I've used here are of that length. The actual size of an instruction on the Intel CPUs can vary considerably, from 1 byte to a theoretical maximum of 12 bytes. Most instructions in common use, however, range from 1 to 5 bytes.

```
Problem
Algorithms
C++
Executable
Hardware
```

Execution Is Everything

Having examined what the compiler does at **compile time** with the preceding little program fragment, the next question is what happens when the compiled program is executed at **run time**. First, let's go over a couple of rules for this part of the "game":

1.   The bold address in the lower block indicates the next instruction to be executed.
2.   We put ?? in the variable and register contents to start out with, to indicate that since we haven't stored anything in them yet, we don't know what they contain.

Now we're ready to start execution. At this point, the sections of RAM we're concerned with will look like Figure 3.11.

```
Register   Contents

ax         ??


Address          Contents          Variable Name

1000        ?? ??                   i

1002        ?? ??                   j


Address    Machine Instruction    Assembly Language
                                       Equivalent

2000        b8 05 00               mov ax,5

2003        a9 00 10               mov [1000],ax

2006        05 03 00               add ax,3

2009        a9 02 10               mov [1002],ax
```

Figure 3.11: Before execution

Figure 3.12 shows the situation after the first instruction, mov ax,5, has been executed.

Problem
Algorithms
C++
Executable
Hardware

```
Register   Contents

ax         5


Address          Contents          Variable Name

1000        ?? ??                   i

1002        ?? ??                   j


Address    Machine Instruction    Assembly Language
                                       Equivalent

2000        b8 05 00               mov ax,5

2003        a9 00 10               mov [1000],ax

2006        05 03 00               add ax,3

2009        a9 02 10               mov [1002],ax
```

Figure 3.12: After the first instruction

Figure 3.13 shows the situation after we have executed the next instruction, mov [1000],ax.

```
Register  Contents

ax        5


Address        Contents          Variable Name

1000      | 05 00 |                  i

1002      | ?? ?? |                  j


Address   Machine Instruction      Assembly Language
                                   Equivalent

2000      | b8 05 00 |              mov ax,5

2003      | a9 00 10 |              mov [1000],ax

2006      | 05 03 00 |              add ax,3

2009      | a9 02 10 |              mov [1002],ax
```

Figure 3.13: After the second instruction

Figure 3.14 shows the situation after we have executed the next
instruction, add ax,3.

```
Register  Contents

ax        8


Address        Contents          Variable Name

1000      | 05 00 |                  i

1002      | ?? ?? |                  j


Address   Machine Instruction      Assembly Language
                                   Equivalent

2000      | b8 05 00 |              mov ax,5

2003      | a9 00 10 |              mov [1000],ax

2006      | 05 03 00 |              add ax,3

2009      | a9 02 10 |              mov [1002],ax
```

```
Problem
Algorithms
C++
Executable
Hardware
```

Figure 3.14: After the third instruction

Finally, Figure 3.15 shows the situation after we have executed the final instruction, mov [1002],ax. As we intended, the variable i has the value 5, and the variable j has the value 8.

```
Register   Contents

ax         8
```

Address	Contents	Variable Name
1000	05 00	i
1002	08 00	j

Address	Machine Instruction	Assembly Language Equivalent
2000	b8 05 00	mov ax,5
2003	a9 00 10	mov [1000],ax
2006	05 03 00	add ax,3
2009	a9 02 10	mov [1002],ax

```
Problem
Algorithms
C++
Executable
Hardware
```

Figure 3.15: After the final instruction

A Cast of Characters

This should give you some idea of how numeric variables and values work. But what about nonnumeric ones?

This brings us to the subject of two new variable types and the values they can contain. These are the char (short for "character") and its relative, the string. What are these good for, and how do they work?

A variable of type char corresponds to 1 byte of storage. Since a byte has 8 bits, it can hold any of 256 (2^8) values; the exact values depend on whether it is signed or unsigned, as with the short variables we have seen before. Going strictly according to this description, you might get the idea that a char is just a "really short" numeric variable. A char indeed can be used for this purpose in cases where no more than 256 different numeric values are to be represented. However, its main purpose is to represent an individual letter, digit, punctuation mark, "special character" (e.g., $, #, %, and so on), or one of the other "printable" and displayable units from which words, sentences, and other textual data such as this paragraph are composed.[11] The 256 different possibilities are plenty to represent any character in English, as well as a number of other European languages; in fact, this is one of the main reasons that there are 8 bits in a byte, rather than some other number.[12] Of course, one char isn't good for much by itself, so we often use groups of them, called strings, to make them easier to handle. Just as with numeric values, these variables can be set to literal values, which represent themselves.

Figure 3.16 is an example of how to specify and use each of these types we've just encountered. This is the first complete program we've seen, so there are a couple of new constructs that I'll have to explain to you. By the way, this program isn't very useful; it's just an example of the syntax of defining and using variables and literal values. However, we'll use these constructs to do useful work later.

Before we get to the code, I should explain that we need the line #include "string6.h" to tell the compiler how to manipulate strings; they aren't built in to its knowledge base. For the moment, it's enough to know that the contents of the file string6.h are needed to tell the compiler how to use strings; we'll get into the details of this mechanism later, starting in Chapter 7.

However, since we're already on the subject of files, this would be a good time to point out that the two main types of files in C++ are implementation files (also known as source files), which in our case have the extension .cc, and header files, which by convention have the extension .h.[13] Implementation files contain statements that result in executable code, while each header file contains information that allows us to access a set of language features.

Problem
Algorithms
C++
Executable
Hardware

---

11. As we will see shortly, not all characters have visible representations; some of these "nonprintable" characters are useful in controlling how our printed or displayed information looks.

12. Of course, the written forms of "ideographic" languages such as Chinese and Korean consist of far more than 256 characters. While these languages have been supported to some extent by schemes that switch among a number of sets of 256 characters each, such clumsy approaches to the problem made programs much more complicated and error prone. As the international market for software is increasing rapidly, it has become more important to have a convenient method of handling large *character sets*; as a result, a standard method of representing the characters of such languages by using 2 bytes per character has been developed. It's called the "Unicode standard".

13. Other compilers sometimes use other extensions for implementation files, such as .cpp, and for header files, such as .hpp.

```
#include "string6.h"

int main()
{
    char c1;
    char c2;
    string s1;
    string s2;

    c1 = 'A';
    c2 = c1;

    s1 = "This is a test ";
    s2 = "and so is this.";

    return 0;
}
```

Figure 3.16: Some real characters and strings (code\basic00.cc)

`Problem`
`Algorithms`
`C++`
`Executable`
`Hardware`

The next construct we have to examine is the line int main(), which has two new components. The first is the "return type", which specifies the type of value that will be returned from the program when it ends. In this case, that type is int, which is an integral type exactly like short except that its size depends on the compiler. With a 32-bit compiler like the one on the CD-ROM in this book, an int is 32 bits, or twice the size of a short. With a 16-bit compiler such as Borland C++ version 3.1, an int is the same size as a short. I don't like to use ints, because I want my code to work in the same way on both 16- and 32-bit compilers. However, we don't have much choice here, because the C++ language specifies that main has to have the return type int.

This brings us to the meaning of main(). This tells the compiler where to start executing the code: C++ has a rule that execution always starts at the place called main. We'll get into this in more detail in Chapter 5. For now, you'll just have to take my word that this is necessary; I promise I'll explain what it really means when you have enough background to understand the explanation.

What does this useless but hopefully instructive program do? As is always the case, we have to tell the compiler what the types of our variables are before we can use them. In this case, c1 and c2 are of type char, whereas s1 and s2 are strings.

After taking care of these formalities, we can start to use the variables. In the first executable statement, c1 = 'A';, we set the char variable c1 to a literal value — in this case a capital *A*. We need to surround this with single quotation marks (') to tell the compiler that we mean the letter *A* rather than a variable named A. In the next line, c2 = c1;, we set c2 to the same value as c1 holds, which of course is 'A' in this case. The next executable statement, s1 = "This is a test ";, as you might expect, sets the string variable s1 to the value "This is a test ",[14] which is a literal of a type called a **C string**. Don't confuse a C string with a string. A C string is a type of literal that we use to assign values to variables of type string; in other words, a string is a variable that can be set to the value of a literal string (C string), but they're not the same type. In the statement s1 = "This is a test "; we use a quotation mark, in this case the double quote ("), to tell the compiler where the literal value starts and ends.

You may be wondering why we need two different kinds of quotes in these two cases. The reason is that there are actually two types of nonnumeric data, *fixed-length data* and *variable-length data*. Fixed-length data is relatively easy to handle in a program, as the compiler can set aside the correct amount of space in advance. Variables of type char are 1 byte long and can thus contain exactly one character; as a result, when we set a char to a literal value, as we do in the line c1 = 'A';, the code that executes that statement has the simple task of copying exactly 1 byte representing the literal 'A' to the address reserved for variable c1.[15]

Problem
Algorithms
C++
Executable
Hardware

However, C string literals such as "This is a test " are variable-length data, and dealing with such data isn't so easy. Since there could be any number of characters in a C string, the code that does the assignment of a literal value like "This is a test " to a string variable has to have some way to tell where the literal value ends. One possible way to provide this needed information would be for the compiler to store the length of the C string literal in the memory location immediately before the first character in the literal. I would prefer

---

14. Please note that there is a *space* (blank) character at the end of that C string literal, after the word *test*. That space is part of the literal value.

15. Warning: Every character inside the quotes has an effect on the value of the literal, whether the quotes are single or double; even "invisible" characters such as the *space* (' ') will change the literal's value. In other words, the line c1 = 'A';, is *not* the same as the line c1 = 'A ';. The latter statement may or may not be legal, depending on the compiler you're using, but it is virtually certain not to give you what you want, which is to set the variable c1 to the value equivalent to the character 'A'. Instead, c1 will have some weird value resulting from combining the 'A' and the space character. In the case of a string value contained in double quotes, multiple characters are allowed, so "A B" and "AB" both make sense, but the space still makes a difference; namely, it keeps the 'A' and 'B' from being next to one another.

this method; unfortunately, it is not the method used in the C language or its descendant, the C++ language.

To be fair, the inventors of C didn't make an arbitrary choice; they had reasons for their decision on how to indicate the length of a string. You see, if we were to reserve only 1 byte to store the actual length in bytes of the character data in the string, then the maximum length of a string would be limited to 255 bytes. This is because the maximum value that could be stored in the length byte, as in any other byte, is 255. Thus, if we had a string longer than 255 bytes, we would not be able to store the length of the string in the 1 byte reserved for that purpose. On the other hand, if we were to reserve 2 bytes for the length of each string, then programs that contain many strings would take more memory than they should.

While the extra memory consumption that would be caused by using a 2-byte length code may not seem significant today, the situation was considerably different when C was invented. At that time, conserving memory was very important; the inventors of C therefore chose to mark the end of a C string by a byte containing the value 0, which is called a **null byte**.[16]

Problem
Algorithms
C++
Executable
Hardware

This solution has the advantage that only one extra byte is needed to indicate the end of a C string of any length. However, it also has some serious drawbacks. First, this solution makes it impossible to have a byte containing the value 0 in the middle of a C string, as all of the C string manipulation routines would treat that null byte as being the end of the C string. Second, it is a nontrivial operation to determine the length of a C string; the only way to do it is to scan through the C string until you find a null byte. As you can probably tell, I'm not particularly impressed with this mechanism; nevertheless, as it has been adopted into C++ for compatibility with C, we're stuck with it for literal strings in our programs. Therefore, the literal string "ABCD" would occupy 5 bytes, 1 for each character, and 1 for the null byte at the end, added automatically by the compiler when it sees the ending ". But we've skipped one step: How do we represent characters in memory? There's no intuitively obvious way to convert the character 'A' into a value that can be stored in 1 byte of memory.

The answer, at least for our purposes in English, is called the **ASCII code** standard. This stands for American Standard Code for

---

16. I don't want to mislead you about this notion of a byte having the value 0; it is *not* the same as the representation of the decimal digit "0". As we'll see, each displayable character (and a number of invisible ones) is assigned a value to represent it when it's part of a string or literal value (i.e., a C string literal or char literal). The 0 byte I'm referring to is a byte with the binary value 0.

Information Interchange, which as the name suggests was invented precisely to allow the interchange of data between different programs and makes of computers. Before the invention of ASCII, such interchange was difficult or impossible, since every manufacturer made up its own code or codes. Here are the specific character codes that we have to be concerned with for the purposes of this book:

1. The codes for the capital letters start with hex 41 for 'A' and run consecutively to hex 5a for 'Z'.
2. The codes for the lowercase letters start with hex 61 for 'a' and run consecutively to hex 7a for 'z'.
3. The codes for the numeric digits start with hex 30 for '0' and run consecutively to hex 39 for '9'.

Given these rules, the memory representation of the C string "ABCD" might look something like Figure 3.17.

```
Address    Hex value

1000       41
1001       42
1002       43
1003       44
1004       00 (null byte; that is, end of C string)
```

Problem
Algorithms
C++
Executable
Hardware

Figure 3.17: Yet another small section of RAM

Now that we see how C strings are represented in memory, I can explain why we need two kinds of quotes. The double quotes tell the compiler to add the null byte at the end of the C string literal, so that when the assignment statement s1 = "This is a test "; is executed, the program knows when to stop copying the value to the string variable.

A Byte by Any Other Name . . .

Have you noticed that I've played a little trick here? The illustration of the C string "ABCD" should look a bit familiar; its memory contents are exactly the same as in Figure 3.2, where we were discussing numeric variables. I did this to illustrate an important point: The contents of memory actually consist of uninterpreted bytes, which have meaning only when used in a particular way by a program. That is, the same bytes can represent numeric data or characters, depending on how they are referred to.

This is one of the main reasons why we need to tell the C++ compiler what types our variables have. Some languages allow variables to be used in different ways at different times, but in C++ any given variable always has the same type. For example, a char variable can't change into a short. At first glance, it seems that it would be much easier for programmers to be able to use variables any way they like; why is C++ so restrictive?

The C++ **type system**, as this feature of a language is called, is specifically designed to minimize the risk of misinterpreting or otherwise misusing a variable. It's entirely too easy in some languages to change the type of a variable without meaning to; the resulting bugs can be very difficult to find, especially in a large program. In C++, the usage of a variable can be checked by the compiler. This **static type checking** allows the compiler to tell you about many errors that otherwise would not be detected until the program is running (**dynamic type checking**). This is particularly important in systems that need to run continuously for long periods of time. While you can reboot your machine if your word processor crashes due to a run-time error, this is not acceptable as a solution for errors in the telephone network, for example.

Problem
Algorithms
C++
Executable
Hardware

Of course, you probably won't be writing programs demanding that degree of reliability any time soon, but strict static type checking is still worthwhile in helping eliminate errors at the earliest possible stage in the development of our programs.

Some Strings Attached

After that infomercial for the advantages of static type checking, we can resume our examination of C strings. You may have noticed that there's a **space** character at the end of the C string "This is a test ". That's another reason why we have to use a special character like " (the double quote) to mark the beginning and end of a string; how else would the compiler know whether that space is supposed to be part of the C string or not? The space character is one of the **nonprinting characters** (or **nondisplay characters**) that controls the format of our displayed or printed information. Imagine how hard it would be to read this book without space characters! While we're on the subject, I should also tell you about some other characters that have special meaning to the compiler. They are listed in Figure 3.18.

Name	Graphic	Use
Single quote	'	Surrounds a single character value
Double quote	"	Surrounds a multicharacter value
Semicolon	;	Ends a statement
Curly braces	{ }	Groups statements together
Parentheses	( )	Surrounds part of a statement[17]
Backslash	\	Tells the compiler that the next character should be treated differently from the way that it would normally be treated[18]

Figure 3.18: Special characters for program text

Our next task, after a little bit of practice with the memory representation of a C string, will be to see how we get the values of our strings to show up on the screen.

Exercises, Second Set

2.   Assume that a C string literal starts at memory location 1001. If the contents of memory are as illustrated in Figure 3.19, what is the value of the C string?

Problem
Algorithms
C++
Executable
Hardware

```
Address    Hex value

1000       44
1001       48
1002       45
1003       4c
1004       4c
1005       4f
1006       00
```

Figure 3.19: A small section of RAM

The answer to this exercise can be found at the end of the chapter.

---

17. I'll be more specific later, when we have seen some examples.

18. For example, if you wanted to insert a " in a string, you would have to use \" because just a plain " would indicate the end of the string. That is, if you were to set a string to the value "This is a \"string\".", it would display as: This is a "string".

In and Out

Most programs need to interact with their users, both to ask them what they want and to present the results when they are available. The computer term for this topic is **I/O** (short for "input/output"). We'll start by getting information from the keyboard and displaying it on the screen. Later, we'll go over the more complex I/O functions that allow us to read and write data on the disk.

Now let's look at Figure 3.20, which shows how to display the text "This is a test and so is this.". The meaning of << is suggested by its arrowlike shape. The information on its right is sent to the "output target" on its left. In this case, we're sending the information to one of the predefined destinations, cout, which stands for "character output".[19] Characters sent to cout are displayed on the screen.[20]

```
#include <iostream.h>
#include "string6.h"

int main()
{
    string s1;
    string s2;

    s1 = "This is a test ";
    s2 = "and so is this.";

    cout << s1;
    cout << s2;

    return 0;
}
```

Problem
Algorithms
C++
Executable
Hardware

Figure 3.20: Some simple output (code\basic01.cc)

This program will send the following output to the screen:

This is a test and so is this.

---

19. The line #include <iostream.h> is necessary here to tell the compiler about cout and how it works. We'll get into this in a bit more detail later in this chapter.

20. By the way, cout is pronounced "see out".

So much for (simple) output. Input from the keyboard is just as simple. Let's modify our little sample to use it, as shown in Figure 3.21.

```cpp
#include <iostream.h>
#include "string6.h"

int main()
{
    string s1;
    string s2;

    cin >> s1;
    cin >> s2;

    cout << s1;
    cout << " ";
    cout << s2;

    return 0;
}
```

Figure 3.21: Some simple input and output (code\basic02.cc)

```
Problem
Algorithms
C++
Executable
Hardware
```

As you might have guessed, cin (shorthand for "character input") is the counterpart to cout, as >> is the counterpart to <<; cin supplies characters from the keyboard to the program via the >> operator.[21] This program will wait for you to type in the first string, ended by hitting the ENTER key, then do the same for the second string. When you hit ENTER the second time, the program will display the first string, then a blank, and then the second string.

if **Only You Knew**

By now, you're probably impatient to get a more useful program running. I don't blame you, but if you can hold on just a little longer, we'll have all the pieces we need to accomplish that goal. First, we need to deal with some program organization concepts.

---

21. Similarly to cout, cin is pronounced "see in" rather than "sin".

In our examples so far, the program always executes the same statements in the same order. However, any real program is going to need to alter its behavior according to the data it is processing. For example, in a banking application, it might be necessary to send out a notice to a depositor whenever the balance in a particular account drops below a certain level; or perhaps the depositor would just be charged some exorbitant fee in that case. Either way, the program has to do something different depending on the balance. This can be accomplished by using an if **statement**. Figure 3.22 shows an example of such a statement.

```
#include <iostream.h>

int main()
{
    short balance;

    cout << "Please enter your bank balance: ";
    cin >> balance;

    if (balance < 10000)
        cout << "Please remit $20 service charge." << endl;
    else
        cout << "Have a nice day!" << endl;

    return 0;
}
```

Problem
Algorithms
C++
Executable
Hardware

Figure 3.22: Using an if statement (code\basic03.cc)

This program starts by displaying the line

Please enter your bank balance:

on the screen. Then it waits for you to type in your balance, followed by the ENTER key (so it knows when you're done). The conditional statement checks whether you're a "good customer". If your balance is less than $10,000, the next statement is executed, which displays the line

Please remit $20 service charge.

The phrase << endl is new here. It means "we're done with this line of output; send it out to the screen". You could also use the special character '\n', which means much the same thing; its official name is "newline".

Now let's get back to our regularly scheduled program. If the condition is false (that is, you have at least $10,000 in the bank), the computer skips the statement that asks you to remit $20. Instead, it executes the statement after the else, which tells you to have a nice day. That's what else is for; it specifies what to do if the condition specified in the if statement is false (that is, not true). If you typed in a number 10,000 or higher, the program would display

Have a nice day!

You don't have to specify an else if you don't want to. In that case, if the if condition isn't true, the program just goes to the next statement as though the if had never been executed.

while **We're on the Subject**

The while statement is another way of affecting the order of program execution. This conditional statement executes the statement under its control as long as a certain condition is true. Such potentially repeated execution is called a **loop**; a loop controlled by a while statement is called, logically enough, a while loop. Figure 3.23 is a program that uses a while loop to challenge the user to guess a secret number from 0 to 9 and keeps asking for guesses until the correct answer is entered.

There are a few wrinkles in this program that we haven't seen before. Although the while statement itself is fairly straightforward, the meaning of its condition != isn't intuitively obvious. However, if you consider the problem we're trying to solve, you'll probably come to the (correct) conclusion that != means "not equal", since we want to keep asking for more guesses while the Guess is not equal to our Secret number.[22] Since there is a comparison operator that tests for "not equal", you might wonder how to test for "equal" as well. As is explained in some detail in the next chapter, in C++ we have to use == rather than = to compare whether two values are equal.

Problem
Algorithms
C++
Executable
Hardware

---

22. You may be wondering why we need parentheses around the expression Guess != Secret. The conditional expression has to be in parentheses so that the compiler can tell where it ends and the statement to be controlled by the while begins.

```
#include <iostream.h>

int main()
{
    short Secret;
    short Guess;

    Secret = 3;

    cout << "Try and guess my number. Hint: It's from 0 to 9" << endl;
    cin >> Guess;

    while (Guess != Secret)
        {
        cout << "Sorry, that's not correct." << endl;
        cin >> Guess;
        }

    cout << "You guessed right!" << endl;

    return 0;
}
```

Problem
Algorithms
C++
Executable
Hardware

Figure 3.23: Using a while statement (code\basic04.cc)

You might also be wondering whether an if statement with an else clause would serve as well as the while; after all, if is used to select one of two alternatives, and the else could select the other one. The answer is that this would allow the user to take only one guess before the program ends; the while loop lets the user try again as many times as needed to get the right answer.

Now you should have enough information to be able to write a simple program of your own. Some exercises that ask you to do just that follow below, right after some instructions on the mechanics of creating a program. The instructions assume that you've installed the software from the CD-ROM in the back of this book. If you haven't, follow the instructions in the back of the book to install the software, and then come back to these instructions.

1.   Change to the "\introcpp\code" directory on the drive where you installed the compiler.
2.   Use EDIT or Notepad to create a text file containing the source code for your program, giving it the extension ".cc". In other words, if you want your program to be called "party", then name this file "party.cc".

3. To compile your program, switch to the "\introcpp\normal" directory and type "mk party", substituting the name of your file for "party". Note: do *not* add the ".cc" to the end of the file name.
4. To run your program normally, make sure you are in the "\introcpp\normal" directory, and then type the name of the program, without the extension. In this case, you would just type "party".
5. To run this program under the debugger, make sure you are in the "\introcpp\normal" directory, and then type "trace party" (substituting the name of your program for "party"). Again, do *not* add the ".cc" to the end of the file name.

Exercises, Third Set

3. Write a program that asks the user to type in the number of people that are expected for dinner, not counting the user. Assuming that the number typed in is n, display a message that says "A table for (n+1) is ready.". For example, if the user types 3, display "A table for 4 is ready.".
4. Modify the program from Exercise 3 to display an error message if the number of guests is more than 20.
5. Write a program that asks the user to type in his or her name and age. If the age is less than 47, then indicate that the user is a youngster; otherwise, that he or she is getting on in years.
6. Write a program that calculates how much extra allowance a teenager can earn by doing extra chores. Her allowance is calculated as $10 if she does no extra chores; she gets $1 additional for each extra chore she does.

```
Problem
Algorithms
C++
Executable
Hardware
```

Answers to the preceding exercises can be found at the end of the chapter.

7. Write a program that calculates the tax and tip for a restaurant check, assuming that the tip is 15% and the tax is 8% on the amount before the tip.
8. When purchasing a new automobile, you will probably be offered an extended warranty to cover problems that may arise after the end of the manufacturer's warranty. Let's assume that a particular warranty covers three systems: the engine, the transmission, and the air conditioner. Let's also assume that the average repair for the engine is $500, the average repair for the

transmission is $200, and the average repair for the air conditioner is $1000. The likelihood of each of these happening some time during the period of the extended warranty is 10%, 20%, and 10%, respectively. Write a program that calculates how much the warranty company will pay out on average for each policy that they sell.

9.   Modify the "number guessing" program in Figure 3.23 to make the number between 0 and 1023 instead of between 0 and 9. To help the user get the number more easily, instead of just reporting "right" or "wrong", have the program indicate whether the guess is too high or too low. Of course, if it's correct, then end the program as before.

Just Up the Block

Problem
Algorithms
C++
Executable
Hardware

A more significant addition to our arsenal of programming weapons is the ability to group several statements into one logical section of a program. That's the function of the **curly braces**, { and }. The first one of these starts such a section, called a **block**, and the second one ends the block. Because the two statements after the while are part of the same block, they are treated as a unit; both are executed if the condition in the while is true, and neither is executed if it is false. A block can be used anywhere that a statement can be used and is treated in exactly the same way as if it were one statement.

At the Fair

Now we're ready to write a program that vaguely resembles a solution to a real problem. We'll start with a simple, rural type of programming problem.

Imagine that you are at a county fair. The contest for the heaviest pumpkin is about to get underway, and the judges have asked for your help in operating the "pumpkin scoreboard". This device has one slot for the current pumpkin weight (the CurrentWeight slot) and another slot for the highest weight so far (the HighestWeight slot). Each slot can hold three digits from 0 to 9 and therefore can indicate any weight from 0 to 999. The judges want you to maintain an up-to-date display of the current weight and of the highest weight seen so far.

The weights are expressed to the nearest pound. How would you go about this task?

Probably the best way to start is by setting the number in both slots to the first pumpkin weight called out. Then, as each new weight is called out, you change the number in the CurrentWeight slot to match the current weight; if it's higher than the number in the HighestWeight slot, you change that one to match as well. Of course, you don't have to do anything to the HighestWeight slot when a weight less than the previous maximum is called out, because that pumpkin can't be the winner. How do we know when we are done? Since a pumpkin entered in this contest has to have a weight of at least 1 pound, the weigher calls out 0 as the weight when the weighing is finished. At that point, the number in the HighestWeight slot is the weight of the winner.

The procedure you have just imagined performing can be expressed a bit more precisely by the following algorithm:

1. Ask for the first weight.
2. Set the number in the CurrentWeight slot to this value.
3. Copy the number in the CurrentWeight slot to the HighestWeight slot.
4. Display both the current weight and the highest weight so far (which are the same, at this point).
5. While the CurrentWeight value is greater than 0 (that is, there are more pumpkins to be weighed), do steps 5a to 5d:
   a. Ask for the next weight.
   b. Set the number in the CurrentWeight slot to this weight.
   c. If the number in the CurrentWeight slot is greater than the number in the HighestWeight slot, copy the number in the CurrentWeight slot to the HighestWeight slot.
   d. Display the current weight and the highest weight so far.
6. Stop. The number in the HighestWeight slot is the weight of the winner.

Problem
Algorithms
C++
Executable
Hardware

Figure 3.24 is the translation of our little problem into C++. By the way, this program contains some C++ constructs that you haven't seen before. These constructs will be defined in the text after the listing.

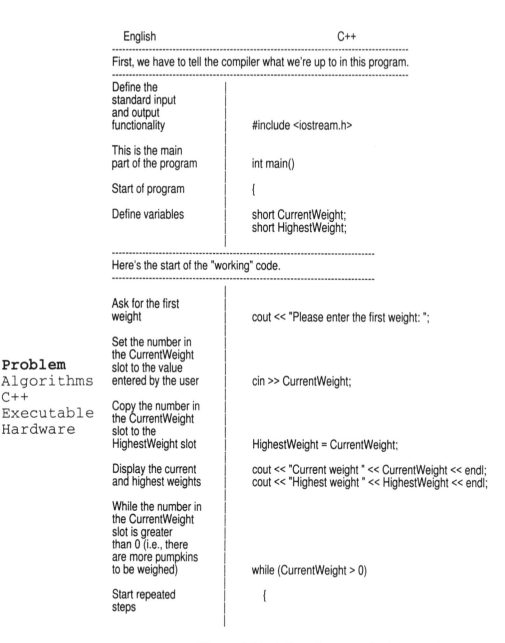

```
English                                  C++
-------------------------------------------------------------------------
First, we have to tell the compiler what we're up to in this program.
-------------------------------------------------------------------------
Define the
standard input
and output
functionality                #include <iostream.h>

This is the main
part of the program          int main()

Start of program             {

Define variables             short CurrentWeight;
                             short HighestWeight;

-------------------------------------------------------------------------
Here's the start of the "working" code.
-------------------------------------------------------------------------

Ask for the first
weight                       cout << "Please enter the first weight: ";

Set the number in
the CurrentWeight
slot to the value
entered by the user          cin >> CurrentWeight;

Copy the number in
the CurrentWeight
slot to the
HighestWeight slot           HighestWeight = CurrentWeight;

Display the current          cout << "Current weight " << CurrentWeight << endl;
and highest weights          cout << "Highest weight " << HighestWeight << endl;

While the number in
the CurrentWeight
slot is greater
than 0 (i.e., there
are more pumpkins
to be weighed)               while (CurrentWeight > 0)

Start repeated                  {
steps
```

Problem
Algorithms
C++
Executable
Hardware

Figure 3.24: A C++ Program (code\pump1.cc)

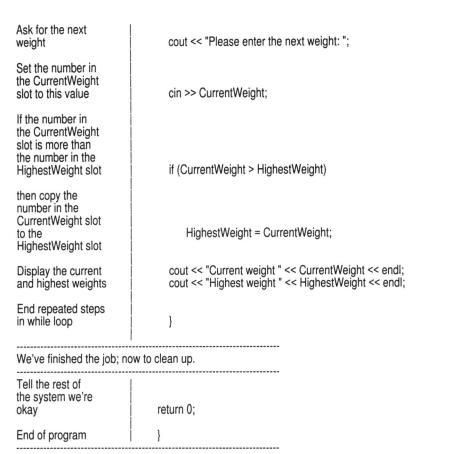

Ask for the next weight	cout << "Please enter the next weight: ";
Set the number in the CurrentWeight slot to this value	cin >> CurrentWeight;
If the number in the CurrentWeight slot is more than the number in the HighestWeight slot	if (CurrentWeight > HighestWeight)
then copy the number in the CurrentWeight slot to the HighestWeight slot	HighestWeight = CurrentWeight;
Display the current and highest weights	cout << "Current weight " << CurrentWeight << endl; cout << "Highest weight " << HighestWeight << endl;
End repeated steps in while loop	}

```
------------------------------------------------------------
We've finished the job; now to clean up.
------------------------------------------------------------
```

| Tell the rest of the system we're okay | return 0; |
| End of program | } |

```
------------------------------------------------------------
```

Problem
Algorithms
C++
Executable
Hardware

Figure 3.24 continued

If you're a programmer in some other language than C, you may wonder why we have to tell the compiler that we want to use the standard I/O library via the #include <iostream.h> statement. Why doesn't the compiler know to use that library automatically? This seeming oversight is actually the result of a decision made very early in the evolution of C: to keep the language itself (and therefore the compiler) as simple as possible, adding functionality with the aid of standard libraries. Since a large part of the libraries can be written in C, this decision reduces the amount of work needed to "port" the C language from one machine architecture or operating system to another. Once the compiler has been ported, it's not too difficult to get the libraries to work on the new machine. In fact, even the C (or

C++) compiler can be written in C (or C++), which makes the whole language quite portable.

This may seem impossible. How do you get started? In fact, the process is called *bootstrapping*, from the impossible task of trying to lift yourself by your own bootstraps.[23] The secret is to have one compiler that's already running; then you use that compiler to compile the compiler for the new machine. Once you have the new compiler running, it is common to use it to compile itself, so that you know it's working. After all, a compiler is a fairly complex program, so getting it to compile and execute properly is a pretty good indication that it's producing the right code.

Most of the rest of the program shown in Figure 3.24 should be fairly easy to understand, except for the two lines int main() and return 0;, which have related functions. Let's start with the line int main(). As we've already seen, the purpose of the main() part of this line is to tell the compiler where to start execution; the C++ language definition specifies that execution always starts at a block called main. This may seem redundant, as you might expect the compiler to assume that we want to start execution at the beginning of the program. However, C++ is intended to be useful in the writing of very large programs;

Problem
Algorithms
C++
Executable
Hardware

such programs can and usually do consist of several implementation files, each of which contains some of the functionality of the program. Without such a rule, the compiler wouldn't know which module should be executed first.

The int part of this same line specifies the type of the *exit code* that will be returned from the program by a return statement when the program is finished executing; in this case, that type is int. The exit code can be used by a *batch file* to determine whether our program finished executing correctly; an exit code of 0, by convention, means that it did.

The final statement in the program is return 0;. This is the return statement just mentioned, whose purpose is to return an exit code of 0 when our program stops running. The value that is returned, 0, is an acceptable value of the type we declared in the line int main(), namely, int. If it didn't match, the compiler would tell us we had made an error.

Finally, the closing curly brace, }, tells the compiler that it can stop compiling the current block, which in this case is the one called main. Without this marker, the compiler would tell us that we have a missing }, which of course would be true.

---

23. If this term sounds familiar, we've already seen it in the context of how we start up a computer when it's turned on, starting from a small *boot program* in the ROM, or Read-Only Memory.

Take It for a Spin

Assuming that you've installed the software from the CD-ROM in the back of this book, you can try out this program. First, you have to compile it by changing to the normal subdirectory under the main directory where you installed the software and typing mk pump1. Then type pump1 to run the program. It will ask you for weights and keep track of the highest weight that has been entered. Type 0 and hit ENTER to end the program.

If just running the program normally doesn't give you a good enough feel for how each statement works, you can run it in under control of the gdb debugger, which shows you each statement as it is to be executed along with the contents of all the variables. To run the program under gdb, make sure you are in the normal subdirectory, then type trace pump1. The program will start up and show you the first line of executable code. Type z and hit ENTER to execute each line of the program. The values of CurrentWeight and HighestWeight will be displayed immediately before the execution of each line. When you are asked for a weight, type one in and hit ENTER just as when executing normally.[24] When you enter a 0 weight, the program will stop looping and execution will take the path to the end of the program. At that point, type q (for *quit*) and hit ENTER to exit from the debugger.[25] This "computer's eye view" of the program should clear up any confusion on your part as to exactly how it works. By the way, if you're confused about the seemingly meaningless values that variables have before they're set to known values, let me assure you that they are indeed meaningless, as we'll see in the next chapter. First, let's practice a little more with chars and strings.

Problem
Algorithms
C++
Executable
Hardware

Exercises, Fourth Set

10. Here are four possible versions of an output statement. Assuming that the value of the string variable called name is "Joe Smith", what does each one of them do?

---

24. The gdb debugger has many commands, but we'll only use a few of them. For more information on gdb, you can type info at a DOS prompt, move down to the entry labeled "GDB", and hit ENTER. Warning: gdb is intended for experienced programmers, so the documentation isn't always as simply written as it might be. If you stick with the gdb commands I've listed here, you shouldn't have any trouble.

25. You can also type q and hit ENTER to leave the debugger at any other point if you get tired of watching the trace.

   a.   cout << "That is very old, " << name << ". " << endl;
   b.   cout << "That is very old, " << name << '. ' << endl;
   c.   cout << "That is very old, " << name << "." << endl;
   d.   cout << "That is very old, " << name << '.' << endl;

Review

Now it's time for some review on what we've covered in this chapter. We started out by discussing the tremendous reliability of computers; whenever you hear "it's the computer's fault", the overwhelming likelihood is that in fact the software is to blame rather than the hardware. Then we took a look at the fact that, although computers are calculating engines, many of the functions for which we use them don't have much to do with numeric calculations. For example, the most common use of computers is probably word processing, which doesn't use much in the way of addition or subtraction. Nevertheless, we started out our investigation of programming with numeric variables, which are easier to understand than non-numeric ones. To use variables, we need to write a C++ program, which consists primarily of a list of operations to be performed by the computer, along with directions that influence how these operations are to be translated into machine instructions.

`Problem`
`Algorithms`
`C++`
`Executable`
`Hardware`

That led us into a discussion of why and how our C++ program is translated into machine instructions by a *compiler*. We examined an example program that contained simple *source code statements*, including some that define variables and others that use those variables and constants to calculate results. We covered the symbols that are used to represent the operations of addition, subtraction, multiplication, division, and *assignment*, which are +, −, *, /, and =, respectively. While the first four of these should be familiar to you, the last one is a programming notion rather than a mathematical one. This may be confusing because the operation of assignment is expressed by the = sign, but is *not* the same as mathematical equality. For example, the statement x = 3; does *not* mean "x is equal to 3", but rather "set the variable x to the value 3."

After this discussion of the structure of statements in C++, we started an exploration of how the CPU actually stores and manipulates data in memory. The topics covered in this section included the order in which multibyte data items are stored in memory and the use of *general registers* to manipulate data efficiently.

Then we spent some time pretending to be a compiler, to improve our understanding of what the compiler does with our programs. This exercise involved keeping track of the addresses of variables and instructions and watching the effect of the instructions on the general registers and memory locations. During this exploration of the machine, we got acquainted with the *machine language* representation of instructions, which is the actual form that our executable programs take in memory. After a thorough examination of what the compiler does with our source code at *compile time*, we followed what would happen to the registers and memory locations at *run time* (that is, if the sample program were actually executed).

Then we began to look at two data types that can hold nonnumeric data, namely, the char and the string. The char corresponds to 1 byte of storage and can hold one character of data. Examples of appropriate values for a char variable include letters (a–z, A–Z), digits (0–9), and special characters (e.g., , . ! @ # $ %). A char can also represent a number of other "nonprintable" characters such as the space, which causes output to move to the next character position on the screen. Actually, a char can also be used as a "really short" numeric variable, but that's mostly a holdover from the days when memory was a lot more expensive and every byte counted.

One char isn't much information, so we often want to deal with groups of them as a single unit; an example would be a person's name. This is the province of the string variable type: variables of this type can handle an indefinitely long group of chars.

Problem
Algorithms
C++
Executable
Hardware

At the beginning of our sample program for strings and chars, we encountered a new construct, the #include *statement*. This tells the compiler where to find instructions on how to handle data types such as strings, about which it doesn't have any built-in knowledge. Then we came across the line int main(), which indicates where we want to start executing our program. A C++ program always starts execution at the place indicated by such a line. We also investigated the meaning of int, which is the *return type* of main. The return type tells the compiler what sort of data this program returns to the operating system when it finishes executing; the return value can be used to determine what action a batch file should take next.

As we continued looking at the sample program for strings and chars, we saw how to assign literal values to both of these types. In this process, we noticed that two different types of quotes are used to mark off the literal values: the single quote ('), which is used in pairs to surround a literal char value consisting of exactly one char, such as 'a'; and the double quote ("), which is used in pairs to surround a literal string value of the *C string* type, such as "This is a test". We also investigated the reason for these two different types of literal values, which involves the notion of a *null byte* (a byte with the value 0). A null byte is used to mark the end of a C string in memory.

This led us to the discussion of the *ASCII code*, which is used to represent characters by binary values. We also looked at the fact that the same bytes can represent either a numeric value or a C string, depending on how we use those bytes in our program. That's why it's so important to tell the compiler which of these possibilities we have in mind when we write our programs. The way in which the compiler regulates our access to variables by their type, defined at compile time, is called the *type system*. The fact that C++ uses this *static type checking* is one of the reasons that C++ programs can be made more robust than programs written in languages that use *dynamic type checking*, where these errors are not detected until run time.

After a short discussion of some of the special characters that have a predefined meaning to the compiler, we took an initial glance at the mechanisms that allow us to get information into and out of the computer, known as *I/O*. We looked at the << function, which provides display on the screen when coupled with the built-in destination called cout. Immediately afterward, we encountered the corresponding input function >> and its partner cin, which team up to give us input from the keyboard.

Problem
Algorithms
C++
Executable
Hardware

Next, we went over some program organization concepts, including the if statement, which allows the program to choose between two alternatives; the while statement, which causes another statement to be executed while some condition is true; and the *block*, which allows several statements to be grouped together into one logical statement. Blocks are commonly used to enable several statements to be controlled by an if or a while statement.

At last we were ready to write a simple program that does something resembling useful work, and we did just that. The starting point for this program, as with all programs, was to define exactly what the program should do; in this case, the task was to keep track of the pumpkin with the highest weight at a county fair. The next step was to define a solution to this problem in precise terms. Next, we broke the solution down into steps small enough to be translated directly into C++. Of course, the next step after that was to do that translation. Finally, we went over the C++ code, line by line, to see what each line of the program did.

Now that the review is out of the way, we're about ready to continue with some more C++. First, though, let's step back a bit to see where we are right now.

Conclusion

We've come a long way from the beginning of this chapter. Starting from basic information on how the hardware works, we've made it through our first actual, runnable program. By now, you should have a much better idea whether you're going to enjoy programming (and this book). Assuming you aren't discouraged on either of these points, let's proceed to gather some more tools so we can undertake a bigger project.

Answers to Selected Exercises

1. 3c43. In case you got a different result, here's a little help:

    a. If you got the result 433a, you started at the wrong address.
    b. If you got the result 433c, you have the bytes in the wrong order.
    c. Finally, if you got 3a43, you made both of these mistakes.

    If you made one or more of these mistakes, don't feel too bad; even experienced programmers have trouble with hexadecimal values once in a while. That's one reason we use compilers and assemblers rather than writing everything in hex!

2. HELLO. See the previous answer if you couldn't figure out what the D at the beginning was for; you started at the wrong place.

3. Figure 3.25 is an answer to this problem.

```
#include <iostream.h>
int main()
{
    short n;
    cout << "Please type in the number of guests ";
    cout << "of your dinner party. ";
    cin >> n;
    cout << "A table for " << n+1 << "is ready. ";
    return 0;
}
```

Figure 3.25: First dinner party program (code\basic05.cc)

Problem
Algorithms
C++
Executable
Hardware

By the way, the reason that this program uses two lines to produce the sentence "Please type in the number of guests of your dinner party." is so that the program listing will fit on the page properly. If you prefer, you can combine those into one line that says cout << "Please type in the number of guests of your dinner party. ";. Of course, this also applies to the next exercise.

4.   Figure 3.26 is an answer to this problem.

```cpp
#include <iostream.h>
int main()
{
    short n;
    cout << "Excluding yourself, please type the ";
    cout << "number of guests in your dinner party.\n";
    cin >> n;
    if (n>20)
        cout << "Sorry, your party is too large. ";
    else
        cout << "A table for " << n+1 << " is ready. ";
    return 0;
}
```

Figure 3.26: Second dinner party program (code\basic06.cc)

Problem
Algorithms
C++
Executable
Hardware

5.   Figure 3.27 is an answer to this problem.

```cpp
#include <iostream.h>
#include "string6.h"
int main()
{
    string name;
    short age;
    cout << "What is your name? ";
    cin >> name;
    cout << "Thank you, " << name << endl;
    cout << "What is your age? ";
    cin >> age;
    if (age < 47)
        cout << "My, what a youngster!" << endl;
    else
        cout << "Hi, Granny!" << endl;
    return 0;
}
```

Figure 3.27: Name and age program (code\basic07.cc)

6.   Figure 3.28 is an answer to this problem.

```
#include <iostream.h>
#include "string6.h"
int main()
{
    short x;
    cout << "Elena can increase her $10 allowance each week ";
    cout << "by adding new chores." << endl;
    cout << "For every extra chore Elena does, she gets ";
    cout << "another dollar." << endl;
    cout << "How many extra chores were done? " << endl;
    cin >> x;
    if (x==0)
        {
        cout << "There is no extra allowance for Elena ";
        cout << "this week. " << endl;
        }
    else
        {
        cout << "Elena will now earn " << 10 + x;
        cout << " dollars this week." << endl;
        }
    return 0;
}
```

Figure 3.28: Allowance program (code\basic09.cc)

Problem
Algorithms
C++
Executable
Hardware

10. None of these is exactly the same as any of the others. However, 1, 3, and 4 will do what you expect, whereas 2 will produce weird-looking output with some bizarre number where the should be. Why is this?

It's not because . is handled specially, but because the space (" "), when inside quotes, either single or double, is a character like any other character. Thus, the expression '. ' in line 2 is a "multicharacter constant", which has a value dependent on the compiler. In this case, you'll get a short value equal to $(256 *$ the ASCII value of the period) + the ASCII value of the space. This comes out to 11808, as I calculate it. So the line you see on the screen may look like this:

That is very old, Joe Smith11808

Now why do all of the other lines work? Well, 1 works because a C string can have any number of characters and be sent to cout correctly; 3 works for the same reason; and 4 works because '.' is a valid one-character constant, another type that << can handle.

I realize it's hard to think of the space as a character when it doesn't look like anything. In addition, you can add spaces freely between variables, expressions, and so forth, in the program text. However, once you're dealing with C strings and literal character values, the space is just like any other character.

```
Problem
Algorithms
C++
Executable
Hardware
```

Chapter 4

More Basics

A Modest Proposal

Now that we have seen how to write a simple program in C++, it's time to acquire some more tools. We'll extend our example program from Chapter 3 for finding the heaviest pumpkin. Eventually, we want to provide the weights of the three heaviest pumpkins so that first, second, and third prizes can be awarded. It might seem that this would require just a minor modification of the previous program, in which we would keep track of the heaviest so far, second heaviest so far, and third heaviest so far, rather than merely the heaviest so far. However, this modification turns out to be a bit more complicated than it seems. Since this book is intended to teach you how to program using C++, rather than just how to use the C++ language, it's worth investigating why this is so. First, though, here are the objectives for this chapter.

Objectives of This Chapter

By the end of this chapter, you should

1. Understand the likelihood of error in even a small change to a program.
2. Be aware that even seemingly small changes in a problem can result in large changes in the program that solves the problem.
3. Have some understanding of the type of thinking needed to solve problems with programming.
4. Understand the selection sorting algorithm for arranging values in order.

5. Understand how to use a vector to maintain a number of values under one name.
6. Be able to use the for statement to execute program statements a (possibly varying) number of times.
7. Be familiar with the arithmetic operators ++ and +=, which are used to modify the value of variables.

Algorithmic Thinking

Let's take our program modification one step at a time, starting with just the top two weights. Figure 4.1 is one possible way to handle this version of the problem.

Problem
Algorithms
C++
Executable
Hardware

```
#include <iostream.h>

int main()
{
    short CurrentWeight;
    short HighestWeight;
    short SecondHighestWeight;

    cout << "Please enter the first weight: ";
    cin >> CurrentWeight;
    HighestWeight = CurrentWeight;
    SecondHighestWeight = 0;
    cout << "Current weight " << CurrentWeight << endl;
    cout << "Highest weight " << HighestWeight << endl;

    while (CurrentWeight > 0)
        {
        cout << "Please enter the next weight: ";
        cin >> CurrentWeight;
        if (CurrentWeight > HighestWeight)
            {
            SecondHighestWeight = HighestWeight;
            HighestWeight = CurrentWeight;
            }
        cout << "Current weight " << CurrentWeight << endl;
        cout << "Highest weight " << HighestWeight << endl;
        cout << "Second highest weight " << SecondHighestWeight << endl;
        }

    return 0;
}
```

Figure 4.1: Finding the top two weights, first try (code\pump1a.cc)

The reasons behind some of the new code should be fairly obvious, but we'll go over them anyway. The new lines are **bold** so you can find them easily. First, of course, we need a new variable, SecondHighestWeight, to hold the current value of the second-highest weight we've seen so far. Then, when the first weight is entered, the statement SecondHighestWeight = 0; sets the SecondHighestWeight to 0. After all, there isn't any second-highest weight when we've only seen one weight. The first nonobvious change is the addition of the statement SecondHighestWeight = HighestWeight;, which copies the old HighestWeight to SecondHighestWeight whenever there's a new highest weight. On reflection, however, this should make sense; when a new high is detected, the old high must be the second-highest value (so far). Also, we have to copy the old HighestWeight to SecondHighestWeight before we change HighestWeight. After we have set HighestWeight to a new value, it's too late to copy its old value into SecondHighestWeight.

Assuming that you've installed the software from the CD-ROM in the back of this book, you can try out this program. First, you have to compile it by changing to the normal subdirectory under the main directory where you installed the software and typing mk pump1a. Then type pump1a to run the program. It will ask you for weights and will keep track of the highest weight and second-highest weight that you've entered. Type 0 and hit ENTER to end the program.

To run the program under gdb, make sure you are in the normal subdirectory, then type trace pump1a. The program will start up and show you the first line of executable code. Type z and hit ENTER to execute each line of the program. The values of CurrentWeight, HighestWeight, and SecondHighestWeight will be displayed below the line that is to be executed next. When you are asked for a weight, type one in and hit ENTER just as when executing normally. When you enter a 0 weight, the program will stop looping and execution will take the path to the end of the program. At that point (or when you're tired of tracing the program), type q (for *quit*) and hit ENTER to exit from the debugger.

Problem
Algorithms
C++
Executable
Hardware

A Prize Catch

This program may seem to keep track of the highest and second-highest weights correctly, but in fact there's a hole in the logic. To be exact, it doesn't work correctly when the user enters a new value that's less than the previous highest value but more than the previous second-highest value. In that case, the new value should be the second-highest value, even though there's no new highest value. For example, suppose that you enter the following weights: 5 2 11 3 7. If we were to update SecondHighestWeight only when we see a new high, our program would indicate that 11 was the high and 5 the second-highest; since neither 3 nor 7 is a new high, SecondHighestWeight would remain as it was when the 11 was entered.

To fix this problem, we have to add an else clause to our if statement, so that the corrected version of the statement looks like Figure 4.2.

```
if (CurrentWeight > HighestWeight)
    {
    SecondHighestWeight = HighestWeight;
    HighestWeight = CurrentWeight;
    }
else
    {
    if (CurrentWeight > SecondHighestWeight)
        SecondHighestWeight = CurrentWeight;
    }
```

Figure 4.2: Using an if statement with an else clause

Problem
Algorithms
C++
Executable
Hardware

In this case, the condition in the first if is checking whether CurrentWeight is greater than the previous HighestWeight; when this is true, we have a new HighestWeight and we can update both HighestWeight and SecondHighestWeight. However, if CurrentWeight is not greater than HighestWeight, the else clause is executed. It contains another if; this one checks whether CurrentWeight is greater than the current value of SecondHighestWeight. If so, SecondHighestWeight is set to the value of CurrentWeight.

What happens if two (or more) pumpkins are tied for the highest weight? In that case, the first one of them to be encountered is going to set HighestWeight, as it will be the highest yet encountered. When the second pumpkin of the same weight is seen, it won't trigger a change to HighestWeight, since it's not higher than the current occupant of that variable. However, it will pass the test in the second if statement, if (CurrentWeight > SecondHighestWeight), which will cause SecondHighestWeight to be set to the same value as HighestWeight. This is reasonable behavior, unlikely to startle the (hypothetical) user of the program, and therefore is good enough for our purposes. In a real application program, we'd have to try to determine what the user of this program would want us to do.

Figure 4.3 shows the corrected program.

```
#include <iostream.h>

int main()
{
    short CurrentWeight;
    short HighestWeight;
    short SecondHighestWeight;

    cout << "Please enter the first weight: ";
    cin >> CurrentWeight;
    HighestWeight = CurrentWeight;
    SecondHighestWeight = 0;
    cout << "Current weight " << CurrentWeight << endl;
    cout << "Highest weight " << HighestWeight << endl;

    while (CurrentWeight > 0)
        {
        cout << "Please enter the next weight: ";
        cin >> CurrentWeight;
        if (CurrentWeight > HighestWeight)
            {
            SecondHighestWeight = HighestWeight;
            HighestWeight = CurrentWeight;
            }
        else
            {
            if (CurrentWeight > SecondHighestWeight)
                SecondHighestWeight = CurrentWeight;
            }
        cout << "Current weight " << CurrentWeight << endl;
        cout << "Highest weight " << HighestWeight << endl;
        cout << "Second highest weight " << SecondHighestWeight << endl;
        }

    return 0;
}
```

Problem
Algorithms
C++
Executable
Hardware

Figure 4.3: Finding the top two weights (code\pump2.cc)

Assuming that you've installed the software from the CD-ROM in the back of this book, you can try out this program. First, you have to compile it by changing to the normal subdirectory under the main directory where you installed the software and typing mk pump2. Then type pump2 to run the program. It will ask you for weights and will keep track of the highest weight and second-highest weight that you've entered. Type 0 and hit ENTER to end the program.

To run the program under gdb, make sure you are in the normal subdirectory, then type trace pump2. The program will start up and show you the first line of executable code. Type z and hit ENTER to execute each line of the program. The values of CurrentWeight, HighestWeight, and SecondHighestWeight will be displayed below the line that is to be executed next. When you are asked for a weight, type one in and hit ENTER just as when executing normally. When you enter a 0 weight, the program will stop looping and execution will take the path to the end }. At that point (or when you're tired of tracing the program), type q (for *quit*) and hit ENTER to exit from the debugger.

By the way, since we've just been using the if statement pretty heavily, this would be a good time to list all of the conditions that it can test. We've already seen some of them, but it can't hurt to have them all in one place. Figure 4.4 lists these conditions, with translations.

Condition symbol	Controlled block will be executed if:
>	First item is larger than second item
<	First item is smaller than second item
>=	First item is larger than or equal to second item
<=	First item is smaller than or equal to second item
!=	First item differs from second item
==	First item has the same value as the second item

Problem
Algorithms
C++
Executable
Hardware

Figure 4.4: What if?

You may wonder why we have to use == to test for equality rather than just =. That's because = means "assign right-hand value to variable on left", rather than "compare two items for equality". This is a "feature" of C++ (and C) that allows us to accidentally write if (a = b) when we mean if (a == b). What does if (a = b) mean? It means the following:

1. Assign the value of b to a.
2. If that value is 0, then the if is false.
3. Otherwise, the if is true.

Some people find this useful; I don't. Therefore, I always enable the compiler warning that tells you when you use a = inside an if statement in a way that looks like you meant to test for equality.

What a Tangled Web We Weave ...

I hope this excursion has given you some appreciation of the subtleties that await in even the simplest change to a working program. Many experienced programmers still underestimate such difficulties and the amount of time that may be needed to ensure that the changes are correct. I don't think it's necessary to continue along the same path with a program that can award three prizes. The principle is the same, although the complexity of the code grows with the number of special cases we have to handle. Obviously, a solution that could handle any number of prizes without special cases would be a big improvement, but it will require some major changes in the organization of the program. That's what we'll take up next.

You May Already Have Won

One of the primary advantages of the method we've used so far to find the heaviest pumpkin(s) is that we didn't have to save the weights of all the pumpkins as we went along. If we don't mind saving all the weights, then we can solve the three-prize problem in a different way. Let's assume for the purpose of simplicity that there are only five weights to be saved, in which case the solution looks like this:

Problem
Algorithms
C++
Executable
Hardware

1. Read in all of the weights.
2. Make a list consisting of the three highest weights in descending order.
3. Award the first, second, and third prizes, in that order, to the three entries in the list of highest weights.

Now let's break those down into substeps that can be more easily translated into C++:

1. Read in all of the weights.
    a. Read first number.
    b. Read next number.
    c. If we haven't read five weights yet, go back to 1b.

Now that we have all the numbers, let's proceed to the calculation phase:

2. Make a list consisting of the three highest weights in descending order.
   a. Find the largest number in the original list of weights.
   b. Copy it to the sorted list.
   c. If we haven't found the three highest numbers, go back to 2a.

Oops! That's not going to work since we'll get the same number each time.[1] To prevent that from happening, we have to mark off each number as we select it. Here's the revised version of step 2:

2. Make a list consisting of the three highest weights in descending order.
   a. Find the largest number in the original list of weights.
   b. Copy it to the sorted list.
   c. Mark it off in the original list of weights so we don't select it again.
   d. If we haven't found the three highest numbers, go back to 2a.

Now we're ready for output:

```
Problem
Algorithms
C++
Executable
Hardware
```

3. Award the first, second, and third prizes, in that order, to the three entries in the list of highest weights.
   a. Write first number.
   b. Write another number.
   c. If we haven't done them all, go back to 3b.

Unlike our previous approach, this obviously can be generalized to handle any number of prizes. However, we have to address two problems before we can use this approach: First, how do we keep track of the weights? Second, how do we select out the highest three weights? Both of these problems are much easier to solve if we don't have a separate variable for each weight.

---

1. I realize I'm breaking a cardinal rule of textbooks: Never admit that the solution to a problem is anything but obvious, so the student who doesn't see it immediately feels like an idiot. In reality, even a simple program is difficult to get right, and indicating the sort of thought processes that go into analyzing a programming problem might help demystify this difficult task.

Variables, by the Numbers

The solution to our first question is to use a vector.[2] This is a variable containing a number of "subvariables" that can be addressed by position in the vector; each of these subvariables is called an **element**. A vector has a name, just like a regular variable, but the elements do not. Instead, each element has a number, corresponding to its position in the vector. For example, we might want to create a vector of short values called Weight, with five elements. To do this, we would write this line: vector<short> Weight(5);.[3]

Now we can refer to the individual elements of the vector called Weight by using their numbers, enclosed in **square brackets** ([ ]); the number in the brackets is called the **index**. Here are some examples:

```
Weight[1] = 123;
Weight[2] = 456;
Weight[3] = Weight[1] + Weight[2];
Weight[i+1] = Weight[i] + 5;[4]
```

As these examples indicate, an element of a vector can be used anywhere a "regular" variable can be used.[5] But the most valuable difference between a regular variable and an element of a vector is that we can vary which element we are referring to in a given statement by varying the index. Take a look at the last sample line, in which two elements of the vector Weight are used; the first one is element i+1 and the other is element i. As this indicates, we don't have to use a constant value for the element number but can calculate it while the program is executing. In this case, if i is 0, the two elements referred to are element 1 and element 0, whereas if i is 5, the two elements are elements 6 and 5, respectively.

The ability to refer to an element of a vector by number rather than by name is extremely powerful since it allows us to write statements that can refer to any element in a vector, depending on the value of the index variable in the statements. This may sound mysterious, but

Problem
Algorithms
C++
Executable
Hardware

---

2. To use vectors, we have to #include the header file vector.h; otherwise, the compiler won't understand that type of variable.

3. A vector actually contains some additional information beyond the elements themselves. Unfortunately, how a vector actually works is too complicated to go into in this book.

4. By the way, if you're wondering how to pronounce Weight[i], it's "weight sub i". "Sub" is short for **subscript**, which is an old term for index.

5. What I'm calling a *regular variable* here is technically known as a **scalar variable**; that is, one with only one value at any given time.

actually it's quite simple. To see how this works in practice, let's look at Figure 4.5, which solves our three-prize problem.

```cpp
#include <iostream.h>
#include "vector.h"

int main()
{
    vector<short> Weight(5);
    vector<short> SortedWeight(3);
    short HighestWeight;
    short HighestIndex;
    short i;
    short k;

    cout << "I'm going to ask you to type in five weights, in pounds." << endl;

    for (i = 0; i < 5; i ++)
      {
      cout << "Please type in weight #" << i+1 << ": ";
      cin >> Weight[i];
      }

    for (i = 0; i < 3; i ++)
        {
        HighestWeight = 0;
        for (k = 0; k < 5; k ++)
            {
            if (Weight[k] > HighestWeight)
                {
                HighestWeight = Weight[k];
                HighestIndex = k;
                }
            }
        SortedWeight[i] = HighestWeight;
        Weight[HighestIndex] = 0;
        }

    cout << "The highest weight was: " << SortedWeight[0] << endl;
    cout << "The second highest weight was: " << SortedWeight[1] << endl;
    cout << "The third highest weight was: " << SortedWeight[2] << endl;

    return 0;
}
```

Problem
Algorithms
C++
Executable
Hardware

Figure 4.5: Using a vector (code\vect1.cc)

Assuming that you've installed the software from the CD-ROM in the back of this book, you can try out this program. First, you have to compile it by changing to the normal subdirectory under the main directory where you installed the software and typing mk vect1. Then type vect1 to run the program. It will ask you for 5 weights and will display the highest 3 of them in descending order.

To run the program under gdb, make sure you are in the normal subdirectory, then type trace vect1. The program will start up and show you the first line of executable code. Type z and hit ENTER to execute each line of the program. The values of k, i, HighestIndex, HighestWeight, Weight, and SortedWeight will be displayed below the line that is to be executed next. When you are asked for a weight, type one in and hit ENTER just as when executing normally. After you've entered 5 weights, the program will start the sorting process. When the sorted results have been displayed (or when you're tired of tracing the program), type q (for *quit*) and hit ENTER to exit from the debugger.

This program uses several new features of C++ that need some explanation. First, of course, there is the line that defines the vector Weight:

```
vector<short> Weight(5);
```

As we have already seen, this means that we want a vector of five elements, each of which is a short. This vector thus has five distinct index values, each of which refers to one element. However, what isn't so obvious is what those five distinct index values actually are. You might expect them to be 1, 2, 3, 4, and 5; actually, they are 0, 1, 2, 3, and 4.

This method of referring to elements in a vector is called **zero-based indexing**. Although it might seem arbitrary to start counting at 0 rather than at 1, assembly language programmers find it perfectly natural because the calculation of the address of an element is simpler with such indexing. The formula is "(address of first element) + (element number) * (size of element)".

This bit of history is relevant because C, the predecessor of C++, was originally intended to replace assembly language so that programs could be moved from one machine architecture to another with as little difficulty as possible. One reason for some of the eccentricities of C++ is that it has to be able to replace C as a "portable assembly language" that doesn't depend on any specific machine architecture. This explains, for example, the great concern of the inventor of C++ for run time efficiency, as he wished to allow programmers to avoid the use of C or assembly language for

Problem
Algorithms
C++
Executable
Hardware

efficiency.[6] Since C++ was intended to replace C completely, it has to be as efficient as possible; otherwise, programmers might switch back from C++ to C whenever they were concerned about the speed and size of their programs.

The last two lines in the variable definition phase define two variables, called i and k, which have been traditional names for **index variables** (i.e., variables used to hold indexes) since at least the invention of FORTRAN in the 1950s. The inventors of FORTRAN used a fairly simple method of determining the type of a variable: If it began with one of the letters I through N, it was an integer. Otherwise, it was a **floating-point variable** (i.e., one that can hold values that contain a fractional part, such as 3.876). This rule was later changed so that the user could specify what type the variable was, as we do in C++, but the default rules were the same as in the earlier versions of FORTRAN so that programs using the old rules would continue to compile and run correctly.

I suspect one reason for the durability of these short names is that they're easy to type, and many programmers aren't very good typists.[7] In C++, the only remnant of this FORTRAN tradition of assigning letters I through N to start the names of integral variables is that i, j, k, m, and n are used as indexes.[8]

Problem
Algorithms
C++
Executable
Hardware

After the variable definitions are out of the way, we can proceed to the executable portion of our program. First, we type out a note to the user, stating what to expect. Then we get to the code in Figure 4.6.

---

6. *Run time efficiency* means the amount of time a program takes to run, as well as how much memory it uses. These issues are very significant when writing a program to be sold to or used by others, as an inefficient program may be unacceptable to the users.

7. I strongly recommend learning how to type (i.e., touch-type). I was a professional programmer without typing skills for over 10 years before agreeing to type (someone else's) book manuscript. At that point, I decided to teach myself to touch-type, so I wrote a *Dvorak keyboard* driver for my Radio Shack Model III computer and started typing. In about a month I could type faster than with my previous two finger method and eventually got up to 80+ words per minute on English text. If you've never heard of the Dvorak keyboard, it's the one that has the letters laid out in an efficient manner; the "home row" keys are AOEUIDHTNS rather than the absurd set ASDFGHJKL;. This "new" (1930s) keyboard layout reduces effort and increases speed and accuracy compared to the old QWERTY keyboard, which was invented in the 1880s to prevent people from typing two keys in rapid succession and jamming the typebars together. This problem has been nonexistent since the invention of the Selectric typewriter (which uses a ball rather than type bars) in the 1960s, but inertia keeps the old layout in use even though it is very inefficient.

In any event, since I learned to type, writing documentation has required much less effort. This applies especially to writing articles or books, which would be a painful process otherwise.

8. By the way, the reason that l (the letter "ell") isn't used very much for this purpose is that it looks too much like a 1 (the numeral one); the compiler doesn't get confused by this resemblance, but programmers very well might.

```
for (i = 0; i < 5; i ++)
    {
    cout << "Please type in weight #" << i+1 << ": ";
    cin >> Weight[i];
    }
```

Figure 4.6: Using a for statement (from code\vect1.cc)

The first line here is called a for **statement**, which is used to control a for **loop**. This is a loop control facility similar to the while loop we encountered in Chapter 3. The difference between these two statements is that a for loop allows us to specify more than just the condition under which the **controlled block** will be repetitively executed.[9]

A for statement specifies three expressions (separated by ";") that control the execution of the for loop: a starting expression, a continuation expression, and a modification expression. In our case, these are i = 0, i < 5, and i ++, respectively. Let's look at the function and meaning of each of these components.

First, the **starting expression**, i = 0. This is executed once before the block controlled by the for statement is executed. In this case, we use it to set our index variable, i, to 0, which will refer to the first element of our Weight vector.

Next, the **continuation expression**, i < 5. This specifies under what conditions the statement controlled by the for will be executed. In this case, we will continue executing the controlled statement as long as the value of i is less than 5. Be warned that the continuation expression is actually executed *before* every execution of the controlled block; thus, if the continuation expression is false when the loop is entered, the controlled block will not be executed at all.

Finally, the **modification expression**, i ++.[10] This is exactly equivalent to i = i + 1, which means "set i to one more than its current value", an operation technically referred to as **incrementing a variable**. You may wonder why we need two ways to say the same thing; actually, there are a few reasons. One is that ++ requires less typing, which as we know isn't a strong point of many programmers. Also, the ++ (pronounced "plus plus") operator doesn't allow the possibility of mistyping such a modification expression as i = j + 1

Problem
Algorithms
C++
Executable
Hardware

---

9. You may sometimes see the term *controlled statement* used in place of *controlled block*; since a block can be used anywhere that a single statement can be used, *controlled statement* and *controlled block* are actually just two ways of saying the same thing.

10. You don't need a space between the variable name and the ++ operator; however, I think it's easier to read this way.

when you really meant to increment i. Another reason why this feature was added to the C language is that, in the early days of C, compiler technology wasn't very advanced and the ++ operator allowed the production of more efficient programs. You see, many machines can add one to a memory location by a single machine language instruction, usually called something like *increment memory*. Even a simple compiler can generate an "increment memory" instruction as a translation of i++, but it takes a bit more sophistication for the compiler to recognize i = i + 1 as an increment operation. Since incrementing a variable is a very common operation in C++, this was worth handling specially.[11]

Now that we have examined all the parts of the for statement, we can see that its translation into English would be something like this:

1.   Set the index variable i to 0.
2.   If the value of i is less than 5, execute the following block (in this case, the block with the cout and cin statements). Otherwise, skip to the next statement after the end of the controlled block; that is, the one following the closing }.
3.   Add one to the value of i and go back to step 2.

Problem
Algorithms
C++
Executable
Hardware

Now let's continue with the next step in the description of our for loop, the modification expression i++. In our example, this will be executed five times. The first time, i will be 0, then 1, 2, 3, and finally 4. When the loop is executed for the fifth time, i will be incremented to 5; therefore, step 2 will end the loop by skipping to the next statement after the controlled block.[12] A bit of terminology is useful here: Each time through the loop is called an *iteration*.

Now that we've examined the for statement in excruciating detail, what about the block it controls? The first statement in the block,

cout << "Please type in weight #" << i+1 << ": ";

doesn't contain anything much we haven't seen before; it just displays a request to enter a weight. The only difference from

---

11. By the way, the name C++ is sort of a pun using this notation; it's supposed to mean "the language following C". In case you're not doubled over with laughter, you're not alone. I guess you had to be there.

12. In case you're wondering why the value of i at the end of this loop will be 5, the reason is that at the end of each pass through the loop, the modification expression (i ++) is executed before the continuation expression that determines whether the next execution will take place (i < 5). Thus, at the end of the fifth pass through the loop, i is incremented to 5 and then tested to see if it is still less than 5. Since it isn't, the loop terminates at that point.

previous uses we've made of the cout facility is that we're inserting a numeric expression containing a variable, i+1, into the output. This causes the expression to be translated into a human-readable form consisting of digits. All of the expressions being sent to cout in one statement are strung together to make one line of output, if we don't specify otherwise. Therefore, when this statement is executed during the first iteration of the loop, the user of this program will see:

Please type in weight #1:

Then the user will type in the first weight. The same request, with a different value for the weight number, will show up each time the user hits ENTER, until five values have been accepted.

The second statement in the controlled block,

cin >> Weight[i];

is a little different. Here, we're reading the number the user has typed in at the keyboard and storing it in a variable. But the variable we're using is different each time through the loop: it's the ith element of the Weight vector. So, on the first iteration, the value the user types in will go into Weight[0]. The value accepted on the second iteration will go into Weight[1], and so on until the fifth and last iteration, when the typed-in value will be stored in Weight[4].

```
Problem
Algorithms
C++
Executable
Hardware
```

A Sorted Tale

Now that we have stored all of the weights, we want to find the three highest of the weights. Here's an English description of the sorting algorithm that we will use, which is technically known as a **selection sort**.

1. Repeat the following steps three times, once through for each weight that we want to select.
2. Search through the list (i.e., the Weight vector), keeping track of the highest weight seen so far in the list and the index of that highest weight.
3. When we get to the end of the list, copy the highest weight we've found to the current element of another list (the "output list", which in this case is the vector SortedWeight). The index i of the current element in the output list is equal to the number of times we have been through the loop before; that is, the true

highest weight, which we will identify first, goes in position 0 of the output list, the next highest in position 1, and so forth.

4. Finally, set the highest weight we've found in the original list to 0, so we won't select it as the highest value again on the next pass through the list.

Figure 4.7 shows the portion of our C++ program that implements this sort.

```
for (i = 0; i < 3; i ++)
    {
    HighestWeight = 0;
    for (k = 0; k < 5; k ++)
        {
        if (Weight[k] > HighestWeight)
            {
            HighestWeight = Weight[k];
            HighestIndex = k;
            }
        }
    SortedWeight[i] = HighestWeight;
    Weight[HighestIndex] = 0;
    }
```

Problem
Algorithms
C++
Executable
Hardware

Figure 4.7: Sorting the weights (from code\vect1.cc)

Let's look at the correspondence between the English description of the algorithm and the code.

1. Repeat the following steps once through for each prize:

    ```
    for (i = 0; i < 3; i ++)
    ```

    (During this process the variable i is the index into the SortedWeight vector where we're going to store the weight for the current prize we're working on. While we're looking for the highest weight, i is 0; for the second-highest weight, i is 1; finally, when we're getting ready to award a third prize, i will be 2.)

2. Search through the input list. For each element of the list Weight, we check whether that element (Weight[k]) is greater than the highest weight seen so far in the list (HighestWeight). If that is the case, then we reset HighestWeight to the value of the current

element (Weight[k]) and the index of the highest weight so far (HighestIndex) to the index of the current element (k).

3. When we get to the end of the input list, HighestWeight is the highest weight in the list and HighestIndex is the index of that element of the list that had the highest weight. Therefore, we can copy the highest weight to the current element of another list (the "output list"). As mentioned earlier, i is the index of the current element in the output list. Its value is the number of times we have been through the outer loop before; that is, the highest weight (which we will identify first) goes in position 0 of the output list, the next highest in position 1, and so on:

SortedWeight[i] = HighestWeight;

4. Finally, set the highest weight in the input list to 0, so we won't select it as the highest value again on the next pass through the list.

Weight[HighestIndex] = 0;

This statement is the reason that we have to keep track of the "highest index"; that is, the index of the highest weight. Otherwise, we wouldn't know which element of the original Weight vector we've used and therefore wouldn't be able to set it to 0 to prevent its being used again.

Problem
Algorithms
C++
Executable
Hardware

By the way, you may have noticed a slight oddity in this code. The block controlled by the for statement consists of exactly one statement; namely, the if that checks for a new HighestWeight value. According to the rules I've provided, that means we don't have to put curly braces ({}) around it to make it a block. While this is true, long experience has indicated that it's a very good idea to make it a block anyway, as a preventive measure. It's very common to revisit old code to fix bugs or add new functions, and in so doing we might add another statement after the if statement at a later time, intending it to be controlled by the for. The results wouldn't be correct, since the added statement would be executed exactly one time after the loop was finished rather than once each time through the loop. Such errors are very difficult to find, because the code looks all right when inspected casually. Therefore, a little extra caution when writing the program in the first place often pays off handsomely.

Details, Details

Now let's go back and look at the steps of the algorithm more closely.[13] Step 1 should be fairly self-explanatory, once you're familiar with the syntax of the for statement; it causes the statements in its controlled block to be executed three times, with the index variable i varying from 0 to 2 in the process.

Step 2 is quite similar to the process we went through to find the highest weight in our previous two programs. Figure 4.8 shows a picture of the situation before the first pass through the data.[14]

Index	Contents of Weight	Contents of SortedWeight
0	5	???
1	2	???
2	11	???
3	3	
4	7	

Figure 4.8: Initial situation

Problem
Algorithms
C++
Executable
Hardware

Here, the highest value is 11 in Weight[2]. After we've located it and copied its value to SortedWeight[0], we set Weight[2] to 0, yielding the situation in Figure 4.9.

Index	Contents of Weight	Contents of SortedWeight
0	5	11
1	2	???
2	0	???
3	3	
4	7	

Figure 4.9: After the first pass

Now we're ready for the second pass. This time, the highest value is the 7 in Weight[4]. After we copy the 7 to SortedWeight[1], we set Weight[4] to 0, leaving the situation in Figure 4.10.

---

13. They're in the section titled "A Sorted Tale".

14. The ??? in SortedWeight indicates that those locations contain unknown data, as they haven't been initialized yet.

Index	Contents of Weight	Contents of SortedWeight
0	5	11
1	2	7
2	0	???
3	3	
4	0	

Figure 4.10: After the second pass

On the third and final pass, we locate the 5 in Weight[0], copy it to SortedWeight[2], and set Weight[0] to 0. As you can see in Figure 4.11, SortedWeight now has the results we were looking for: the top three weights, in descending order.

Index	Contents of Weight	Contents of SortedWeight
0	0	11
1	2	7
2	0	5
3	3	
4	0	

Figure 4.11: Final situation

Problem
Algorithms
C++
Executable
Hardware

To Err Is Human . . .

The reason for the HighestIndex variable should be more evident after that simulation of the sorting algorithm. We need to keep track of which element of the original vector (i.e., Weight) we have decided is the highest so far, so that this element won't be selected as the highest weight on *every* pass through the Weight vector. To prevent this error, step 4 sets each "highest" weight to a value that won't be selected on a succeeding pass. Since we know there should be no 0 weights in the Weight vector, we can set each selected element to 0 after it has been selected to prevent its reselection.

That accounts for all of the steps in the sorting algorithm. However, our implementation of the algorithm has a weak spot that we should fix. If you want to try to find it yourself, look at the code and explanation again before going on. Ready?

The key word in the explanation is "should" in the following sentence: "Since we know there *should* be no 0 weights in the Weight vector, we can set each selected element to 0 after it has been selected to prevent its reselection." How do we *know* that there are no 0 weights? We don't, unless we screen for them when we accept input. In the first pumpkin-weighing program, we stopped the input when we got a 0, but in the programs in this chapter, we ask for a set number of weights. If one of them is 0 (or even negative), the program will continue along happily. Of course, this doesn't make any sense, but it's a good idea to try to prevent errors rather than assuming that users of a program will always act sensibly. Before we change the program, though, let's try to figure out what would happen if the user types in a 0 for every weight.

You can try this scenario out yourself. To run it, just change to the normal subdirectory under the main directory where you installed the software and type vect1. When it asks for weights, enter a 0 for each of the five weights. In case you're reading this away from your computer, here's what will happen (although the element number in the message may not be the same):

You have tried to use element 51082 of a vector which has only 5 elements.

Problem
Algorithms
C++
Executable
Hardware

Why doesn't the program work in this case? Because we have an **uninitialized variable**; that is, one that has never been set to a valid value. In this case, it's HighestIndex. Let's look at the sorting code one more time, in Figure 4.12.

```
for (i = 0; i < 3; i ++)
    {
    HighestWeight = 0;
    for (k = 0; k < 5; k ++)
        {
        if (Weight[k] > HighestWeight)
            {
            HighestWeight = Weight[k];
            HighestIndex = k;
            }
        }
    SortedWeight[i] = HighestWeight;
    Weight[HighestIndex] = 0;
    }
```

Figure 4.12: Sorting the weights, again (from code\vect1.cc)

It's clear that HighestWeight is **initialized** (i.e., given a valid value) before it is ever used; the statement HighestWeight = 0; is the first statement in the block controlled by the outer for loop. However, the same is not true of HighestIndex. Whenever the condition in the if statement is true, both HighestWeight and HighestIndex will indeed be set to legitimate values: HighestWeight will be the highest weight seen so far on this pass, and HighestIndex will be the index of that weight in the Weight vector. However, what happens if the condition in the if statement never becomes true? In that case, HighestIndex will have whatever random value it started out with at the beginning of the program. It's very unlikely that such a value will be correct or even refer to an actual element in the Weight vector.

It should be fairly obvious that if the user types in even one weight greater than 0, the if statement will be true when that weight is encountered, so the program will work. However, if the user typed in all 0 weights, the program would fail, as we saw before, because the condition in the if statement would never become true. To prevent this from causing program failure, all we have to do is to add one more line, the one in **bold** in Figure 4.13.

```
for (i = 0; i < 3; i ++)
    {
    HighestWeight = 0;
    HighestIndex = 0;
    for (k = 0; k < 5; k ++)
        {
        if (Weight[k] > HighestWeight)
            {
            HighestWeight = Weight[k];
            HighestIndex = k;
            }
        }
    SortedWeight[i] = HighestWeight;
    Weight[HighestIndex] = 0;
    }
```

```
Problem
Algorithms
C++
Executable
Hardware
```

Figure 4.13: Sorting the weights, with correct initialization (from code\vect2.cc)

Now we can be sure that HighestIndex always has a value that corresponds to some element of the Weight vector, so we won't see the program fail as the previous one would.

Assuming that you've installed the software from the CD-ROM in the back of this book, you can run the corrected program to test that it works as advertised. First, you have to compile it by changing to the normal subdirectory under the main directory where you installed the software and typing mk vect2.   Now you can run the corrected program by typing vect2 at the DOS prompt in the normal subdirectory. This time, entering five 0 weights will produce the expected result: The top three weights will all be 0.

To run the program under gdb, make sure you are in the normal subdirectory, then type trace vect2. The program will start up and show you the first line of executable code. Type z and hit ENTER to execute each line of the program. The values of k, i, HighestIndex, HighestWeight, Weight, and SortedWeight will be displayed below the line that is to be executed next. When you are asked for a weight, type one in and hit ENTER just as when executing normally. After you've entered 5 weights, the program will start the sorting process. When the sorted results have been displayed (or when you're tired of tracing the program), type q (for *quit*) and hit ENTER to exit from the debugger.

By the way, it's also possible to initialize a variable at the same time as you define it. For example, the statement short i = 12; defines a short variable called i and sets it to the value 12 at the same time. This is generally a good practice to follow when possible. If you initialize the variable when you define it, you don't have to remember to write a separate statement to do the initialization.

```
Problem
Algorithms
C++
Executable
Hardware
```

To Really Foul Things Up Requires a Computer

We should pay some more attention to the notion of program failure, as it's very important. The first question, of course, is what it means to say that a program "fails". The simplest answer is that it doesn't work correctly, but we should delve into this topic a bit deeper.

In the specific case that we've just seen, we'll probably get an error message while trying to access a nonexistent element of the Weight vector. However, it's entirely possible for a program to just "hang" (run endlessly), "crash" your system, produce an obviously ridiculous answer, or worst of all, provide a seemingly correct but actually erroneous result.

The causes of program failures are legion. A few of the possibilities are these:

1.   Problems isolated to our code
     a.   The original problem could have been stated incorrectly.

b. The algorithm(s) we're using could have been inappropriate for the problem.
c. The algorithm(s) might have been implemented incorrectly.
d. The input to the program might be outside the expected range.

And so on . . .

2. Problems interacting with other programs
    a. We might be misusing a function supplied by the system, like the << operator.
    b. The documentation for a system function might be incorrect or incomplete. This is especially common in "guru"-oriented operating systems, where the users are supposed to know everything.
    c. A system function might be unreliable. This is more common than it should be.
    d. The compiler might be generating the wrong instructions. I've seen this on a few rare occasions.
    e. Another program in the system might be interfering with our program. This is quite common in some popular operating environments that allow several programs to be executing concurrently.

Problem
Algorithms
C++
Executable
Hardware

And so on . . .

With a simple program such as the ones we're writing here, errors such as the ones listed under problems with our code are more likely, as we have relatively little interaction with the rest of the system. As we start to use more sophisticated mechanisms in C++, we're more likely to run into instances of interaction problems.

What, Me Worry?

After that excursion into the sources of program failure, let's get back to our question about initializing variables. Why do we have to worry about this at all? It would seem perfectly reasonable for the compiler to make sure that our variables were always initialized to some reasonable value; in the case of numeric variables such as a short, 0 would be a good choice. Surely Bjarne Stroustrup, the designer of C++, didn't overlook this.

No, he didn't; he made a conscious decision not to provide this facility. It's not due to cruelty or unconcern with the needs of programmers. On the contrary, he stated in the Preface to the first edition of *The C++ Programming Language* that "C++ is a general-purpose programming language designed to make programming more enjoyable for the serious programmer".[15] To allow C++ to replace C completely, he could not add features that would penalize efficiency for programs that do not use these features. Adding initialization as a built-in function of the language would make programs larger and slower if the programmer had already initialized all variables as needed. This may not be obvious, but we'll see in a later section why it is so.

Garbage in, Garbage Out

In the meantime, there's something else we should do if we want the program to work as it should. As the old saying "garbage in, garbage out" suggests, by far the best solution to handling spurious input values is to prevent them from being entered in the first place. What we want to do is to check each input value and warn the user if it's invalid. Figure 4.14 illustrates a new input routine that looks like it should do the trick.

`Problem`
`Algorithms`
`C++`
`Executable`
`Hardware`

```
for (i = 0; i < 5; i ++)
   {
   cout << "Please type in weight #" << i+1 << ": ";
   cin >> Weight[i];
   if (Weight[i] <= 0)
      {
      cout << "I'm sorry, " << Weight[i] << " is not a valid weight.";
      cout << endl;
      }
   }
```

Figure 4.14: Garbage prevention, first attempt (from code\vect2a.cc)

Assuming that you've installed the software from the CD-ROM in the back of this book, you can try out this program. First, you have to compile it by changing to the normal subdirectory under the main directory where you installed the software and typing mk vect2a. Then type vect2a to run the program. It will ask you for 5 weights and will display the highest 3 of them in descending order.

---

15. *The C++ Programming Language, 2nd Edition*, Addison-Wesley, 1991. v.

To run the program under gdb, make sure you are in the normal subdirectory, then type trace vect2a. The program will start up and show you the first line of executable code. Type z and hit ENTER to execute each line of the program. The values of k, i, HighestIndex, HighestWeight, Weight, and SortedWeight will be displayed below the line that is to be executed next. When you are asked for a weight, type one in and hit ENTER just as when executing normally. After you've entered 5 weights, the program will start the sorting process. When the sorted results have been displayed (or when you're tired of tracing the program), type q (for *quit*) and hit ENTER to exit from the debugger.

Most of this should be familiar; the only line that has a new construct in it is the if statement. The condition <= means "less than or equal to", which is reasonably intuitive.

Unfortunately, this program won't work as we intended. The problem is what happens after the error message is displayed; namely, the loop continues at the top with the next weight, and we never correct the erroneous input.

To fix this problem completely, we need a slightly different approach, which can be coded as illustrated in Figure 4.15.

Problem
Algorithms
C++
Executable
Hardware

```
for (i = 0; i < 5; )
  {
  cout << "Please type in weight #" << i+1 << ": ";
  cin >> Weight[i];
  if (Weight[i] <= 0)
    {
    cout << "I'm sorry, " << Weight[i] << " is not a valid weight.";
    cout << endl;
    }
  else
    i ++;
  }
```

Figure 4.15: Garbage prevention (from code\vect3.cc)

Putting it all together, we get the final version of this program, which is shown in Figure 4.16.

Assuming that you've installed the software from the CD-ROM in the back of this book, you can try out this program. First, you have to compile it by changing to the normal subdirectory under the main directory where you installed the software and typing mk vect3. Then type vect3 to run the program. It will ask you for 5 weights; any illegal values you type in will be discarded and you will be asked to re-enter them.

```cpp
#include <iostream.h>
#include "vector.h"

int main()
{
    vector<short> Weight(5);
    vector<short> SortedWeight(3);
    short HighestWeight;
    short HighestIndex;
    short i;
    short k;

    cout << "I'm going to ask you to type in five weights, in pounds." << endl;

    for (i = 0; i < 5; )
      {
      cout << "Please type in weight #" << i+1 << ": ";
      cin >> Weight[i];
      if (Weight[i] <= 0)
        {
        cout << "I'm sorry, " << Weight[i] << " is not a valid weight.";
        cout << endl;
        }
      else
        i ++;
      }

    for (i = 0; i < 3; i ++)
      {
      HighestIndex = 0;
      HighestWeight = 0;
      for (k = 0; k < 5; k ++)
          {
          if (Weight[k] > HighestWeight)
              {
              HighestWeight = Weight[k];
              HighestIndex = k;
              }
          }
      SortedWeight[i] = HighestWeight;
      Weight[HighestIndex] = 0;
      }

    cout << "The highest weight was: " << SortedWeight[0] << endl;
    cout << "The second highest weight was: " << SortedWeight[1] << endl;
    cout << "The third highest weight was: " << SortedWeight[2] << endl;

    return 0;
}
```

Problem
Algorithms
C++
Executable
Hardware

Figure 4.16: Finding the top three weights using vectors (code\vect3.cc)

To run the program under gdb, make sure you are in the normal subdirectory, then type trace vect3. The program will start up and show you the first line of executable code. Type z and hit ENTER to execute each line of the program. The values of k, i, HighestIndex, HighestWeight, Weight, and SortedWeight will be displayed below the line that is to be executed next. When you are asked for a weight, type one in and hit ENTER just as when executing normally. After you've entered 5 weights, the program will start the sorting process. When the sorted results have been displayed (or when you're tired of tracing the program), type q (for *quit*) and hit ENTER to exit from the debugger.

Now let's look at the changes that we've made to the program from the last revision. The first change is that the for loop has only two sections rather than three in its control definition (inside the ()). As you may recall, the first section specifies the initial condition of the index variable; in this case, we're starting i out at 0, as is usual in C and C++. The second section indicates when we should continue executing the loop; here, it's as long as i is less than 5. But the third section, which usually indicates what to do to the index variable, is missing. The reason for this is that we're going to adjust the index variable manually in the loop, depending on what the user enters.

In this case, if the user enters an invalid value (i.e., less than or equal to 0), we display an error message and leave i as it was, so that the next time through the loop the value will go into the same element in the Weight vector. However, if the user enters a valid value, the else clause increments i so that the next value will go into the next element in the vector. This fixes the error in our previous version that left incorrect entries in the vector.

Now that we have beaten the pumpkin-weighing example to a pulp,[16] let's review the mass of information to which I've subjected you so far in this chapter.

> Problem
> **Algorithms**
> C++
> Executable
> Hardware

Review

We started out by extending our pumpkin-weighing program to tell us the highest two weights rather than just the highest one. During this exercise, we learned the use of the else clause of an if statement. We also saw that making even an apparently simple change to a working program can introduce an error; in this case we were copying the highest weight to the next highest-weight only when a new highest weight was detected. This would produce an incorrect result if a value higher than the previous second-highest but lower than the current highest weight were entered.

---

16. Pumpkin pie, anyone?

After fixing this problem, we continued by extending the program again, this time to handle any number of prizes to be given to the highest weight, second-highest weight, third-highest weight, and so on. This required a complete reorganization of the program. The new version used the *selection sort* algorithm to produce a list of as many of the highest weights as we need, in descending order. To do this, we had to use a vector, or set of values with a common name, to store all of the weights as they were read in. When they had all been entered, we searched through them three times, once to find each of the top three elements. A vector, just like a regular variable, has a name. However, unlike a regular variable, a vector does not have a single value but rather consists of a number of *elements*, each of which has a separate value. An element is referred to by a number, called an *index*, rather than by a unique name; each element has a different index. The lowest index is 0, and the highest index is 1 less than the number of elements in the vector. For example, with a 10-element vector, the legal indexes are 0 through 9. The ability to refer to an element by its index allows us to vary the element we are referring to in a statement by varying the index. We put this facility to good use in our implementation of the selection sort, which we'll review shortly.

Problem
Algorithms
C++
Executable
Hardware

We then added the for statement to our repertoire of loop control facilities. This statement provides more precise control than the while statement. Using for, we can specify a *starting expression*, a *continuation expression*, and a *modification expression*. The starting expression sets up the initial conditions for the loop. Before each possible execution of the controlled block, the continuation expression is checked. If it is true, the controlled block will be executed; otherwise, the for loop will terminate. Finally, the modification expression is executed after each execution of the controlled block. Most commonly, the starting expression sets the initial value of a variable, the continuation expression tests whether that variable is still in the range we are interested in, and the modification expression changes the value of the variable. For example, in the for statement

for (i = 0; i < 5; i ++)

the starting expression is i = 0, the continuation expression is i < 5, and the modification expression is i ++. Therefore, the block controlled by the for statement will be executed first with the variable i set to 0. At the end of the block, the variable i will be incremented by 1, and the loop will continue if i is still less than 5.

Then we used the for statement and a couple of vectors to implement a *selection sort*. This algorithm goes through an "input list" of n elements once for each desired "result element". In our case, we want the top three elements of the sorted list, so the input list has to be scanned three times. On each time through, the algorithm picks the highest value remaining in the list and adds that to the end of a new "output list". Then it removes the found value from the input list. At the end of this process, the output list has all of the desired values from the input list, in descending order of size. When going over the program, we found a weak spot in the first version: If all the weights the user typed were less than or equal to 0, the program would fail because one of the variables in the program would never be *initialized*; that is, set to a known value.

This led to a discussion of why variable initialization isn't done automatically in C++. Adding this feature to programs would make them slower and larger than C programs doing the same task, and C++ was intended to replace C completely. If C++ programs were significantly less efficient than equivalent C programs, this would not be possible, so Bjarne Stroustrup (the designer of C++) omitted this feature.

While it's important to ensure that our programs work correctly even when given unreasonable input, it's even better to prevent this situation from occurring in the first place. So the next improvement we made to our pumpkin-weighing program was to tell the user when an invalid value had been entered and ask for a valid value in its place. This involved a for loop without a modification expression, since we wanted to increment the index variable i to point to the next element of the vector only when the user typed in a valid entry. If an illegal value was typed in, we requested a legal value for the same element of the vector.

Problem
Algorithms
C++
Executable
Hardware

Exercises

So that you can test your understanding of this material, here are some exercises.

1.   If the program in Figure 4.17 is run, what will be displayed?

```
#include <iostream.h>
#include "vector.h"
int main()
{
    vector<short> x(5);
    short Result;
    short i;
    for (i = 0; i < 5; i ++)
        {
        x[i] = 2 * i;
        }
    for (i = 0; i < 5; i ++)
        {
        Result = Result + x[i];
        }
    cout << Result << endl;
    return 0;
}
```

Figure 4.17: Exercise 1 (code\morbas00.cc)

Problem
Algorithms
C++
Executable
Hardware

2. If the program in Figure 4.18 is run, what will be displayed?

```
#include <iostream.h>
#include "vector.h"
int main()
{
    vector<short> x(4);
    short Result;
    short i;
    x[0] = 3;
    for (i = 1; i < 4; i ++)
        x[i] = x[i-1] * 2;
    Result = 0;
    for (i = 0; i < 4; i ++)
        Result = Result + x[i];
    cout << Result << endl;
    return 0;
}
```

Figure 4.18: Exercise 2 (code\morbas01.cc)

3. Write a program that asks the user to type in a weight, and display the weight on the screen.

4. Modify the program from Exercise 3 to ask the user to type as many weights as desired, stopping as soon as a 0 is entered. Add up all of the weights entered and display the total on the screen at the end of the program.

Answers to the preceding exercises can be found at the end of the chapter.

5. When a child has a fever, the amount of medication needed to reduce the fever depends on two variables: the weight of the child and the child's temperature. Here is a table showing the dose in teaspoons of ibuprofen needed for a child of a given weight and given temperature.

		Temperature	
		Under 102.5 F	Over 102.5 F
W			
e			
i	12-17	1/4 tsp	1/2 tsp
g			
h	18-23	1/2 tsp	1 tsp
t			
	24-35	3/4 tsp	1 1/2 tsp
i			
n	36-47	1 tsp	2 tsp
p	48-59	1 1/4 tsp	2 1/2 tsp
o			
u	60-71	1 1/2 tsp	3 tsp
n			
d	72-95	2 tsp	4 tsp
s			

Figure 4.19: Ibuprofen dosage

Problem
Algorithms
C++
Executable
Hardware

Write a program that will ask for the weight and temperature of the child and will display the correct dose of ibuprofen for that situation.

Conclusion

We've covered a lot of material in this chapter in our quest for better pumpkin weighing, ranging from sorting data based on numeric value through the anatomy of vectors. Next, we'll take up some more of the language features you will need to write significant C++ programs.

Answers to Selected Exercises

1. The correct answer is: "Who knows?" If you said "30", you forgot that the loop variable values are from 0 through 4, rather than from 1 through 5. On the other hand, if you said "20", you had the right total of the numbers 0, 2, 4, 6, and 8, but didn't notice that the variable Result was never initialized. Of course, adding anything to an unknown value makes the final value unpredictable. Most current compilers, including the one on the CD-ROM in the back of this book, are capable of warning you about such problems. If you compiled the program with this warning turned on, you'd see a message something like this:

    morbas00.cc:7: warning: 'short result' may be used uninitialized in this function.

    This is the easiest way to find such errors, especially in a large program. Unfortunately, the compiler may produce such warnings even when they are not valid, so the final decision is still up to you.

Problem
Algorithms
C++
Executable
Hardware

   Assuming that you've installed the software from the CD-ROM in the back of this book, you can try this program out. First, you have to compile it by changing to the normal subdirectory under the main directory where you installed the software and typing mk morbas00. Running this program normally isn't likely to give you much information. To run the program under gdb, make sure you are in the normal subdirectory, then type trace morbas00. The program will start up and show you the first line of executable code. Type z and hit ENTER to execute each line of the program; the values of x[i], i, and Result will be displayed immediately before the execution of each line. When the results have been displayed (or when you're tired of tracing the program), type q (for *quit*) and hit ENTER to exit from the debugger.

2. The correct answer is 45. In case this isn't obvious, consider the following:

    a. The value of x[0] is set to 3.
    b. In the first for loop, the value of i starts out at 1.
    c. Therefore, the first execution of the assignment statement x[i] = x[i–1] * 2; is equivalent to x[1] = x[0] * 2;. This clearly sets x[1] to 6.

   d.   The next time through the loop i is 2, so that same assignment statement x[i] = x[i–1] * 2; is equivalent to x[2] = x[1] * 2;. This sets x[2] to 12.

   e.   On the last pass through the loop, the value of i is 3, so that assignment statement x[i] = x[i–1] * 2; is equivalent to x[3] = x[2] * 2;. This sets x[3] to 24.

   f.   The second for loop just adds up the values of all the entries in the x vector; this time, we remembered to initialize the total, Result, to 0, so the total is calculated and displayed correctly. Aren't vectors wonderful?

Running this program normally isn't likely to give you much information, but you might want to run it under control of the gdb debugger. You can do this in exactly the same way as you did the previous program, except that you would type trace morbas01 rather than trace morbas00.

3.   Figure 4.20 shows a solution to this problem.

```
#include <iostream.h>                              Problem
int main()                                         Algorithms
{                                                  C++
    short weight;                                  Executable
    cout << "Please write your weight here: ";     Hardware
    cin >> weight;
    cout << "I wish I only weighed " << weight << " pounds.";
    return 0;
}
```

Figure 4.20: The weight program (code\morbas03.cc)

4.   Figure 4.21 shows a solution to this problem. In case you were wondering, the reason we have to duplicate the statements to read in the weight is that we need an initial value for the variable weight before we start the while loop so that the condition in the while will be calculated correctly.

By the way, there's another way to write the statement total = total + weight; that uses an operator analogous to ++, the increment operator: total += weight;. This new operator, +=, means "add what's on the *right* to what's on the *left*". The motivation for this shortcut, as you might imagine, is the same as that for ++: It requires less typing, is more likely to be correct, and is easier to compile to efficient code. Just like the "increment memory" instruction, many machines have an "add (something) to memory" instruction, and it's easier to figure out that such an instruction should be used for an expression like x += y than in the case of the equivalent x = x + y.

```
#include <iostream.h>
int main()
{
    short weight;
    short total;
    cout << "Please type in your weight, typing 0 to end:";
    cin >> weight;
    total = weight;
    while (weight > 0)
        {
        cout << "Please type in your weight, typing 0 to end:";
        cin >> weight;
        total = total + weight;
        }
    cout << "The total is: " << total << endl;
    return 0;
}
```

Problem
Algorithms
C++
Executable
Hardware

Figure 4.21: The weight totaling program (code\morbas04.cc)

Running this program normally isn't likely to give you much information, so you might want to run it under control of the gdb debugger. You can do this in exactly the same way as you did the previous two programs, except that you would type trace morbas04 to start.

Chapter 5

Functional Literacy

Form Follows Function

C++ was intended to be useful in writing large programs. Such programs are usually composed of many *implementation file*s, as I mentioned in Chapter 3.

In such a case, we must have some way of creating an executable program (sometimes abbreviated to just an *executable*) from a number of implementation files. We also need some way for code in one module to refer to code in another one. Similarly, we have to be able to specify where execution of our program should start; this is taken care of by the C++ rule that execution always starts at the block called main.

As we've already seen, the computer can't execute source code. Therefore, any implementation files we write have to be translated into object code. The result of such translation is an object code module. One other kind of module we're interested in is the library module, which contains the object code from several implementation files. Here's a list of these different kinds of modules, with a little more detail:

1. An **implementation file** is a file that contains source code for a program. Almost every part of every program starts out as an implementation file.
2. Compilation of an implementation file produces a file called an **object code module** (or **object file**), which contains object (machine) code.
3. Several object code modules of a generally useful nature can be combined to make a file called a **library module**, usually abbreviated to **library**.

Actually, I've misused C++ terminology a little here in the interest of comprehensibility. The term *block* isn't quite correct as applied to main(); the correct term is *function*. Let's take a look at the difference between these two concepts, some other related definitions, and the objectives for this chapter.

Definitions

A **block** is a section of code that acts like one statement, as far as the language is concerned; that is, wherever a statement can occur, a block can be substituted and will be treated as one statement for the purposes of program organization.

A **function** is also a section of code, but its characteristics are different from those of a block. For one thing, you can't substitute a function for a statement. Also, a function has a name, whereas blocks are anonymous. This name enables one function to start execution of another one.

```
Problem
Algorithms
C++
Executable
Hardware
```

A **function call** (or just "call" for short) causes execution to be transferred temporarily from the current function to the one named in the call.

A **called function** is a function that starts execution as a result of a function call.

A **calling function** is a function that suspends execution as a result of a function call.

A return **statement** is the mechanism used by a called function to return to the calling function, which picks up just where it left off.

Objectives of This Chapter

By the end of this chapter, you should

1. Understand how and when to use functions to reduce the amount of code you have to write.
2. Understand what software really is.

3. Understand how your source code is turned into an executable program.
4. Understand how storage is assigned to different types of variables.
5. Understand how functions can call one another.

Functioning Normally

Why would we want to use a function? To answer that question, let's take a look at the program in Figure 5.1. It has some duplicated code, so a function could be helpful.

```
#include <iostream.h>

int main()
{
    short FirstWeight;
    short SecondWeight;
    short FirstAge;
    short SecondAge;
    short AverageWeight;
    short AverageAge;

    cout << "Please type in the first weight: ";
    cin >> FirstWeight;

    cout << "Please type in the second weight: ";
    cin >> SecondWeight;

    AverageWeight = (FirstWeight + SecondWeight) / 2;

    cout << "Please type in the first age: ";
    cin >> FirstAge;

    cout << "Please type in the second age: ";
    cin >> SecondAge;

    AverageAge = (FirstAge + SecondAge) / 2;

    cout << "The average weight was: " << AverageWeight << endl;
    cout << "The average age was: " << AverageAge << endl;

    return 0;
}
```

Problem
Algorithms
C++
Executable
Hardware

Figure 5.1: A sample program with duplicated code (code\nofunc.cc)

I'd like you to look particularly at this line,

AverageWeight = (FirstWeight + SecondWeight) / 2;

and this one,

AverageAge = (FirstAge + SecondAge) / 2;

These two lines are awfully similar; the only difference between them is that one of them averages two weights and the other averages two ages. While this particular example doesn't take too much code to duplicate, it may not be too difficult for you to imagine the inefficiency and nuisance of having to copy and edit many lines of code every time we want to do exactly the same thing with different data. Instead of copying the code and editing it to change the name of the variables, we can write a function that averages whatever data we give it.

When we call a function, we usually have to provide it with input (in this case, the values to be averaged) and it usually produces output that we use in further processing (in this case, the average of the input values). Some functions, though, have only one or the other. For example, some pairs of functions consist of one **storage function** and one **retrieval function**; the first stores data for the second to retrieve later. In that case, the storage function may not give us anything back when we call it, and the retrieving function may not need any input from us.

Problem
Algorithms
C++
Executable
Hardware

A picture is often worth 1024 words, so I've drawn Figure 5.2, a picture of a function call. The calling function **(1)** is main; the function call is at position **(2)**. The called function is Average **(3)**, and the return is at position **(4)**. The returned value is stored in the variable AvgAge, as indicated by the assignment operator = in the statement AvgAge = Average(FirstAge,SecondAge);. The calling function, main, resumes execution at line **(5)**.[1]

By the way, it's important to distinguish between returning a value from a function, which is optional, and returning control from the called function to the calling function, which always happens at the end of the called function (unless the program has terminated due to an error in the called function).

---

1. If you provide no return statement, then the called function will just return to the calling function when it gets to its closing }. However, this is not legal for a function that is defined to return a value. This of course leads to the question of why we'd call a function that **doesn't** return a value. One possibility is that the function exists only to produce output on the screen, rather than to return any results. The actions that a function performs other than returning a value are called **side effects**.

```
short Average(short First, short Second)          (3)

{

   short Result;

   Result = (First + Second) / 2;

   return Result;                                 (4)

}
```

```
int main()                                        (1)

{

   short FirstAge;

   short SecondAge;

   short AvgAge;

   FirstAge = 5;

   SecondAge = 9;

   AvgAge = Average(FirstAge,SecondAge);          (2)

   cout << k << endl;                             (5)

   return 0;

}
```

Problem
Algorithms
C++
Executable
Hardware

Figure 5.2: A function call

In the event that you're wondering why we started the example at the beginning of main, it's because every C++ program starts executing at that point. When the main function calls another function, such as Average, then main is suspended until Average is finished. When Average finishes, main resumes where it left off.

This isn't limited to one "level" of calls. The same thing can happen if Average (for example) calls another function, let's say Funcx; Average will wait until Funcx returns before continuing. Then when Average finishes, it will return to main, which will take up where it left off.

Above Average

I think it's time for a more detailed example of how we would use a function. Suppose we want to average sets of two numbers and we don't want to write the averaging code more than once. The Average function just illustrated provides this service; its input is the two numbers we want to average, and its output is the average. Figure 5.3 shows the code for the function Average without all the lines and arrows.

```
short Average(short First, short Second)
{
    short Result;

    Result = (First + Second) / 2;

    return Result;
}
```

Problem
Algorithms
C++
Executable
Hardware

Figure 5.3: A function to average two values

Assuming that you've installed the software from the CD-ROM in the back of this book, you can try out this function in a running program.[2] First, you have to compile it by changing to the normal subdirectory under the main directory where you installed the software and typing mk func1. Then type func1 to run the program. When it asks you to type a number in, type one in and hit ENTER. To run it under gdb, make sure you are in the normal subdirectory, then type trace func1. The program will start up and show you the first line of executable code. Type z and hit ENTER to execute each line. The values of all the variables in main will be displayed immediately before the execution of each line in that function. When you get to the end of the program (or when you're tired of tracing), type q (for *quit*) and hit ENTER to exit from the debugger.

---

2. If you want to see the whole program that this function is used in, it's in Figure 5.5.

By the way, if you trace through this program, please don't be confused by the seemingly random values that all of the variables start out with when tracing the program. These are just the garbage values that happen to be lying around in memory where those variables reside. As we've already seen, variables that haven't yet been assigned a value are called *uninitialized variables*. The variables in this program are all initialized before they are used, but the tracing program starts to display them before the initializing statements have been executed; therefore, they appear uninitialized at the beginning of the trace. We'll see later in this chapter exactly why we have to initialize all of our variables before we use them.

To analyze this piece of code, let's start at the beginning. Every function starts with a **function declaration**, which tells the compiler some vital statistics of the function. The function declaration consists of three parts:

1. A return type
2. The function's name
3. An argument list

In the case of our Average function, the function declaration is short Average(short First, short Second). The return type is short, the name of the function is Average, and the argument list is (short First, short Second). Let's take these one at a time.

```
Problem
Algorithms
C++
Executable
Hardware
```

Return to Sender

The first part of the function declaration is the **return type**, in this case short. This indicates that the function Average will provide a value of type short to the calling function when the Average function returns. Looking at the end of the function, you will see a statement that says return Result;. Checking back to the variable definition part of the function, we see that Result is indeed a short, so the value we're returning is of the correct type. If that were not the case, the compiler would tell us that we had a discrepancy between the declared return type of our function and the type actually returned in the code. This is another example where the compiler helps us out with *static type checking*, as mentioned in Chapter 3. If we say we want to return a short and then return some other incompatible type such as a string, we've made a mistake.[3] It's much easier for the compiler to catch this and warn us than it is for us to locate the error ourselves when the program doesn't work correctly.

The function name (in this case, Average) follows the same rules as a variable name. This is not a coincidence, because both function names and variable names are identifiers, which is a fancy word for "user-defined names". The rules for constructing an identifier are pretty simple, as specified in the C++ *Draft Standard*: "An identifier is an arbitrarily long sequence of letters and digits. The first character is a letter; the underscore _ counts as a letter. Upper- and lower-case letters are different. All characters are significant." In other words:

1. Your identifiers can be as long as you wish.[4]
2. They can be made of any combination of letters and digits, as long as the first character is a letter. For historical reasons, the underscore character _ counts as a letter.[5]
3. The upper- and lowercase version of the same character aren't considered equal as far as names are concerned; that is, the variable xyz is a different variable from Xyz, while XYZ is yet another variable. Of course, *you* may get confused by having three variables with those names, but the compiler considers them all distinct.
4. The compiler is required to distinguish between two identifiers, no matter how many identical characters they contain, as long as at least one character is different in the two names.

Problem
Algorithms
C++
Executable
Hardware

By the way, the reason that the first character of an identifier can't be a digit is to make it easier for the compiler to figure out what is a number and what isn't. Another rule is that user-defined names cannot conflict with names defined by the C++ language (keywords); some examples of keywords that we've already seen are if, for, and short.

---

3. What do I mean by an *incompatible type*? C++ has rules that, for example, allow us to return a char variable where a short (or an int) is expected; the compiler will convert the char into either of those types for us automatically. This is convenient sometimes, but it reduces the chances of catching an error of this kind and therefore is less safe than it could be. This practice is a legacy from C, which means that it can't be changed for practical reasons, even though it is less than desirable theoretically.

4. You don't have to worry about wasting space in your program by using long identifiers. They go away when your program is compiled and are replaced by addresses of the variables or functions to which they refer.

5. You should avoid starting your variable or function names with an underscore, as such names are "reserved" for use by compiler writers and other language implementers.

Finally, we have the **argument list**. In this case, it contains two arguments. The first is a short called First, which holds the first number that our Average function uses to calculate its result. The second argument is a short called Second, which of course is the other number needed to calculate the average. In other cases, there might be several entries in the argument list, each of which provides some information to the called function. But what exactly *is* an argument?

For the Sake of Argument

The question of what is an argument is more subtle than it may appear. An argument is a value that is supplied by a function (the *calling function*) that wishes to use the services of another function (the *called function*). For example, the calling function might be our main function, and the called function might be our Average function, while the arguments are two short values to be averaged. Arguments like the ones here are actually copies of values from the calling function; that is, the compiler will set the variable named in the argument list of the called function to the value supplied by the calling function. This process of making a copy of the calling function's argument is referred to as *call by value*, and the resulting copy is called a **value argument**.[6]

Problem
Algorithms
C++
Executable
Hardware

Figure 5.4 is an example of this argument-passing mechanism at work with only one argument. In this program, main sets x to 46 and then calls Birthday with x as the argument. When Birthday starts, a new variable called age is created and set to 46, because that's the value of x, the argument with which main called Birthday. Birthday adds one to its variable age and then returns the new value of that variable to main. What will be printed by the line cout << x << endl;? Answer: 46, because the variable age in Birthday was a *copy* of the argument from main, not the actual variable x named in the call to Birthday. On the other hand, the value of y in the main program will be 47, because that is the return value from Birthday.

The same analysis that we have just applied to the Birthday function applies also to the Average function that we started out with; the arguments First and Second are copies of the values specified in the call to Average.

---

6. This discussion might make you wonder whether there's another type of argument besides a value argument. There is, and we'll find out about it in Chapter 7.

```
#include <iostream.h>

short Birthday(short age)
{
   age ++;
   return age;
}

int main()
{
   short x;
   short y;

   x = 46;
   y = Birthday(x);

   cout << "Your age was: " << x << endl;
   cout << "Happy Birthday: your age is now " << y << endl;

   return 0;
}
```

Figure 5.4: Argument passing with one argument (code\birthday.cc)

Problem
Algorithms
C++
Executable
Hardware

General Delivery

Now that we have accounted for the Average function's input and output, we can examine how it does its work. First, we have a variable definition for Result, which will hold the value we will return to the calling function; namely, the average of the two input values.

Then we calculate that average, with the statement Result = (First + Second) / 2;. Once the average has been calculated, we're ready to return it to the calling program, which is accomplished by the line return Result;. Finally, we reach the closing }, which tells the compiler that the function is done.

Using a Function

Now that we have seen how to write the Average function, let's see how to use it to solve our original problem. The program in Figure 5.5 uses our Average function twice, once to average two weights and once to average two ages.

```
#include <iostream.h>

short Average(short First, short Second)
{
    short Result;

    Result = (First + Second) / 2;

    return Result;
}

int main()
{
    short FirstWeight;
    short SecondWeight;
    short FirstAge;
    short SecondAge;
    short AverageWeight;
    short AverageAge;

    cout << "Please type in the first weight: ";
    cin >> FirstWeight;

    cout << "Please type in the second weight: ";
    cin >> SecondWeight;

    AverageWeight = Average(FirstWeight, SecondWeight);

    cout << "Please type in the first age: ";
    cin >> FirstAge;

    cout << "Please type in the second age: ";
    cin >> SecondAge;

    AverageAge = Average(FirstAge, SecondAge);

    cout << "The average weight was: " << AverageWeight << endl;
    cout << "The average age was: " << AverageAge << endl;

    return 0;
}
```

Problem
Algorithms
C++
Executable
Hardware

Figure 5.5: Using the Average function (code\func1.cc)

As before, calling a function requires specifying its name and its argument(s) and doing something with the return value, if any. In this case, we call Average with the arguments FirstWeight and SecondWeight, and store the result in AverageWeight. This is accomplished via the line AverageWeight = Average(FirstWeight, SecondWeight);. Later, we call Average with the arguments FirstAge and SecondAge, and store the result in AverageAge. We do this via the line AverageAge = Average(FirstAge, SecondAge);.

A Convincing Argument

As you can see, using a function isn't very difficult. We have to provide it with the material to work on (its input arguments) and can store its return value in a variable for further processing (or use it directly, if we wish). But there's a little more here than meets the eye. How does the variable FirstWeight, for example, get transformed into the variable First that we used when writing the function?

This explanation requires us to look at some more underlying software technology. To be precise, we're going to spend some time examining the infrastructure that makes computers usable for programmers. First, though, we have to consider a more general notion, that of a "virtual computer".

```
Problem
Algorithms
C++
Executable
Hardware
```

The Man Behind the Curtain

Unlike many words in the vocabulary of computing, *virtual* has more or less retained its standard English definition: "That is so in essence or effect, although not formally or actually; admitting of being called by the name so far as the effect or result is concerned."[7] In other words, a virtual computer would be something that acts just like a computer, but really isn't one. Who would want such a thing?

Apparently everyone, since *virtual computer* is just another name for what we have been calling *software*. This may seem a rash statement, but it really isn't. One of the most important mathematical discoveries (inventions?) of the twentieth century was Alan Turing's demonstration that it was possible to create a fairly simple computing device (called a *Turing machine* for some reason) that could imitate *any* other computing device. This machine works in the following way: You provide it with a description of the other computer you want it to imitate, and it follows those directions. Suppose we want a computer that calculates only trigonometric functions. Then we could theoretically write a set of instructions as to how such a computer

---

7. *Oxford English Dictionary*, first current definition (4).

would behave, feed it into a Turing machine, and have the Turing machine imitate the behavior of this theoretical "trigonometric computer".

This is undoubtedly interesting, but you may be wondering what it has to do with programming. Well, what do we do when we write a program? In the case of our pumpkin-weighing program, we're describing the actions that would be taken by a hypothetical "pumpkin-weighing computer". When we run the program, the real computer simulates these actions. In other words, we have created a virtual pumpkin-weighing computer.

The same analysis applies to any program. A program can most fundamentally be defined as instructions to a "universal computer", telling it how to simulate the specialized computer you actually want to use. When the universal computer executes these instructions, it behaves exactly as the hypothetical specialized computer would behave.

Of course, real computers aren't really universal; they have limits in the amount of memory or disk space they contain and the speed of their execution. However, for problems that can be solved within those limits, they are truly universal computing devices that can be tailored to a particular problem by programming.

Problem
Algorithms
C++
Executable
Hardware

The Object of My Affections

Now let's take a look at one of these areas of software technology. We've already seen that the function of a compiler is to convert our human-readable C++ program into machine instructions that can be executed by the computer but the compiler doesn't actually produce an executable program that can stand by itself; instead, it translates each implementation file into a machine language file called an *object code module* (or *object file*). This file contains the instructions that correspond to the source code statements you've written, but not the "infrastructure" needed to allow them to be executed. We'll see what that infrastructure does for us shortly.

The creation of an object file rather than a complete executable program isn't a universal characteristic of compilers, dictated by nature. In fact, one of the most popular compilers in the early history of the PC, the Turbo Pascal™ compiler, did create an executable file directly from source code. This appears much simpler, so we have to ask why this approach has been abandoned with C++. As I've mentioned before, C++ was intended to be useful in writing large programs. Such programs can consist of hundreds or even thousands of modules (sections of source code), each containing hundreds or thousands of lines of code. Once all the modules are compiled, the object files resulting from the compilation are run through a program called the *linker*. The linker combines information from all of the object files, along with some previously prepared files called *library modules* (or *libraries*), to produce an executable program; this is called **linking** the program. One reason for this two-step approach is that we wouldn't want to have to recompile every module in a large program every time we made a change in one section. Therefore, only those modules that have been affected are recompiled.

By the way, in the event that you're wondering why I said "those modules that have been affected" rather than "those modules that have been changed", the reason is that even if we don't change a particular module, we will have to recompile it if a header file that it uses is changed. This can be a serious maintenance problem in large systems; there are special programming methods used to alleviate it, which are outside the scope of this book. When all of the affected modules have been recompiled, the program is relinked to produce an updated executable.

Figure 5.6 is a picture of the process of turning your source code into an executable file.

Problem
Algorithms
C++
Executable
Hardware

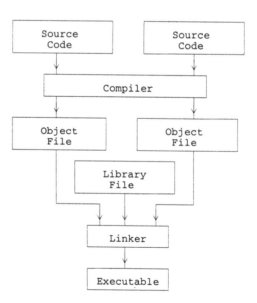

Figure 5.6: Making an executable

To make such a system work, it's necessary to set up conventions as to which parts will be executed first, where data needed by more than one module will be stored, and so on. Also, a lot of operations aren't supplied as part of the language itself but are very handy in writing programs, such as the I/O functions that we've already seen. These make up the infrastructure needed to execute C++ programs.

Operating Systematically

As is often the case in programming, this infrastructure is divided into several layers, the higher ones depending on the lower ones for more fundamental services. The lowest level of the infrastructure is supplied by the **operating system**, a program that deals with the actual hardware of your computer. By far the most common operating system for Intel CPUs, as this is written, is MS-DOS (which is also the basis for Windows 95), followed by OS/2 and Windows NT. All of these provide some of the same facilities. For example, you are accustomed to dealing with files and directories when using application programs such as word processors and spreadsheets. However, the disk drive in your computer doesn't know anything about files or directories. As we have seen in Chapter 2, all it can do is to store and retrieve fixed-size pieces of data called *sectors*, given an absolute address on the disk described by a platter, track number, and sector number. Files are a creation of the operating system, which keeps track of which parts of which files are stored where on the disk. As this suggests, we can think of files as a figment of the operating system's imagination; however, their "virtual" nature doesn't detract from their usefulness.[8]

```
Problem
Algorithms
C++
Executable
Hardware
```

A modern operating system provides many more facilities than just keeping track of file storage. For example, it arranges for code and data to be stored in separate areas of RAM with different *access rights*, so that code can't be accidentally overwritten by a runaway program; that is, one that writes outside the memory areas it is supposed to use. This is a valuable service, as errors of this kind are quite difficult to find and can cause havoc when they occur.

That's the good news. The bad news is that MS-DOS was created before the widespread availability of reasonably priced CPUs with memory protection facilities and therefore doesn't take advantage of

---

8. This reminds me of the story about the man who went to a doctor, complaining that his brother had thought he was a hen for many years. The doctor asked why the family hadn't tried to help the brother before, and the man replied, "We needed the eggs".

these facilities, although they are present in Windows 3.1 and Windows 95, which run "on top of" MS-DOS. Running under plain MS-DOS, it's entirely possible for a runaway program to destroy anything else in memory. Theoretically, we should all be running "real" operating systems by the time you read this; so far, though, the rumors of the demise of MS-DOS have been greatly exaggerated.

Using Your Library Card

The next level of the infrastructure is supplied by the aforementioned *library modules*, which contain standardized segments of code that can perform I/O, mathematical functions, and other commonly used operations. So far, we have used the iostreams library, which provided the keyboard input and screen output in our example programs. We've also relied implicitly on the "startup" library, which sets up the conditions necessary for any C++ program to execute properly, as well as the string and vector libraries for those data types.

To understand the necessity for the startup library, we have to take a look at the way variables are assigned to memory locations. So far, we have just assumed that a particular variable had a certain address, but how is this address determined in the real world?

Problem
Algorithms
C++
Executable
Hardware

There are several possible ways for this to occur; the particular one employed for any given variable is determined by the variable's **storage class**. The simplest of these is the static **storage class**; variables of this class are assigned memory addresses in the executable program when the program is linked. The most common way to put a variable in the static storage class is to define it outside any function.[9] Such a variable will be initialized only once before main starts executing. We can specify the initial value if we wish; if we don't specify it, a default value (0 for numeric variables) will be assigned. An example of such a definition would be writing the line short x = 3; outside any function; this would cause x to be set to 3 before main starts executing. We can change the value of such a variable whenever we wish, just as with any other variable. The distinction I'm making here is that a static variable is always initialized before main begins executing. As you will see, this seemingly obvious characteristic of static variables is not shared with variables of other storage classes.

---

9. Another way to make a variable static is to state explicitly that the variable is static. However, this only works for variables defined inside functions. For the time being, we'll restrict the discussion to statically allocated variables defined outside any function.

Automatic Pilot

The notion of storage classes is essential to the solution of another mystery. You may recall that I mentioned some time ago that C++ doesn't provide automatic initialization of all variables because that facility would make a program bigger and slower. I'll admit that the truth of this isn't intuitively obvious to the casual observer. After all, a variable (or more exactly, the storage location it occupies) has to have *some* value, so why not something reasonable? As we have just seen, this *is* done for static variables. However, there is another storage class for which such a facility isn't quite as easy or efficient to implement; that's the auto (short for "automatic") **storage class**, which is the default class used for variables defined in functions. An auto variable is not initialized until the function in which it is defined starts execution and even then has no known value until we specifically assign a value to it.[10]

So far, all of our variables have been auto, and in most programs the vast majority of all variables are of this class. We haven't seen this keyword before only because auto is the default storage class, which means that we don't have to explicitly mark variables as auto. However, this doesn't explain why we should use these variables when static ones have that handy initialization feature built in.

Problem
Algorithms
C++
Executable
Hardware

The first clue to this mystery is in the name auto. When we define a variable of the auto class, its address is assigned *auto*matically when its function is entered; the address is valid for the duration of that function. By the way, this explains why variables defined outside a function are static rather than auto; if they were auto, when would their addresses be assigned?

Since the address of an auto variable isn't known until its function is entered, it can't be initialized until then (unlike the case with static variables). Therefore, every function would have to start with some extra code to initialize every auto variable, which would make the program both slower and larger. Since Bjarne Stroustrup's design goals required that a C++ program should have the same run time performance as a C program and as little space overhead as possible, such a feature was unacceptable. Luckily, forgetting to initialize an auto variable is something that can be detected at compile time, so it's possible for the compiler to warn us if we make this error. In general,

---

10. I'm oversimplifying a bit here. Variables can actually be declared inside any block, not just any function. An auto variable that is declared inside a block is born when the block is entered and lives until that block is finished executing. A static variable that is declared inside a block is initialized when that block is entered for the first time. It retains its value from that point on unless it is explicitly changed, as with any other statically allocated variable.

it's a good idea to tell the compiler to warn you about dubious practices. Although not all of them may be real errors, some will be, and this is by far the fastest and best way to find them.[11]

Now we've seen why auto variables aren't initialized by default: Their addresses aren't known until entering the function in which they're defined. But that doesn't explain the advantage of assigning the addresses then. Wouldn't it be simpler (and faster) to assign them all during the linking process, as is done with static variables?

Stacking the Deck

To understand why auto variables aren't assigned addresses during the linking process, we have to look at the way functions relate to one another. In particular, it is very common for a statement in one function to call another function; this is called *nesting* functions and can continue to any number of levels.

Although functions can call one another, it is very unlikely that every function in a large program will be in the midst of execution at any given time. This means that reserving space in the executable program for all of the variables in all of the functions will make that executable considerably larger than it otherwise would be.

```
Problem
Algorithms
C++
Executable
Hardware
```

If we had only static variables, this wasteful situation would indeed occur. The alternative, of course, is to use auto variables, which as we have just noted are assigned storage at run time. But where is that storage assigned, if not in the executable program?

While all static variables are assigned storage when the executable program is linked, auto variables are instead stored in a data structure called a **stack**; the name is intended to suggest the notion of stacking clean plates on a spring-loaded holder such as you might see in a cafeteria. The last plate deposited on the stack of plates will be the first one to be removed when a customer needs a fresh plate. Back in the world of programming, a stack with one entry might look something like Figure 5.7.[12]

---

11. There are also commercial tools that help locate errors of this type, as well as other errors that can be found by analyzing the source code for inconsistencies.

12. The actual memory locations used to hold the items in the stack are just like any other locations in RAM. What makes them part of the stack is how they are used. Of course, as always, one memory location can hold only one item at a given time, so the locations used to hold entries on the stack cannot be simultaneously used for something else like machine instructions.

TOP	1234

Figure 5.7: A stack with one entry

If we add (or **push**) another value on to the stack, say 999, the result would look like Figure 5.8.

TOP	999
2nd	1234

Figure 5.8: A stack with two entries

If we were to push one more item, this time with the value 1666, the result would look like Figure 5.9.

TOP	1666
2nd	999
3rd	1234

Problem
Algorithms
C++
Executable
Hardware

Figure 5.9: A stack with three entries

Now, if we retrieve (or **pop**) a value, we'll get the one on top; namely, 1666. Then the stack will look like it did in Figure 5.8. The next value to be popped off the stack will be the 999, leaving us with the situation in Figure 5.7 again. If we continue for one more round, we'll get the value 1234, leaving us with an **empty stack**.

The reason that stacks are used to store auto variables is that the way items are pushed onto or popped off a stack exactly parallels what happens when one function calls another. Let's look at this stack idea again, but this time from the point of view of keeping track of where we are in one function when it calls another one, as well as allocating storage for auto variables.

Don't Call Me, I'll Call You

In Figure 5.5, there are two calls to the function Average: The first one is used to average two weights and the other to average two ages. One point I didn't stress was exactly how the Average function "knew" which call was which; that is, how did Average return to the right place after each time it was called? In principle, the answer is fairly simple: The calling function somehow notifies the called function of the address of the next instruction that should be executed after the called function is finished (the **return address**). There are several possible ways to solve this problem. The simplest solution is to store the return address at some standardized position in the code of the called function. At the end of the called function, that address is used to get back to the caller. While this used to be standard practice, it has a number of drawbacks that have relegated it to the history books. A major problem with this approach is that it requires changing data that is stored with the code of the called routine. As we've already seen, when running a program on a modern CPU under a modern operating system, code and data areas of memory are treated differently, and changing the contents of code areas at run time is not allowed.

Problem
Algorithms
C++
Executable
Hardware

Luckily, there is another convenient place to store return addresses: on the stack. This is such an important mechanism that all modern CPUs have a dedicated register, usually called the **stack pointer**, to make it easy and efficient to store and retrieve return addresses and other data that are of interest only during the execution of a function. In the case of the Intel CPUs, the stack pointer's name is esp.[13] A machine instruction named call is designed to push the return address on the stack and jump to the beginning of the function being called.[14] The call **instruction** isn't very complex in its operation, but before going into that explanation, you'll need some background information about the working of the CPU when it executes instructions.

How does the CPU "know" what instruction is the next to be executed? By using another dedicated register that we haven't discussed before, the **program counter**, which holds the address of the next instruction to be executed. Normally, this is the instruction physically following the one currently being executed. However,

---

13. That's the 32-bit stack pointer; as in the case of the other registers, there's a 16-bit stack pointer called sp, which consists of the 16 lower bits of the "real" stack pointer esp.

14. That is, its name is call on Intel machines and many others; all modern CPUs have an equivalent instruction, although it may have a different name.

when we want to change the sequence of execution, as in an if statement or a function call, the program counter is loaded with the address of the instruction that *logically* follows the present one. Whatever instruction is at the address specified in the program counter is by definition the next instruction that will be executed. Therefore, changing the address in the program counter to the address of any instruction causes that instruction to be the next one to be executed.

Here are the actual steps that the call instruction performs:

1. It saves the contents of the program counter on the stack.
2. Then it loads the program counter with the address of the first instruction of the called function.

What does this sequence of events achieve? Well, since the program counter always points to the next instruction to be executed, the address stored on the stack by the first step is the address of the next instruction after the call. Therefore, the last instruction in the called function can resume execution of the calling function by loading the program counter with the stored value on the stack. This will restart execution of the calling function at the next instruction after the call, which is exactly what we want to achieve.

The effect of the second step is to continue execution of the program with the first instruction of the called function; that's because the program counter is the register that specifies the address of the next instruction to be executed.

Problem
Algorithms
C++
Executable
Hardware

How It All Stacks Up

As we'll see, the actual way that a stack is implemented is a bit different than is suggested by the "stack of plates" analogy, although the effect is exactly the same. Rather than keeping the top of the stack where it is and moving the data (a slow operation), the data is left in place and the address stored in the stack pointer is changed, which is a much faster operation. In other words, whatever address the stack pointer is pointing to is by definition the "top of the stack".[15]

---

15. Please note that the address that the stack occupies in these diagrams is arbitrary. The actual address where the stack is located in your program is determined by the linker and the operating system.

For example, suppose that we start with an empty stack with the stack pointer at 20001ffe. Thus, the stack will look like Figure 5.10.

```
Address              Contents              Meaning

20001ffe          ┌─────────────┐
                  │    ????     │         (none)
                  └─────────────┘
```

Figure 5.10: An empty stack

Then, the user types in the two values "2" and "4" as the values of FirstWeight and SecondWeight, and the first call to Average occurs; let's suppose that call is at location 10001000. As usual, all addresses are in hexadecimal.

Although the details will vary with the compiler, the sequence of events will be something like this:

Problem
Algorithms
C++
Executable
Hardware

1. The address of the next instruction to be executed (say, 10001005) is pushed onto the stack, along with the values for the arguments First and Second, which are copies of the arguments FirstWeight and SecondWeight. In the process, the CPU will subtract 8 (the size of one address added to the size of two shorts, in bytes) from the stack pointer (which is then 20001ff6) and store the return address at the address currently pointed to by the stack pointer. Thus, the stack will look like Figure 5.11.[16]

```
Address              Contents              Meaning

20001ff2          ┌─────────────┐
                  │    ????     │         (none)
20001ff4          ├─────────────┤
                  │    ????     │         (none)
20001ff6          ├─────────────┤
                  │  10001005   │         return address in main
20001ffa          ├─────────────┤
                  │    0004     │         Second
20001ffc          ├─────────────┤
                  │    0002     │         First
20001ffe          ├─────────────┤
                  │    ????     │         (none)
                  └─────────────┘
```

Figure 5.11: The stack immediately after the call to Average

16. The "Top of Stack" address, that is, the address where the stack pointer is pointing, will be **bold**. Also note that when we push items on the stack the stack pointer will move upward in the diagram. That's because lower addresses appear first in the diagram, and new items pushed onto the stack go at lower addresses. Anything in the diagram "above" the stack pointer (i.e., at a lower address than the stack pointer's current value) is not a meaningful value, as indicated in the "meaning" column.

2. Execution starts in the Average function. However, before the code we write can be executed, we have to reserve space on the stack for the auto variable(s) defined in Average (other than the arguments First and Second, which have already been allocated). In this case, there is only one — Result. Since this variable is a short, it takes 2 bytes, so the stack pointer has to be reduced by 2. After this operation is completed, the stack will look like Figure 5.12.

Address	Contents	Meaning
20001ff2	????	(none)
20001ff4	????	Result
20001ff6	10001005	return address in main
20001ffa	0004	Second
20001ffc	0002	First
20001ffe	????	(none)

Figure 5.12: The stack after auto variable allocation

Problem
Algorithms
C++
Executable
Hardware

Wait a minute. What are those ???? doing at location 20001ff4? They represent an uninitialized memory location. We don't know what's in that location, because that depends on what it was used for previously, which could be almost anything. The C++ compiler uses stack-based addressing for auto variables, as well as copies of arguments passed in from the calling function. That is, the addresses of such variables are relative to the stack pointer, rather than being fixed addresses. In this case, the address of Result would be [esp], or the current value of the stack pointer; Second would be referred to in the object file as [esp+6] (i.e, 6 more than the current value of the stack pointer, to leave room for the return address and Result). Similarly, the address of First would be [esp+8], or 8 more than the current value of the stack pointer.[17] Since the actual addresses occupied by these variables aren't known until the setup code at the beginning of the function is actually executed, there's no way to clear the variables out before then. That's why auto variables aren't automatically initialized.

---

17. The actual mechanism used to refer to variables on the stack in a real compiler is likely to be different from this one and indeed can vary among compilers. However, this implementation would work.

Scoped Out

This is a good place to mention another related but distinct way to categorize variables — by their scope. The **scope** of a variable is the part of the program in which it can be accessed. The scopes we are concerned with here are *local scope* and *global scope*. Variables with **global scope** are called *global variables*. These variables are defined outside any function and can be accessed from any function.[18] Global variables are always in the static storage class, as we have already seen.[19] Variables with **local scope** are called *local variables*. These variables are defined in a function and are accessible only while that function is executing; they can be either static or auto and are auto by default.

Figure 5.13 is a table of the allowable combinations of scope and storage class.

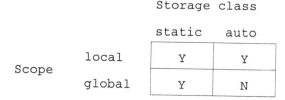

Figure 5.13: Scope vs. storage class

Before we get deeper into the notion of scope, I think we should revisit the question of variable initialization in the light of the notion of global and local variables.

static **Cling**

What makes a variable static or auto is when its storage is assigned and therefore when its address is known. In the case of a static variable, this happens at link time. In the case of an auto variable, it happens

---

18. Variables can be defined either inside a function (local variables) or outside a function (global variables); by contrast, code must always be inside a function.

19. However, do **not** use the keyword static when defining global variables that you want to be statically allocated. That keyword, when applied to a global variable, means something else entirely; an approximate translation of specifying the keyword static for a function or a global variable is that the function or variable is available for use only in the same file where it is defined, following the point of its definition.

when the function where it is defined is entered. If this sounds as though you are responsible for keeping track of the address of every variable, you can breathe easy; that's the compiler's problem, not yours. The important distinction between a static and an auto variable is *when* the address is assigned, not what the actual address is.

This distinction affects initialization because it's impossible to initialize something until you know where it is. Therefore, an auto variable cannot be initialized until the function where it is defined is entered. This also means that it is impossible for an auto variable to retain its value from one execution of the function where it's defined to the next execution of that function, because the variable might be at a different location the next time.

These rules do not apply to static variables, because their addresses are known at link time and don't change thereafter. A variable defined outside all functions (a *global* variable) is automatically in the static storage class, because otherwise its address would never be assigned. Since its address is known at link time, the initialization of such a variable is performed before the start of main.

A static variable that is defined inside a function is different from one defined globally, in that it is not initialized until the function where it is defined is entered for the first time. However, its value is retained from one execution of its function to another, because its address is fixed rather than possibly varying from one call of the function to the next, as can occur with an auto variable. For this property to be of use, the initialization of a static variable in a function must be performed only once. If it were performed on each entry to the function, the value from the previous execution would be lost. Therefore, that initialization is done only once, when the function is first entered.

Problem
Algorithms
C++
Executable
Hardware

Let's pause here to look at a sample program, Figure 5.14, that includes global, local, static, and auto variables. This might help you to visualize how and where each of these variables might be used.

Assuming that you've installed the software from the CD-ROM in the back of this book, you can try out this program. First, you have to compile it by changing to the normal subdirectory under the main directory where you installed the software and typing mk scopclas. Then type scopclas to run the program. Figure 5.15 is the output that results from running this program normally. To run it under gdb, make sure you are in the normal subdirectory, then type trace scopclas. The program will start up and show you the first line of executable code. Type z and hit ENTER to execute each line. The values of all the variables in main will be displayed immediately before the execution of each line in that function, and the variables in func1 will be displayed as they are when the program is run normally. When you get to the end of the program (or when you're tired of tracing), type q (for *quit*) and hit ENTER to exit from the debugger.

```
#include <iostream.h>

short count1; // A global variable, not explicitly initialized
short count2 = 5; // A global variable, explicitly initialized

short func1()
{
    short count3; // A local auto variable, not explicitly initialized
    short count4 = 22; // A local auto variable, explicitly initialized
static short count5; // A local static variable, not explicitly initialized
static short count6 = 9; // A local static variable, explicitly initialized

    count1 ++; // Incrementing the global variable count1.
    count2 ++; // Incrementing the global variable count2.
    count3 ++; // Incrementing the local uninitialized auto variable count3.
    count4 ++; // Incrementing the local auto variable count4.
    count5 ++; // Incrementing the local static variable count5.
    count6 ++; // Incrementing the local static variable count6.

    cout << "count1 = " << count1 << endl;
    cout << "count2 = " << count2 << endl;
    cout << "count3 = " << count3 << endl;
    cout << "count4 = " << count4 << endl;
    cout << "count5 = " << count5 << endl;
    cout << "count6 = " << count6 << endl;
    cout << endl;

    return 0;
}

int main()
{
    func1();
    func1();

    return 0;
}
```

Problem
Algorithms
C++
Executable
Hardware

Figure 5.14: Using variables of different scopes and storage classes
(code\scopclas.cc)

```
count1 = 1
count2 = 6
count3 = -32768
count4 = 23
count5 = 1
count6 = 10

count1 = 2
count2 = 7
count3 = -32767
count4 = 23
count5 = 2
count6 = 11
```

Figure 5.15: The results of using variables of different scopes and storage classes (code\scopclas.out)

The results shown should help to answer the question of when we would want to use a static variable rather than an auto variable: whenever we need a variable that keeps its value from one execution of a function to another. You may be wondering where that weird value for count3 came from. Since we never initialized it, we can't complain when its value is meaningless.

Think Globally?

The next topic we'll take up is the distinction between global and local variables. First, though, I want to make sure that we've cleared up the question of when different types of variables are initialized. Here is an exercise that might help drive this point home.

Problem
Algorithms
C++
Executable
Hardware

Exercises, First Set

1.   What will each of the programs in Figures 5.16 through 5.21 do
      when run?

```cpp
//auto local variable, initialized

#include <iostream.h>

short mess()
{
  short xyz;

  xyz = 5;

  return 0;
}

short counter()
{
  short count = 0;

  count ++;

  cout << count << " ";

  return 0;
}

int main()
{
  short i;

  for (i = 0; i < 10; i ++)
    {
    mess();
    counter();
    }

  cout << endl;

  return 0;
}
```

```
Problem
Algorithms
C++
Executable
Hardware
```

Figure 5.16: Exercise 1a (code\inita.cc)

//auto local variable, uninitialized

#include <iostream.h>

```cpp
short mess()
{
    short xyz;

    xyz = 5;

    return 0;
}
short counter()
{
    short count;

    count ++;

    cout << count << " ";

    return 0;
}
int main()
{
    short i;

    for (i = 0; i < 10; i ++)
        {
        mess();
        counter();
        }

    cout << endl;

    return 0;
}
```

Problem
Algorithms
C++
Executable
Hardware

Figure 5.17: Exercise 1b (code\initb.cc)

```
//static local variable, explicitly initialized

#include <iostream.h>

short mess()
{
    short xyz;

    xyz = 5;

    return 0;
}

short counter()
{
    static short count = 0;

    count ++;

    cout << count << " ";

    return 0;
}

int main()
{
    short i;

    for (i = 0; i < 10; i ++)
        {
        mess();
        counter();
        }

    cout << endl;

    return 0;
}
```

Problem
Algorithms
C++
Executable
Hardware

Figure 5.18: Exercise 1c (code\initc.cc)

```
//static local variable, not explicitly initialized

#include <iostream.h>

short mess()
{
    short xyz;

    xyz = 5;

    return 0;
}
short counter()
{
    static short count;

    count ++;

    cout << count << " ";

    return 0;
}
int main()
{
    short i;

    for (i = 0; i < 10; i ++)
        {
        mess();
        counter();
        }

    cout << endl;

    return 0;
}
```

```
Problem
Algorithms
C++
Executable
Hardware
```

Figure 5.19: Exercise 1d (code\initd.cc)

```
//global variable, explicitly initialized

short count = 0;

#include <iostream.h>

short mess()
{
   short xyz;

   xyz = 5;

   return 0;
}

short counter()
{
   count ++;

   cout << count << " ";

   return 0;
}

int main()
{
   short i;

   for (i = 0; i < 10; i ++)
      {
      mess();
      counter();
      }

   cout << endl;

   return 0;
}
```

```
Problem
Algorithms
C++
Executable
Hardware
```

Figure 5.20: Exercise 1e (code\inite.cc)

```
//global variable, not explicitly initialized

short count;

#include <iostream.h>

short mess()
{
  short xyz;

  xyz = 5;

  return 0;
}
short counter()
{
  count ++;

  cout << count << " ";

  return 0;
}
int main()
{
  short i;

  for (i = 0; i < 10; i ++)
    {
    mess();
    counter();
    }

  cout << endl;

  return 0;
}
```

Problem
Algorithms
C++
Executable
Hardware

Figure 5.21: Exercise 1f (code\initf.cc)

Answers to this exercise can be found at the end of the chapter.

A BASIC Difficulty

Let me tell you a little story about the "power" of global variables. Unlike the one about the funny odometers, this one is true. You may be surprised that a programmer would accept the limitation of allowing certain variables to be accessed only in certain functions. Surely it's more powerful to be able to access anything anywhere. Isn't it?

In the late 1970s, I worked for a (very) small software house that was developing a database program for the Radio Shack TRS-80 Model III computer. This computer was fairly powerful for the time; it had two 79K floppy disks and a maximum of 48K memory. The database program had to be able to find a subset of the few thousand records in the database in a minute or so. The speed of the floppy drive was the limiting factor. The only high-level language that was available was a BASIC interpreter clearly related by ancestry to QBASIC, the BASIC that comes with MS-DOS, but much more primitive. For example, the interpreter considered only the first two characters of a variable name, so names that were the same in their first two characters were considered to refer to the same variable. There was also an assembler, but even at that time I wasn't thrilled with the idea of writing a significant application program in assembly language. So we were stuck with BASIC.

Problem
Algorithms
C++
Executable
Hardware

Actually, that wasn't so bad. Even then, BASIC had pretty good string manipulation functions (much better than the ones that come with C) and the file access functions, although primitive, weren't too hard to work with for the application in question. You could read or write a fixed number of bytes anywhere in a disk file, and since all of the records in a given database were in fact the same length, that was good enough for our purposes. However, there were a couple of (related) glaring flaws in the language: there were no named subroutines (analogous to functions in C++), and all variables were global.

Subroutines were addressed by line number instead of by name. In TRS-80 BASIC, each line had a number, and you could call a subroutine that started at line 1000 by writing "GOSUB 1000". At the end of the subroutine, a "RETURN" statement would cause control to return to the next statement after the GOSUB.

While this was functional in a moronic way, it had some serious drawbacks. First, of course, a number isn't as mnemonic as a name. Remembering that line 1000 is the beginning of the invoice printing routine, for example, isn't as easy as remembering the name PrintInvoice. In addition, if you "renumbered" the program to make room for inserting new lines between previously existing lines, the line numbers would change. The second drawback was that, as the example suggests, there was no way to pass arguments to a subroutine when it was called. Therefore, the only way for a subroutine to get input or produce output was by using and changing global variables. Yet another problem with this line-numbered subroutine facility was that you could call any line as a subroutine; no block structure such as we have in C++ was available to impose some order on the flow of control.

With such an arrangement, it was almost impossible to make a change anywhere in even a moderately large program without breaking some subroutine. One reason for this fragility was that a variable could be used or changed anywhere in the program. Another was that it was impossible to identify subroutines except by adding comments to the program, which could be out of date. For both these reasons, almost any change could have effects throughout the program.

I Say "Live It, or Live with It"

After some time struggling with this problem, I decided to end it, once and for all, by adding named subroutines with arguments and local variables to the language. This made it possible to maintain the program, and we ended up selling several hundred copies of it over the course of a couple of years. Besides, fixing the language was fun.

Problem
Algorithms
C++
Executable
Hardware

The moral? There's almost always a way around a limitation of a computer language, although it may not be worth the effort to find it. Luckily, with C++, adding functionality is a bit easier than patching BASIC in assembly language.

Nesting Instinct

After that (theoretically) instructive anecdote, it's time to get back to our regularly scheduled text, where we were examining the function of the stack in storing information needed during execution of a function. The next statement in our example program (Figure 5.5) is Result = (First + Second) / 2;. Since we've assumed that First is 2, and Second is 4, the value of Result will be (4 + 2)/2, or 3. After this statement is executed, the stack looks like Figure 5.22.

Address	Contents	Meaning
20001ff2	????	(none)
20001ff4	0003	Result
20001ff6	10001005	Return address in main
20001ffa	0004	Second
20001ffc	0002	First
20001ffe	????	(none)

Figure 5.22: The stack after the initialization of Result

Finally, at the end of the function, the stack pointer will be incremented to point to the stored return address. Then the return instruction will reload the program counter with the stored return address, which in this case is 10001005. Then the value of Result will be made available to the calling function and the stack pointer will be adjusted so the stack looks as it did before we called Average.

After the return, the stack will be empty, as we no longer need the arguments, the auto variable Result, or the return address from the Average function. Figure 5.23 shows what the stack looks like at this point.

Problem
Algorithms
C++
Executable
Hardware

Address	Contents	Meaning
20001ff2	????	(none)
20001ff4	0003	(none)
20001ff6	10001005	(none)
20001ffa	0004	(none)
20001ffc	0002	(none)
20001ffe	????	(none)

Figure 5.23: The stack after exiting from Average

Do not be fooled by the casual statement "the stack is empty". That means only that the stack pointer (esp) is pointing to the same place it was when we started our excursion into the Average function; namely, 20001ffe. The values that were stored in the memory locations used by Average for its auto variables haven't been erased by changing the stack pointer. This illustrates one very good reason why we can't rely on the values of auto variables until they've been initialized; we don't know how the memory locations they occupy might have been used previously.

The previous discussion of how arguments are copied into local variables when a function is called applies directly to our Average function. If we try to change the input arguments, we will change only the copies of those arguments; the corresponding variables in the calling function won't be altered. That's perfectly acceptable here, since we don't want to change the values in the calling function; we just want to calculate their average and provide the result to the calling function. An argument that is handled this way is called a *value argument*, as its value is copied into a newly created variable in the called function, rather than allowing the called function access to the "real" argument in the calling function.[20]

One thing we haven't really discussed here is how the return value gets back to the caller. In the cases we've examined so far, using the compiler that accompanies this book, it's stored in a register (eax, to be precise), which is then available to the calling routine after we get back.[21] This is a very easy and fast way to pass a return value back to the caller. However, it has a drawback: A register can only hold one value of 32 bits. Sometimes this is not enough, in which case another mechanism will have to be used; unfortunately, we won't get a chance to cover it in this book. In any event, it's time to go over the material we've covered in this chapter.

```
Problem
Algorithms
C++
Executable
Hardware
```

Review

First, we added the fundamental programming concept of the *function*. A function is a piece of code that can "stand alone"; it can be compiled separately from other functions and provides some service that we can use via a mechanism known as a *function call*. The function that makes the call is known as the *calling function*, and the one it calls is known as the *called function*. Before we can call a function, we need to know what input values it needs and what it

---

20. It's also possible to define a function that has access to an actual variable in the calling function; we'll see how and when to do that at the appropriate time.

21. In case you're wondering how I know which register is used to pass back the return value, it's simple. I cheated by examining the compiled code with a utility program. Different compilers do this differently, but luckily you don't have to worry about this detail when writing C++ programs.

returns. This information is provided by a *function declaration* at the beginning of each function. This includes an *argument list*, which specifies input values that the called function uses (if any), and a *return type*, which specifies the type of the value that it produces when it's finished (if any). When we call a function, it executes until it reaches the end of its code or reaches a return statement, whichever comes first. When either of these events happens, the program continues execution in the calling function immediately after the place where the function call occurs. Ordinarily, as in our example, an argument to a function is actually a copy of the variable in the calling program, so that the called function can't modify the "real" value in the caller. Such an argument is called a *value argument*.

We also saw that function and variable names can be of any length, consisting of upper- or lowercase characters (or both), digits, and the special character underscore (_). To make it easier for the compiler to distinguish numbers from variable names, the first character can't be a digit. Also, a variable name can't be the same as a *keyword*, or name defined by the language. Examples of keywords we've seen so far include if, for, and short.

Problem
Algorithms
C++
Executable
Hardware

After finishing the construction of our Average function, we saw how to use it by making a function call. Then we launched into an examination of the way that values in the calling function are converted into arguments in the called function, which required a detour into the software infrastructure.

We started this excursion by looking at the *linker*, which is used to construct programs from a number of functions compiled into separate *object files*. Next, we explored the notion of *storage class*, which determines the working lifetime of a variable. The simplest storage class is static. Variables of this class, which includes all variables defined outside any function, have storage assigned to them by the linker and retain the same address during the lifetime of the program. On the other hand, auto (for "automatic") variables are always defined in a function and are assigned storage on the *stack* when that function starts execution. The stack is the data structure that stores function arguments and *return addresses* during the execution of a function; it's called that because it behaves like a spring-loaded stack of plates in a cafeteria, where the last one put on the top is the first one to be removed. Don't take this analogy too literally; most of the diagrams in this chapter show data being added and removed at the bottom rather than the top of the stack, but that doesn't affect its behavior.

Then we noted that each variable, in addition to a storage class, has a *scope*, which is the part of a program in which the variable can be accessed. At this point, the scopes that are important to us are *local scope* and *global scope*. As you might guess, a global variable can be referred to anywhere, while a local variable can be accessed only in the function where it is defined. Although it may seem limiting to use local variables rather than global ones, programs that rely on global variables are very difficult to maintain, as a change anywhere can affect the rest of the program. Programs that limit the scope of their variables, on the other hand, minimize the amount of code that can be affected by a change in one place. Because local variables are only usable while in the function where they are defined, they can be stored on the stack. Therefore, they don't occupy memory during the entire lifetime of the program.

Of course, local variables take up room while they're being used, which means that the stack has to have enough storage to hold all of the local variables for the current function and all of the functions that haven't finished executing. That is, the stack has to have enough room for all of the variables in the current function, the function that called the current function, the one that called that one, and so on up to the main function, which is always the top-level function in a C++ program. Since the amount of memory that is allocated to the stack is not unlimited, it's possible to run out of space, in which case your program will stop working. This is called a *stack overflow*, by analogy with what happens if you put too many plates on the cafeteria plate stack: It falls over and makes a mess. When using the DJGPP compiler that comes with this book, it's unlikely that you'll ever run out of stack space unless you have a bug in your program. Other compilers aren't as generous in their space allotments, so the likelihood of a stack overflow is less remote. The solution to this problem, should it arise, is to use another kind of storage allocation called *dynamic storage*; we'll see an example of this mechanism in Chapter 7.

```
Problem
Algorithms
C++
Executable
Hardware
```

Exercises, Second Set

It's time for some more exercises.

2.   When the program in Figure 5.24 is run, what will be displayed?

```cpp
#include <iostream.h>

short i;

short Calc(short x, short y)
{
static short j = 0;

    cout << "The value of j in Calc is: " << j << endl;

    i ++;

    j = x + y + j;

    return j;
}

int main()
{
    short j;

    for (i = 0; i < 5; i ++)
        {
        j = Calc(i + 5, i * 2) + 7;
        cout << "The value of j in main is: " << j << endl;
        }

    return 0;
}
```

```
Problem
Algorithms
C++
Executable
Hardware
```

Figure 5.24: Exercise 2 (code\calc1.cc)

The answer to the preceding exercise can be found at the end of the chapter.

3. Rewrite the program you wrote for Exercise 5 in Chapter 4, using a function to look up the dose of ibuprofen.

Conclusion

We've covered a lot of material in this chapter, ranging from the anatomy of functions through a lot more information on what's going on "underneath the covers" of even a fairly simple C++ program. Next, we'll see how to write a realistic, although simplified, application program using some more advanced concepts in C++.

Answers to Selected Exercises

1. Here are the answers for each of the programs in Figures 5.16 through 5.21, Exercises 1a–1f:
    a. 1 1 1 1 1 1 1 1 1 1
    b. 6 6 6 6 6 6 6 6 6 6
    c. 1 2 3 4 5 6 7 8 9 10
    d. 1 2 3 4 5 6 7 8 9 10
    e. 1 2 3 4 5 6 7 8 9 10
    f. 1 2 3 4 5 6 7 8 9 10

Why are these the way they are? Well, let's take them in order — except for 1b, which I'll take up last.

a. The reason for these results should be fairly obvious. Since we set the variable count to 0 every time we enter the counter function, incrementing it always gives the answer 1.

Problem
Algorithms
C++
Executable
Hardware

As for 1c–1f, they all produce the same answer; namely, the output value starts at 1 and increments by 1 each time. This is because the variable named count is statically allocated in each of these cases. This has two consequences: The initialization of the variable is done only once and it retains its value from one call of the counter function to the next. However, the reason for this behavior differs slightly in each of these cases, as follows:

c. In initc.cc, count is a static variable defined in the counter function, which is explicitly initialized to 0.
d. In initd.cc, count is a static variable defined in the counter function, which is not explicitly initialized. Statically allocated numeric variables are initialized to 0 if no other initial value is specified.[22]
e. In inite.cc, count is a global variable explicitly initialized to 0. Note that the keyword static is **not** used to specify that this variable is statically allocated. Since globals are always

---

22. You can count on this, because it's part of the language definition, although it's nicer for the next programmer if you specify what you mean rather than leaving it to the compiler.

statically allocated, the keyword static means something different when applied to a global variable.

f.   In initf.cc, count is a global variable not explicitly initialized. As in initd.cc, this will work because the default value of a statically allocated numeric variable is 0.

Now what about 1b? Well, the result of running that program will vary from one compiler to the next, because the program contains a logic error; namely, we're using an *uninitialized variable*. Here's where we see why there's a mess function that apparently has no function; it's there to provide some garbage to fill in the memory that the count variable will use later. In other words, in the DJGPP compiler that comes with this book, the variable xyz in the mess function happens to land in the same memory location that the variable count occupies in the counter function. Therefore, whatever value happened to be in xyz at the end of the mess function will appear as if by magic in count when counter starts. If we were to initialize count before we used it in counter, we would never see this leftover value, but since we just use count without initializing it, we get whatever value that memory location had left in it from before.

In case this point isn't yet apparent to you, I've drawn a set of pictures that might help clear it up. At the point in main where mess is about to be called, let's suppose that the stack is empty, with the stack pointer pointing to 20001ffe. The call instruction is at location 10001000 and is 5 bytes long, so the next instruction after the call starts at location 10001005. Before the call to mess occurs, the stack looks like Figure 5.25.[23]

Problem
Algorithms
C++
Executable
Hardware

Address	Contents	Meaning
20001ff2	????	(none)
20001ff4	????	(none)
20001ff6	????	(none)
20001ff8	????	(none)
20001ffa	????	(none)
20001ffe	????	(none)

Figure 5.25: The stack immediately before the call to mess

---

23. As usual, the **bold** address indicates the current value of the stack pointer.

Then the call to mess occurs, which leaves the stack looking like Figure 5.26.

Address	Contents	Meaning
20001ff2	????	(none)
20001ff4	????	(none)
20001ff6	????	(none)
20001ff8	????	(none)
20001ffa	10001005	Return address in main
20001ffe	????	(none)

Figure 5.26: The stack immediately before the execution of the first instruction in mess

Then mess declares a variable called xyz, which is an auto variable and therefore has to be stored on the stack. Since xyz is a short, it occupies 2 bytes on the stack, so the stack now looks like Figure 5.27.

Address	Contents	Meaning
20001ff2	????	(none)
20001ff4	????	(none)
20001ff6	????	(none)
20001ff8	????	xyz (uninitialized)
20001ffa	10001005	Return address in main
20001ffe	????	(none)

Problem
Algorithms
C++
Executable
Hardware

Figure 5.27: The stack after mess has declared the auto variable xyz

So far, so good. Now xyz is assigned the value 5, which leaves the stack looking like Figure 5.28.

Address	Contents	Meaning
20001ff2	????	(none)
20001ff4	????	(none)
20001ff6	????	(none)
20001ff8	0005	xyz
20001ffa	10001005	Return address in main
20001ffe	????	(none)

Figure 5.28: The stack after the auto variable xyz in mess is assigned the value 5

Then mess returns to main, so the stack is empty again. But here's the tricky part: to say "the stack is empty" merely means that the stack pointer has been reset back to 20001ffe. The data stored in locations 20001ff8–20001ffc has not been changed in any way.[24] So, before counter is called, the situation looks like Figure 5.29.

Problem
Algorithms
C++
Executable
Hardware

Address	Contents	Meaning
20001ff2	????	(none)
20001ff4	????	(none)
20001ff6	????	(none)
20001ff8	0005	(none)
20001ffa	10001005	(none)
20001ffe	????	(none)

Figure 5.29: The stack before counter is called

When counter is called, let's assume the return address in main is now 10001013. After this is stored on the stack, we have the situation illustrated in Figure 5.30 upon entry to counter.

---

24. This statement is true when running the DJGPP compiler on an Intel machine; it may not be true on other systems. However, that possibility only reinforces the point that you should not rely on such behavior, as it is outside the definition of the C++ language.

Address	Contents	Meaning
20001ff2	????	(none)
20001ff4	????	(none)
20001ff6	????	(none)
20001ff8	0005	(none)
20001ffa	10001013	New return address in main
20001ffe	????	(none)

Figure 5.30: The stack immediately before the execution of the first instruction in counter

The first thing that counter does is to allocate storage for its one auto variable, count, by subtracting 2 from the stack pointer. After this is done, the situation is as illustrated in Figure 5.31.

Address	Contents	Meaning
20001ff2	????	(none)
20001ff4	????	(none)
20001ff6	????	(none)
20001ff8	0005	count (uninitialized)
20001ffa	10001013	New return address in main
20001ffe	????	(none)

Problem
Algorithms
C++
Executable
Hardware

Figure 5.31: The stack when counter is entered

That is, the variable count is assigned the storage location that previously held the value of xyz; this storage location (20001ff8) still has the value 5 left over from xyz. Of course, if we initialize count as we should, we'll never see that old value. However, this program doesn't initialize count; thus, count starts out with the leftover value 5 from xyz before counter increments count.

The moral of the story is "always initialize your auto variables before use"; otherwise, you'll get whatever junk happens to be lying around in memory at the location where they are assigned when the function starts.

2.   If you got this one right, congratulations! It's just *filled* with tricks, but they're all things that you might run into in a real (poorly written) program. Here's the answer:

```
The value of j in Calc is: 0
The value of j in main is: 12
The value of j in Calc is: 5
The value of j in main is: 23
The value of j in Calc is: 16
The value of j in main is: 40
```

Let's see how this came about. The first question is why there are only three values displayed by each output statement. The for loop that calls the Calc routine and displays the results should execute 5 times, shouldn't it?

This is the first trick. Since i is a global variable, the statement i ++; in the Calc function affects its value. Therefore, i starts out at 0 in the main function, as usual, but when the Calc function is called, i is incremented to 1. So the next time the modification expression i ++ in the for statement is executed, i is already 1 and is changed to 2. Now the controlled block of the for statement is executed again, with i set to 2. Again, the call to Calc results in i being incremented an extra time, to 3, so the next execution of the for loop sets i to 4. The final call to Calc increments the value of i to 5, so the for loop terminates, having executed only three times rather than the five you would expect by looking at it. Now you can see why global variables are dangerous!

Now what about the values of j? Well, since the j in Calc is a static variable, it is initialized only once. Because it is a local static variable, that initialization is performed when Calc is called for the first time. So the first time Calc is called, j is set to 0. The arguments specified by main on the first call to Calc are 5 and 0; this means that inside Calc, x and y have those values, respectively. Then the new value of j is calculated by the statement j = x + y + j;, or 5 in total. The return j; statement specifies this as the return value of Calc; this value is then added to 7 as specified by the assignment statement j = Calc(i + 5, i * 2) + 7; in main. That explains why the output statement in main displays the value of j as 12 the first time.

It's very important to note that the variable j in main is completely unrelated to the variable j in Calc. Since they are local variables, they have nothing in common but their names. There is no risk of confusion (at least on the compiler's part), since we can access a local variable only in the function in which it is defined. Therefore,

```
Problem
Algorithms
C++
Executable
Hardware
```

when we refer to j in main, we mean the one defined there. Likewise, when we refer to j in Calc, we mean the one defined there.

Next, we call Calc again with the arguments 7 and 4. To compute these arguments from the expressions i + 5 and i * 2, you have to remember that i has been modified by Calc and is now 2, not 1 as we would expect normally. When we get to Calc, it displays the old value of j (5), left over from the previous execution of this function. This is because j is a local static variable. Thus, the initialization statement static short j = 0; is executed only once, upon the first call to the function where it is defined. Once j has been set to a value in Calc, it will retain that value even in a subsequent call to Calc; this is quite unlike a normal auto variable, which has no known value at the beginning of execution of the function where it is defined. A new value of j is now calculated as 7 + 4 + 5, or 16, and returned to main.

On return from Calc, the value of j in main is 23, as set by the assignment statement j = Calc(i + 5, i * 2) + 7;. We also don't want to forget that i is now 3, having been changed in Calc.

Exactly the same steps occur for the last pass through the for loop: We call Calc with the new values of i + 5 and i * 2, which are 9 and 8, respectively, since i has been incremented to 4 by the for statement's modification expression i ++. Then Calc displays the old value of j, which is 16, and calculates the new value, which is 33. This is added to the literal value 7 and stored in j in main, resulting in the value 40, which is then displayed by the output statement.

Don't get discouraged if you didn't get this one, especially the effects caused by a global i. Even experienced programmers can be taken by surprise by programs that use global variables in such error prone ways.

```
Problem
Algorithms
C++
Executable
Hardware
```

Chapter 6

Taking Inventory

A class **Act**

Now we have enough of the fundamentals of programming under our belts to look at some of the more powerful features of C++. As I've mentioned before, C++ is the successor to C. What I haven't told you is *why* it was invented. One of the main reasons was to improve on C's support for user-defined data types. What are these, and why are they so important?

As is the case with C++, the data types available in C are divided into two groups: **native** (i.e., defined in the language itself) and **user-defined** (i.e., defined by the programmer, the user of the language). However, there is a major difference between C and C++ in the support provided to user-defined types. In C, variables of the native types are fully supported by the language, while variables of user-defined types are not. The native types that we've been using are char, short, and unsigned short (and int, but only for the return type of main), all of which have been inherited from C.[1]

By fully supported, I mean that native variables in both C and C++ can be defined, initialized, assigned values, passed as arguments and return values, and compared to other values of the same type. Such a variable can be assigned storage in either the static or auto storage classes. If a variable is auto, the storage is assigned at entry to the function where it is defined, and released automatically at exit from

---

1. There are actually several other native C++ types that we haven't used: long, float, double, and bool. The long type is useful for storing whole-number values that are larger than will fit into a short (hence the name), while float and double are able to store values that have fractional parts as well as integral values. These are useful in scientific and engineering calculations; I'll go into these types in somewhat more detail in the Appendix. The bool type, recently added to C++, is useful for keeping track of a true/false condition. We'll see how to use the bool variable type later in this chapter.

that function; if it is static, it is initialized to some reasonable value either at link time (for a *global* variable) or upon the first entry to the function where it is defined (for a *local* variable). However, most of these facilities aren't available to user-defined data types in C. For example, they can't be compared; of course, this limitation is understandable, since the compiler has no idea how to compare two variables of a type that you define. Similarly, what is a reasonable default value for a variable of a user-defined type? Presumably, the user (i.e., the programmer) knows, but the compiler doesn't.

In this chapter, we'll see how to give the compiler enough information to allow data types that we define to behave just like the native types. Let's start out with some definitions and objectives.

Definitions

A class is a user-defined type.[2]

A class **interface** tells the compiler what facilities the class provides. This interface is usually found in a header file, which by convention has the extension .h.

Problem
Algorithms
C++
Executable
Hardware

A class **implementation** tells the compiler how to implement the facilities defined in the class interface. This is usually found in an implementation file, which in the case of the compiler on the CD-ROM in the back of this book usually has the extension .cc.

An **object** is a variable of a class type. Its behavior is defined by the code that implements the class.

A **member function** is a function that is part of the definition of a class.

A **member variable** is a variable that is part of the definition of a class.

Object-oriented programming is the organization of programs as collections of objects, rather than as collections of functions operating on variables of native data types.

---

2. Please note that the terms class and *storage class* have nothing to do with one another. This is another case where C++ reuses the same word for different concepts.

Encapsulation is the concept of hiding the details of a class inside the implementation of that class rather than exposing them in the interface. This is one of the primary organizing principles that characterize object-oriented programming.

A **concrete data type** is a class whose objects behave like variables of native data types. That is, the class gives the compiler enough information that its objects can be created, copied, assigned, and automatically destroyed just as native variables are. The StockItem class that we will construct in this chapter is a concrete data type.

A **constructor** is a member function that creates new variables of the class type. All constructors have the same name as the class for which they are constructors; therefore, the constructors for StockItem variables also have the name StockItem.

A **default constructor** is a constructor that is used when no initial value is specified for an object. Because it is a constructor, it has the same name as the class. Since it is used when no initial value is specified, it has no arguments. Thus, StockItem() is the default constructor for the StockItem class.

A **copy constructor** is a constructor that makes a new object with the same contents as an existing object of the same type.

An **assignment operator** is a member function that sets a pre-existing object to the same value as another object of the same type.

A **destructor** is a member function that cleans up when an object expires. For a local object, this occurs at the end of the function where that object is defined.

Problem
Algorithms
C++
Executable
Hardware

Objectives of This Chapter

By the end of this chapter, you should

1. Understand what a user-defined type (a class) is, and how it is defined.
2. Understand how variables of some simple classes are created, destroyed, and copied.
3. Understand how and why access to the internals of a class is controlled.

Pay Some Attention to the Man Behind the Curtain

In C++, a user-defined variable is called an *object*. Each object has a type, just like variables of native types (short, char, etc.). For example, if we define a class called StockItem (as we will do in this chapter), then an object can be of type StockItem, just as a native variable can be of type short. However, an additional step is required when we want to use user-defined types. Since the compiler has no intrinsic knowledge of these types, we have to tell it exactly what they are and how they work. We do this by defining a class, which specifies both the data contained in the user-defined variable and what operations can be performed on this data.

To use C++ in the most effective way, rather than merely as a "better C", it is necessary to make up data types and tell the compiler how to treat them as though they were native data types. So far in this book, we have been using data types that were previously defined, either by the compiler and language (native types, e.g., short, char) or by libraries (class types, e.g., string). Now we're going to actually make up our own types that will be usable just like those of a native type. The difference between using variables and making up new variable types is analogous to the difference between using a program and writing a program, but carried to the next higher level.

Before we get back to the technical explanation of how we create new data types, I'm sure one more question is burning in your mind: *Why* should we do this? What's wrong with the native types like char and short? The answer is simple: We make up types so that we can match the language to the needs of the problem we're trying to solve. For example, suppose we want to write a program to do inventory control for a small business like a grocery store. Such a program needs objects representing items in the store, which have prices, names, and so on. We'd need to define each of these types of objects so that it can display the behavior appropriate to the thing it represents. The availability of objects that have relevance to the problem being solved makes it much easier to write (and *read*) a program to handle inventory than if everything has to be made of shorts and chars.

I suspect that the advantages of making up one's own data types may still not be apparent to you, so let me make an analogy with natural languages. Making up new data types in C++ is in some ways quite similar to making up new words in English (for example). You might think that if everyone made up new words, the result would be

Problem
Algorithms
C++
Executable
Hardware

chaos. Actually, this is correct, with the very important exception of technical jargon and other vocabularies that are shared by people who have more in common than simply being speakers of English. For example, physicians have their own "language" in the form of medical terminology. Of course, a cynical observer might conclude that the reason for such specialized vocabulary is to befuddle or impress the naive listener, and of course it can be used for that purpose. However, there is also a much more significant and valid reason: To make it possible for experts in a field to communicate with one another quickly and precisely. The same is true of creating our own data types; they enable us to write programs that are more understandable to those who are conversant with the problems being solved. It's much easier to talk to a store owner about inventory objects than about shorts and chars!

Assuming that I've sold you on the advantages of making up our own data types, let's see how we can actually do it. Each data type is represented by a class, whose full definition is composed of two parts: the **interface** definition (usually contained in a file with the extension .h), and the **implementation** definition (usually contained in a file with the extension .cc). The interface definition tells the compiler (and the class user) *what* the class does, while the implementation definition tells the compiler *how* the objects of that class actually perform the functions specified in the interface definition. Let's take a look at a step-by-step description of how to create and use a class.

Problem
Algorithms
C++
Executable
Hardware

1. Write the class interface definition, which will be stored in a file with the extension .h. In our example of a StockItem class, we'll use item1.h to hold our first version of this interface definition. This definition tells the compiler the names and types of the member functions and variables that make up the objects of the class, which gives the compiler enough information to create objects of this class in a user's program.

2. Write the class implementation definition, which will be stored in a file with the extension .cc. In our example, the first one of these will be stored in the file item1.cc. This definition is the code that tells the compiler how to perform the operations that the interface definition refers to. The implementation definition file must #include the interface definition file (item1.h, in this case) so that the compiler has access to the interface that is being implemented.

3. Write the program that uses objects in the class to do some work. The first such program we'll write will be itemtst1.cc. This

program also needs to #include the interface definition file so that the compiler can tell how to create objects of this class.

4.   Compile the class implementation definition to produce an object file (item1.o). This makes the class available for use by the user program.
5.   Compile the user program to produce an object file (itemtst1.o).
6.   Link the object file from the user program, the object file from the class implementation definition, and the standard libraries together to form a finished executable. Our first sample will be called itemtst1.exe.

Taking Stock

Now let's start on our first class definition, which is designed to help solve the problem of maintaining inventory in a small grocery store. We need to keep track of all the items that we carry, so we're going to define a class called StockItem. The StockItem class, like other classes, is composed of a number of functions and variables. To make this more concrete, think of something like Lego blocks, which you can put together to make parts that can in turn be used to build bigger structures. The smallest Legos are the native types, and the bigger, composite ones are class types.

Problem
Algorithms
C++
Executable
Hardware

For the compiler to be able to define an object correctly, we'll have to tell it the names and types of the member variables that will be used to store the information about each StockItem. This enables the compiler to allocate memory for a StockItem.

So how do we identify these member variables? By considering what member variables each StockItem object will need to keep track of its corresponding item in the stock of the store. After some thought, I've come up with the following list of member variables.

1.   The name of the item (m_Name)
2.   The number in stock (m_InStock)
3.   The distributor that we purchase it from (m_Distributor)
4.   The price we charge (m_Price)
5.   The item number, or UPC (m_UPC)

What I mean by *an item* is actually something like "chunky chicken soup, 16 oz.", rather than a specific object like a particular can of soup. In other words, every can of soup with the same item number is considered equivalent to every other can of soup with the same item number, so all we have to keep track of for each item can be described by the above data. For the item number, we'll use the Universal Product Code (UPC), which is printed as a bar code on almost every product other than fresh produce; it's a 10-digit number, which we'll represent as a string for convenience.

Let's recap what we know about a StockItem so far. We know that we need a member variable in the class definition for each value in the above description. Each StockItem object will store the name of the item (m_Name), its price (m_Price), the number of items in stock (m_InStock), the name of the distributor (m_Distributor), and the UPC (m_UPC) of the item.

Of course, merely storing this data isn't very useful unless we can do something with it. Therefore, objects of the StockItem class also need to be able to perform several operations on their data. We'll start by giving them the ability to display their contents. Figure 6.1 illustrates a very simple way that this class might be used.

```
#include <iostream.h>
#include "string6.h"
#include "item1.h"

int main()
{
    StockItem soup;

    soup = StockItem("Chunky Chicken",32,129,
    "Bob's Distribution","123456789");

    soup.Display();

    return 0;
}
```

Problem
Algorithms
C++
Executable
Hardware

Figure 6.1: The initial sample program for the StockItem class
(code\itemtst1.cc)

This program defines a StockItem named soup, assigns it some data, displays it on the screen via a function called Display, and finally terminates normally. By the time we're done with this chapter, you'll understand exactly how every operation in this program is performed by the StockItem class. Before we get too deeply into this particular class, however, we should look at the functions that almost all classes have in common. These are the *concrete data type* functions described in Figure 6.2.

The Native Problem	A Concrete Plan
Here are the essential facilities that the compiler provides for every native type:	To make a concrete data type, we have to provide each of these facilities for our new type. By no coincidence, there is a specific type of member function to provide each of them. Here are the official names and descriptions of each of these four functions:

```
Problem
Algorithms
C++
Executable
Hardware
```

1. The ability to create a variable with no specified initial value (an uninitialized variable), e.g., short x;.

2. The ability to pass a variable as an argument to a function; in this case, the compiler has to make a copy of the variable so that the called function doesn't change the value of the variable in the calling function.

3. The ability to assign a value of an appropriate type to a variable that already exists, such as x = 22; or x = z;.

4. Reclaiming the storage assigned to a variable when it ceases to exist, so that those memory addresses can be reallocated to other uses. In the case of auto variables, this is at the end of the function where they were created; with static variables, it's at the end of execution of the program.

1. A *default constructor* that can create an object when there is no initial value specified for the object.

2. A *copy constructor* that can make a new object with the same contents as an existing object of the same type.

3. An *assignment operator* that is used to set an existing object to the value of another object of the same type.

4. A *destructor* that cleans up when an object expires, including releasing the memory that the object has occupied; for a local object, this occurs at the end of the function where the object was created.

Figure 6.2: Comparison of native and class types

Common Behavior

While different classes vary considerably in the facilities that they provide, there are significant benefits to a class whose objects behave like those of native types. Such a class is called a concrete data type. To make a class a concrete data type, we must define certain member functions that allow creation, copying, and deletion to behave as with a native variable.

The easiest way to figure out what the compiler needs to handle a concrete data type is to look at what the compiler does for a native type. We have to supply the same functionality for our own new data type, as shown in Figure 6.2.

Because these member functions are so fundamental to the proper operation of a class, the compiler will generate a version of each of them for us if we don't write them ourselves, just as the corresponding behavior is automatically supplied for the native types. As we will see in Chapter 7, the compiler-generated functions are generally too simplistic to be used in a complex class; in such a case we need to create our own versions of these functions. I'll illustrate how to do that at the appropriate time. However, with a simple class such as the one we're creating here, the compiler-generated versions of the assignment operator, copy constructor, and destructor are perfectly adequate, so we won't be creating our own versions of these functions for StockItem.

```
Problem
Algorithms
C++
Executable
Hardware
```

Before we can implement the member functions for our StockItem class, we have to define what a StockItem is in more detail than my previous sketch.[3] Let's start with the simplified version of the interface specification for that class in Figure 6.3, which includes the specification of the default constructor, the display function, and another constructor that is specific to the StockItem class.

I strongly recommend that you print out the files that contain this interface and its implementation, as well as the test program, for reference as you are going through this part of the chapter; those files are item1.h, item1.cc, and itemtst1.cc, respectively.

---

3. By the way, in using a functional class such as StockItem to illustrate these concepts, I'm violating a venerable tradition in C++ tutorials. Normally, example classes represent zoo animals, or shapes, or something equally useful in common programming situations.

```
class StockItem
{
public:
    StockItem();

    StockItem(string Name, short InStock, short Price,
    string Distributor, string UPC);

    void Display();

private:
    short m_InStock;
    short m_Price;
    string m_Name;
    string m_Distributor;
    string m_UPC;
};
```

Figure 6.3: The initial interface of the StockItem class (code\item1.h)

Problem
Algorithms
C++
Executable
Hardware
Your first reaction is probably something like "What a bunch of malarkey!" Let's take it a little at a time, and you'll see that this seeming gibberish actually has a rhyme and reason to it. First we have the line class StockItem. This tells the compiler that what follows is the definition of a class interface, which as we have already seen is a description of the operations that can be performed on objects of a given user-defined type;[4] in this case, the type is StockItem. So that the compiler knows where this description begins and ends, it is enclosed in {}, just like any other block of information that is to be treated as one item.

After the opening {, the next line says public:. This is the first time we've seen the keyword public, which is a type of **access specifier**. When an access specifier appears in a class interface definition followed by a :, it tells the compiler the "security classification" of the item(s) following it, up to the next access specifier. This particular access specifier, public, means that any part of the program, whether or not it is defined in this class, can use the items starting immediately after the public declaration and continuing until there is another access specifier. In the current case, all of the items following the public specifier are operations that we wish to perform

---

4. For the implementation of the functions in this interface specification, see the following figures:
    1.   For StockItem(), see Figure 6.4.
    2.   For StockItem(string Name, short InStock, short Price, string Distributor, string UPC), see Figure 6.7.
    3.   For Display(), see Figure 6.8.

on StockItem objects. Since they are public, we can use them anywhere in our programs. You may be wondering why everything isn't public; why should we prevent ourselves (or users of our classes) from using everything in the classes? It's not just hardheartedness; it's actually a way of improving the reliability and flexibility of our software, as I'll explain later.

Now we're up to the line that says StockItem();. This is the declaration for a function called a *constructor*, which tells the compiler what to do when we define a variable of a user-defined type since, as we have already seen, there's no way for it to know this otherwise. This particular constructor is the *default constructor* for the StockItem class. It's called the "default" constructor because it is used when no initial value is specified by the user. The empty parentheses after the name of the function indicate the lack of arguments to the function. The name of the function is the clue that it's a constructor; the name of a constructor is always the same as the name of the class for which it's a constructor, to make it easier for the compiler to identify constructors among all of the possible functions in a class.

Why do we need to write our own default constructor? After all, the compiler can figure out the size of a variable of our class, as it can for any other static or auto variable, so it can allocate storage for a variable of our class.[5] However, that isn't enough information for the compiler to know how to initialize the objects of the class correctly. Unlike a native variable, the compiler can't set a newly created StockItem to a reasonable value since it doesn't understand what the member variables of a StockItem are used for. That is, it can't do the initialization without help from us. In the code for our default constructor, we will initialize the member variables to legitimate values, so that we don't have to worry about having an uninitialized StockItem lying around as we did with a short in a previous example. Figure 6.4 shows what the code to our first default constructor looks like.

Problem
Algorithms
C++
Executable
Hardware

---

5. In case it isn't obvious how the compiler can figure out the size of the object, consider that the class definition specifies all of the variables that are used to implement the objects of the class. Since the compiler already knows the definitions of all of these components, it can calculate the size of our class variables based on the sizes and types of those components. By the way, the size of our object isn't necessarily the sum of the sizes of its components; the compiler often has to add some space to the objects for reasons that are, unfortunately, beyond the scope of this book.

```
StockItem::StockItem()
: m_InStock(0), m_Price(0), m_Name(), m_Distributor(), m_UPC()
{
}
```

Figure 6.4: The default constructor for the StockItem class (from code\item1.cc)

Let's use this example of a StockItem class to illuminate the distinction between interface and implementation. As I've already mentioned, the implementation of a class is the code that is responsible for actually doing the things promised by the interface of that class. The interface was laid out in Figure 6.3. With the exception of the test program that illustrates the use of the StockItem class, all of the code that we will examine in this chapter is part of the implementation: This includes the constructors and the Display member function.

So you can keep track of where this fits into the "big picture", the code in Figure 6.4 is the implementation of the function StockItem::StockItem() (i.e., the default constructor for the class StockItem), whose interface was defined in Figure 6.3.

Problem
Algorithms
C++
Executable
Hardware

Now, how does it work? Actually, this function isn't all that different from a "regular" function, but there are some important differences. First of all, the name looks sort of funny: Why is StockItem repeated?

The answer is that, unlike "regular" (technically, *global*) functions, a *member function* always belongs to a particular class. That is, such a function has special access to the data and other functions in the class. To mark its membership, its name consists of the name of the class (in this case, StockItem), followed by the class *membership* operator ::, followed by the name of the function (which in this case, is also StockItem). Figure 6.5 shows how each component of the function declaration contributes to the whole.

```
This function belongs to the StockItem class;

                    it is a constructor, because its name is the
                    same as the name of the class;

                               and it has no arguments.
                                  In other words, it is the
                                  default constructor for
                                  its class.


   StockItem ::  StockItem   ()
```

Figure 6.5: The declaration of the default constructor for the StockItem class

As we have already seen, the name of a constructor is always the same as the name of its class. However, if you've really been paying attention, there's one thing that you may have noticed about this declaration as compared with the original declaration of this function in the class interface definition for StockItem (Figure 6.3). In that figure, we declared this same function as StockItem();, without the additional StockItem:: on the front.[6] Why didn't we need to use the StockItem:: class membership notation in the class interface definition? Because inside the declaration of a class, we don't have to specify what class the member functions belong to; by definition, they belong to the class we're defining. Thus, StockItem() in the class interface declaration means "the member function StockItem, having no arguments"; i.e., the default constructor for the StockItem class.

Now let's look at the part of the constructor that initializes the member variables of the StockItem class, the **member initialization list**. The start of a member initialization list is signified by a : after the closing) of the constructor declaration, and the expressions in the list are separated by commas; it can be used only with constructors, not any other type of functions. In the case of the default StockItem constructor, the member initialization list consists of the following line:

`: m_InStock(0), m_Price(0), m_Name(), m_Distributor(), m_UPC()`

Problem
Algorithms
C++
Executable
Hardware

What does this mean exactly? Well, as its name indicates, it is a list of expressions each of which initializes one member variable. In the case of a native variable type, it is equivalent to creating the variable with the initial value specified in the parentheses. In the case of a class type, it is equivalent to creating the variable by calling the constructor that matches the type(s) of argument(s) specified in the parentheses, or the default constructor if there are no arguments specified. So the expression m_InStock(0) is analogous to the creation of a local variable by the statement short m_InStock = 0;, and the expression m_Name() is analogous to the creation of a local variable by the statement string m_Name;, which initializes the string m_Name to the empty C string "".

Using a member initialization list is the best way to set up member variables in a constructor, for two reasons. First, it's more efficient than using assignment statements to set the values of member

---

6. By the way, spaces between components of the name aren't significant; that is, we can have them, as in Figure 6.5, or leave them out, as we did in Figure 6.4.

variables. For example, suppose that we were to write this constructor as shown in Figure 6.6.

```
StockItem::StockItem()
{
    m_InStock = 0;
    m_Price = 0;
    m_Name = "";
    m_Distributor = "";
    m_UPC = "";
}
```

Figure 6.6: Another possible default constructor for the StockItem class

If we wrote the constructor that way, before we got to the opening { of the constructor, all of the member variables that had constructors (here, the strings) would be initialized to their default values. After the {, they would be set to the values we specified in the code for the constructor. It's true that we could solve this problem in this specific example by simply not initializing the strings at all, as that would mean that they would be initialized to their default values anyway. However, that solution wouldn't apply in other constructors such as the one in Figure 6.7, where the member variables have specified values rather than default ones.

Problem
Algorithms
C++
Executable
Hardware

The second reason that we should use a member initialization list to initialize our member variables is that some member data items aren't variables at all but constants. We'll see how to define consts, as they are called in C++, in a later chapter. For now, it's enough to know that you can't assign a value to a const, but you can (and indeed have to) initialize it; therefore, when dealing with member consts, a member initialization list isn't just a good idea, it's the law.

There is one fine point that isn't obvious from looking at the code for this constructor: The expressions in a member initialization list are executed in the order in which the member variables being initialized are declared in the class definition, which is **not** necessarily the order in which the expressions appear in the list. In our example, since m_InStock appears before m_Name in the class definition, the member initialization expression for m_InStock will be executed before the expression initializing m_Name. This doesn't matter right now, but it will be important in Chapter 7, where we will be using initialization expressions whose order of execution is important.

You may have noticed that the executable part of the function (Figure 6.4) is empty, because all of the work has already been done by the member initialization list. This is fairly common, but not universal; as we'll see in Chapter 7, sometimes a constructor has to do something other than initialize member variables, in which case we need some code inside the {}.

Now let's get back to the member variables of StockItem. One important characteristic of any variable is its scope, so we should pay attention to the scope of these variables. In Chapter 5, we saw two scopes in which a variable could be defined: *local* (i.e., available only within the function where it was defined) and *global* (i.e., available anywhere in the program). Well, these variables aren't arguments (which have local scope) since they don't appear in the function's header. Since they aren't defined in the function itself, they aren't local variables. Surely they can't be global variables, after I showed you how treacherous those can be.

Go to the Head of the class

I haven't misled you on that point; there is another scope called class **scope**, which applies to all member variables of a class.[7] class scope means that each object of a given class has one set of member variables. In the case of StockItem, this set of variables consists of m_InStock, m_Price, m_Name, m_Distributor, and m_UPC. Member functions of a class can access member variables of that class without defining them, as though they were global variables.

In addition to scope, each member variable has another attribute we have already encountered: an access specifier. The access of nonmember functions to any member variable or member function depends on the access specifier in effect when the member variable or function was defined. If you look back at Figure 6.3, you'll see that the line private: precedes the definition of the member variables in the StockItem class. The keyword private is an access specifier like public. However, where a public access specifier allows any function to access the items that follow it, a private access specifier allows only member functions to access items that follow it.

In the event that this sounds like our previous discussion of scopes, it's not quite the same. Scope defines where a variable is visible, whereas access specifiers control where a variable (or function) is accessible. That is, if you write a program that tries to read or modify a private variable from outside the class implementation, the compiler knows what you're trying to do but won't let you do it. On the other

```
Problem
Algorithms
C++
Executable
Hardware
```

---

7. Actually, I'm describing "normal" member variables here. There is another kind that we won't be covering.

hand, if you try to access a local variable from a function where it isn't defined, the compiler just tells you it never heard of that variable, which indeed it hasn't in that context.

For example, let's suppose that the local variable x defined in function abc has no existence in any other function; in that case, if you try to access a variable named x in another function, say def, where it hasn't been defined, you'll get an error message from the compiler telling you that there is no variable x in function def. However, if there is a private member variable called x defined in class ghi and you try to access that member variable from a nonmember function, the compiler will tell you that you're trying to do something illegal. It knows which x you mean, but it won't let you access it because you don't have permission.

Of course, the constructor StockItem::StockItem(), by virtue of being a member function, has access to all member variables, so the private access specifier doesn't apply to it. We'll see later how that access specifier comes into play.

Now that we know what kind of variables the StockItem::StockItem() function deals with, its behavior isn't very mysterious. It simply initializes the member variables to 0 or "", whichever is appropriate to their types. That's all very well, but it doesn't answer a very important question: What exactly do these member variables do? The answer is that they don't do anything by themselves; rather, they are the "raw material" the member functions use to implement the behavior that we want a StockItem to display. If you recall the discussion of interface vs. implementation, then you'll appreciate that the private member variables are also essentially part of the implementation and not part of the interface because even though they are defined in the header file the user of the class can't access them directly.

That's why we call variables that are declared inside the class definition *member variables* and functions that are declared inside the class definition *member functions*: They "belong" to the class that we're defining. The member functions set, change, and use the values of the member variables in the course of implementing the behaviors that the StockItem class interface definition promises. As an aside, the special status of member functions and variables as implementation aids explains why you cannot apply an access specifier such as public to data or functions declared outside a class; the purpose of access specifiers is to control "outside" access to variables and functions used to implement a class. In case you were wondering, we can't apply access specifiers to native types because the way they are implemented is not accessible to the programmer.

Problem
Algorithms
C++
Executable
Hardware

So much for the "high-altitude" description of what a class does. Now let's get back to the details that make it work, starting with a little puzzle: figuring out where the StockItem::StockItem() function is used in the test program in Figure 6.1. Believe it or not, this constructor is actually used in that program. To be exact, the line StockItem soup; calls it. Remember that the basic idea of constructing a class is to add data types to the language that aren't available "out of the box". One of the functions that we have to help the compiler with is initialization; a main purpose for the StockItem::StockItem() constructor is to initialize variables of the StockItem type that have no values explicitly assigned to them. That's why it's called a *default constructor*.

You should generally write a default constructor for every class you define, so that the state of any "default-constructed" variable will be known. As with the other fundamental functions of a concrete data type, if you don't define a default constructor, the compiler will supply one for you. However, since it doesn't know much about your class, it won't be able to guarantee very much about the initial state of one of your variables. The moral is that you should define your own default constructor. As you can see from our example, it's not much work.

So why did I say "generally", rather than "always"? Because there are some times when you don't want to allow an object to be created unless the "real" data for it is available. As with the copy constructor, the compiler will generate a default constructor for you automatically. To prevent this, you can declare a private default constructor, which will cause a compiler error in any user code that tries to define an object of that class without specifying any initial values. You don't actually have to implement this private constructor because a program that tries to use it will fail in the compile stage; thus, the link phase won't ever be executed.

Problem
Algorithms
C++
Executable
Hardware

Shop till You Drop

Now let's continue with our analysis of the class interface (Figure 6.3). Before we can do anything with an inventory record, we have to enter the inventory data. This means that we need another constructor that actually sets the values into the object. We also need some way to display the data for a StockItem on the screen, which means writing a Display function.

The next line of Figure 6.3 is the declaration of the constructor that creates an object with actual data:

StockItem(string Name, short InStock, short Price, string Distributor, string UPC);

We can tell that this function is a constructor because its name, StockItem, is the same as the name of the class. If you're a C programmer, you may be surprised to see two functions that have the same name, differing only in the types of their arguments. This is not legal in C, but it is in C++; it's called **function overloading**. As you'll see, it's a very handy facility that isn't limited to constructors. The combination of the function name and argument types is called the **signature** of a function; two functions that have the same name but differ in the type of at least one argument are distinct functions.

Note that the names of the arguments are not part of the signature; in fact, you don't have to specify them in the function declaration at all. However, I strongly recommend that you use the same argument names in the function declaration and in the function implementation. This makes it easier for the user of the function to understand what the arguments to the function are. After all, the declaration StockItem(string,short,short,string,string); doesn't provide much information on what its arguments actually mean.

In the case of the default constructor, there are no arguments, so that constructor is used where no initial data is specified for the object. The statement StockItem soup; fits that description, so the default constructor is used. However, in the next line of the sample program, we have the expression

Problem
Algorithms
C++
Executable
Hardware

StockItem("Chunky Chicken",32,129,"Bob's Distribution","123456789");

This is clearly a call to a constructor, because the name of the function is the name of a class, StockItem. Therefore, the compiler looks for a constructor that can handle the set of arguments in this call, and it finds

StockItem(string Name, short InStock, short Price, string Distributor, string UPC);

The first argument to the constructor is a string, the second is a short, the third is another short, the fourth is a string, and the fifth is another string. These types all match those specified in the expression in the sample program. Therefore, the compiler can translate that expression into a call to this constructor.

Figure 6.7 shows the code for that constructor.

```
StockItem::StockItem(string Name, short InStock,
short Price, string Distributor, string UPC)
: m_Name(Name), m_InStock(InStock), m_Price(Price),
  m_Distributor(Distributor), m_UPC(UPC)
{
}
```

Figure 6.7: Another constructor for the StockItem class (from code\item1.cc)

As you can see, nothing about this constructor is terribly complex; it merely uses the member initialization list to set the member variables of the object being constructed to the values of their corresponding arguments.

Once the expression that calls the constructor has been translated, the compiler has to figure out how to assign the result of the expression to the StockItem object called soup, as requested in the whole statement:

```
soup = StockItem("Chunky Chicken",32,129,"Bob's Distribution","123456789");
```

Since the compiler has generated its own version of the assignment operator = for the StockItem class, it can translate that part of the statement as well, which results in the StockItem object named soup having the value produced by the constructor.

Problem
Algorithms
C++
Executable
Hardware

Finally, we have the line soup.Display();, which displays the value of soup on the screen. Figure 6.8 shows the code for that function.

```
void StockItem::Display()
{
    cout << "Name: ";
    cout << m_Name << endl;
    cout << "Number in stock: ";
    cout << m_InStock << endl;
    cout << "Price: ";
    cout << m_Price << endl;
    cout << "Distributor: ";
    cout << m_Distributor << endl;
    cout << "UPC: ";
    cout << m_UPC << endl;
}
```

Figure 6.8: Display member function for the StockItem class (from code\item1.cc)

This is also not very complicated; it just uses << to copy each of the parts of the StockItem object to cout, along with some identifying information that makes it easier to figure out what the values represent.

That should clear up most of the potential problems with the meaning of this Display function. However, it does contain one construct that we haven't seen before: void. This is the return type of the Display function, as might be apparent from its position immediately before the class name StockItem. But what sort of return value is a void? In this context, it means simply that this function doesn't supply a return value at all.

Price Fixing

That takes care of the public part of the class definition. Now what about the private part?

As I mentioned before in the discussion of how a class is defined, the access specifier private means that only member functions of the class can access the items after that specifier. It's almost always a good idea to mark all the member variables in a class as private, for two reasons.

```
Problem
Algorithms
C++
Executable
Hardware
```

1. If we know that only member functions of a class can change the values of member data, then we know where to look if the values of the data are incorrect. This can be extremely useful when debugging a program.
2. Marking member variables as private simplifies the task of changing or deleting those member variables should that become necessary. You see, if the member variables are public, then we have no idea what functions are relying on their values. That means that changing or deleting these member variables can cause havoc anywhere in the system. Allowing access only by member functions means that we can make changes freely as long as all of the member functions are kept up to date.

Both of these advantages of keeping member variables private can be summed up in the term **encapsulation**, which means "hiding the details inside the class implementation rather than exposing them in the interface". This is one of the primary organizing principles that characterize object-oriented programming.

There's only one more point about the member variables in the StockItem class that needs clarification; surely the price of an object in the store should be in dollars and cents, and yet we have only a short to represent it. As you know by now, a short can hold only a whole number, from −32768 to 32767. What's going on here?

Not much; I've just decided to store the price in cents rather than dollars and cents. That is, when someone types in a price, I'll assume that it's in cents, so "246" would mean 246 cents, or $2.46. This would of course not be acceptable in a real program, but for now it's OK.

This allows prices up to $327.67 (as well as negative numbers for things like coupons), which should be acceptable for a grocery store. In a big hardware store that sells items like diesel generators and expensive plumbing fixtures, this wouldn't be a big enough range. In the Appendix, I'll give you some tips on how to solve that problem by using a different kind of numeric variable that can hold a greater variety of values. For now, though, let's stick with the short.

There's one more point that I should emphasize about defining a class: Make very sure that you have a ; at the end of the definition, after the closing }. If you don't, you'll get all kinds of weird errors when you try to use the class in your programs.

Now that we've covered all of the member functions and variables of the StockItem class, Figure 6.9 shows the interface for the StockItem class again. As noted previously, the test program for this class, itemtst1.cc, is shown in Figure 6.1.

Problem
Algorithms
C++
Executable
Hardware

```
class StockItem
{
public:
    StockItem();

    StockItem(string Name, short InStock, short Price,
    string Distributor, string UPC);

    void Display();

private:
    short m_InStock;
    short m_Price;
    string m_Name;
    string m_Distributor;
    string m_UPC;
};
```

Figure 6.9: The initial interface of the StockItem class (code\item1.h)

Figure 6.10 shows the initial implementation for the StockItem class.

```
#include <iostream.h>
#include "string6.h"
#include "item1.h"

StockItem::StockItem()
: m_Name(), m_InStock(0), m_Price(0), m_Distributor(), m_UPC()
{
}

StockItem::StockItem(string Name, short InStock,
short Price, string Distributor, string UPC)
: m_Name(Name), m_InStock(InStock), m_Price(Price),
  m_Distributor(Distributor), m_UPC(UPC)
{
}

void StockItem::Display()
{
    cout << "Name: ";
    cout << m_Name << endl;
    cout << "Number in stock: ";
    cout << m_InStock << endl;
    cout << "Price: ";
    cout << m_Price << endl;
    cout << "Distributor: ";
    cout << m_Distributor << endl;
    cout << "UPC: ";
    cout << m_UPC << endl;
}
```

Problem
Algorithms
C++
Executable
Hardware

Figure 6.10: The initial implementation of the StockItem class (code\item1.cc)

Assuming that you've installed the software from the CD-ROM in the back of this book, you can try out this program. First, you have to compile it by changing to the normal subdirectory under the main directory where you installed the software and typing mk itemtst1. Then type itemtst1 to run the program. You'll see that it indeed prints out the information in the StockItem object.

That's good as far as it goes, but how do we use this class to keep track of all of the items in the store? Surely we aren't going to have a separately named StockItem variable for each one!

Vectoring In

This is another application for our old friend the vector; specifically, we need a vector of StockItems to store the data for all the StockItems in the store. In a real application we would need to be able to vary the number of elements in the vector. After all, the number of items in a store isn't constant. However, in our example program we'll ignore this complication and just use a vector that can hold 100 StockItems. Even with this limitation, we will have to keep track of the number of items that are in use, so that we can store each new StockItem in its own vector element and keep track of how many items we may have to search through to find a particular StockItem. Finally, we need something to read the data for each StockItem from the inventory file where it's stored when we're not running the program.

Figure 6.11 shows the code necessary to read the data for the StockItem vector into memory when the program starts.

```
#include <iostream.h>
#include <fstream.h>
#include "vector.h"
#include "string6.h"
#include "item2.h"

int main()
{
    ifstream ShopInfo("shop2.in");
    vector<StockItem> AllItems(100);
    short i;
    short InventoryCount;

    for (i = 0; i < 100; i ++)
        {
        AllItems[i].Read(ShopInfo);
        if (ShopInfo.fail() != 0)
            break;
        }

    InventoryCount = i;

    for (i = 0; i < InventoryCount; i ++)
        {
        AllItems[i].Display();
        }

    return 0;
}
```

Problem
Algorithms
C++
Executable
Hardware

Figure 6.11: Reading and displaying a vector of StockItems (code\itemtst2.cc)

This program has a number of new features that need examination. First, we've had to add the "file stream" header file fstream.h to the list of #include files, so that we will be able to read data in from a file. The way we do this is to create an ifstream object that is "attached" to a file when the object is constructed. In this case, the line ifstream ShopInfo("shop2.in"); creates an ifstream object called ShopInfo and connects it to the file named shop2.in.

The next line is AllItems[i].Read(ShopInfo);, which calls the function Read for the ith StockItem in the AllItems vector, passing the ShopInfo ifstream object to a new StockItem member function called Read, which uses ShopInfo to get data from the file and store it into its StockItem (i.e., the ith element in the vector).

Figure 6.12 is the new interface to the StockItem class, showing the declaration of the new Read member function. I strongly recommend that you print out the files that contain this interface and its implementation, as well as the test program, for reference as you are going through this part of the chapter; those files are item2.h, item2.cc, and itemtst2.cc, respectively.

Problem
Algorithms
C++
Executable
Hardware

```
class StockItem
{
public:
        StockItem();

        StockItem(string Name, short InStock, short Price,
        string Distributor, string UPC);

        void Display();
        void Read(ifstream& s);

private:
        short m_InStock;
        short m_Price;
        string m_Name;
        string m_Distributor;
        string m_UPC;
};
```

Figure 6.12: The second version of the interface for the StockItem class
(code\item2.h)

And Figure 6.13 is the implementation of the new Read function.

```
void StockItem::Read(ifstream& s)
{
    s >> m_Name;
    s >> m_InStock;
    s >> m_Price;
    s >> m_Distributor;
    s >> m_UPC;
}
```

Figure 6.13: The Read function for the StockItem class (from code\item2.cc)

As you can see, this Read function is pretty simple; it just reads the data for one StockItem in from the file by way of the ifstream object s, using one >> expression to read each member variable's value. However, there's one construct here we haven't seen before: the & in ifstream&. What does that mean?

The &, in this context, means that the argument to which it refers is a **reference argument**, rather than a "normal" argument. It's important to understand this concept thoroughly, so let's go into it in detail.

Problem
Algorithms
C++
Executable
Hardware

References Required

As you may recall from Chapter 5, when we call a function, it doesn't ordinarily operate on actual variables in the calling function. Instead, a new local variable is created and initialized to the value of each expression from the calling function, and the called function works on that local variable. Such a local variable is called a *value argument*, because it is a new variable with the same value as the caller's original argument. There's nothing wrong with this in many cases; sometimes, though, as in the present case, we have to do it a bit differently. A reference argument, such as the ifstream& argument to Read, is *not* a copy of the caller's argument, but another name for the actual argument passed by the caller.

Why would we want to use a reference argument? For several reasons. First, it's more efficient than using a value argument, because the overhead of making a copy for the called function isn't necessary. Second, any changes made to the reference argument change the caller's argument as well.[8] The use of this mechanism should be limited to those cases where it is really necessary, since it can confuse the readers of the calling function; there's no way to tell just by looking at the calling function that some of its variables can be changed by calling another function.

In this case, however, it *is* necessary to change the ifstream object that is the actual argument to the Read function, because that object contains the information about what data we've already read from the stream. If we passed the ifstream as a value argument, then the internal state of the "real" ifstream in the calling function wouldn't be altered to reflect the data we've read in our Read function, so every time we called Read, we would get the same input again. Therefore, we have to pass the ifstream as a reference argument.

The complete decoding of the function declaration void StockItem::Read(ifstream& s) is shown in Figure 6.14.

This means that the function we're defining doesn't return anything;

    it belongs to the StockItem class;

        its name is Read;

        and its argument is a reference to an ifstream.

Problem
Algorithms
C++
Executable
Hardware

```
void  StockItem::  Read  (ifstream& s)
```

Figure 6.14: The declaration of the function StockItem::Read (in code\item2.h)

Putting it all together, we're defining a void function (one that doesn't return a value) called Read, which belongs to class StockItem. This function takes an argument named s that's a reference to an ifstream. That is, the argument s is another name for the ifstream passed to us by the caller, not a copy of the caller's ifstream.

There is one point that we haven't examined yet, though: How does this routine determine that it's finished reading from the input file? With keyboard input, we process each line separately when it's

8. This characteristic of references means that the caller's actual argument corresponding to a reference argument must be a variable, not an expression like x + 3, as changing the value of such an expression wouldn't make much sense.

typed in, but that won't do the job with a file, where we want to read all the items in until we get to the end of the file.

We actually handle this detail in the main program itemtst2.cc, by asking ShopInfo whether there is any data left in the file. To be more precise, we call the ifstream member function fail() to ask the ShopInfo ifstream whether we have tried to read past the end of the file. If we have, then the result of that call to ShopInfo.fail() will be nonzero (which signifies true). If we haven't yet tried to read past the end of the file, then the result of that call will be 0 (which signifies false). How do we use this information?

We use it to decide whether to execute a break **statement**. This is a loop control device that interrupts processing of a loop whenever it is executed. The flow of control passes to the next statement after the end of the controlled block of a for statement, a while loop, or some other types of control mechanisms that we won't get to.

The loop will terminate in one of two ways. Either 100 records have been read, in which case i will be 100; or the end of the file is reached, in which case i is the number of records that have been read successfully.

Whether there are 100 records in the file or fewer than that number, obviously the number of items in the vector is equal to the current value of i. Or is it?

Problem
Algorithms
C++
Executable
Hardware

Don't Fence Me In

Let's examine this a bit more closely. It's actually quite easy to make a mistake in counting objects when writing a program. It's quite common to make the mistake of thinking you have one more or one less than the actual number of objects. In fact, this error is common enough to have a couple of widely known nicknames: an **off-by-one error**, also known as a **fencepost error**. The former name should be fairly evident, but the latter name may require some explanation. First, let's try it as a "word problem". If you have to put up a fence 100 feet long, and each section of the fence is 10 feet long, how many sections of fence do you need? Obviously, the answer is 10. Now how many fenceposts do you need? 11. The confusion caused by counting fenceposts when you should be counting segments of the fence (and vice-versa) is the cause of a fencepost error.

That's fine as a general rule, but what about this specific example? Well, let's start out by supposing that we have an empty file, so the sequence of events in the upper loop is as follows:

1. Set i to 0.
2. Is i less than 100? If not, exit. If so, continue.
3. Use the Read function to try to read a record into the ith element of the AllItems vector.
4. Call ShopInfo.fail() to find out whether we've tried to read past the end of the file.
5. If so, execute the break statement to exit the loop.

The answer to the question in step 4 is that in fact nothing was read, so we do execute the break and leave the loop. The value of i is clearly 0 here, because we never went back to the top of the loop; since we haven't read any records, setting count to i works in this case.

Now let's try the same thing, but this time assuming that there is one record in the file. Here's the sequence of events:

1. Set i to 0.
2. Is i less than 100? If not, exit. If so, continue.
3. Use the Read function to try to read a record into the ith element of the AllItems vector.
4. Call ShopInfo.fail() to find out whether we've tried to read past the end of the file.

Problem
Algorithms
C++
Executable
Hardware

5. If so, execute the break statement to exit the loop. In this case, we haven't run off the end of the file, so we go back to the top of the loop, and continue with step 6.
6. Increment i to 1.
7. Is i less than 100? If not, exit. If so, continue.
8. Use the Read function to try to read a record into the AllItems vector.
9. Call ShopInfo.fail() to find out whether we've tried to read past the end of the file.
10. If so, execute the break statement to exit the loop.

The second time through, we do execute the break. Since i is 1 and the number of elements read was also 1, it's correct to set the count of elements to i.

It should be pretty clear that this same logic applies to all the possible numbers of elements up to 99. But what if we have 100 elements in the file? Don't worry; I'm not going to go through these steps 100 times! But I think we should start out from the situation that would exist after reading 99 elements to see if we get the right answer in this case too. After the 99th element has been read, i will be 99; we know this from our previous analysis that indicates that whenever we start executing the statements in the controlled block of the loop, i is always equal to the number of elements previously read. So here's the 100th iteration of the loop:

1.   Increment i to 100.
2.   Is i less than 100? If not, exit. If so, continue.

Since i is not less than 100, we exit.

At this point, we've read 100 records and i is 100, so these two numbers are still the same. Therefore, we can conclude that setting count equal to i when the loop is finished is correct; we have no fencepost error here.

Actually, this whole procedure we've just been through reminds me of the professor who claimed that some point he was making was obvious. This was questioned by a student, so the professor spent 10 minutes absorbed in calculation and finally emerged triumphantly with the news that it was indeed obvious.

Assuming that you've installed the software from the CD-ROM in the back of this book, you can try out this program. First, you have to compile it by changing to the normal subdirectory under the main directory where you installed the software and typing mk itemtst2. Then type itemtst2 to run the program. You'll see that it indeed prints out each StockItem object read from the file.

Problem
Algorithms
C++
Executable
Hardware

Our current itemtst example is getting to be enough like a real program that I'm going to start using the term *application program* (or equivalently, *application*) to refer to it sometimes. As is generally true of C++ programs, the responsibility for doing the user's work is divided up into a main program (or application program) and a set of classes (sometimes called *infrastructure*) used in the application. In this case, itemtst2.cc is the main program, or application program, whereas the other two files (item2.h and item2.cc) are the infrastructure.

Can I Help You?

Of course, this isn't all we want to do with the items in the store's inventory. Since we have a working means of reading and displaying the items, let's see what else we might want to do with them. Here are a few possible transactions at the grocery store:

1.   George comes in and buys 3 bags of marshmallows; the price is marked on the bags. We have to adjust the inventory for the sale.

2.   Sam comes up to the checkout counter carrying a can of string beans with no price marked on it, so we have to look up the price in the inventory.
3.   Judy comes in and asks if we have any chunky chicken soup; there's none on the shelf where it should be, so we have to check the inventory to see if we're supposed to have any cans of that soup.

What do all of these scenarios have in common? The need to find a StockItem object given some information about it. Let's start with the first example, which we might state as a programming task in the following manner: "Given the UPC from the bag of marshmallows and the number of bags purchased, adjust the inventory by subtracting the number purchased from the previous quantity on hand."

To break this down further, the steps should look something like this:

1.   Take the UPC from the item.
2.   For every item in the inventory list, check whether its UPC is the same as the one from the item.
3.   If it doesn't match, go back to step 2.
4.   If it does match, subtract the number purchased from the inventory.

Problem
Algorithms
C++
Executable
Hardware

Figure 6.15 is a program that looks as though it should solve this problem. There's nothing really new here except for the bool variable type (which we'll get to in a moment) and the -= operator that the program uses to adjust the inventory; -= is just like +=, except that it subtracts the right-hand value from the left-hand variable instead of adding as += does.

The bool variable type is a new addition to C++. Expressions and variables of this type are limited to the two values true and false.[9] This is a new data type that was added to C++ in the draft standard and will be implemented by any compiler that conforms to the actual standard. We've been using the terms true and false to refer to the result of a logical expression such as if (x < y); similarly, a bool variable or function return value can be either true or false. However, there's something wrong with this program; can you spot what it is?

---

9. The type bool is short for "Boolean", which means "either true or false". The derivation of the term "Boolean" is interesting but not relevant here.

```
#include <iostream.h>
#include <fstream.h>
#include "vector.h"
#include "string6.h"
#include "item2.h"

int main()
{
    ifstream ShopInfo("shop2.in");
    vector<StockItem> AllItems(100);
    short i;
    short InventoryCount;
    string PurchaseUPC;
    short PurchaseCount;
    bool Found;

    for (i = 0; i < 100; i ++)
        {
        AllItems[i].Read(ShopInfo);
        if (ShopInfo.fail() != 0)
            break;
        }

    InventoryCount = i;

    cout << "What is the UPC of the item?" << endl;
    cin >> PurchaseUPC;
    cout << "How many items were sold?" << endl;
    cin >> PurchaseCount;

    Found = false;
    for (i = 0; i < InventoryCount; i ++)
        {
        if (PurchaseUPC == AllItems[i].m_UPC)
            {
            Found = true;
            break;
            }
        }

    if (Found == true)
        {
        AllItems[i].m_InStock -= PurchaseCount;
        cout << "The inventory has been updated." << endl;
        }
    else
        cout << "Can't find that item. Please check UPC" << endl;

    return 0;
}
```

Problem
Algorithms
C++
Executable
Hardware

Figure 6.15: First attempt to update inventory of StockItems
(code\itemtst3.cc)

If you compile this program, you'll find that it is not valid. The problem is that we're trying to access private member variables of the StockItem class, namely m_UPC and m_InStock, from function main. Since main is not a member function of StockItem, this is not allowed. The error message from the compiler should look something like this:

```
itemtst3.cc: In function 'int main()':
itemtst3.cc:34: member 'm_UPC' is a private member of class 'StockItem'
itemtst3.cc:43: member 'm_InStock' is a private member of class 'StockItem'
```

Does this mean that we can't accomplish our goal of updating the inventory? Not at all. It merely means that we have to do things "by the book" rather than going in directly and reading or changing member variables that belong to the StockItem class. Of course, we could theoretically "solve" this access problem by simply making these member variables public rather than private. However, this would allow anyone to mess around with the internal variables in our StockItem objects, which would defeat one of the main purposes of using class objects in the first place — that they behave like native types as far as their users are concerned. We want the users of this class to ignore the internal workings of its objects and merely use them according to their externally defined interface; the implementation of the class is our responsibility, not theirs.

Problem
Algorithms
C++
Executable
Hardware

As it happens, we can easily solve our access problem without exposing the implementation of our class to the user. All we have to do is to add a couple of new member functions called CheckUPC and DeductSaleFromInventory to the StockItem class. The first of these allows us to check whether a given UPC belongs to a given StockItem, and the second allows us to adjust the inventory level of an item.

Figure 6.16 shows the new, improved interface definition. I strongly recommend that you print out the files that contain this interface and its implementation, as well as the test program, for reference as you are going through this part of the chapter; those files are item4.h, item4.cc, and itemtst4.cc, respectively. The declarations of the two new functions CheckUPC and DeductSaleFromInventory should be pretty easy to figure out. CheckUPC takes the UPC that we want to find and compares it to the UPC in its StockItem. Here's a good place to use the bool data type; the only possible results of the CheckUPC function are that the UPC in the StockItem matches the one we've supplied (in which case we return true) or it doesn't match (in which case we return false). DeductSaleFromInventory takes the number of items sold and subtracts it from the previous inventory. But where did those other two member functions GetInventory and GetName come from?

```
class StockItem
{
public:
    StockItem();

    StockItem(string Name, short InStock, short Price,
    string Distributor, string UPC);

    void Display();
    void Read(ifstream& s);

    bool CheckUPC(string ItemUPC);
    void DeductSaleFromInventory(short QuantitySold);
    short GetInventory();
    string GetName();

private:
    short m_InStock;
    short m_Price;
    string m_Name;
    string m_Distributor;
    string m_UPC;
};
```

```
Problem
Algorithms
C++
Executable
Hardware
```

Figure 6.16: An enhanced interface for the StockItem class (code\item4.h)

The Customer Is Always Right

I added those functions because I noticed that the itemtst program wasn't very user-friendly. Originally it followed these steps:

1. Ask for the UPC.
2. Ask for the number of items purchased.
3. Search through the list to see whether the UPC is legitimate.
4. If so, adjust the inventory.
5. If not, give an error message.
6. Exit.

What's wrong with this picture? Well, for one thing, why should the program make me type in the number of items sold if the UPC is no good? Also, it never told me the new inventory or even what the name of the item was. It may have known these things, but it never bothered to inform me. So I changed the program to work as follows:

1. Ask for the UPC.
2. Search through the list to see whether the UPC was legitimate.
3. If not, give an error message and exit.
4. If the UPC was OK, then
    a. Display the name of the item and the number in stock.
    b. Ask for the number of items purchased.
    c. Adjust the inventory.
    d. Display a message with the name of the item and number of remaining units in inventory.
5. Exit.

To do this, I needed those two new functions GetInventory and GetName, so as you've seen I added them to the class declaration. Figure 6.17 shows the implementation of all of these new functions. Figure 6.18 shows the new, improved version of our application, which updates the inventory and actually tells the user what it's doing.

Problem
Algorithms
C++
Executable
Hardware

```cpp
bool StockItem::CheckUPC(string ItemUPC)
{
    if (m_UPC == ItemUPC)
        return true;

    return false;
}

void StockItem::DeductSaleFromInventory(short QuantitySold)
{
    m_InStock -= QuantitySold;
}

short StockItem::GetInventory()
{
    return m_InStock;
}

string StockItem::GetName()
{
    return m_Name;
}
```

Figure 6.17: Some new functions for the StockItem class (from code\item4.cc)

```
#include <iostream.h>
#include <fstream.h>
#include "vector.h"
#include "string6.h"
#include "item4.h"

int main()
{
    ifstream ShopInfo("shop2.in");
    vector<StockItem> AllItems(100);
    short i;
    short InventoryCount;
    short OldInventory;
    short NewInventory;
    string PurchaseUPC;
    string ItemName;
    short PurchaseCount;
    bool Found;

    for (i = 0; i < 100; i ++)
        {
        AllItems[i].Read(ShopInfo);
        if (ShopInfo.fail() != 0)
            break;
        }

    InventoryCount = i;
    cout << "What is the UPC of the item? ";
    cin >> PurchaseUPC;
    Found = false;

    for (i = 0; i < InventoryCount; i ++)
        {
        if (AllItems[i].CheckUPC(PurchaseUPC) == true)
            {
            Found = true;
            break;
            }
        }

    if (Found == true)
        {
        OldInventory = AllItems[i].GetInventory();
        ItemName = AllItems[i].GetName();

        cout << "There are currently " << OldInventory << " units of "
        << ItemName << " in stock." << endl;
        cout << "How many items were sold? ";
        cin >> PurchaseCount;
```

Figure 6.18: Updating StockItem inventory (code\itemtst4.cc)

Problem
Algorithms
C++
Executable
Hardware

```
        AllItems[i].DeductSaleFromInventory(PurchaseCount);
        cout << "The inventory has been updated." << endl;
        NewInventory = AllItems[i].GetInventory();
        cout << "There are now " << NewInventory << " units of "
        << ItemName << " in stock." << endl;
        }
    else
        cout << "Can't find that item. Please check UPC" << endl;

    return 0;
}
```

Figure 6.18 continued

This code should be pretty easy to follow; it simply implements the first item purchase scenario I outlined in the list in the section titled "Can I Help You?".

Assuming that you've installed the software from the CD-ROM in the back of this book, you can try out this program. First, you have to compile it by changing to the normal subdirectory under the main directory where you installed the software and typing mk itemtst4. Then type itemtst4 to run the program normally. To run it under gdb, make sure you are in the normal subdirectory, then type trace itemtst4. The program will start up and ask you for the UPC; you can use 7904886261, which is the (made-up) UPC for "antihistamines". Type in that number and hit ENTER. Then the program will stop at the line that determines whether the UPC has been found, if (Found == true). Type z and hit ENTER to execute each line from then on. The values of the relevant variables will be displayed immediately before the execution of each remaining line in main.[10] When you get to the end of the program (or when you're tired of tracing), type q (for *quit*) and hit ENTER to exit from the debugger.

Problem
Algorithms
C++
Executable
Hardware

Next Customer, Please?

Now let's consider what might be needed to handle some of the other possibilities, starting with the second scenario in that same list. To refresh your memory, here it is again: "Sam comes up to the checkout counter carrying a can of string beans with no price marked on it, so we have to look up the price in the inventory".

---

10. Note that the Found variable will be displayed as 0 for false and 1 for true, due to limitations of gdb.

How would this be expressed as a programming task? Perhaps in this way: "Given a UPC, look up the price of the item in the inventory".

Here is a set of steps to solve this problem:

1. Ask for the UPC.
2. Search through the list to see whether the UPC is legitimate.
3. If not, give an error message and exit.
4. If the UPC is OK, then display the name and price of the item.
5. Exit.

These steps are very similar to those for the first problem. It seems wasteful to duplicate code rather than reusing it, and in fact we've seen how to avoid code duplication by using a function. Now that we're doing object-oriented programming, perhaps we should write a member function instead of a global one.

This is a good idea, except that the search function can't be a member function of StockItem because we don't have the right StockItem yet; if we did, we wouldn't need to search for it. Therefore, we have to create a new class that contains a member variable that is a vector of StockItems and a member function that will look through that vector to find the StockItem we want. Then we can use the member functions of StockItem to do the rest of the work. Figure 6.19 shows the interface (class declaration) for this new class, called Inventory.

Problem
Algorithms
C++
Executable
Hardware

```
#include "vector.h"

class Inventory
{
public:
    Inventory();

    short LoadInventory(ifstream& InputStream);
    StockItem FindItem(string UPC);
    bool UpdateItem(StockItem Item);

private:
    vector<StockItem> m_Stock;
    short m_StockCount;
};
```

Figure 6.19: Interface of Inventory class (code\invent1.h)

I strongly recommend that you print out the files that contain this interface and its implementation, as well as the test program, for reference as you are going through this part of the chapter; those files are invent1.h, invent1.cc, and itemtst5.cc, respectively.

Most of this should be fairly self-explanatory by this point. We start out with the default constructor, which makes an empty Inventory.[11] Figure 6.20 has the implementation for the default constructor.

```
Inventory::Inventory()
: m_Stock (vector<StockItem>(100)),
  m_StockCount(0)
{
}
```

Figure 6.20: Default constructor for Inventory class (from code\invent1.cc)

There's nothing complex here; we're using the member initialization list to initialize the m_Stock variable to a newly constructed vector of 100 StockItems and the number of active StockItems to 0. The latter value, of course, is appropriate because we haven't yet read any data in from the file.

Then we have a couple of handy functions. The first is LoadInventory, which will take data from an ifstream and store it in its Inventory object, just as we did with the AllItems vector in our application itemtst4.cc.

Figure 6.21 shows the implementation of LoadInventory.

Problem
Algorithms
C++
Executable
Hardware

```
short Inventory::LoadInventory(ifstream& InputStream)
{
        short i;

        for (i = 0; i < 100; i ++)
            {
            m_Stock[i].Read(InputStream);
            if (InputStream.fail() != 0)
                    break;
            }

        m_StockCount = i;
        return m_StockCount;
}
```

Figure 6.21: LoadInventory function for Inventory class (from code\invent1.cc)

---

11. As before, we can count on the compiler to supply the other three standard member functions needed for a concrete data type: the copy constructor, the assignment operator =, and the destructor.

Now we come to the FindItem member function. Its declaration is pretty simple: It takes an argument of type string, which contains the UPC that we're looking for. Its implementation is pretty simple, too: It will search the Inventory object for the StockItem that has that UPC and return a copy of that StockItem, which can then be interrogated to find the price or whatever other information we need.

However, there's a serious design issue here: What should this function return if the UPC doesn't match the UPC in any of the StockItem entries in the Inventory object? The application program has to be able to determine whether or not the UPC is found. In the original program this was no problem because the main program maintained that information itself. But in this case, the member function FindItem has to communicate success or failure to the caller somehow.

Of course, we could use a return value of true or false to indicate whether the UPC is found, but we're already using the return value to return the StockItem to the calling function. We could add a reference argument to the FindItem function and use it to set the value of a variable in the caller's code, but that's very nonintuitive; functions that use arguments only for input are easier to use and less likely to cause surprises.

Nothing Ventured, Nothing Gained

There's one more possibility. We can return a **null object** of the StockItem class; that is, an object that exists solely to serve as a placeholder, representing the desired object that we couldn't find.

I like this solution because when the member function terminates, the application program has to test something anyway to see if the desired StockItem was found. Why not test whether the returned object is a null StockItem? This solution, while quite simple, requires a minor change to our implementation of StockItem: We have to add an IsNull member function to our StockItem class so that we can tell whether the returned StockItem is a null StockItem or a "normal" one. We have to add the line bool IsNull(); to the class interface and provide the implementation as shown in Figure 6.22. I strongly recommend that you print out the files that contain this interface and its implementation, as well as the test program, for reference as you are going through this part of the chapter; those files are item5.h, item5.cc, and itemtst5.cc, respectively.

Problem
Algorithms
C++
Executable
Hardware

```
bool StockItem::IsNull()
{
      if (m_UPC == "")
            return true;

      return false;
}
```

Figure 6.22: The implementation of IsNull (from code\item5.cc)

As you can see, not much rocket science is involved in this member function. All we do is check whether the UPC is the null string "". If it is, we return true; otherwise, we return false. Since no real item can have a UPC of "", this should work well.

Figure 6.23 shows the implementation of FindItem, which uses CheckUPC to check whether the requested UPC is the one in the current item and returns a null StockItem if the desired UPC isn't found in the inventory list.

Problem
Algorithms
C++
Executable
Hardware

```
StockItem Inventory::FindItem(string UPC)
{
      short i;
      bool Found = false;

      for (i = 0; i < m_StockCount; i ++)
            {
            if (m_Stock[i].CheckUPC(UPC) == true)
                  {
                  Found = true;
                  break;
                  }
            }

      if (Found == true)
            return m_Stock[i];

      return StockItem();
}
```

Figure 6.23: FindItem function for Inventory class (from code\invent1.cc)

After we get a copy of the correct StockItem and update its inventory via DeductSaleFromInventory, we're not quite done; we still have to update the "real" StockItem in the Inventory object. This is the task of the last function in our Inventory class: UpdateItem. Figure 6.24 shows its implementation.

```
bool Inventory::UpdateItem(StockItem Item)
{
    string UPC = Item.GetUPC();

    short i;
    bool Found = false;

    for (i = 0; i < m_StockCount; i ++)
        {
        if (m_Stock[i].CheckUPC(UPC) == true)
            {
            Found = true;
            break;
            }
        }

    if (Found == true)
        m_Stock[i] = Item;

    return Found;
}
```

Figure 6.24: UpdateItem function for Inventory class (from code\invent1.cc)

Problem
Algorithms
C++
Executable
Hardware

Why do we need this function? Because we are no longer operating on the "real" StockItem, as we had been when we accessed the inventory vector directly in the previous version of the application program. Instead, we are getting a copy of the StockItem from the Inventory object and changing that copy; thus, to have the final result put back into the Inventory object, we need to use the UpdateItem member function of Inventory, which overwrites the original StockItem with our changed version.

This function needs another function in the StockItem class to get the UPC from a StockItem object, so that UpdateItem can tell which object in the m_Stock vector is the one that needs to be updated. This additional function is the GetUPC function. Its declaration is string GetUPC();, and its implementation is shown in Figure 6.25.

```
string StockItem::GetUPC()
{
     return m_UPC;
}
```

Figure 6.25: The implementation of GetUPC (from code\item5.cc)

The application program also needs one more function to be added to the interface of StockItem, to retrieve the price from the object once we have found it. This is also very simple, as you might imagine. The interface of this function is short GetPrice();, and its implementation is shown in Figure 6.26.

```
short StockItem::GetPrice()
{
     return m_Price;
}
```

Figure 6.26: The implementation of GetPrice (from code\item5.cc)

We're almost ready to examine the revised test program. First, though, let's pause for another look at all of the interfaces and implementations of the StockItem and Inventory classes. The interface for the Inventory class is in Figure 6.27.

```
#include "vector.h"

class Inventory
{
public:
     Inventory();

     short LoadInventory(ifstream& InputStream);
     StockItem FindItem(string UPC);
     bool UpdateItem(StockItem Item);

private:
     vector<StockItem> m_Stock;
     short m_StockCount;
};
```

Figure 6.27: Current interface for Inventory class (code\invent1.h)

Figure 6.28 contains the implementation for Inventory.

```
#include <iostream.h>
#include <fstream.h>
#include "vector.h"
#include "string6.h"
#include "item5.h"
#include "invent1.h"

Inventory::Inventory()
: m_Stock (vector<StockItem>(100)),
  m_StockCount(0)
{
}

short Inventory::LoadInventory(ifstream& InputStream)
{
    short i;

    for (i = 0; i < 100; i ++)
        {
        m_Stock[i].Read(InputStream);
        if (InputStream.fail() != 0)
            break;
        }

    m_StockCount = i;
    return m_StockCount;
}

StockItem Inventory::FindItem(string UPC)
{
    short i;
    bool Found = false;

    for (i = 0; i < m_StockCount; i ++)
        {
        if (m_Stock[i].CheckUPC(UPC) == true)
            {
            Found = true;
            break;
            }
        }

    if (Found == true)
        return m_Stock[i];

    return StockItem();
}

bool Inventory::UpdateItem(StockItem Item)
{
    string UPC = Item.GetUPC();
```

Problem
Algorithms
C++
Executable
Hardware

Figure 6.28: Current implementation for Inventory class (code\invent1.cc)

```
        short i;
        bool Found = false;

        for (i = 0; i < m_StockCount; i ++)
            {
            if (m_Stock[i].CheckUPC(UPC) == true)
                {
                Found = true;
                break;
                }
            }

        if (Found == true)
            m_Stock[i] = Item;

        return Found;
        }
```

Figure 6.28 continued

Figure 6.29 shows the interface for StockItem.

Problem
Algorithms
C++
Executable
Hardware

```
class StockItem
{
public:
        StockItem();

        StockItem(string Name, short InStock, short Price,
        string Distributor, string UPC);

        void Display();
        void Read(ifstream& s);

        bool CheckUPC(string ItemUPC);
        void DeductSaleFromInventory(short QuantitySold);
        short GetInventory();
        string GetName();
        bool IsNull();
        short GetPrice();
        string GetUPC();

private:
        short m_InStock;
        short m_Price;
        string m_Name;
        string m_Distributor;
        string m_UPC;
};
```

Figure 6.29: Current interface for StockItem class (code\item5.h)

The implementation for StockItem is in Figure 6.30.

```
#include <iostream.h>
#include <fstream.h>
#include "string6.h"
#include "item5.h"

StockItem::StockItem()
: m_InStock(0), m_Price(0), m_Name(),
   m_Distributor(), m_UPC()
{
}

StockItem::StockItem(string Name, short InStock,
short Price, string Distributor, string UPC)
: m_InStock(InStock), m_Price(Price), m_Name(Name),
   m_Distributor(Distributor), m_UPC(UPC)
{
}

void StockItem::Display()
{
     cout << "Name: ";
     cout << m_Name << endl;
     cout << "Number in stock: ";
     cout << m_InStock << endl;
     cout << "Price: ";
     cout << m_Price << endl;
     cout << "Distributor: ";
     cout << m_Distributor << endl;
     cout << "UPC: ";
     cout << m_UPC << endl;
     cout << endl;
}

void StockItem::Read(ifstream& s)
{
     s >> m_Name;
     s >> m_InStock;
     s >> m_Price;
     s >> m_Distributor;
     s >> m_UPC;
}

bool StockItem::CheckUPC(string ItemUPC)
{
     if (m_UPC == ItemUPC)
          return true;
```

Problem
Algorithms
C++
Executable
Hardware

Figure 6.30: Current implementation for StockItem class (code\item5.cc)

```
          return false;
      }

      void StockItem::DeductSaleFromInventory(short QuantitySold)
      {
          m_InStock -= QuantitySold;
      }

      short StockItem::GetInventory()
      {
          return m_InStock;
      }

      string StockItem::GetName()
      {
          return m_Name;
      }


      bool StockItem::IsNull()
      {
          if (m_UPC == "")
              return true;

          return false;
      }

      short StockItem::GetPrice()
      {
          return m_Price;
      }

      string StockItem::GetUPC()
      {
          return m_UPC;
      }
```

Problem
Algorithms
C++
Executable
Hardware

Figure 6.30 continued

To finish this stage of the inventory control project, Figure 6.31 is the revised test program that uses the Inventory class rather than doing its own search through a vector of StockItems. This program can perform either of two operations, depending on what the user requests. Once the UPC has been typed in, the user is prompted to type either "C" for price check or "S" for sale. Then an if statement selects which of the two operations to perform. The code for the S (i.e., sale) operation is the same as it was in the previous version of this application, except that, of course, at that time it was the only possible operation so it wasn't controlled by an if statement. The code for the C (i.e., price check) operation is new, but it's very simple. It merely displays both the item name and the price.

```cpp
#include <iostream.h>
#include <fstream.h>
#include "string6.h"
#include "item5.h"
#include "invent1.h"

int main()
{
    ifstream InputStream("shop2.in");
    string PurchaseUPC;
    short PurchaseCount;
    string ItemName;
    short OldInventory;
    short NewInventory;
    Inventory MyInventory;
    StockItem FoundItem;
    string TransactionCode;

    MyInventory.LoadInventory(InputStream);

    cout << "What is the UPC of the item? ";
    cin >> PurchaseUPC;

    FoundItem = MyInventory.FindItem(PurchaseUPC);
    if (FoundItem.IsNull() == true)
        {
        cout << "Can't find that item. Please check UPC." << endl;
        return 0;
        }

    OldInventory = FoundItem.GetInventory();
    ItemName = FoundItem.GetName();

    cout << "There are currently " << OldInventory << " units of "
    << ItemName << " in stock." << endl;

    cout << "Please enter transaction code as follows:\n";
    cout << "S (sale), C (price check): ";
    cin >> TransactionCode;

    if (TransactionCode == "C" || TransactionCode == "c")
        {
        cout << "The name of that item is: " << ItemName << endl;
        cout << "Its price is: " << FoundItem.GetPrice();
        }
```

Problem
Algorithms
C++
Executable
Hardware

Figure 6.31: Updated inventory application (code\itemtst5.cc)

```
else if (TransactionCode == "S" || TransactionCode == "s")
    {
    cout << "How many items were sold? ";
    cin >> PurchaseCount;
    FoundItem.DeductSaleFromInventory(PurchaseCount);
    MyInventory.UpdateItem(FoundItem);
    cout << "The inventory has been updated." << endl;

    FoundItem = MyInventory.FindItem(PurchaseUPC);
    NewInventory = FoundItem.GetInventory();

    cout << "There are now " << NewInventory << " units of "
    << ItemName << " in stock." << endl;
    }

    return 0;
}
```

Figure 6.31 continued

Problem
Algorithms
C++
Executable
Hardware

The only part of the program that might not be obvious at this point is the expression in the if statement that determines whether the user wants to enter a price check or sale transaction. The first part of the test is if (TransactionCode == "C" || TransactionCode == "c"). The || is the "logical OR" operator. An approximate translation of this expression is "if at least one of the two expressions on its right or left is true, then produce the result true; if they're both false, then produce the result false".[12] In this case, this means that the if statement will be true if the TransactionCode variable is either C or c. Why do we have to check for either a lower- or uppercase letter, when the instructions to the user clearly state that the choices are C or S?

This is good practice because users generally consider upper- and lowercase letters to be equivalent. Of course, as programmers, we know that the characters c and C are completely different; however, we should humor the users in this harmless delusion. After all, they're our customers!

Assuming that you've installed the software from the CD-ROM in the back of this book, you can try out this program. First, you have to compile it by changing to the normal subdirectory under the main directory where you installed the software and typing mk itemtst5. Then type itemtst5 to run the program normally. To run it under gdb,

---

12. The reason it's only an approximate translation is that there is a special rule in C++ governing the execution of the || operator: if the expression on the left is true, then the answer must be true and the expression on the right is not executed at all. The reason for this *short-circuit evaluation* rule is that in some cases you may want to write a right-hand expression that will only be legal if the left-hand expression is true.

make sure you are in the normal subdirectory, then type trace itemtst5. The program will start up and show you the first line of executable code. Type z and hit ENTER to execute each line from then on; when the program asks for a UPC, you can use 7904886261, which is the (made-up) UPC for "antihistamines". The values of the relevant variables will be displayed immediately before the execution of each remaining line in main. When the program asks you for a transaction code, type S for "sale" or C for "price check", and then hit ENTER. When you get to the end of the program (or when you're tired of tracing), type q (for *quit*) and hit ENTER to exit from the debugger.

Paging Rosie Scenario

By this point, you very understandably might have gotten the notion that we have to make changes to our classes every time we need to do anything slightly different in our application program. In that case, where's the advantage of using classes instead of just writing the whole program in terms of shorts, chars, and so on?

Well, this is your lucky day. It just so happens that the next (and last) scenario we are going to examine requires no more member functions at all; in fact, we don't even have to change the application program. Here it is, for reference: "Judy comes in and asks if we have any chunky chicken soup; there's none on the shelf where it should be, so we have to check the inventory to see if we're supposed to have any cans of that soup".

```
Problem
Algorithms
C++
Executable
Hardware
```

The reason we don't have to do anything special for this scenario is that we're already displaying the name and inventory for the item as soon as we find it. Of course, if we hadn't already handled this issue, there are many other ways that we could solve this same problem. For example, we could use the Display member function of StockItem to display an item as soon as the UPC lookup succeeds, rather than waiting for the user to indicate what operation our application is supposed to perform.

For that matter, we'd have to consider a number of other factors in writing a real application program, even one that does such a simple task as this one. For example, what would happen if the user indicated that 200 units of a particular item had been sold when only 100 were in stock? Also, how would we find an item if the UPC isn't available? The item might very well be in inventory somewhere, but the current implementation of Inventory doesn't allow for the possibility of looking up an item by any information other than the UPC.

Although these topics and many others are essential to the work of a professional programmer, they would take us too far afield from our purpose in this book, which is to teach you how to program using C++. Therefore, we will leave them for another day (and another book). Now let's review what we've covered in this chapter.

Review

The most important concept in this chapter is the idea of creating user-defined data types. In C++, this is done by defining a class for each such data type. Each class has both a class *interface*, which describes the behavior that the class displays to the "outside world" (i.e., other, unrelated functions), and a class *implementation*, which tells the compiler how to perform the behaviors promised in the interface definition. A variable of a class type is called an *object*. With proper attention to the interface and the details of implementation, it is possible to make objects behave just like native variables; that is, they can be initialized, assigned, compared, passed as function arguments, and returned as function return values.

```
Problem
Algorithms
C++
Executable
Hardware
```

Both the interface and the implementation of a class are described in terms of the functions and variables of which the class is composed. These are called *member functions* and *member variables*, because they belong to the class rather than being "free-floating" or localized to one function like the global functions or local variables we encountered earlier.

Of course, one obvious question is why we need to make up our own variable types. What's wrong with char, short, and the rest of the native types built into C++? The answer is that it's easier to write an inventory control program, for example, if we have data types representing items in the stock of a store rather than having to express everything in terms of the native types. An analogy is the universal preference of professionals to use technical jargon rather than "plain English": Jargon conveys more information, more precisely, in less time.

The idea of using objects rather than functions as the fundamental building blocks of programming is the basis of the object-oriented programming paradigm.[13]

---

13. Purists may not approve of this use of the term *object-oriented programming*, as I'm not using this term in its strictest technical sense. We'll see what else the concept of object-oriented programming implies in later chapters; however, since we are already using objects and classes as our central organizing ideas, I think we can start using the term here.

Then we examined how creating classes differs from using classes, as we have been doing throughout the book. A fairly good analogy is that creating your own classes is to using classes as writing a program is to using a program.

Next, we went through the steps needed to actually create a new class; our example is the StockItem class, which is designed to allow tracking of inventory for a small grocery store. These steps include writing the interface definition, writing the implementation, writing the program that uses the class, compiling the implementation, compiling the program that uses the class, and linking the object files resulting from these compilation steps together with the standard libraries to produce the final executable program.

Then we moved from the general to the specific, analyzing the particular data and functions that the StockItem class needed to perform its duties in an application program. The member variables needed for each StockItem object included the name, count, distributor, price, and UPC. Of course, merely having these member variables doesn't make a StockItem object very useful if it can't do anything with them. This led us to the topic of what member functions might be needed for such a class.

Rather than proceed immediately with the specialized member functions that pertain only to StockItem, however, we started by discussing the member functions that nearly every class needs to make its objects act like native variables. A class that has (at least) the capabilities of a native type is called a *concrete data type*. Such a class requires the following member functions:

Problem
Algorithms
C++
Executable
Hardware

1. A *default constructor*, which makes it possible to create an object of that class without supplying any initial data.
2. A *copy constructor*, which makes it possible to create a new object of this type with the same contents as an existing object of the same type.
3. An *assignment operator*, which copies the contents of one object of this type to another object of the same type.
4. A *destructor*, which performs whatever cleanup is needed when an object of this type "dies".

Since these member functions are so important to the proper functioning of a class, the compiler will create a version of each of them for us if we don't write them ourselves. In the case of StockItem, these compiler-generated member functions are perfectly acceptable, with the exception of the default constructor. The compiler-generated default constructor doesn't initialize a new StockItem object to a valid state, so we had to write that constructor ourselves to be sure of what a newly created StockItem contains.

Next, we looked at the first version of a class interface specification for StockItem (Figure 6.3), which tells the user (and the compiler) exactly what functions objects of this class can perform. Some items of note in this construct are:

1. The *access specifiers* public and private, which control access to the implementation of a class by functions not in the class (*nonmember functions*). Member variables and functions in the public section are available for use by nonmember functions, whereas member variables and functions in the private section are usable only by member functions.

2. The declarations of the *constructor* functions, which construct a new object of the class. The first noteworthy point about constructors is that they have the same name as the class, which is how the compiler identifies them as constructors. The second point of note is that there can be more than one constructor for a given class; all constructors have the same name and are distinguished by their argument lists. This facility, called *function overloading*, is applicable to C++ functions in general, not just constructors. That is, you can have any number of functions with the same name as long as they have different argument lists; the difference in argument lists is enough to make the compiler treat them as different functions. In this case, we have written two constructors: the default constructor, which is used to create a StockItem when we don't specify an initial value, and a constructor that has arguments to specify values for all of the member variables.[14]

3. The declaration of a "normal" member function (that is, not a constructor or other predefined function) named Display, which, as its name indicates, is used to display a StockItem on the screen.

4. The declaration of the member variables of StockItem, which are used to keep track of the information for a given object of the StockItem class.

Once we'd defined the class interface, we started on the class implementation by writing the default constructor for the StockItem class: StockItem::StockItem(). The reason for the doubled name is that when we write the implementation of a member function, we have to

```
Problem
Algorithms
C++
Executable
Hardware
```

---

14. The compiler has also supplied a copy constructor for us so that we can use StockItem objects as function arguments and return values.

specify what class that member function belongs to. In this example, the first StockItem is the name of the class, whereas the second StockItem is the name of the function, which, as always with constructors, has the same name as the class. By contrast, we didn't have to specify the class name when declaring member functions in the interface definition because all functions defined there are automatically member functions of that class. During this discussion, we saw that the preferred way to set the values of member variables is by using a member initialization list.

The next topic we visited was the scope of member variables, which is class scope. Each object of a given class has one set of member variables, which live as long as the object does. These member variables can be accessed from any member function as though they were global variables.

Then we examined how the default constructor was actually used in the example program, discovering that the line StockItem soup; was enough to cause it to be called. This is appropriate because one of the design goals of C++ was to allow a class object to be as easy to use as a native variable. Since a native variable can be created simply by specifying its type and name, the same should be true of a class object.

As this suggests, the person who writes a class isn't always the person who uses it. One reason for this is that the skills required to write a program using a class are not the same as those required to create the class in the first place.

Next, we covered the other constructor for the StockItem class. This one has arguments specifying the values for all of the member variables that make up the data part of the class.

Then we got to the final function of the first version of the StockItem class: the Display function, which, as its name indicates, is used to display the contents of a StockItem on the screen. This function uses the preexisting ability of << to display the shorts and strings that hold the contents of the StockItem. The return type of this function is a type we hadn't seen before, void, which simply means that there is no return value from this function. We don't need a return value from the Display function because we call it solely for its *side effect*: displaying the value of its StockItem on the screen.

Next, we took up the private part of the StockItem class definition, which contains the member variables. We covered two reasons why it is a good idea to keep the member variables private. First, it makes debugging easier, because only the member functions can modify the member variables. Second, we can change the names or types of our member variables or delete them from the class definition much more

```
Problem
Algorithms
C++
Executable
Hardware
```

easily if we don't have to worry about what other functions might be relying on them. While we were on the subject of the member variables of StockItem, we saw how we could use a short to store a price. By expressing the price in cents, rather than dollars and cents, any price up to $327.67 could be stored in such a variable.

As we continued with the analysis of how the StockItem objects would be used, we discovered that our example program actually needed a vector of such objects, one for each different item in the stock. We also needed some way to read the information for these StockItem objects from a disk file, so we wouldn't have to type it in every time we started the program up. So the next program we examined provided this function via a C++ library class we hadn't seen before: ifstream (for input from a file). We also added a new function called Read to use this new class to read information for a StockItem from the file containing that information.

While looking at the implementation of the new Read member function, we ran into the idea of a *reference argument*. This is an argument that is another name for the caller's variable, rather than a copy of that variable (a *value argument*). This makes it possible to change the caller's variable by changing the value of the argument in the function. In most cases, we don't want to be able to change the caller's variable, but it is essential when reading from a stream. Otherwise, we'd get the same data every time we read something from the stream. Therefore, we have to use a reference argument in this case, so that the stream's internal state will be updated correctly when we retrieve data from it.

Then we got to the question of how we could tell when there was no data left in the input file; the answer was to call the ifstream member function fail, which returns nonzero if we have tried to read past the end of the file and zero if we haven't. We used a nonzero return value from fail to trigger a break statement, which terminates whatever loop contains the break. In this case, the loop was the one that read data from the input file, so the loop would stop whenever we got to the end of the input file or when we had read 100 records, whichever came first.

This led to a detailed investigation of whether the number of records read was always calculated correctly. The problem under discussion was the potential for a *fencepost error*, also known as an *off-by-one error*. After careful consideration, we concluded that the code as written was correct.

Having cleared up that question, we proceeded to some other scenarios that might occur in the grocery store for which this program theoretically was being written. All of the scenarios we

Problem
Algorithms
C++
Executable
Hardware

looked at had a common requirement: to be able to look up a StockItem, given some information about it. We first tried to handle this requirement by reading the UPC directly from each StockItem object in the vector. When we found the correct StockItem, we would display and update the inventory for that StockItem. However, this didn't compile, because we were trying to access private member variables of a StockItem object from a nonmember function, which is illegal. While we could have changed those variables from private to public, that would directly contradict the reason that we made them private in the first place; that is, to prevent external functions from interfering in the inner workings of our StockItem objects. Therefore, we solved the problem by adding some new member functions (CheckUPC and DeductSaleFromInventory) to check the UPC of a StockItem and manipulate the inventory information for each StockItem, respectively. At the same time, we examined a new data type, bool, which is limited to the two values true and false. The bool type is handy for keeping track of information such as whether we have found the StockItem object we are seeking and for communicating such information back to a calling function.

While making these changes, we noticed that the original version of the test program wasn't very helpful to its user; it didn't tell the user whether the UPC was any good, the name of the item, or how much inventory was available for sale. So we added some more member functions (GetInventory and GetName) to allow this more user-friendly information to be displayed.

Then we progressed to the second of the grocery store scenarios, in which the task was to find the price of an item, given its UPC. This turned out to be very similar to the previous problem of finding an item to update its inventory. Therefore, it was a pretty obvious step to try to make a function out of the "find an item by UPC" operation, rather than writing the code for the search over again. Since we're doing object-oriented programming, such a function should probably be a member function. The question was "of which class?" It couldn't be a member function of StockItem, because the whole idea of this function was to locate a StockItem. A member function of StockItem needs a StockItem object to work on, but we didn't have the StockItem object yet.

The solution was to make another class, called Inventory, which had member functions to load the inventory information in from the disk file (LoadInventory) and search it for a particular StockItem (FindItem). Most of this class was pretty simple, but we did run into an interesting design question: What should the FindItem function return if the UPC didn't match anything in the inventory? After some consideration, we

Problem
Algorithms
C++
Executable
Hardware

decided to use a *null object* of the class StockItem; that is, one that exists solely to serve as a placeholder representing a nonexistent object. This solution required adding an IsNull member function to the StockItem class, so that the user of FindItem could determine whether the returned object was "real" or just an indication of an incorrect UPC.

Then we updated the test program to use this new means of locating a StockItem. Since the new version of the test program could perform either of two functions (price check or sale), we also added some output and input statements to ask the user what he wanted to do. To make this process more flexible, we allowed the user to type in either an upper- or lowercase letter to select which function to perform. This brought up the use of the "logical OR" operator || to allow the controlled block of an if statement to be executed if either (or both) of two expressions is true. We also saw how to combine an else with a following if statement, when we wanted to select among more than two alternatives.

We needed two more functions to make this new version of the application program work correctly: one to update the item in the inventory (Inventory::UpdateItem(StockItem Item)) and one to get the UPC of a StockItem (StockItem::GetUPC()). The reason that we had to add these new functions to the interfaces of Inventory and StockItem, respectively, is that we were no longer operating on the "real" StockItem, as we had been when we accessed the inventory vector directly in the previous version of the application program. Instead, we were getting a copy of the StockItem from the Inventory object and changing that copy. Thus, to have the final result put back into the Inventory object, we had to add the UpdateItem member function of Inventory, which overwrote the original StockItem with our changed version. The GetUPC function's role in all this was to allow the UpdateItem function to look up the correct StockItem to be replaced without the main program having to pass the UPC in explicitly; instead, the GetUPC function allowed the UpdateItem function to retrieve the correct UPC from the updated object provided by the main program.

This brought us to the final scenario, which required us to look up the inventory for an item, given its UPC. As it happened, we had already solved that problem by the simple expedient of displaying the name and inventory of the StockItem as soon as it was located.

Finally, I mentioned a few other factors, such as alternative means of looking up an item without knowing its UPC, that would be important in writing a real application program and noted that we couldn't go into them here due to space limitations.

Problem
Algorithms
C++
Executable
Hardware

Exercises

1. In a real inventory control program, we would need to do more than merely read the inventory information in from a disk file, as we have done in this chapter. We'd also want to be able to write the updated inventory back to the disk file. This requires the use of an ofstream object, which is exactly analogous to an ifstream object except that it allows us to write to a file rather than reading from one as an ifstream allows. Modify the header files item5.h and invent1.h to include the declarations of the new functions StockItem::Write and Inventory::StoreInventory, which are needed to support this new ability.

2. Implement the new functions that you declared in Exercise 1. Then update the test program to write the changed inventory to a new file. To connect an ofstream called OutputStream to a file named test.out, you could use the line

    ofstream OutputStream("test.out");

Answers to the preceding exercises can be found at the end of the chapter.

Problem
Algorithms
C++
Executable
Hardware

3. Suppose that the store that is using our inventory control program adds a new pharmacy department. Most of their items are nonprescription medications that can be handled with the StockItem class we've already created, but their prescription drug items need to be handled more carefully. This means that the DeductSaleFromInventory member function has to ask for a password before allowing the sale to take place. Create a DrugStockItem class that enforces this new rule.

4. The store also needs some way to keep track of its employees' hours so it can calculate their pay. We'll assume that the employees are paid their gross wages, ignoring taxes. These wages are calculated as follows:

    1. Managers are paid a flat amount per week, calculated as their hourly rate multiplied by 40 hours.
    2. Hourly employees are paid a certain amount per hour, no matter how many hours are worked (i.e., overtime is not paid at a higher rate).

    Write an Employee class that allows the creation of Employee objects with a specified hourly wage level and either "manager" or "hourly" salary rules. The pay for each object is to be calculated via a CalculatePay member function that uses the "manager" or "hourly" category specified when the object was created. You should use the float data type to store the pay rate and to calculate the total pay; this behaves just like a short except that it can store values with fractional parts as well as whole numbers.

Conclusion

In this chapter, we've delved into the concepts and implementations of classes and objects, which are the constructs that make C++ an object-oriented language. Of course, we have only scratched the surface of these powerful topics; in fact, we'll spend the rest of this book on the fundamentals of classes and objects. Unfortunately, it's impossible to cover these constructs and all of their uses in any one book, no matter how long or detailed it may be, and I'm not going to try to do that. Instead, we'll continue with our in-depth examination of the basics of object-oriented programming. In the next chapter, we'll start on the task of creating a string class like the one that we've been using so far in this book.

```
Problem
Algorithms
C++
Executable
Hardware
```

Answers to Selected Exercises

1. Here is the new function declaration that needs to be added to the StockItem interface definition (from code\item6.h):

    void Write(ofstream& s);

    and the one to be added to the Inventory interface definition, (from code\invent2.h):

    void StoreInventory(ofstream& OutputStream);

2. Figure 6.32 shows the implementation of the Write member function for StockItem.

```
void StockItem::Write(ofstream& s)
{
    s << m_Name << endl;
    s << m_InStock << endl;
    s << m_Price << endl;
    s << m_Distributor << endl;
    s << m_UPC << endl;
}
```

Figure 6.32: The Write member function for the StockItem class (from code\item6.cc)

Figure 6.33 is the implementation of the StoreInventory member function of the Inventory class.

```
void Inventory::StoreInventory(ofstream& OutputStream)
{
    short i;

    for (i = 0; i < m_StockCount; i ++)
        m_Stock[i].Write(OutputStream);
}
```

Problem
Algorithms
C++
Executable
Hardware

Figure 6.33: The StoreInventory member function for the Inventory class (from code\invent2.cc)

As you can see, neither of these is tremendously complex or, for that matter, very different from its counterpart used to read the data in from the file in the first place.

Finally, Figure 6.34 shows the changes needed to the application program to write the updated inventory back to a new file.

```
ofstream OutputStream("shop2.out");
MyInventory.StoreInventory(OutputStream);
```

Figure 6.34: The changes to the application program (from code\itemtst6.cc)

Of course, in a real program, it would probably be better to write the updated inventory back to the original file, so that the next time we ran the program the updated inventory would be used. However, in the case of a test application, it's simpler to

avoid modifying the input file so we can run the same test again
if necessary.

Assuming that you've installed the software from the CD-
ROM in the back of this book, you can try out my solution to
these two exercises. First, you have to compile it by changing to
the normal subdirectory under the main directory where you
installed the software and typing mk itemtst6. Then type itemtst6 to
run the program normally. To run it under gdb, make sure you
are in the normal subdirectory, then type trace itemtst6. The
program will start up and show you the first line of executable
code. Type z and hit ENTER to execute each line from then on;
when the program asks for a UPC, you can use 7904886261,
which is the (made-up) UPC for "antihistamines". The values of
the relevant variables will be displayed immediately before the
execution of each remaining line in main. When you get to the
end of the program (or when you're tired of tracing), type q (for
quit) and hit ENTER to exit from the debugger.

```
Problem
Algorithms
C++
Executable
Hardware
```

Chapter 7

Stringing Along

You may recall the discussion near the beginning of Chapter 6 of *native* vs. *user-defined* variable types. I provided a list of native C++ variable types; namely, char, short, long, float, double, bool, and int. A logical question to ask is, What about strings and vectors? After all, we've been using those data types for a long time.[1] One possible explanation is that C++ has added these very useful data types to the list of types provided in C, but that's not the case. No, as I've hinted earlier, string is actually a class like StockItem rather than a native type. In this chapter we're going to see exactly how to implement the string class we've been using.

Objectives of This Chapter

By the end of this chapter, you should

1. Understand how variables of the string class are created, destroyed, and assigned to one another.
2. Understand how to assign memory to variables where the amount of memory needed is not known until run time.
3. Understand how literal C strings can be used to initialize variables of the string class.

---

1. To be very precise, vector isn't a data type, but a specification from which a number of data types can be constructed as needed. In C++, such a specification is called a template; unfortunately, we won't be able to examine the construction of templates in this book, due to space limitations.

Playing Out the string

Before we get into how to create the string class we've been using in this book, I should explain why string isn't a native type in the first place: It's to keep the C++ language itself as simple as possible. One of the design goals of C++, as of C, was to allow the language to be moved (**ported**, in the jargon) from one machine type to another as easily as possible. Since strings, vectors, and so on can be written in C++ (i.e., created out of the more elementary parts of the language), they don't have to be built in. This reduces the amount of effort needed to port C++. In addition, some applications don't need and can't afford anything but the barest essentials. The biggest class of such applications runs on "embedded" CPUs such as those in cameras, VCRs, elevators, or microwave ovens, which are much more common than "real" computers. However, this still leaves the question of why these data types aren't part of a standard library that can be used when necessary. Bjarne says in his book *Design and Evolution of C++* that it might very well have been a mistake to have released C++ to the general public without this library; I tend to agree. In any event, this situation will be remedied when the C++ standard is adopted, which as mentioned is scheduled to occur sometime next year (1998).

```
Problem
Algorithms
C++
Executable
Hardware
```

Even though strings aren't native, we've been using them for some time already without realizing that they're not native variables. Thus it should be fairly obvious that this class has to provide the facilities of a concrete data type; that is, one whose objects can be created, copied, assigned, and destroyed as though they were native variables. You may recall from the discussion starting in the section titled "Common Behavior" in Chapter 6 that such data types must have certain member functions. Here's the description of each of these member functions:

1. A *default constructor* creates an object when there is no initial value specified for the object.
2. A *copy constructor* makes a new object with the same contents as an existing object of the same type.
3. An *assignment operator* sets an existing object to the value of another object of the same type.
4. A *destructor* cleans up when an object expires; for a local object, this occurs at the end of the block where it was created.

In our StockItem and Inventory class definitions, the compiler-generated versions of these functions were fine for all but the default constructor. In the case of the string class, though, we're going to have to create our own versions of all four of these functions, for reasons that will become apparent as we examine their implementations in this chapter and the next one.

Before we can implement these member functions for our string class, we have to define exactly what a string is. The string class is a data type that gives us the following capabilities in addition to those facilities that every concrete data type provides.

1. We can set a string to a literal value like "abc".
2. We can display a string on the screen with the << operator.
3. We can read a string in from the keyboard with the >> operator.
4. We can compare two strings to find out whether they are equal.
5. We can compare two strings to find out which is "less than" the other; that is, which one would come first in the dictionary.

We'll see how all of these capabilities work sometime in this chapter or the next one, but for now let's start with Figure 7.1, a simplified version of the interface specification for the string class, which includes the specification of the four member functions needed for a concrete data type as well as a special constructor that is specific to the string class. I strongly recommend that you print out the files that contain this interface and its implementation, as well as the test program, for reference as you are going through this part of the chapter; those files are string1.h, string1.cc, and strtst1.cc, respectively.

Problem
Algorithms
C++
Executable
Hardware

```
class string
{
public:
    string();
    string(const string& Str);
    string& operator = (const string& Str);
    ~string();

    string(char* p);

private:
    short m_Length,
    char* m_Data;
};
```

Figure 7.1: The string class interface, initial version (code\string1.h)

The first four member functions in that interface are the standard concrete data type functions. In order, they are

1.   The *default constructor*
2.   The *copy constructor*
3.   The *assignment operator*, operator =
4.   The *destructor*

Figure 7.2 shows all of the code that implements this initial
version of our string class at once, before we start to analyze it.

```cpp
#include <string.h>
#include "string1.h"

string::string()
: m_Length(1),
  m_Data(new char [m_Length])
{
    memcpy(m_Data,"",m_Length);
}

string::string(const string& Str)
: m_Length(Str.m_Length),
  m_Data(new char [m_Length])
{
    memcpy(m_Data,Str.m_Data,m_Length);
}

string::string(char* p)
: m_Length(strlen(p) + 1),
  m_Data(new char [m_Length])
{
    memcpy(m_Data,p,m_Length);
}

string& string::operator = (const string& Str)
{
   if (&Str != this)
      {
      delete [ ] m_Data;
      m_Length = Str.m_Length;
      m_Data = new char [m_Length];
      memcpy(m_Data,Str.m_Data,m_Length);
      }
   return *this;
}

string::~string()
{
    delete [ ] m_Data;
}
```

Problem
Algorithms
C++
Executable
Hardware

Figure 7.2: The initial implementation for the string class (code\string1.cc)

Now let's start by looking at the default constructor. Figure 7.3 shows its implementation.

```
string::string()
: m_Length(1),
    m_Data(new char [m_Length])
{
    memcpy(m_Data,"",m_Length);
}
```

Figure 7.3: The default constructor for the string class (from code\string1.cc)

The member initialization list in this constructor contains two expressions. The first of them, m_Length(1), isn't very complicated at all. It simply sets the length of our new string to 1. However, this may seem a bit odd: Why do we need any characters at all for a string that has no value? The answer to this riddle is quite simple: To make our strings as compatible as possible with preexisting C functions that work on C strings, we need to include the null byte that terminates all C strings. So we need to reserve one more byte of memory for a string's data than is needed to hold the characters that we actually want to store. In the current case of a zero-character string, this means that even though we have no actual data, we need one byte of storage for the null byte.

It's important to note that this is an example where the order of execution of member initializer expressions is important: we definitely want m_Length to be initialized before m_Data, because the amount of data being assigned to m_Data depends on the value of m_Length. As you may remember from Chapter 6, the order in which the initialization expressions are executed is dependent **not** on the order in which they are written in the list but on the order in which the member variables being initialized are declared in the class interface definition. Therefore, it's important to make sure that the order in which those member variables are declared is correct. In this case, it is, because m_Length is declared before m_Data in the interface file string1.h.

Before proceeding to the next member initialization expression, let's take a look at the characteristics of the variables that we're using here. The scope of these variables, as we know from our previous discussion of the StockItem class, is class scope; hence, each object of the string class has a set of these variables, accessible from member functions of the class as though they were global variables.

However, an equally important characteristic of each of these variables is its data type. The type of m_Length is short, which is a type

Problem
Algorithms
C++
Executable
Hardware

we've encountered before — a 16-bit integer variable that can hold a number between -32768 and 32767. But what about the type of the other member variable, m_Data, which is listed in Figure 7.1 as char*? We know what a char is, but what does that * mean?

Passing Along a Few Pointers

The star means **pointer**, which is just another term for a memory address. In particular, char* (pronounced "char star") means "pointer to a char".[2] This is considered one of the most difficult concepts for beginning programmers to grasp, but you shouldn't have any trouble understanding its definition if you've been following the discussion so far: A pointer is the address of some data item in memory. That is, to say "a variable points to a memory location" is almost exactly the same as saying "a variable's value is the address of a memory location". In the specific case of a variable x of type char*, for example, to say "x points to a C string" is exactly the same as saying "x contains the address of the first byte of the C string."[3] The m_Data variable is used to hold the address of the first char of the data that a string contains; the rest of the characters follow the first character at consecutively higher locations in memory.

Problem
Algorithms
C++
Executable
Hardware

If this sounds familiar, it should; a literal C string like "hello" (Chapter 3) consists of a number of chars in consecutive memory locations. It should come as no surprise then when I tell you that a literal C string has the type char*.

As you might infer from these cases, our use of one char* to refer to multiple chars isn't an isolated example. Actually, it's quite a widespread practice in C++, which brings up an important point: A char*, or any other type of pointer for that matter, has two different possible meanings in C++.[4] One of these meanings is the obvious one of signifying the address of a single item of the type the pointer points to. In the case of a char*, that means the address of a char.

---

2. By the way, char* can also be written as char *, but I find it clearer to attach the * to the data type being pointed to.

3. C programmers are likely to object that a pointer has some properties that differ from those of a memory address. Technically, they're right, but in the specific case of char* the differences between a pointer and a memory address will never matter to us. Even when we use other types of pointers in later chapters, the differences still won't matter, so we can safely avoid adding yet another source of complexity to this discussion.

4. As this implies, it's possible to have a pointer to any type of variable, not just to a char. For example, a pointer to a short would have the type short*, and similarly for pointers to any other data type, as we'll see later in this book.

However, in the case of a literal C string, as well in the case of our m_Data member variable, we use a char* to indicate the address of the first char of an indeterminate number of chars. Any chars after the first one occupy consecutively higher addresses in memory. Most of the time, this distinction has little effect on the way we write programs, but sometimes we have to be sensitive to this "multiple personality" of pointers; we'll run across one of these cases later in this chapter.

While we're on the subject of that earlier discussion of literal C strings, you may recall that I bemoaned the fact that such literal C strings use a 0 byte to mark the end of the literal value rather than keeping track of the length separately. Nothing can be done about that decision now, at least as it applies to literal C strings. In the case of the string class, however, the implementation is under our control rather than the language designer's. Therefore, I've decided to use a length variable (m_Length) along with the variable that holds the address of the first char of the data (m_Data).

In other words, what we're doing in this exercise is synthesizing a new data type called string. A string needs a length and a set of characters to represent the actual data in the string. The short named m_Length is used in the string class to keep track of the number of characters in the data part of the string. The char* named m_Data is used to hold the address of the first character of the data part of the string.

Problem
Algorithms
C++
Executable
Hardware

The next member initialization expression, m_Data(new char [m_Length]), takes us on another of our side trips. This one has to do with the dreaded topic of dynamic memory allocation.

The Dynamic Duo: new **and** delete

So far, we've encountered two storage classes: static and auto. As you might recall from the discussion in Chapter 5, static variables are allocated memory when the program is linked, while the memory for auto variables is assigned to them at entry to the block where they are defined. However, both mechanisms have a major limitation: The amount of memory needed is fixed when the program is compiled. In the case of a string, we need to allocate an amount of memory that cannot be known until the program is executed, so we need another storage class.

As you will be happy to learn, there is indeed another storage class called **dynamic storage** which enables us to decide the amount of memory to allocate at run time.[5] To allocate memory dynamically, we use the new operator, specifying the data type of the memory to be allocated and the number of elements that we need. In our example member initialization expression, m_Data(new char [m_Length]), the type is char and the count is m_Length. The result of calling new is a *pointer* to the specified data type. In this case, since we want to store chars, the result of calling new is a pointer to a char, that is, a char*. This is a good thing, because char* is the type of the variable m_Data that we're initializing to the address that is returned from new. So the result of the member initialization expression we're examining is to set m_Data to the value returned from calling new. That value is the address of a newly assigned block of memory that can hold m_Length chars. In the case of the default constructor, we've asked for a block of 1 byte, which is just what we need to hold the contents of the zero-length C string that represents the value of our empty string.

It may not be obvious why we need to call new to get the address where we will store our data. Doesn't a char* always point to a byte in memory? Yes, it does; the problem is *which* byte. We can't use static (link time) or auto (function entry time) allocation for our string class, because each string can have a different number of characters.

Problem
Algorithms
C++
Executable
Hardware

Therefore, we have to assign the memory after we find out how many characters we need to store the value of the string. The new operator reserves some memory and returns the address of the beginning of that memory. In this case, we assign that address to our char* variable called m_Data. An important point to note here is that in addition to giving us the address of a section of memory, new also gives us the right to use that memory for our own purposes. That same memory area will not be made available for any other use until we say we're done with it by calling another operator called delete.

The purpose of the only statement inside the default constructor proper, memcpy(m_Data,"",m_Length);, is to copy the null byte from the C string "" to our newly allocated area of memory. The function memcpy (short for "memory copy") is one of the C *standard library* functions for C string and memory manipulation. As you can see, it takes three arguments. The first argument is a pointer to the destination; that is, the address that will receive the data. The second argument is a pointer to the source of the data; this, of course, is the address that we're copying from (i.e., the address of the null byte in the "", in our example). The last argument is the number of bytes to copy.

---

5. This terminology doesn't exactly match the official nomenclature used by Bjarne Stroustrup to describe dynamic memory allocation. However, every C and C++ programmer will understand you if you talk about dynamic storage, and I believe that this terminology is easier to understand than the official terminology.

In other words, memcpy reads the bytes that starts at the address specified by its input argument (in this case, "") and writes a copy of those bytes to addresses starting at the address specified by its output argument (in this case, m_Data). The amount copied is specified by the length argument (in this case, m_Length). Effectively, therefore, memcpy copies a certain amount of data from one place in memory to another. In this case, it copies 1 byte from the address of the literal C string "" to the address pointed to by m_Data (that is, the place where we're storing the data that makes up the value of our string).

As the call to memcpy is the only statement in the constructor proper, it's time to see what we have accomplished. The constructor has initialized a string by

1. Setting the length of the string to the effective length of a null C string, "", including the terminating null byte (i.e., 1 byte).
2. Allocating memory for a null C string.
3. Copying the contents of a null C string to the allocated memory.

Now let's continue with our examination of the string::string() constructor. Its final result is a string with the value "", whose memory layout might look like Figure 7.4.[6]

Problem
Algorithms
C++
Executable
Hardware

Address	Name	string n
12340000	m_Length	0001
12340002	m_Data	1234febc
1234febc	(none)	00

Figure 7.4: An empty string in memory

Using the default constructor is considerably easier than defining it. As we have seen in Chapter 6, the default constructor is called whenever we declare an object without specifying any data to initialize it with; for example, in the line string s; in Figure 7.5, which

---

6. By the way, Figure 7.4 is pretty close to the representation of an empty string in memory, although the details will vary according to the compiler you're using. Also, the reason for the different numbers of digits in the representations of m_Length, m_Data, and the data for the null C string is to indicate how long those data items are.

is the first test program that we will use to illustrate the functioning of the string class.[7]

```
#include "string1.h"

int main()
{
    string s;
    string n("Test");
    string x;

    s = n;
    n = "My name is: ";

    x = n;
    return 0;
}
```

Figure 7.5: Our first test program for the string class (code\strtst1.cc)

In case it's still not clear why the line string s; calls the default constructor string::string(), here's the detailed explanation.

Problem
Algorithms
C++
Executable
Hardware

1.   The line string s; means that we want to create a variable of type string with the name s.
2.   Therefore, since string is not a native data type, the compiler looks for a function called string::string, which would create a string. It finds one because we've included the file string1.h in our example program; the contents of that file are listed in Figure 7.1.
3.   However, we can have several functions named string::string, with different argument lists, because there are several possible ways to supply the initial data for a string we're creating. In this case, we aren't supplying any initial data, so the default constructor string::string() is the only possibility.
4.   Since that function string::string() is declared in the header file, the line string s; is translated to a call to that function.

I should point out here that the only file that the compiler needs to figure out how to compile the line string s; is the header file, string1.h. The actual implementation of the string class in string1.cc isn't required, because all the compiler cares about when compiling a program

---

7. Although this test program doesn't do anything useful, it does illustrate how we can use the member functions that we're analyzing in this chapter, so pay attention.

using classes is the contract between the class implementer and the user; that is specified by the header file. The actual implementation in string1.cc that fulfills this contract isn't needed until the program is linked to make an executable. At that point, the linker will complain if it can't find an implementation of any function that we've referred to.

Caution: Construction Area

Now that we've disposed of the default constructor, let's take a look at the line in the string interface definition (Figure 7.1) that says string(char* p);.[8] This is the declaration for another constructor. Unlike the default constructor we've examined, this one has an argument, char* p.[9]

As we saw in Chapter 6, the combination of the function name and argument types is called the *signature* of a function. Two functions that have the same name but differ in the type of at least one argument are distinct functions, and the compiler will use the difference(s) in the type(s) of the argument(s) to figure out which function with a given name should be called in any particular case. Of course, this leads to the question of why we would need more than one string constructor; they all make strings, don't they?

Yes, they do, but not from the same "raw material". It's true that every constructor in the string class makes a string, but each constructor has a unique argument list, which determines exactly how the new string will be constructed. The default constructor always makes an empty string (like the C string ""), whereas the constructor string(char* p) takes a C string as an argument and makes a string that has the same value as that argument.

Figure 7.6 shows the implementation for the constructor that takes a char* argument.

Problem
Algorithms
C++
Executable
Hardware

---

8. I know we've skipped the copy constructor, the assignment operator, and the destructor. Don't worry; we'll get to them later.

9. There's nothing magical about the name p for a pointer. You could call it George if you wanted to, but it would just confuse people. The letter p is often used for pointers, especially by programmers who can't type, which unfortunately is fairly common.

```
string::string(char* p)
: m_Length(strlen(p) + 1),
  m_Data(new char [m_Length])
{
    memcpy(m_Data,p,m_Length);
}
```

Figure 7.6: The char* constructor for the string class (from code\string1.cc)

You should be able to decode the header string::string(char* p): This function is a constructor for class string (because its class is string and its name is also string); its argument, named p, is of type char*. The first member initialization expression is m_Length(strlen(p) + 1). This is obviously initializing the string's length (m_Length) to something, but it's not quite as obvious what that something is. In particular, what's strlen?

As you may recall, C strings are stored as a series of characters terminated by a null byte (i.e., one with a 0 value). Therefore, unlike the case with our strings, where the length is available by looking at a member variable (m_Length), the only way to find the length of a C string is to search from the beginning of the C string until you get to a null byte. Since this is such a common operation in C, the C *standard library* provides the function strlen (short for "string length") for this purpose; it returns a result indicating the number of characters in the C string, *not* including the null byte.[10] So the member initialization expression m_Length(strlen(p) + 1), initializes our member variable m_Length to the length of the C string p, which we compute as the length reported by strlen (which doesn't include the terminating null byte) + 1 for the terminating null byte. We need this

Problem
Algorithms
C++
Executable
Hardware

---

10. This is probably a good place to clear up any confusion you might have about whether there are native and user-defined functions; there is no such distinction. However, the reason might not be what you expect. Rather than there being no user-defined functions, it's just the opposite. That is, functions are never native in the way that variables are: built into the language. Quite a few functions such as strlen and memcpy come *with* the language; that is, they are supplied in the standard libraries that you get when you buy the compiler. However, these functions are not privileged relative to the functions you can write yourself, unlike the case with native variables in C. In other words, you can write a *function* in C or C++ that looks and behaves exactly like one in the library, whereas it's impossible in C to add a type of *variable* that has the same appearance and behavior as the native types. The knowledge of the native variable types is built into the C compiler and cannot be changed by the programmer.

But *why* aren't there any native functions? Because the language was designed to be easy to move (or **port**) from one machine to another. This is easier if the compiler is simpler; hence, most of the functionality of the language is provided by functions that can be written in the "base language" the compiler knows about. This includes basic functions such as strlen and memcpy, which can be written in C. For purposes of performance, they are often written in assembly language instead, but that's not necessary to get the language running on a new machine.

information because we've decided to store the length explicitly in our string class rather than relying solely on a null byte to mark the end of the string, as is done in C.[11]

The next member initialization expression in the constructor, m_Data(new char [m_Length]), is the same as the corresponding expression in the default constructor. In this case, of course, the amount of memory being allocated is equal to the length of the input C string (including its terminating null byte) rather than the fixed value 1.

Now that we have the address of some memory that belongs to us, we can use it to hold the characters that make up the value of our string. The literal value that our test program uses to call this constructor is "Test", which is four characters long, not counting the null byte at the end. Since we have to make room for that null byte, the total is 5 bytes, so that's what we'd ask for from new. Assuming that the return value from new was 1234febc, Figure 7.7 illustrates what our new string looks like at this point.

Address	Name	string n
12340000	m_Length	0005
12340002	m_Data	1234febc
1234febc	(none)	????

Problem
Algorithms
C++
Executable
Hardware

Figure 7.7: string n during construction

The reason for the ???? is that we haven't set the data at that location to any value yet, so we don't know what it contains. Actually, this brings up a point we've skipped so far — where new gets the memory it allocates. The answer is that all of the "free" memory in your machine (i.e., memory that isn't used to store the operating system, the code for your program, statically allocated variables, and the stack) is lumped into a large area called the **heap**.

---

11. You may wonder why we even need to include the null byte if we're going to store the length also. Isn't this redundant? Yes, it is, but if we want to be able to use the gdb debugger to look at our strings, we have to include that null byte at the end. Otherwise, gdb won't know how to display them in an intelligible format.

This is where dynamically allocated memory "lives".[12] That's a loose way of stating what actually happens, which is that new cordons off part of the heap as being "in use" and returns a pointer to that portion.

So at this point, we have allocated m_Length bytes of memory, which start at the address in the pointer variable m_Data. Now we need to copy the current value of the input C string (pointed to by p) into that newly allocated area of memory. This is the job of the sole statement inside the constructor proper {}, memcpy(m_Data,p,m_Length);, which copies the data from the C string pointed to by p to our newly allocated memory.

The final result is that we have made (constructed) a string variable and set it to a value specified by a C string. To see what our string might look like in memory, see Figure 7.10. But how would this string::string(char* p) constructor operate in a program? To answer that question, Figure 7.8 gives us another look at our sample program.

```
#include "string1.h"

int main()
{
    string s;
    string n("Test");
    string x;

    s = n;
    n = "My name is: ";

    x = n;
    return 0;
}
```

Problem
Algorithms
C++
Executable
Hardware

Figure 7.8: A simple test program for the string class (code\strtst1.cc)

---

12. This is a bit of an oversimplification. In a "real" operating system, the heap will occupy most or all of the free memory in your computer. However, in MS-DOS, this is not true; the problem is that MS-DOS was devised to run on a very limited processor called the 8088, which had a maximum of 640K of available memory for programs. As a result of this historical limitation, a program that runs under MS-DOS can't access most of the memory in today's machines. Even if you have 32 MB of RAM, you'll run out of memory if you try to allocate more than a few hundred KB from the heap under MS-DOS. You'll be happy to know that the programs you compile with the compiler on the CD-ROM in the back of this book don't have this limitation, as they run under a "DOS extender", an operating system extension that was invented largely to solve this problem.

Constructive Criticism?

How does the compiler interpret the line string n("Test");? First, it determines that string is the name of a class. A function with the name of a class, as we have already seen, is always a constructor for that class. The question is which constructor to call; the answer is determined by the type(s) of the argument(s). In this case, the argument is a literal C string, which has the type char*. Therefore, the compiler looks for a constructor for class string that has an argument of type char*. Since there is such a constructor, the one we have just examined, the compiler generates a call to it. Figure 7.9 shows it again for reference while we analyze it.

```
string::string(char* p)
: m_Length(strlen(p) + 1),
    m_Data(new char [m_Length])
{
    memcpy(m_Data,p,m_Length);
}
```

Figure 7.9: The char* constructor for the string class, again (from code\string1.cc)

Problem
Algorithms
C++
Executable
Hardware

When the program executes, string::string(char* p) is called with the argument "Test". Let's trace the execution of the constructor, remembering that member initialization expressions are executed in the order in which the member variables being initialized are listed in the class interface, not necessarily in the order in which they are written in the member initialization list.

1. The first member initialization expression is m_Length(strlen(p) + 1). This initializes the member variable m_Length to the length of the C string whose address is in p, including the null byte that terminates the string. In this case, the C string is "Test", and its length, including the null byte, is 5.
2. Next, the member initialization expression m_Data(new char [m_Length]) is executed. This allocates m_Length (5, in this case) bytes of memory from the heap and initializes the variable m_Data to the address of that memory.
3. Finally, the statement memcpy(m_Data,p,m_Length); copies m_Length bytes (5, in this case) of data from the C string pointed to by p to the memory pointed to by m_Data.

When the constructor is finished, the string variable n has a length, 5, and contents, "Test", as shown in Figure 7.10. It's now ready for use in the rest of the program.

Tricky Assignment

Now let's look at the next line: s = n;. That looks harmless enough; it just copies one string, n, to another string, s.[13] But wait a second; how does the compiler know how to assign a value to a variable of a type we've made up?

Just as the compiler will generate a version of the default constructor if we don't define one (because every object has to be initialized somehow), the ability to assign one value of a given type to a variable of the same type is essential to being a data type. Therefore, the compiler will supply a version of operator =, the *assignment operator*, if we don't define one ourselves. In Chapter 6, we were able to rely on the compiler-generated operator =, which simply copies every member variable from the source object to the target object, but here we'll have to define our own.

Problem
Algorithms
C++
Executable
Hardware

Before we get into the details of writing our own operator =, I should mention that there are actually three ways that an assignment operator can be implemented:

1. (Native assignment) The knowledge of how to assign values of every native type is built into the compiler; whenever such an assignment is needed, the compiler emits prewritten code that copies the value from the source variable to the destination variable.

2. (Compiler-generated assignment) The knowledge of how to create an assignment operator for any class type is built into the compiler; the compiler generates code for an assignment operator that merely copies all of the members of the source variable to the destination variable. Note that this is slightly different from 1, where the compiler writes the instructions directly into the object file whenever the assignment is done. Here, it generates an assignment operator and then uses that operator whenever an assignment is done.

3. (User-defined assignment) This does exactly what we define it to do.

---

13. By the way, in case you're wondering what useful function this statement serves in the sample program, the answer is none. It's just to illustrate how operator = works.

Clearly the first of these is not relevant to the string class, because it isn't a native type. However, since the compiler-generated assignment operator was perfectly fine for our StockItem and Inventory objects, wouldn't it do the job here?

Unfortunately, no. The reason is that the member variable m_Data isn't really the data for the string; it's a pointer to (i.e., the address of) the data. The compiler-generated =, however, doesn't know how we're using m_Data, so it copies the pointer rather than the data. In our example, s = n;, the member variable m_Data in s would end up pointing to the same place in memory as the member variable m_Data in n. Thus, if either s or n did something to change "its" data, both strings would have their values changed, which isn't how we expect variables to behave.

To get a better handle on this problem, let's suppose that our string object n looks like Figure 7.10 in memory.

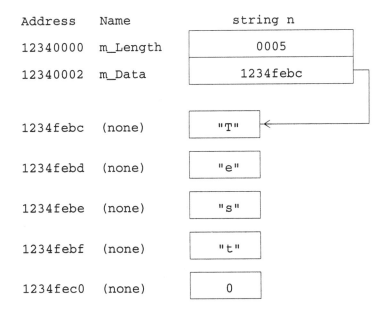

Figure 7.10: string n in memory

If we use the compiler-generated operator = to execute the statement s = n;, the result looks like Figure 7.11.

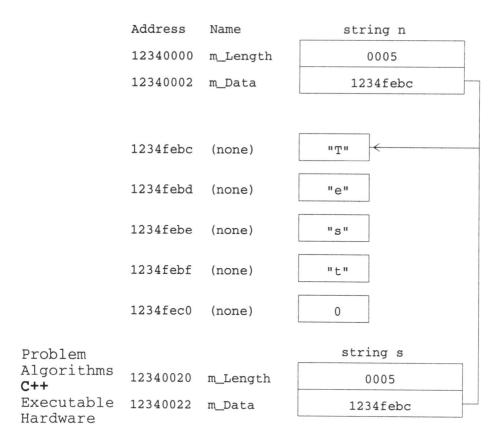

Figure 7.11: strings n and s in memory after compiler-generated =

In other words, the two strings s and n are like Siamese twins; whatever affects one of them affects the other since they share one copy of the data "Test". What we really want is two strings that are independent of one another so that we can change the contents of one without affecting the other one. Very shortly, we'll see how to accomplish this.

Assignment of Responsibility

Although it's actually possible to get the effect of two independent strings without the extra work of allocating memory and copying data every time an assignment is done, the mechanisms needed to do that are beyond the scope of this discussion.[14] By far the easiest way to have the effect of two independent strings is to actually make another copy of a string's data whenever we copy the string, and that's how we'll do it here. The results will be as indicated in Figure 7.12.

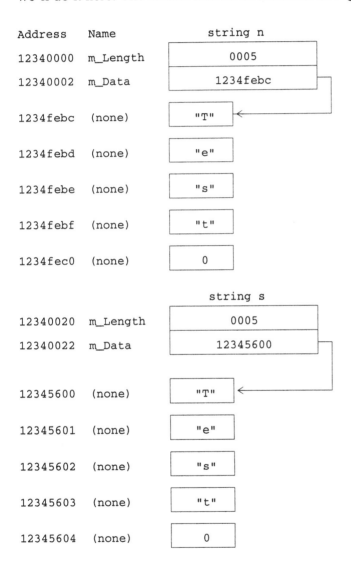

Problem
Algorithms
C++
Executable
Hardware

Figure 7.12: strings n and s in memory after custom =

---

14. However, it's an exercise in a later chapter, so it wouldn't hurt you to keep the possibility in mind.

With this arrangement, a change to one of the string variables will leave the other one unaffected, as the user would expect. To make this happen, we have to implement our own operator =, which will copy the data rather than just the pointer to the data. That's the operator declared in Figure 7.1 by the following line:

```
string& operator = (const string& Str);
```

What exactly does this mean? Well, as with all function declarations, the first part of the function declaration indicates the return type of the function. In this case, we're going to return a reference to the string to which we're assigning a value; that is, the string on the left of the = sign in an assignment statement. While this may seem reasonable at first glance, actually it's not at all obvious why we should return anything from operator =. After all, if we say a = b;, after a has been set to the same value as b, we're done. That operation is performed by the = operator, so no return value is needed after the assignment is completed.

However, there are two reasons why assignment of native types returns a value equal to the value that was assigned to the left-hand argument of =. First, it allows us to write an if statement such as if (a = b), when we really meant if (a == b). Of course, this will cause a bug in the program since these two statements don't have the same meaning. The first one sets a to b and returns the value of a; if a isn't 0, then the if condition is considered true. The latter statement, of course, compares a and b for equality and makes the if condition true if they are equal. To help prevent the error of substituting = for == in this situation, many compilers have a warning that indicates your use of, say, if (a = b). Unfortunately, this is a legal construction with native types and so cannot generate a compiler error. As it happens, using = in this way is an illegal operation with class objects, so even if you want to use this error prone construction, you can't. Since I never use that construction with native variables, I don't mind not having it for class objects.

The other potential use of the return value from operator = is to allow statements such as a = b = c; where the current value of c is assigned to b and the return value from that assignment is assigned to a. Although I don't use that construction either, since I find it more confusing than useful, I have been told that this ability will be required to use some of the library facilities specified in the forthcoming C++ standard. Therefore, it is my obligation to teach you the "right" way to write assignment operators so that you will be able to use these standard facilities with your classes.

Problem
Algorithms
C++
Executable
Hardware

Now we're up to the mysterious-looking construct operator =. This portion of the function declaration tells the compiler the name of the function we're defining; namely, operator =. The operator keyword lets the compiler know that the "name" of this function is actually an operator name, rather than a "normal" function name. We have to say operator = rather than merely =, for two reasons. First, normal function names can't have a = character in them, but are limited to upper- and lowercase letters, numbers, and the underscore (_). Second, when we're redefining *any* operator, even one (like new) whose name is made of characters allowed in identifiers, we have to tell the compiler that we're doing that on purpose. Otherwise, we'll get an error telling us that we're trying to define a function or variable with the same name as a keyword. By the way, as this explanation may suggest, we can't make up our own operators with strange names by prefixing those names with operator; we're limited to those operators that already exist in the C++ language.

We're ready to look at the argument to this function, specified by the text inside the parentheses, const string& Str. We've already seen in Chapter 6 that & in this context means that the argument to which it refers is a *reference argument* rather than a *value argument*.[15] In other words, the variable Str is actually just another name for the argument provided by the caller of this function, rather than being a separate local variable with the same value as the caller's argument. However, there is a new keyword in this expression, const, which is short for "constant". In this context, it means that we promise that this function will not modify the argument to which const refers, namely, string& Str. This is essential in the current situation, but it will take some discussion to explain why.

Problem
Algorithms
C++
Executable
Hardware

References Required

As you may recall from Chapter 5, when you call a function using a *value argument*, the argument that you give in the calling function isn't the one that the called function receives. Instead, a copy is made of the calling function's argument, and the called function works on

---

15. In this section, you're going to see a lot of hedging of the form "in this context, *x* means *y*". The reason is that C and C++ both reuse keywords and symbols in many different situations, often with different meanings in each situation. In my opinion, this is a flaw in the design of these languages, as it makes learning them more difficult. The reason for this reuse is that every time you add a keyword, it's possible that formerly working code will break as a result. Personally, I think this is an overrated problem compared to the problems caused by overuse of the same keywords. However, I don't have a lot of old C or C++ code to maintain, so maybe I'm biased.

the copy. While this is fine most of the time, in this case it won't work properly (for reasons that will be apparent shortly); instead, we have to use a reference argument. As we saw in the discussion of reference arguments in Chapter 6, such an argument is *not* a copy of the caller's argument but another name for the actual argument provided by the caller. This has a number of consequences. First, it's more efficient than a "normal" argument because the usual processing time needed to make a copy for the called function isn't required. Second, any changes made to the reference argument change the caller's argument as well. The use of this mechanism should be limited to those cases where it is really necessary, since it can confuse the readers of the calling function. There's no way to tell just by looking at the calling function that some of its variables can be changed by calling another function.

In this case, however, we have no intention of changing the input argument. All we want to do is to copy its length and data into the output string, the one for which operator = was called. Therefore, we tell the compiler, by using the const modifier, that we aren't going to change the input argument. This removes the drawback of non-const reference arguments, which is that they can change variables in the calling function with no indication of that possibility in the calling function. Therefore, using const reference arguments is quite a useful and safe way to reduce the number of time-consuming copying operations needed to make function calls.

Problem
Algorithms
C++
Executable
Hardware

The use of a const reference argument in this case is more than just efficient, however. As we'll see in the discussion in Chapter 8 under the heading "Temporary Help Wanted", such an argument allows us to assign a C string (i.e., bytes pointed to by a char*) to one of our string variables without having to write a special operator = for that purpose.

We now have enough information to decode the function declaration

string& string::operator = (const string& Str)

as illustrated in Figure 7.13.

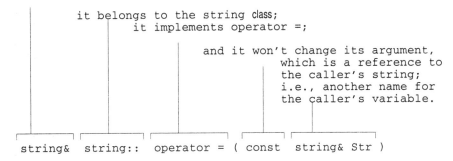

This function returns a reference to a string;

      it belongs to the string class;
           it implements operator =;

               and it won't change its argument,
                     which is a reference to
                     the caller's string;
                     i.e., another name for
                     the caller's variable.

```
string&  string::  operator = ( const  string& Str )
```

Figure 7.13: The declaration of operator = for the string class

Putting it all together, we're defining a function belonging to class string that returns a reference to a string. This function implements operator = and takes an argument named Str that's a constant reference to a string. That is, the argument Str is another name for the string passed to us by the caller rather than being a copy of the caller's string. Furthermore, we're vowing not to use this argument to change the caller's variable.

Hello, operator?

Problem
Algorithms
C++
Executable
Hardware

Now that we've dissected the header into its atomic components, the actual implementation of the function should be relatively trivial by comparison. But first there's a loose end to be tied up. That is, why was this function named string::operator = called in the first place? The line that caused the call was very simple: s = n;. There's no explicit mention of string or operator.

This is another of the ways in which C++ supports classes. Because you can use the = operator to assign one variable of a native type to another variable of the same type, C++ provides the same syntax for user-defined variable types. Similar reasoning applies to operators like >, <, and so on, for classes where these operators make sense.

When the compiler sees the statement s = n;, it proceeds as follows:

1. The variable s is an object of class string.
2. The statement appears to be an assignment statement (i.e., an invocation of the C++ operator named operator =) setting s equal to the value of another string variable named n.

3. Is there a definition of a member function of class string that implements operator = and takes one argument of class string?
4. Yes, there is. Therefore, translate the statement s = n; into a call to operator = for class string.
5. Compile that statement as though it were the one in the program.

Following this procedure, the correspondence between the tokens in the original program and the call to the member function should be fairly obvious, as we see them in Figure 7.14.[16]

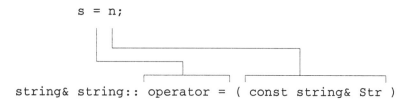

Figure 7.14: Calling the operator = implementation

Problem
Algorithms
C++
Executable
Hardware

But we've left out something. What does the string s correspond to in the function call to operator =?

What Is the Meaning of this?

The string s corresponds to a hidden argument whose name is the keyword this. Such an argument is automatically included in every call to a member function in C++.[17] Its type is always a constant pointer to an object of the class that a member function belongs to. In this case its type is const string*; that is, a constant pointer to a string. The const means that we can't change the value of this by assigning a new value to it. The value of this is the address of the class object for which the member function call was made. In this case, the statement s = n; was translated into s.operator = (n); by the compiler. Therefore, when the statement s = n; is being executed, the value of this is the address of the string s.

---

16. A **token** is the smallest part of a program that the compiler treats as a separate unit. It's analogous to a word in English, with a statement being more like a sentence. For example, string is a token, as are :: and (. On the other hand, x = 5; is a statement.

17. Actually, there is a kind of member function, called a static member function, that doesn't have a this pointer passed to it. We'll see how those functions work later, in Chapter 9.

To see why we need to be concerned about this, let's start analyzing the implementation of operator =. Figure 7.15 shows the code for that function.[18]

```
string& string::operator = (const string& Str)
{
    if (&Str != this)
        {
        delete [ ] m_Data;
        m_Length = Str.m_Length;
        m_Data = new char [m_Length];
        memcpy(m_Data,Str.m_Data,m_Length);
        }
    return *this;
}
```

Figure 7.15: The assignment operator (operator =) for the string class (from code\string1.cc)

Equality Now!

In the case of the string class, as in most cases, the only reasons why we have to worry about this are to be able to determine whether two objects that are referred to by different names are actually the same object and to return a reference to the left-hand object in an assignment statement. You can see both uses of this in the code for string::operator = (const string& Str). The first use is illustrated by the following line:

```
    if (&Str != this)
```

Most of this statement should be familiar by now. Like other if statements, it tests a condition for truth or falsity. The != is the comparison operator that tests for "not equal", and of course we've just seen that this is the address of the variable for which the operator = function was called. In the expression s = n, this would be the address of the variable s. However, that still leaves the expression &Str.

Problem
Algorithms
C++
Executable
Hardware

---

18. If you don't believe that the apparently mysterious argument this makes life a lot easier for us, look at Figure 7.16, which shows what Figure 7.15 might look like without the automatic provision of this by the compiler.

Unfortunately, & is one of the tokens that is used in several different ways depending on context; when it precedes the name of a variable without itself being preceded by a data type like string, it means "the address of the following variable". In this case, &Str means "the address of Str". The variable Str is the argument passed to us by the caller. Remember, as a reference argument Str is another name for the caller's variable, rather than a copy of it. Therefore, &Str is the address of the caller's variable (n, in our example).

Clearly, then, the expression if (&Str != this) is comparing the address of the caller's string (i.e., &Str) to this. As we just saw, this represents the address of the object that we're operating on; in the case of operator =, it's the address of (i.e., a pointer to) the string that is going to be changed by operator =. Therefore, this if statement is checking whether the string that was passed to us by the caller is a different string from the one to which the assignment is supposed to be made. For example, if the source line that caused operator = to be called was a = a;, then the if statement would be false and therefore the block controlled by the if wouldn't be executed. Of course, there's no reason to do anything other than return the value of a in that case. However, there are good reasons besides efficiency to check for the attempt to assign a string to itself; those reasons are the subject of one of the exercises in this chapter. For now, let's continue with the contents of the block controlled by the if, assuming that the two strings are actually distinct.

Problem
Algorithms
C++
Executable
Hardware

The first statement in the controlled block of the if statement is delete [ ] m_Data;. This corresponds to the new statement that we used to allocate memory in a constructor that explicitly allocates memory in which to store characters for a string, such as string::string(char* p) (Figure 7.6). That is, the delete operator returns the memory to the available pool called the *heap*. There are actually two versions of the delete operator: One version frees memory for a single data item, and the other frees memory for a group of items that are stored consecutively in memory. Here, we're using the version of the delete operator that frees a group of items rather than a single item, which we indicate by means of the [ ] after the keyword delete. The version of delete that frees only one item doesn't have the [ ].[19] So after this statement is executed, the memory that was allocated in the

---

19. By the way, this is one of the previously mentioned times when we have to explicitly deal with the difference between a pointer used as "the address of an item" and one used as "the address of some number of items"; the [ ] after delete tells the compiler that the latter is the current situation. The C++ standard specifies that any memory that was allocated via a new expression containing [ ] must be deleted via delete [ ].

constructor to hold the characters in our string has been handed back to the memory allocation routines for possible reuse at a later time.

Please delete Me, Let Me Go

A point that we should not overlook is the possibility of calling delete for a pointer that has never been assigned a value. Calling delete on a pointer that doesn't point to a valid block of memory allocated by new will cause the system to malfunction in some bizarre way, usually at a time considerably after the improper call to delete.[20] This occurs because the dynamic memory allocation system will try to reclaim the "allocated" memory pointed to by the invalid pointer by adding it back to the heap. Eventually, some other function will come along, ask for some memory, and be handed a pointer to this "available" block that is actually nothing of the sort. The result of trying to use this area of memory depends on which of three cases the erroneous address falls into: The first is that the memory at that address is inaccessible, the second is that the memory is already in use for some other purpose, and the third is that the invalid address points to data that is already in the heap.

Problem
Algorithms
C++
Executable
Hardware

In the first case, the function that tries to store its data in this inaccessible area of memory will cause a system crash or error message, depending on the system's ability and willingness to check for such errors. The "General Protection Fault" message so familiar to Windows users is caused by this sort of error. In the second case, the function that is the "legal" owner of the memory will find its stored values changed mysteriously and will misbehave as a result. In the third case, the heap management routines will probably get confused and start handing out wrong addresses. Errors of this kind are common in programs that use pointers heavily and are extremely difficult to find.

Another way to go wrong with dynamic memory allocation is the opposite one. Instead of trying to delete something that was never dynamically allocated, you can forget to delete something that *has* been dynamically allocated. This is called a **memory leak**; it's very insidious, because the program appears to work correctly when tested casually. The usual way to find these errors is to notice that the program runs apparently correctly for a (possibly long) time and then fails due to running out of available memory. I should mention here

---

20. There's an exception to this rule: Calling delete for a pointer with the value 0 will not cause any untoward effects, as such a pointer is recognized as "pointing to nowhere".

how we can tell that we've run out of memory: The new operator returns a pointer with a 0 value. By convention, a pointer with the value 0 means "a pointer that doesn't point to anything". Hence, 0 is a reasonable value to return when there is no memory left. Our sample programs don't check the return value from new, so they will go along merrily as though they have actually allocated memory successfully. The result will be a spectacular failure when we actually try to use the "allocated" memory at location 0. Of course, a real program should check for this problem and tell the user that no more memory is left (if no better solution is available). However, plenty of programs that have supposedly been working for a long time fail to check this situation sometimes.[21]

Given all of the ways to misuse dynamic memory allocation, we'll use it only when its benefits clearly outweigh the risks. To be exact, we'll restrict its use to controlled circumstances inside class implementations, to reduce the probability of such errors.

Problem
Algorithms
C++
Executable
Hardware

The error prone nature of dynamic memory allocation is ironic, since it would be entirely possible for the library implementers (that is, the people who write the functions that are used by new and delete) to prevent or at least detect the problem of deleting something you haven't allocated or failing to delete something that you have allocated. After all, those routines handle all of the memory allocation and deallocation for a C++ program, so there's no reason that they couldn't keep track of what has been allocated and not released.

Of course, an ounce of prevention is worth a pound of cure, so avoiding these problems by proper design is the best solution. As we'll see, it is possible to write programs so that this type of error is much less likely. Basically, this approach requires keeping all dynamic memory allocation inside class implementations, rather than exposing it to the application programmer. We're following this approach with our string class, and will see later how it can also be applied to other situations where it is less straightforward.

The Next Assignment

Having discussed some of the possible problems with dynamic allocation, let's continue with the code for operator = (Figure 7.15).

---

21. The forthcoming standard for the C++ language will change the behavior of new when no more memory is left. Instead of returning 0, new will notify the application programmer via a mechanism called an *exception*. Unfortunately, this mechanism is outside the scope of this book.

The next statement is m_Length = Str.m_Length;. This the first time we've used the . operator to access a member variable of an object other than the one for which the member function was called. Up until now, we've been satisfied to refer to a member variable such as m_Length just by that simple name, as we would with a local or global variable. The name m_Length is called an **unqualified name** because it doesn't specify which object we're referring to. The expression m_Length by itself refers to the occurrence of the member variable m_Length in the object for which the current function was called; i.e., the string whose address is this (the string s in our example line s = n;).

If you think about it, this is a good default because member functions refer to member variables of their "own" object more than any other kinds of variables. Therefore, to reduce the amount of typing the programmer has to do, whenever we refer to a member variable without specifying the object to which it belongs, the compiler will assume that we mean the variable that belongs to the object for which the member function was called (i.e, the variable whose address is the current value of this). However, when we want to refer to a member variable of an object other than the one pointed to by this, we have to indicate which object we're referring to, which we do by using the . operator. This operator means that we want to access the member variable (or function) whose name is on the right of the . for the object whose name is on the left of the .. Hence, the expression Str.m_Length specifies that we're talking about the occurrence of m_Length that's in the variable Str, and the whole statement m_Length = Str.m_Length; means that we want to set the length of "our" string (i.e., the one pointed to by this) to the length of the argument string Str.

Problem
Algorithms
C++
Executable
Hardware

Next, we use the statement m_Data = new char [m_Length]; to acquire the address of some memory that we will use to store our new copy of the data from Str. Along with the address, new gives us the right to use that memory until we free it with delete.

Then we use memcpy to copy the data from Str (i.e., the group of characters starting at the address stored in Str.m_Data) to our newly allocated memory, which of course is pointed to by m_Data (i.e., the occurrence of m_Data in the string being assigned to). Now our target string is a fully independent entity with the same value as the string that was passed in.

Finally, we return *this, which means "the object to which this points", i.e., a reference to the string whose value we have just set, so that it can be used in further operations.

Figure 7.16 shows what the code for operator = might look like if the this pointer weren't supplied automatically, both in the function declaration and as a qualifier for the member variable names.

By the way, I've introduced another new notation here: the operator –>. This does the same thing for pointer variables that . does for objects. That is, if the token on the right of –> is a member variable, that token refers to the specific member variable belonging to the object pointed to by the pointer on the left of –>. If the token on the right of –> is a member function, then it is called for the object pointed to by the pointer on the left of –>. For example, this–>m_Data means "the m_Data that belongs to the object pointed to by this".

```
string& string::operator = (const string* this, const string& Str)
{
    if (&Str != this)
        {
        delete [ ] this->m_Data;
        this->m_Length = Str.m_Length;
        this->m_Data = new char [this->m_Length];
        memcpy(this->m_Data,Str.m_Data,this->m_Length);
        }
    return *this;
}
```

Problem
Algorithms
C++
Executable
Hardware

Figure 7.16: A hypothetical assignment operator (operator =) for the string class with explicit this

Note that every reference to a member variable of the current object would have to specify this. That would actually be more significant in writing the code than the fact that we would have to supply this in the call. Of course, how we would actually supply this when calling the operator = function is also a good question. Clearly the necessity of passing this explicitly would make for a messier syntax than just s = n;.

The Terminator

Now that we have seen how operator = works in detail, let's look at the next member function in the initial version of our string class, the *destructor*. A destructor is the opposite of a constructor; that is, it is responsible for deallocating any memory allocated by the constructor and performing whatever other functions have to be done before a variable dies. It's quite rare to call the destructor for a variable explicitly; as a rule, the destructor is called automatically when the variable goes out of scope. As we've seen, the most common way for this to happen is that a function returns to its calling function. At that time, destructors are called for all local variables that have destructors, whereas local variables that don't have destructors, such as those of native types, just disappear silently.[22]

Because destructors are almost always called automatically when a variable goes out of scope rather than by an explicit statement written by the programmer, the only information guaranteed to be available to a destructor is the address of the variable to be destroyed. For this reason, the C++ language specifies that a destructor cannot have arguments. This in turn means that there can be only one destructor for any class, since there can be at most one function in a given class with a given name and the same type(s) of argument(s) (or, as in this case, no arguments).

As with the constructor(s), the destructor has a special name to identify it to the compiler. In this case, it's the name of the class with the token ~ (the tilde) prefixed to it, so the destructor for class string is named ~string.[23] The declaration of this function is the next line in Figure 7.1, ~string();. Its implementation looks like Figure 7.17.

Problem
Algorithms
C++
Executable
Hardware

```
string::~string()
{
    delete [ ] m_Data;
}
```

Figure 7.17: The destructor for the string class (from code\string1.cc)

This function doesn't use any new constructs; we've already seen that the delete [ ] operator frees the memory allocated to the pointer variable it operates on. In this case, that variable is m_Data, which holds the address of the first one of the group of characters that make up the actual data contained by the string.

Now that we've covered nearly all of the member functions in the initial version of the string class, it's time for some review.

---

22. If we use new to allocate memory for a variable that has a destructor, then the destructor is called when that variable is freed by delete, as we'll see in Chapter 10.

23. In case you're wondering, this somewhat obscure notation was chosen because the tilde is used to indicate logical negation; that is, if some expression x has the logical value true, then ~x will have the logical value false, and vice-versa.

Review

We've almost finished building a concrete data type called the string class, which provides a means of storing and processing a group of characters similar to the facilities provided by a *C string*, but without some of the drawbacks of the latter data type. The fact that string is a concrete data type means that a string that is defined as a local variable in a function should be created when the function starts up and automatically deleted when the function ends. Also, we need to be able to copy a string to another string and have the two copies behave like independent variables, not linked together in the manner of Siamese twins.

The creation of an object is performed by a special member function called a *constructor*. Any class can have several constructors, one for each possible way that a newly created object can be initialized. So far, we've examined the interface and implementation of the *default constructor*, which takes no arguments, and a constructor that takes a char* argument. The former is needed to create a string that doesn't have an initial value, whereas the latter allows us to create a string that has the same contents as a C string. The default constructor is one of the required member functions in a concrete data type.

`Problem`
`Algorithms`
`C++`
`Executable`
`Hardware`

We've also seen that in the case of our string constructors, we need to know the order in which the member initialization expressions are executed; since this is dependent on the order of declaration of member variables, we have to make sure that those member variables are declared in the correct order for our member initialization expressions to work properly.

Continuing with the requirements for a concrete data type, we've implemented our own version of operator =, which can set one string to the same value as another string while leaving them independent of one another.

We've also created one other required member function for a concrete data type, the *destructor*, which is used to clean up after a string when it expires. This member function is called automatically for an auto variable at the end of the function where that variable is defined.

We're still short a *copy constructor*, which can create a string that has the same value as another preexisting string. This may sound just like operator =, but it's not exactly the same. While operator = is used to set a string that already exists to the same value as another extant string, the copy constructor creates a brand-new string with the same value as one that already exists. We'll see how this works in the next chapter.

In the meantime, let's take a look at some exercises intended to test your understanding of this material.

Exercises

1. What would happen if we compiled the program in Figure 7.18? Why?

```
class string
{
public:
    string();
    string(const string& Str);
    string(char* p);
    string& operator = (const string& Str);
    ~string();
private:
    short m_Length;
    char* m_Data;
};

int main()
{
    string s;
    string n("Test");
    string x;
    short Length;

    Length = n.m_Length;

    s = n;
    n = "My name is: ";

    x = n;
    return 0;
}
```

Problem
Algorithms
C++
Executable
Hardware

Figure 7.18: Exercise 1 (code\strex1.cc)

2. What would happen if we compiled the program in Figure 7.19? Why?

```
class string
{
public:
    string(const string& Str);
    string(char* p);
    string& operator=(const string& Str);
    ~string();
private:
    string();
    short m_Length;
    char* m_Data;
};

int main()
{
    string s("Test");
    string n;

    n = s;

    return 0;
}
```

Figure 7.19: Exercise 2 (code\strex2.cc)

Problem
Algorithms
C++
Executable
Hardware

3. What would happen if we compiled the program in Figure 7.20?
    Why?

```
class string
{
public:
    string();
    string(const string& Str);
    string(char* p);
    string& operator=(const string& Str);
private:
    ~string();
    short m_Length;
    char* m_Data;
};

int main()
{
    string s("Test");

    return 0;
}
```

Figure 7.20: Exercise 3 (code\strex3.cc)

4. What would happen if a user of our string class wrote an
    ·expression that tried to set a string variable to itself (e.g., a = a;)
    and we hadn't bothered to check for that situation in our
    operator = (Figure 7.15)?
5. What would happen if we compiled the program in Figure 7.21?
    Why?

```
class string
{
public:
    string(const string& Str);
    string(char* p);
    string& operator = (const string& Str);
    ~string();
private:
    string();
    short m_Length;
    char* m_Data;
};

int main()
{
    string n("Test");
    string x = n;

    n = "My name is: ";

    return 0;
}
```

Problem
Algorithms
C++
Executable
Hardware

Figure 7.21: Exercise 5 (code\strex5.cc)

Answers to the preceding exercises can be found at the end of the
chapter.

6. Write an essay explaining, in your own words, exactly why the
    compiler-generated assignment operator is acceptable for the
    StockItem class but not for the string class.
7. Write a version of operator = for the string class that copies a C
    string literal (i.e., the characters pointed to by a char*) to a string.
8. Consider the following function, and explain how it can produce
    the same result as the previous versions of operator < in fewer
    lines of code.

```
bool string::operator < (const string& Str)
{
    short Result;
    short CompareLength;
    short i;

    if (Str.m_Length < m_Length)
        CompareLength = Str.m_Length;
    else
        CompareLength = m_Length;

    i = 0;
    while ((i < CompareLength) && (m_data[i] == Str.m_data[i]))
        i++;

    if (i < CompareLength)
        return m_data[i] < Str.m_data[i];
    else
        return m_Length < Str.m_Length;
}
```

Figure 7.22: Exercise 9 (code\fastcomp.cc)

Problem
Algorithms
C++
Executable
Hardware

Conclusion

We've covered a lot of material about how a real, generally useful class such as string works in this chapter. In the next chapter, we'll continue with the saga of the string class.

Answers to Selected Exercises

1.   The output of the compiler should look something like this:

     strex1.cc: In function 'int main()':
     strex1.cc:21: member 'm_Length' is a private member of class 'string'

     This one is simple; since m_Length is a private member variable of string, a nonmember function such as main can't access it.

2.   The output of the compiler should look something like this:

     strex2.cc: In function 'int main()':
     strex2.cc:9: constructor 'string::string()' is private
     strex2.cc:17: within this context

strex2.cc:17: in base initialization for class 'string'

This is also pretty simple. Since the default constructor string::string() is in the private area, it's impossible for a nonmember function such as main to use it. Notice that there was no error message about string::string(char* p); that constructor is in the public area, so main is permitted to create a string from a C string. It's just the default constructor that's inaccessible.

3. The output of the compiler should look something like this:

strex3.cc:12: warning: 'class string' only defines a private destructor and has no friends[24]
strex3.cc: In function 'int main()':
strex3.cc:16: destructor for type 'string' is private in this scope

This answer is considerably less obvious than the previous ones. To be sure, the destructor is private and can't be called from main, but that doesn't explain why main is trying to call the destructor in the first place. The reason is that every auto variable of a type that has a destructor must have its destructor called at the end of that function.[25] That's part of the mechanism that makes our objects act like "normal" variables, which also lose their values at the end of the function where they are declared. In the case of a user-defined variable, though, more cleanup may be required. This is certainly true for strings, which have to deallocate the memory that they allocated to store their character data.

Therefore, you cannot create an object of a class whose destructor is private as an auto variable, as the automatic call of the destructor at the end of the scope would be illegal.

4. Let's take a look at the sequence of events that would have transpired if the user had typed a = a; and we hadn't taken the precaution of checking for that situation in the operator = code.[26]

The first statement to be executed would be delete [ ] m_Data;. This gives the memory that had been allocated to store characters in string a back to the operating system.

Problem
Algorithms
C++
Executable
Hardware

---

24. In case you're wondering what a friend is, it's a class or a function that has special access to the internal workings of another class. We'll get into that mechanism in Chapter 8.

25. To be more precise, the destructor is called at the end of the *scope* in which the variable was defined. It's possible for a variable to have scope smaller than an entire function; in that case, the variable is destroyed when its scope expires.

26. See Figure 7.15 for the code.

The second statement to be executed would be m_Length = Str.m_Length;. Since m_Length and Str.m_Length are actually the same memory location in this case, this statement wouldn't do anything.

The third statement to be executed would be m_Data = new char [m_Length];. This would allocate memory for the target string and assign it to the member variable m_Data.

The fourth statement to be executed would be memcpy(m_Data, Str.m_Data, m_Length);. This would copy m_Length bytes of data to the address stored in m_Data, which points to the newly allocated piece of memory, from the address stored in Str.m_Data, which points to . . . the same address. Remember, if this and &Str are the same, as they are in this case, then m_Data and Str.m_Data are two names for the same memory location. Therefore, this operation will have no effect. Furthermore, the preceding step has assigned the address of the newly allocated memory to m_Data, overwriting the previous contents of m_Data; that is, the address of the original contents of the string a. Therefore, the original value of a, which was pointed to by m_Data when we started, is no longer accessible. Even if we had a copy of that address, we couldn't use it because the memory to which it refers has already been returned to the operating system and no longer belongs to us.

The net result of all of this is that the m_Data member variable of string a would point to uninitialized data.

```
Problem
Algorithms
C++
Executable
Hardware
```

5. This one was a little tricky. I'll bet you thought that making the default constructor private would keep this from compiling, but it turns out that we're not using the default constructor. That should be obvious in the line string n("Test");, which clearly uses string::string(char* p). But what does the compiler do with the line string x = n;? You might think that it calls the default constructor to make x and then uses operator = to copy the value of n into it. If that were true, the private status of the default constructor would prevent the program from compiling. However, what actually happens is that the copy constructor string::string(const string&) is used to make a brand-new string called x with the same value as n. So, in this case, the private access specifier on the default constructor doesn't get in the way.

However, this leaves one question unanswered: Since there's an = sign in the statement string x = n;, why is a constructor called instead of operator =? Because we can't assign a value to a variable that doesn't exist before the beginning of the statement. Thus, when we define a variable and provide an initial value for it, as this statement does, we're actually calling a constructor to create the variable with that initial value, rather than constructing the variable first with no value and then calling operator =.

```
Problem
Algorithms
C++
Executable
Hardware
```

Chapter 8

Down the Garden Path

In this chapter we will complete our implementation of the string class. Along the way, we'll encounter a number of features of the C++ language that are often considered difficult and dangerous to use. However, as we'll see, when used properly these features of C++ can enable us as class designers to create classes that are safe and easy to use for our customers, the application programmers.

Objectives of This Chapter

By the end of this chapter, you should

1. Understand how to implement all the concrete data type functions for a class that uses pointers.
2. Have a string class that is useful in some real programming situations.
3. Understand how to write appropriate input and output functions (operator >> and operator <<) to handle the objects of our string class.
4. Understand how to use some additional C library functions such as memcmp and memset.
5. Understand the *array* data type and some of its hazards.
6. Understand how to use the friend declaration, which allows access to private members by selected nonmember functions.

For Reference Only

Now we're finally ready to examine exactly why the code for our operator = needs a *reference argument* rather than a *value argument*.

I've drawn two diagrams that illustrate the difference between a value argument and a reference argument. First, Figure 8.1 illustrates what happens when we call a function with a value argument of type string using the compiler-generated copy constructor.[1]

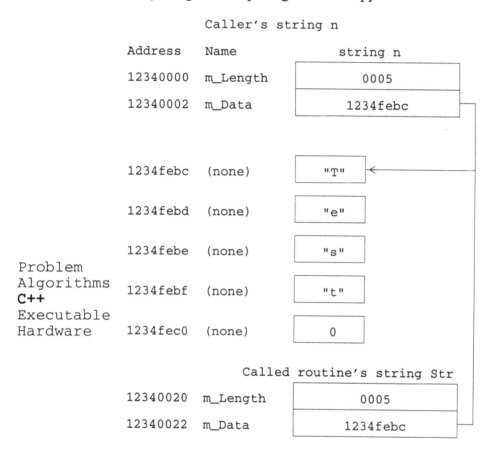

Figure 8.1: Call by value ("normal argument") using the compiler-generated copy constructor

In other words, with a value argument, the called routine makes a copy of the argument on its stack. This won't work properly with a string argument. Instead, it will destroy the value of the caller's variable upon return to the calling function. Why is this?

---

1. In case you were wondering where you'd seen this diagram before, it's the same as the one illustrating the problem with the compiler-generated operator =, Figure 7.11.

Unfair Copy

The problem occurs when the destructor is called at the end of a function's execution to dispose of the copy that was made of the input argument during the function call. Since the copy points to the same data as the caller's original variable, the destruction of the copy causes the memory allocated to the caller's variable to be freed prematurely.

This is due to the way in which a variable is copied in C++ by the compiler-generated *copy constructor*. This mechanism for variable copying uses the same basic approach as the compiler-generated operator =; it makes a copy of all of the parts of the variable (a so-called **memberwise copy**). In the case of our string variable, this results in copying only the length m_Length and the pointer m_Data, not the data that m_Data points to. That is, both the original and the copy refer to the same data, as indicated by Figure 8.1. If we were to implement our operator = with a string argument rather than a string&, then the following sequence of events would take place during the execution of the statement s = n;:

1. A default copy like the one illustrated by Figure 8.1 would be made of the input argument n, so that the variable Str in the operator = code would point to the same data as the caller's variable n.
2. The Str variable would be used in the operator = code.
3. The Str variable would be destroyed at the end of the operator = function. During this process, the destructor would free the memory that Str.m_Data points to by calling delete [].

Problem
Algorithms
C++
Executable
Hardware

Since Str.m_Data holds the same address as the caller's variable n.m_Data, the latter now points to memory that has been freed and may be overwritten or assigned to some other use at any time. This is a bug in the program caused by the string destructor being called for a temporary copy of a string that shares data with a caller's variable.

Figure 8.2 shows the same call with a reference argument instead of a value argument. As this diagram indicates, because we're using a reference argument the "variable" Str in the called function is nothing more (and nothing less) than another name for the caller's variable. No copy is made on entry to the operator = code; therefore, the destructor is not called on exit. This allows the caller's variable n to remain unmolested after operator = finishes executing.

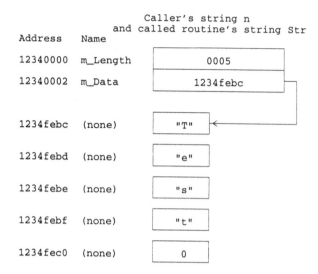

Figure 8.2: Call by reference

Problem
Algorithms
C++
Executable
Hardware

Running Out the String

Finally, we're finished examining the intricacies that result from the apparently simple statement s = n;. Now let's take a look at the next statement in our little test program, n = "My name is: ";. Figure 8.3 shows the entire test program again, for your convenience.

```
#include "string1.h"

int main()
{
    string s;
    string n("Test");
    string x;

    s = n;
    n = "My name is: ";

    x = n;
    return 0;
}
```

Figure 8.3: Our first test program for the string class (code\strtst1.cc)

The type of the expression "My name is: " is char*; that is, the compiler stores the character data somewhere and provides a pointer to it. In other words, this line is attempting to assign a char* to a string. Although the compiler has no built-in knowledge of how to do this, we don't have to write any more code to handle this situation because the code we've already written is sufficient. That's because if we supply a value of type char* where a string is needed, the constructor string::string(char*) is automatically invoked, much as the default constructor is invoked when we create a string with no arguments. Such automatic conversion is another of the features of C++ that makes our user-defined types more like native types.[2]

The sequence of events during compilation of the line n = "My name is: "; is something like this:

1. The compiler sees a string on the left of an =, which it interprets as a call to some version of string::operator =.
2. It looks at the expression on the right of the = and sees that it is a char*.
3. Therefore, it looks for a user-defined function that has the signature string::operator = (char*). If it finds one, it compiles the statement as n.operator = ("My name is: ").
4. In this case, we have not defined such an operator. Therefore, the compiler checks to see whether we have defined a constructor for the string class that has exactly one argument of type char* and no other arguments of any type; that is, whose signature is string::string(char*).
5. Yes, there is such a constructor. Therefore, the compiler interprets the statement as n.operator = (string("My name is: "));. If there were no such constructor, then the line would be flagged as an error.

So the actual interpretation of n = "My name is: "; is n.operator = (string("My name is: "));. What exactly does this do? Figure 8.4 is a picture that I hope will illuminate what the compiler does in this situation; that is, when we assign a C string with the value "My name is: " to a string called n via the constructor string::string(char*).[3]

---

2. There are situations, however, where this usually helpful feature is undesirable. For this reason, the new draft standard for C++ provides a way of preventing the compiler from supplying such conversions automatically.

3. Rather than showing each byte address of the characters in the strings and C strings as I've done in previous diagrams, I'm just showing the address of the first character in each group so that the figure will fit on one page.

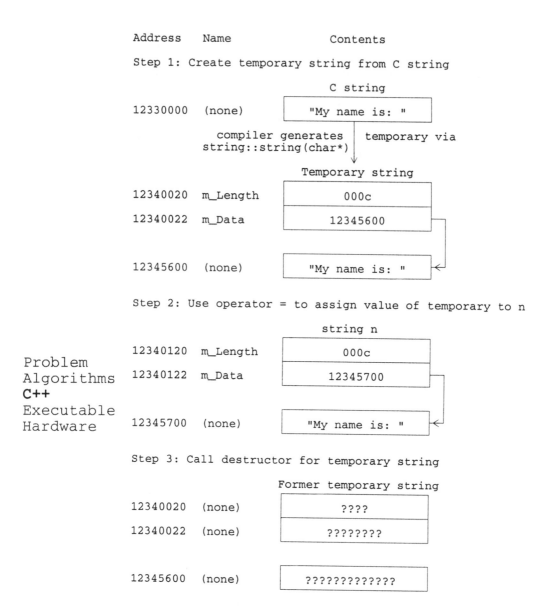

Figure 8.4: Assigning a C string to a string via string::string(char*)

Temporary Help Wanted

Let's go over Figure 8.4, step by step. The first thing that the compiler does is to call the constructor string::string(char*) to create a

temporary (jargon for **temporary variable**) of type string, having the value "My name is: ". This temporary is then used as the argument to the function string::operator = (const string& Str) (see Figure 7.15). Since the argument is a reference, no copy is made of the temporary; the variable Str in the operator = code actually refers to the (unnamed) temporary variable. When the operator = code is finished executing, the string n has been set to the same value as the temporary (i.e., "My name is: "). Upon return from the operator = code, the temporary is automatically destroyed by a destructor call inserted by the compiler.

This sequence of events also holds the key to understanding why the argument of string::operator = should be a const string& (that is, a constant reference to a string) rather than just a string& (that is, a reference to a string). You see, if we declared the function string::operator = to have a string& argument rather than a const string& argument, then it would be possible for that function to change the value of the argument. However, any attempt to change the caller's argument wouldn't work properly if, as in the current example, the argument turned out to be a temporary string constructed from the original argument (the char* value "My name is: "). Clearly, changing the temporary string would have no effect on the original argument. Therefore, if the argument to string::operator = were a string&, the line n = "My name is: "; would produce a compiler warning to the effect that we might be trying to alter an argument that was a temporary value. The reason that we don't get this warning is that the compiler knows that we aren't going to try to modify the value of an argument that has the specification const string&. Therefore, constructing a temporary value and passing it to string::operator = is guaranteed to have the behavior that we want.[4]

Here is a more compact listing of the possibilities when a string& argument is specified in a function:

1. If we specify the argument type as string& *and* a temporary has to be created because the actual argument is a char* rather than a string, then the compiler will warn us that changes to that temporary would not affect the original argument.
2. If we specify the argument type as const string& *and* a temporary has to be created because the actual argument is a char*, then the compiler won't warn us that our (hypothetical) change would be ineffective, because it knows that we aren't going to make such a change.

---

4. By the way, the compiler doesn't just take our word that our operator = function isn't going to modify an argument with the const specifier; if we wrote an operator = that tried to modify such an argument, it wouldn't compile.

Problem
Algorithms
C++
Executable
Hardware

3. However, if the actual argument is a string, then no temporary needs to be made in either of these cases (string& or const string&). Therefore, the argument that we see in the function is actually the real argument, not a temporary, and the compiler won't warn us about trying to change a (nonexistent) temporary.

Copy Cat

Assuming you've followed this so far, you might have noticed one loose end. What if we want to pass a string as a value argument to a function? As we have seen, with the current setup bad things will happen, since the compiler-generated copy constructor doesn't copy strings correctly. Well, you'll be relieved to learn that this, too, can be fixed. The answer is to implement our own version of the *copy constructor*, created precisely to solve the problem of copying variables of a given class — in this case, string. Let's take another look at the header file, now in Figure 8.5.

```
Problem        class string
Algorithms     {
C++            public:
Executable         string();
Hardware           string(const string& Str);
                   string& operator = (const string& Str);
                   ~string();

                   string(char* p);

               private:
                   short m_Length;
                   char* m_Data;
               };
```

Figure 8.5: The string class interface (code\string1.h)

The line we're interested in here is string(const string& Str);. This is a constructor, since its name is the class name string. It takes one argument, which is a const string&, that is, a reference to a constant string. This means that we're not going to change the argument's value "through" the reference, as would be possible if it were a non-const reference. Figure 8.6 has the code that implements this new constructor.

```
string::string(const string& Str)
: m_Length(Str.m_Length),
   m_Data(new char [m_Length])
{
     memcpy(m_Data,Str.m_Data,m_Length);
}
```

Figure 8.6: The copy constructor for the string class (from code\string1.cc)

This function's job is similar to that of operator =, since both of these functions are in the copying business. However, there are also some differences; otherwise, we wouldn't need two separate functions.

Of course, the first difference is that because a copy constructor is a constructor, we can use a member initialization list to initialize the member variables; this convenience is not available to operator =, as it is not a constructor.

The next difference is that we don't have to check whether the argument refers to the same string as this. That's because a constructor always creates a new, never-before-seen object of whatever class it's a constructor for. There's no equivalent of the statement a = a; that can cause trouble for operator = without special handling.

Finally, we don't have to delete any previously held storage that might have been assigned to m_Data. Of course, this is also because we're building a new string, not reusing one that already exists. Therefore, we know that m_Data has never had any storage assigned to it previously.

One fine point that might have slipped past you is why we can't use a value argument rather than a reference argument to our copy constructor. The reason is that using a value argument of a class type requires a copy of the actual argument to be made, using a ... copy constructor! Obviously this won't work when we're writing the copy constructor for that type, and the compiler will let us know if we try to do this accidentally.

Now that we have a correct copy constructor, we can use a string as a value argument to a function, and the copy that's made by the compiler when execution of the function starts will be an independent string, not connected to the caller's variable. When this copy is destroyed at the end of the function, it will go away quietly and the caller's original variable won't be disturbed.

This is all very well in theory, but it's time to see some practice. Let's write a function that we can call with a string to do some useful work, like displaying the characters in the string on the screen.

Problem
Algorithms
C++
Executable
Hardware

Screen Test

As I hope you remember from the previous chapters, we can send output to the screen via cout, a predefined output destination. For example, to write the character 'a' to the screen we could use the statement cout << 'a';. Although we have previously used cout and << to display string variables, our current version of the string class doesn't support this facility. If we want it, we'll have to provide it ourselves. Since variables that can't be displayed are limited in usefulness, we're going to start to add it right now. Figure 8.7 is the updated header file.

I strongly recommend that you print out the files that contain this interface and its implementation, as well as the test program, for reference as you are going through this part of the chapter; those files are string3.h, string3.cc, and strtst3.cc, respectively.

```
class string
{
public:
     string();
     string(const string& Str);
     string& operator = (const string& Str);
     ~string();

     string(char* p);
     void Display();

private:
     short m_Length;
     char* m_Data;
};
```

Problem
Algorithms
C++
Executable
Hardware

Figure 8.7: The string class interface, with Display function (code\string3.h)

As you can see, the new function is declared as void Display();. This means that it returns no value, its name is Display, and it takes no arguments. This last characteristic may seem odd at first, because surely Display needs to know which string we want to display. However, as we've already seen, each object has its own copy of all of the variables defined in the class interface. In this case, the data to be displayed is the set of characters pointed to by m_Data.

Figure 8.8 is an example of how Display can be used.

```
#include <iostream.h>
#include "string3.h"

int main()
{
    string s;
    string n("Test");
    string x;

    s = n;
    n = "My name is: ";

    n.Display();

    return 0;
}
```

Figure 8.8: The string class test program, using the Display function
(code\strtst3.cc)

See the line that says, n.Display();? That is how our new Display function is called. Remember, it's a member function of the string class, so it is always called with respect to a particular string variable; in this case, that variable is n. Now, let's look at the implementation of this new member function in Figure 8.9.

Problem
Algorithms
C++
Executable
Hardware

```
void string::Display()
{
    short i;

    for (i = 0; i < m_Length-1; i ++)
        cout << m_Data[i];
}
```

Figure 8.9: The string class implementation of the Display function (from
code\string3.cc)

This should be looking almost sensible by now; here's the play-by-play. We start out with the function declaration, which says we're defining a void function (i.e., one that returns no value) that is a member function of the class string. This function is named Display, and it takes no arguments. Then we define a short called i. The main part of the function is a for loop, which is executed with the index starting at 0 and continuing while the index is less than the number of displayable characters that we use to store the value of our string. Of course, we don't need to display the null byte at the end of the string.

So far, so good. Now comes the tricky part. The next statement, which is the controlled block of the for loop, says to send something to cout; that is, display it on the screen. This makes sense, because after all that's the purpose of this function. But what is it that is being sent to cout?

A Character Study

It's just a char but that may not be obvious from the way it's written. The expression m_Data[i] looks just like a vector element, doesn't it? In fact, m_Data[i] is an element, but not of a vector. Instead, it's an element of an *array*, the C equivalent of a C++ vector.

What's an array? Well, it's a bunch of data items (elements) of the same type; in this case, it's an array of chars. The array name, m_Data in this case, corresponds to the address of the first of these elements; the other elements follow the first one immediately in memory. If this sounds familiar, it should; it's very much like our old nemesis, a pointer. However, like a vector, we can also refer to the individual elements by their indexes. So m_Data[i] refers to the ith element of the array, which in the case of a char array is, oddly enough, a char. Now it should be clear that each time through the loop, we're sending out the ith element of the array of chars where we stored our string data.

That's all very well, but where did that array come from? We defined m_Data as a char*, which is a pointer to (i.e., the address of) a char. As is common in C and C++, this particular char* is the first of a bunch of chars one after the other in memory.

Problem
Algorithms
C++
Executable
Hardware

Array of Hope?

Brace yourself for this one. In C++, a pointer and the address of an array are for almost all purposes the same thing. You can treat an array address as a pointer and a pointer as an array address, pretty much as you please. This is a holdover from C, necessary for compatibility with C programs.

People who like C will tell you how "flexible" the equivalence of pointers and arrays in C is. That's true, but it's also extremely dangerous, because arrays have no error checking whatsoever. You can use whatever index you feel like, and you'll end up referring to whatever happens to be at the address to which that index would have corresponded. The program in Figure 8.10 is an example of what can go wrong when using arrays.

```
#include <iostream.h>

int main()
{
    char High[10];
    char Middle[10];
    char Low[10];
    char* Alias;
    short i;

    for (i = 0; i < 10; i ++)
        {
        Middle[i] = 'A' + i;
        High[i] = '0';
        Low[i] ='1';
        }

    Alias = Middle;

    for (i = 10; i < 20; i ++)
        {
        Alias[i] = 'a' + i;
        }

    cout << "Low: ";
    for (i = 0; i < 10; i ++)
        cout << Low[i];

    cout << endl;

    cout << "Middle: ";
    for (i = 0; i < 10; i ++)
        cout << Middle[i];

    cout << endl;

    cout << "Alias: ";
    for (i = 0; i < 10; i ++)
        cout << Alias[i];

    cout << endl;

    cout << "High: ";
    for (i = 0; i < 10; i ++)
        cout << High[i];

    cout << endl;
}
```

Problem
Algorithms
C++
Executable
Hardware

Figure 8.10: Dangerous characters (code\dangchar.cc)

Let's look at what this program does when it's executed. First, we define three variables High, Middle, and Low, each as an array of 10 chars. Then we define a variable Alias as a char*; as you may recall, this is how we specify a pointer to a char. Such a pointer is essentially equivalent to a plain old memory address.

In the next part of the program, we use a for loop to set each element of the arrays High, Middle, and Low to a value. So far, so good, except that the statement Middle[i] = 'A' + i; may look a bit odd. How can we add a char value like 'A' and a short value such as i?

A Slippery Character

Let us return to those thrilling days of yesteryear (Chapter 3). Since then, we've been using chars to hold ASCII values, which is their most common use. However, every char variable actually has a "double life"; it can also be thought of as a "really short" numeric variable, which can take on any of 256 values. Thus, we can add and subtract chars and shorts as long as we're careful not to try to use a char to hold a number greater than 255 (or greater than 127, for a signed char). In this case, there's no problem with the magnitude of the result, since we're starting out with the value A and adding a number between 0 and 9 to it. The highest possible result is J, which is still well below the maximum value that can be stored in a char.

With that detail taken care of, let's proceed with the analysis of this program. The next statement after the end of the first for loop is the seemingly simple line alias = middle;. This is obviously an assignment statement, but what is being assigned?

The value that Alias receives is the address of the first element of the array Middle. That is, after the assignment statement is executed, Alias is effectively another name for Middle. Therefore, the next loop, which assigns values to elements 10 through 19 of the "array" Alias, actually operates on the array Middle, setting those elements to the values k through t.

The rest of the program is pretty simple. It just displays the characters from each of the Low, Middle, Alias, and High arrays. Of course, Alias isn't really an array, but it acts just like one; to be precise, it acts just like Middle, since it points to the first character in Middle. Therefore, the Alias and Middle loops will display the same characters. Then the final loop displays the values in the High array.

Problem
Algorithms
C++
Executable
Hardware

Overwrought

That's pretty simple, isn't it? Not quite as simple as it looks. If you've been following along closely, you're probably thinking I've gone off the deep end. First, I said that the array Middle had 10 elements (which are numbered 0 through 9, as always in C++); now I'm assigning values to elements numbered 10 through 19. Am I nuts?

No, but the program is. When you run it, you'll discover that it produces output similar to Figure 8.11.

Low: 1111111111
Middle: ABCDEFGHIJ
Alias: ABCDEFGHIJ
High: mnopqrst00

Figure 8.11: Reaping the whirlwind

Most of these results are pretty reasonable: Low is just as it was when we initialized it, and Middle and Alias have the expected portion of the alphabet. But look at High. Shouldn't it be all 0s?

Problem
Algorithms
C++
Executable
Hardware

Yes, it should. However, we have broken the rules by writing "past the end" of an array, and the result is that we have overwritten some other data in our program, which in this case turned out to be the original values of High. You may wonder why we didn't get an error message, as we did when we tried to write to a nonexistent vector element in an earlier chapter. The reason is that, in C, an array is no more (and no less) than the address of some data. In other words, it's just like a pointer, except that the address it refers to can't be changed at run time. Because of this near-identity between pointers and arrays, the compiler does not and cannot keep track of how many elements are in an array. To the compiler, keeping track of such information makes no sense, any more than it can tell how many elements there are "in a pointer".

This is why pointers and (equivalently) arrays are the single most error prone construct in C (and C++, when they're used recklessly). It's also why we're not going to use either of these constructs except when there's no other reasonable way to accomplish our goals. Even then, we'll confine them to tightly controlled circumstances in the implementation of a user-defined data type. For example, we don't have to worry about going "off the end" of the array in our Display function, because we know exactly how many characters we've stored (m_Length), and we've written the function to send exactly that many characters to the screen via cout. In fact, all of the member functions of our string class are carefully designed to allocate, use, and dispose of the memory pointed to by m_Data so that the user of this class doesn't have to worry about pointers or arrays, or the problems they can cause. After all, one of the main benefits of using C++ is that the users of a class don't have to concern themselves with the way it works, just with what it does.

Assuming that you've installed the software from the CD-ROM in the back of this book, you can try out this program. First, you have to compile it by changing to the normal subdirectory under the main directory where you installed the software and typing mk dangchar. Then type dangchar to run the program normally. You can run this program under gdb by switching to the normal subdirectory, then typing trace dangchar. The program will start up and show you the first line of executable code. Type z and hit ENTER to execute each line. The values of the relevant variables will be displayed immediately before the execution of each line in main. When you get to the end of the program (or when you're tired of tracing), type q (for *quit*) and hit ENTER to exit from the debugger.

```
Problem
Algorithms
C++
Executable
Hardware
```

private **Property: Keep Out!**

Now that we have disposed of the correspondence between arrays and pointers, it's time to return to our discussion of the private access specifier that we've used to control access to the member variables of the class. First of all, let me refresh your memory as to what this access specifier means: only member functions of the string class can refer to variables or functions marked private. As a rule, no member variables of a class should be public, for reasons that we'll get into later. By contrast, most member functions are public, because such functions provide the interface that is used by programmers who need the facilities of the class being defined. While private member functions are sometimes useful for handling implementation details that aren't of interest or use to the "outside world" beyond the class boundaries, they aren't needed in most classes, including the classes defined in this book.

Now that I've clarified the role of these access specifiers, let's take a look at the program in Figure 8.12, which won't compile because it tries to refer to m_Length, a private member variable of string.

```
#include <iostream.h>
#include "string3.h"

int main()
{
    string n("Test");

    n.m_Length = 12;

    n.Display();

    return 0;
}
```

Figure 8.12: Attempted privacy violation (code\strtst3a.cc)

Here's the result of trying to compile this program:

```
strtst3a.cc: In function 'int main()':
strtst3a.cc:8: member 'm_Length' is a private member of class 'string'
```

Why would we want to prevent access to a member variable? Because public member variables have problems similar to those of global variables. To begin with, we want to guarantee consistent, safe behavior of our strings, which is impossible if a nonmember function outside our control can change one of our variables. In the example program, assigning a new value to the m_Length member variable would trick our Display member function into trying to display 11 characters, when our string contains only four characters of displayable data. Similar bad results would occur if a nonmember function were to change the value of m_Data; we wouldn't have any idea of what it was pointing to or whether we should call delete in the destructor to allow reuse of memory formerly used for our string data.

While this may be a convincing argument against letting nonmember functions change our member variables, could we let them at least retrieve the values of member variables?

Problem
Algorithms
C++
Executable
Hardware

Maintenance Required

Unfortunately this would be hazardous too. The problem here is akin to the other difficulty with global variables: Removing or changing the type of a global variable can cause repercussions everywhere in the program. If we reimplemented our string class by a different mechanism than a char* and a short, or even changed the names of the member variables from m_Data and m_Length, any programs that relied on those types or names would have to be changed. If our string class were to become popular, this might amount to dozens or even hundreds of programs that would need to be changed if we were to make the slightest change in our member variables. Therefore, allowing nonmember functions even to retrieve the values of member variables reduces the maintainability of programs using classes.

However, it is sometimes useful for a program that is using an object to find out something about the object's internal state. For example, a user of a string variable might very well want to know how long the string is; that is, how many characters it is storing at the moment. For example, when formatting a report, you might want to pad each string with blanks to the same length so that the columns would line up.

It is indeed possible to provide such a service while preserving the safety and maintainability of our class by writing a function that tells the user how long the string is. Figure 8.13 has the new interface definition that includes the GetLength function.

I strongly recommend that you print out the files that contain this interface and its implementation, as well as the test program, for reference as you are going through this part of the chapter; those files are string4.h, string4.cc, and strtst4.cc, respectively.

Problem
Algorithms
C++
Executable
Hardware

```
class string
{
public:
      string();
      string(const string& Str);
      string& operator = (const string& Str);
      ~string();

      string(char* p);
      void Display();
      short GetLength();

private:
      short m_Length;
      char* m_Data;
};
```

Figure 8.13: Yet another version of the string class interface (code\string4.h)

As you can see, all we have to do here is to add the declaration of the new function, GetLength. The implementation in Figure 8.14 is extremely simple: it merely returns the number of chars in the string, deducting 1 for the null byte at the end.

```
short string::GetLength()
{
    return m_Length-1;
}
```

Figure 8.14: The string class implementation of the GetLength function (from code\string4.cc)

This solves the problem of letting the user of a string variable find out how long the string is without allowing functions outside the class to become dependent on our implementation. It's also a good example of how we can provide the right information to the user more easily by creating an access function rather than letting the user get at our member variables directly. After all, we know that m_Length includes the null byte at the end of the string's data, which is irrelevant to the user of the string, so we can adjust our return value to indicate the "visible length" rather than the actual one.

With this mechanism in place, we can make whatever changes we like in how we store the length of our string, as long as we don't change the name or return type of GetLength. Of course, we actually don't have free rein to change the implementation of the string class, because if we were to allow strings longer than 32767 bytes, we would have to change the return type of GetLength to something more capacious than a short. Even so, we still have a lot more leeway to make changes in the implementation than if we allowed direct access to our member variables. The example program in Figure 8.15 illustrates how to use this new function.

```
Problem
Algorithms
C++
Executable
Hardware
```

```
#include <iostream.h>
#include "string4.h"

int main()
{
    short len;
    string n("Test");

    len = n.GetLength();

    cout << "The string has " << len << " characters." << endl;

    return 0;
}
```

Figure 8.15: Using the GetLength function in the string class (code\strtst4.cc)

Pulling a Few Strings

At this point, we have a fairly minimal string class. We can create a string, assign it a literal value in the form of a C string, and copy the value of one string to another. We can even pass a string as a value argument. Now we'll use the techniques that we've already covered (along with others that we find necessary in the process) to improve the facilities that the string class provides.

To make this goal more concrete, let's suppose that we want to modify the sorting program of Chapter 4 to sort strings, rather than shorts. To use the sorting algorithm from that program, we'll need to be able to compare two strings to see which would come after the other in the dictionary. This is exactly analogous to comparing two shorts to see which is greater. We also want to be able to use cout and << to display strings on the screen, and cin and >> to read them from the keyboard. While our Display function provides the first of these facilities, it's not nearly as nice to use as <<, and we want our types to be as easy to use as the native ones. Let's see what is involved in adding these facilities to the string class.

```
Problem
Algorithms
C++
Executable
Hardware
```

A Pleasant Sort

Before we go into the changes needed in the string class to allow us to write a string sorting program, Figure 8.16 shows our goal: The selection sort algorithm adapted to sort a vector of strings rather than shorts.

Assuming that you've installed the software from the CD-ROM in the back of this book, you can try out this program. First, you have to compile it by changing to the normal subdirectory under the main directory where you installed the software and typing mk strsort1. To run it under gdb, type trace strsort1. The program will start up and show you the first line of executable code. Type z and hit ENTER to execute each line. The values of the relevant variables will be displayed immediately before the execution of each line in main. When you get to the end of the program (or when you're tired of tracing), type q (for *quit*) and hit ENTER to exit from the debugger.

```
#include <iostream.h>
#include "string6.h"
#include "vector.h"

int main()
{
    vector<string> Name(5);
    vector<string> SortedName(5);
    string FirstName;
    short FirstIndex;
    short i;
    short k;
    string HighestName = "zzzzzzzz";

    cout << "I'm going to ask you to type in five last names." << endl;

    for (i = 0; i < 5; i ++)
      {
      cout << "Please type in name #" << i+1 << ": ";
      cin >> Name[i];
      }

    for (i = 0; i < 5; i ++)
        {
        FirstName = HighestName;
        FirstIndex = 0;
        for (k = 0; k < 5; k ++)
            {
            if (Name[k] < FirstName)
                {
                FirstName = Name[k];
                FirstIndex = k;
                }
            }
        SortedName[i] = FirstName;
        Name[FirstIndex] = HighestName;
        }

    cout << "Here are the names, in alphabetical order: " << endl;
    for (i = 0; i < 5; i ++)
        cout << SortedName[i] << endl;

    return 0;
}
```

Problem
Algorithms
C++
Executable
Hardware

Figure 8.16: Sorting a vector of strings (code\strsort1.cc)

As you can see, this program looks very similar to the code that sorts short values, which is good because that's what we wanted to achieve. Let's take a look at the differences between this program and the original one in Figure 4.5.

1.   One difference is that we're sorting the names in ascending alphabetical order, rather than descending order of weight as with the original program. This means that we have to start out by finding the name that would come first in the dictionary (the "lowest" name). By contrast, in the original program we were looking for the highest weight, not the lowest one; therefore, we have to do the sort "backward" from the previous example.

2.   The next difference is that the vectors Name and SortedName are collections of strings; the corresponding vectors Weight and SortedWeight in the first program were shorts.

3.   We've added a new variable called HighestName, which plays the role of the value 0 that was used to initialize HighestWeight in the original program. That is, it is used to initialize the variable FirstName to a value that will certainly be replaced by the first name we find, just as 0 was used to initialize the variable HighestWeight to a value that had to be lower than the first weight we would find. The reason we need a "really high" name rather than a "really low" one is that we're sorting the "lowest" name to the front, rather than sorting the "highest" weight to the front as we did originally.

Problem
Algorithms
C++
Executable
Hardware

You may think these changes to the program aren't very significant. That's a correct conclusion; we'll spend much more time on the changes we have to make to our string class before this program will run (or even compile). The advantage of making up our own data types (like strings) is that we can make them behave in any way we like. Of course, the corresponding disadvantage is that we have to provide the code to implement that behavior and give the compiler enough information to use that code to perform the operations we request. In this case, we'll need to tell the compiler how to compare strings, read them in via >>, and write them out via <<. Let's start with the header file that provides the new interface specification of the string class, including all of the new member functions needed to implement the comparison and I/O operators. We find this in Figure 8.17.[5]

---

5. I've also thrown in the declaration of operator ==, which we'll implement later in the chapter.

I strongly recommend that you print out the files that contain this interface and its implementation, as well as the test program, for reference as you are going through this part of the chapter; those files are string5.h, string5.cc, and strtst5.cc, respectively.

```
class string
{
friend ostream& operator << (ostream& s, const string& Str);
friend istream& operator >> (istream& s, string& Str);

public:
    string();
    string(const string& Str);
    string& operator = (const string& Str);
    ~string();

    string(char* p);
    short GetLength();
    bool operator < (const string& Str);
    bool operator == (const string& Str);

private:
    short m_Length;
    char* m_Data;
};
```

Problem
Algorithms
C++
Executable
Hardware

Figure 8.17: The updated string class interface, including comparison and I/O operators (code\string5.h)

Let's start by implementing operator < (the "less than" operator) so that we can compare two strings. This will enable us to use the selection sort to arrange strings by their dictionary order. The signature of this operator is bool string::operator < (const string& Str), which isn't that much different from the signature of operator =, the assignment operator. The difference is that rather than defining what it means to say x = y; for two strings x and y, we are defining what it means to say x < y. Of course, we want this "less-than" operator to act analogously to the < operator for short values; that is, our operator will compare two strings and return true if the first string would come before the second string in the dictionary and false otherwise. Thus, after defining operator < for the string class, we could write something like Figure 8.18.

```
#include <iostream.h>
#include "string5.h"

int main()
{
    string x;
    string y;

    x = "post";
    y = "poster";

    if (x < y)
       cout << x << " comes before " << y << endl;
    else
       cout << x << " doesn't come before " << y << endl;

    return 0;
}
```

Figure 8.18: Using operator < for strings (code\strtst5.cc)

Problem
Algorithms
C++
Executable
Hardware

Less Than Obvious

All right, then, how do we actually implement this undoubtedly
useful facility? Let's start by examining the function declaration bool
string::operator < (const string& Str) a little more closely. This means that
we're declaring a function that returns a bool and is a member
function of class string; its name is operator < and it takes a constant
reference to a string as its argument. As we've seen before, operators
don't look the same when we use them as when we define them. In
the example program in Figure 8.18, the line if (x < y) actually means if
(x.operator < (y)). In other words, if the return value from the call to
operator < is false, then the if expression will also be considered false
and the controlled block of the if won't be executed. On the other
hand, if the return value from the call to operator < is true, then the if
expression will also be considered true and the controlled block of the
if will be executed. To make this work correctly, our version of
operator < will return the value true if the first string is less than the
second string and the value false otherwise.

Now that we've seen how the compiler will use our new function,
let's see how it does its work. The basic approach we will use to
compare two strings is as follows:

1. Determine the length of the shorter of the two strings.
2. Compare a character from the first string with the corresponding character from the second string.
3. If the character from the first string is less than the character from the second string, then we know that the first string precedes the second in the dictionary, so we're done and the result is true.
4. If the character from the first string is greater than the character from the second string, then we know that the first string follows the second in the dictionary, so we're done and the result is false.
5. If the two characters are the same and we haven't come to the end of the shorter string, then move to the next character in each string and go back to step 2.
6. When we run out of characters to compare, if the strings are the same length, then the answer is that they are identical, so we're done and the result is false.
7. On the other hand, if the strings are different in length and we run out of characters in the shorter string before finding a difference between the two strings, then the longer string follows the shorter one in the dictionary. In this case, the result is true if the second string is longer and false if the first string is longer.

One question that might occur to you on looking over the preceding explanation is why we care whether two strings differ in length. Wouldn't it be simpler just to compare up to the length of the longer string?

Problem
Algorithms
C++
Executable
Hardware

Down for the Count

As it happens, the comparison would work properly so long as both of the strings we're comparing have a null byte at their ends *and* neither of them has a null byte anywhere else. To see why this restriction is necessary, let's look at what the memory layout might look like for two string variables x and y, with the contents "post" and "poster", respectively. In Figure 8.19, the letters in the box labeled "string contents" represent themselves, while the 0s represent the null byte, not the digit 0.

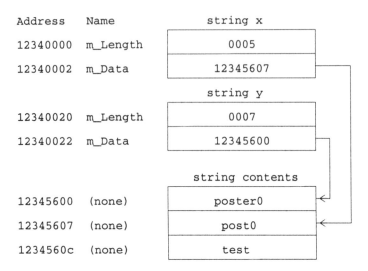

Figure 8.19: strings x and y in memory

If we were to compare the strings up to the longer of the two lengths with this memory layout, the sequence of events would go like this:

Problem
Algorithms
C++
Executable
Hardware

1. Get character p from location 12345600.
2. Get character p from location 12345607.
3. They are the same, so continue.
4. Get character o from location 12345601.
5. Get character o from location 12345608.
6. They are the same, so continue.
7. Get character s from location 12345602.
8. Get character s from location 12345609.
9. They are the same, so continue.
10. Get character t from location 12345603.
11. Get character t from location 1234560a.
12. They are the same, so continue.
13. Get character e from location 12345604.
14. Get a null byte from location 1234560b.
15. The character e from the first string is higher than the null byte from the second string, so we conclude (correctly) that the first string comes after the second one.

The reason this works is that the null byte, having an ASCII code of 0, in fact is less than any byte that might be in the corresponding position of the other string.

However, one reason we're storing the actual length of the string rather than relying on the null byte to mark the end of a string (as is done with C strings) is that keeping the length separately makes it possible to have a string that has any characters whatever in it, even nulls. For example, we could add a string constructor that takes an array of bytes and a length and copies the specified number of bytes from the array.[6] Since an array of bytes can contain any characters in it, including nulls, that new constructor would obviously allow us to create a string with a null in the middle of it. If we tried to use the preceding comparison mechanism, it wouldn't work reliably. To see why, let's change the memory layout slightly to stick a null byte in the middle of string y. Figure 8.20 shows the modified layout.

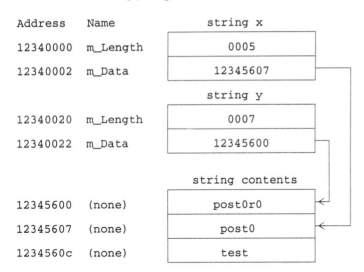

Problem
Algorithms
C++
Executable
Hardware

Figure 8.20: strings x and y in memory, with an embedded null byte

If we were to compare the strings up to the longer of the two lengths with this memory layout, the sequence of events would go like this:

1. Get character p from location 12345600.
2. Get character p from location 12345607.

---

6. In fact, this is an exercise at the end of the chapter.

3.   They are the same, so continue.
4.   Get character *o* from location 12345601.
5.   Get character *o* from location 12345608.
6.   They are the same, so continue.
7.   Get character *s* from location 12345602.
8.   Get character *s* from location 12345609.
9.   They are the same, so continue.
10.   Get character *t* from location 12345603.
11.   Get character *t* from location 1234560a.
12.   They are the same, so continue.
13.   Get a null byte from location 12345604.
14.   Get a null byte from location 1234560b.
15.   They are the same, so continue.
16.   Get character *r* from location 12345605.
17.   Get character *t* from location 1234560c.
18.   The character *r* from the first string is less than the character *t* from the second string, so we conclude that the first string comes before the second one.

Problem
Algorithms
C++
Executable
Hardware

Unfortunately, this conclusion is completely fallacious; what we have actually done is run off the end of the second string and started retrieving data from the next location in memory. Since we want to be able to handle the situation where one of the strings has one or more embedded nulls, we have to stop the comparison as soon as we get to the end of the shorter string. Whatever happens to be past the end of that string's data, it's not anything relevant to our comparison of the two strings.

Dare to Compare

Now that we've examined why the algorithm for operator < works the way it does, Figure 8.21 shows one way to implement it. The variables used in this function are:

1.   i, which is used as a loop counter in the for loop that steps through all of the characters to be compared.
2.   Result, which is used to hold the true or false value that we'll return to the caller.
3.   ResultFound, which we'll use to keep track of whether we've found the result yet.
4.   CompareLength, which we'll use to determine the number of characters to compare in the two strings.

```
bool string::operator < (const string& Str)
{
      short i;
      bool Result;
      bool ResultFound;
      short CompareLength;

      if (Str.m_Length < m_Length)
            CompareLength = Str.m_Length;
      else
            CompareLength = m_Length;

      ResultFound = false;
      for (i = 0; (i < CompareLength) && (ResultFound == false); i ++)
            {
            if (m_Data[i] < Str.m_Data[i])
                  {
                  Result = true;
                  ResultFound = true;
                  }
            else
                  {
                  if (m_Data[i] > Str.m_Data[i])
                        {
                        Result = false;
                        ResultFound = true;
                        }
                  }
            }

      if (ResultFound == false)
            {
            if (m_Length < Str.m_Length)
                  Result = true;
            else
                  Result = false;
            }

      return Result;
}
```

```
Problem
Algorithms
C++
Executable
Hardware
```

Figure 8.21: The implementation of operator < for strings (from code\string5a.cc)

It will probably be easier to understand the code if we follow an example, and I've written a program called strtst5x.cc for this purpose. Figure 8.22 has the code for that program.

```
#include <iostream.h>
#include "string5.h"

int main()
{
    string x;
    string y;

    x = "ape";
    y = "axes";

    if (x < y)
        cout << x << " comes before " << y << endl;
    else
        cout << x << " doesn't come before " << y << endl;

    return 0;
}
```

Figure 8.22: Using operator < for strings (code\strtst5x.cc)

Problem
Algorithms
C++
Executable
Hardware

In case this looks awfully familiar, it's exactly the same as Figure 8.18, except that the string values are different. This change is to reduce the number of steps we'll have to go through in the blow-by-blow explanation. You can see that in this program the two strings are "ape" and "axes", which are assigned to strings x and y, respectively. We've already seen that the line if (x < y) calls our function string::operator < (const string& Str).

Now back to our implementation of operator < in Figure 8.21. After variable definition, the next four lines of the code determine how many characters from each string we actually have to compare. The value of CompareLength is set to the lesser of the lengths of our string and the string referred to by Str. In this case, that value is 4, the length of our string (including the terminating null byte).

Now we're ready to do the comparison. This takes the form of a for loop that steps through all of the characters to be compared in each string. The header of the for loop is for (i = 0; (i < CompareLength) && (ResultFound == false); i ++). The first and last part of the expression controlling the for loop should be familiar by now; we're setting i, the index variable, to 0 and incrementing i each time through the loop. But what about the continuation expression (i < CompareLength) && (ResultFound == false)?

For Better or Worse?

What we're doing here is specifying a two-part condition for continuing the loop. The first part, (i < CompareLength), is the usual condition that allows the program to execute the loop as long as the index variable is within the correct range. The second part, (ResultFound == false) should also be fairly clear; we want to test whether we've already found the result we're looking for and continue only as long as that isn't the case (i.e., ResultFound is still false). The () around each of these expressions are used to tell the compiler that we want to evaluate each of these expressions first, before the && is applied to their results. That leaves the && symbol as the only mystery.

It's really not too mysterious. The && operator is the symbol for the "logical AND" operation, which means that we want to combine the truth or falsity of two expressions, each of which has a logical value of true or false. The result of using && to combine the results of these two expressions will also be a logical value. Here is the way the value of that expression is determined:

1. If both of the expressions connected by the && are true, then the value of the expression containing the && will also be true.
2. Otherwise, the value of the expression containing the && will be false.

Problem
Algorithms
C++
Executable
Hardware

If you think about it for a minute, this should be comprehensible. We want to continue the loop as long as both of the conditions are true; that is,

1. i is less than CompareLength; *and*
2. ResultFound is false (i.e, we haven't found what we're looking for yet).

That's why the && operator is called logical AND; it checks whether condition 1 *and* condition 2 are both true. If either is false, we want to stop the loop, and this continuation expression will do just that.[7]

Now let's trace the path of execution through the for loop in Figure 8.21. On the first time through the loop, the index i is 0 and ResultFound is false. Therefore, the continuation expression allows us

---

7. This operator follows a rule analogous to the one for ||: if the expression on the left is false, then the answer must be false and the expression on the right is not executed at all. The reason for this short-circuit evaluation rule is that in some cases you may want to write a right-hand expression that will only be legal if the left-hand expression is true.

to execùte the statements in the loop, where we test whether the current character in the current string, m_Data[i], is less than the corresponding character from the string Str, Str.m_Data[i].[8] Figure 8.23 shows the code for that test.

```
if (m_Data[i] < Str.m_Data[i])
    {
    Result = true;
    ResultFound = true;
    }
```

Figure 8.23: Is our character less than the other one? (from code\string5a.cc)

In the event that the current character in our string is indeed less than the corresponding character in Str, we have our answer: Our string is less than the other string. If that were the case, we would set Result to true and ResultFound to true, and we would be finished with this execution of the for loop.

As it happens, in our current example both m_Data[0] and Str.m_Data[0] are equal to *a*, so they're equal to each other as well.

Problem
Algorithms
C++
Executable
Hardware

What happens when the character from our string is the same as the one from the string Str? In that case, the first if, whose condition is stated as if (m_Data[i] < Str.m_Data[i]), is false. So we continue with the else clause of that if statement, which looks like Figure 8.24.

```
else
    {
    if (m_Data[i] > Str.m_Data[i])
        {
        Result = false;
        ResultFound = true;
        }
    }
```

Figure 8.24: The else clause in the comparison loop (from code\string5a.cc)

As you can see, this clause contains another if statement that checks whether the character from our string is greater than the one

---

8. In case the expression in the if statement doesn't make sense immediately, perhaps I should remind you that the array notation m_Data[i] means the ith character of the data pointed to by m_Data; an index value of 0 means the first character, as is always the case when using an array. We've already covered this earlier in the chapter, starting in the section called "A Character Study". You should go back and reread that part of the chapter if you're not comfortable with the equivalence between pointers and arrays.

from Str. Since the two characters are the same, this if also comes out false, so the controlled block of the if, which sets Result and ResultFound, isn't executed. After that if statement, we've reached the end of the controlled block of the for statement. Therefore, we have to go back to the top of the for loop, where the modification expression i ++ increments i to 1. Then the continuation expression is evaluated again; i is still less than CompareLength and ResultFound is still false, so we get to execute the controlled block of the loop again, this time with i equal to 1.

On this pass through the for loop, m_Data[1], the character from our string, is *p*, and Str.m_Data[1], the character from the other string, is *x*. Therefore, the condition in the first if statement (that the character from our string is less than the character from the other string) is true, so we execute the controlled block of the if statement. This sets both Result and ResultFound to true, as you can see in Figure 8.23.

We're now at the end of the for loop, so we return to the for statement to continue execution. First, i is incremented again, to 2. Then the continuation expression (i < CompareLength) && (ResultFound == false) is evaluated. The first part of the condition, i < CompareLength is true, since i is 2 and CompareLength is 4. However, the second part of the condition, ResultFound == false, is false, because we've just set ResultFound to true. Since the && that connects the two parts of the condition requires both to be true for the overall condition to be true and that is not the case here, the for loop terminates. As always occurs when a loop terminates, control passes to the next statement after the controlled block of the loop. In this case, that next statement is the if statement that looks like Figure 8.25.

Problem
Algorithms
C++
Executable
Hardware

```
if (ResultFound == false)
    {
    if (m_Length < Str.m_Length)
        Result = true;
    else
        Result = false;
    }
```

Figure 8.25: Handling the return value (from code\string5a.cc)

In the current scenario, ResultFound is true because we have found a character from m_Data that differs from the corresponding character from Str.m_Data. Therefore, the condition in the first if is false, and we proceed to the next statement after the end of the if statement, return Result;. This shouldn't come as too much of a surprise; we know the answer to the comparison, namely, that our string is less than the other string, so we're ready to tell the caller the information that he requested by calling our routine.

A Greater Cause

The path of execution is almost exactly the same if the first time we find a mismatch between the two strings, the character from our string is greater than the character from the other string. The only difference is that the if statement that handles this scenario sets Result to false rather than true (Figure 8.24), because our string is not less than the other string. Of course, it still sets ResultFound to true, since we know the result that will be returned.

There's only one other possibility: That the two strings are the same up to the length of the shorter one (e.g., "post" and "poster"). In that case, the for loop will expire of natural causes when i gets to be greater than or equal to CompareLength. Then the final if statement shown in Figure 8.25 will evaluate to true, because ResultFound is still false. In this case, if the length of our string is less than the length of the other string, we will set Result to true because a shorter string will precede a longer one in the dictionary if the two strings are the same up to the length of the shorter one.

Otherwise, we'll set Result to false because our string is at least as long as the other one. Since they're equal up to the length of the shorter one, our string can't precede the other string. In this case, either they're identical, or our string is longer than the other one and therefore should follow it. Either of these two conditions means that the result of operator < is false, so that's what we tell the caller via our return value.

Problem
Algorithms
C++
Executable
Hardware

Simple Pleasures

This implementation of operator < for strings definitely works. However, there's a much simpler way to do it. Figure 8.26 shows the code. This version starts out in the same way as our previous one, by figuring out how much of the two strings we actually need to compare character by character. Right after that calculation, though, the code is very different; where's that big for loop?

It's contained in the standard library function memcmp, a carryover from C, which does exactly what that for loop did for us. Although C doesn't have the kind of strings that we're implementing here, it does have primitive facilities for dealing with arrays of characters, including comparing one array with another, character by character. One type of character array supported by C is the C string, which we've already encountered. However, C strings have a serious drawback for our purposes here — their use of a null byte to mark the end of a group of characters. This isn't suitable for our strings, whose length is explicitly stored. As noted previously, our strings could theoretically have null bytes in them. There are several C functions that compare C strings, but they rely on the null byte for their proper operation, so we can't use them.

```cpp
bool string::operator < (const string& Str)
{
    short Result;
    short CompareLength;

    if (Str.m_Length < m_Length)
        CompareLength = Str.m_Length;
    else
        CompareLength = m_Length;

    Result = memcmp(m_Data,Str.m_Data,CompareLength);

    if (Result < 0)
        return true;

    if (Result > 0)
        return false;

    if (m_Length < Str.m_Length)
        return true;

    return false;
}
```

Problem
Algorithms
C++
Executable
Hardware

Figure 8.26: Implementing operator < for strings (from code\string5.cc)

However, these limitations of C strings are so evident that the library writers have supplied another set of functions that act almost identically to the ones used for C strings, except that they don't rely on null bytes to determine how much data to process. Instead, whenever you use one of these functions, you have to tell it how many characters to manipulate. In this case, we're calling memcmp, which compares two arrays of characters up to a specified length. The first argument is the first array to be compared (corresponding to our string), the second argument is the second array to be compared (corresponding to the string Str), and the third argument is the length for which the two arrays are to be compared. The return value from memcmp is calculated by the following rules:

1. It's less than 0 if the first array would precede the second in the dictionary.
2. It's 0 if they are the same up to the length specified.
3. It's greater than 0 if the first array would follow the second in the dictionary.

This is very convenient for us, because if the return value from memcmp is less than 0, we know that our result will be true. If the return value from memcmp is greater than 0, then our result will be false. The only complication, which isn't very complicated, is that if the return value from memcmp is 0, meaning that the two arrays are the same up to the length of the shorter character array, we have to see which is longer. If the first one is shorter, then it precedes the second one; therefore, our result is true. Otherwise, it's false.

One small point that shouldn't be overlooked is that in this version of the operator < code, we have more than one return statement; in fact, we have four! That's perfectly legal and should be clear to a reader of this function. It's usually not a good idea to scatter return statements around in a large function, because it's easy to overlook them when trying to follow the flow of control through the function. In this case, though, that's not likely to be a problem; any reasonably fluent reader of C++ code will find this organization easy to understand.

Problem
Algorithms
C++
Executable
Hardware

Equalization of Opportunity

Although our current task requires only operator <, another comparison operator, operator ==, will make an interesting contrast in implementation. In addition, a concrete data type that allows comparisons should really implement more than just operator <. Since we've just finished one comparison operator, we might as well knock this one off now. Figure 8.27 shows the code.

This function is considerably simpler than the previous one. Why is this, since they have almost the same purpose? It's because in this case we don't care which of the two strings is greater than the other, just whether they're the same or different. Therefore, we don't have to worry about comparing the two char arrays if they're of different lengths. Two arrays of different lengths can't be the same, so we can just return false. Once we have determined that the two arrays are the same length, we do the comparison via memcmp. This gives us the answer directly because if Result is 0, then the two strings are equal; otherwise, they're different.

```
bool string::operator == (const string& Str)
{
    short Result;

    if (m_Length != Str.m_Length)
        return false;

    Result = memcmp(m_Data,Str.m_Data,m_Length);

    if (Result == 0)
        return true;

    return false;
}
```

Figure 8.27: Implementing operator == for strings (from code\string5.cc)

Displaying Expertise

Problem
Algorithms
C++
Executable
Hardware

Before moving on to see how we will display a string on the screen via operator <<, I should bring up a couple of points that otherwise might pass you by. First, we didn't have to change our interface header file string5.h (Figure 8.17) just because we changed the implementation of operator <. Since the *signature* of this function didn't change, neither the header file nor the user program had to change. Second, we didn't even implement operator == in the string5a.cc version of the string class, yet our test program still compiled without difficulty. How can this be?

In C++, you can declare all of the functions you want to, whether they are member functions or global functions, without actually defining them. As long as no one tries to actually use the functions, everything will work fine. In fact, the compiler doesn't even care whether any functions you *do* refer to are available; that's up to the linker to worry about. This is very handy when you know that you're going to add functions in a later revision of a class, as was the case here. Of course, you should warn your class users if you have listed functions in the interface header file that aren't available. It's true that they'll find out about the missing functions the first time they try to link a program that uses one of these functions, because the linker will report that it can't find the function. However, if they've spent a lot of time writing a program using one of these functions, they're likely to get mad at you for misleading them. So let them know what's actually implemented and what's "for later".

Now let's continue with our extensions to the string class, by looking at how we send a string out to the screen.

Down by the Old cout stream

We've been using cout and its operator << for quite awhile now, but have just taken them for granted. Now we have to look under the hood a bit.

The first question is what type of object cout is. The answer is that it's an ostream (short for "output stream"), which is an object that you can use to send characters to some output device. I'm not sure of the origin of this term, but you can imagine that you push the characters out into a "stream" that leads to the output device.

As you may recall from our uses of cout, you can chain a bunch of << expressions together in one statement, as in Figure 8.28.

```
Problem
Algorithms
C++
Executable
Hardware
```

```cpp
#include <iostream.h>

int main()
{
    short x;
    char y;

    x = 1;
    y = 'A';

    cout << "On test #" << x << ", your mark is: " << y << endl;

    return 0;
}
```

Figure 8.28: Chaining several operator << expressions together
(code\cout1.cc)

If you compile and execute that program, it will produce the following output:

On test #1, your mark is: A

Notice that it displays the short as a number and the char as a letter, just as we want it to do. This desirable event occurs because there's a separate version of << for each type of data that can be displayed; in other words, operator << uses function overloading, just like the constructors for the StockItem class and the string class. We'll also use function overloading to add support for our string class to the I/O facilities supplied by the iostreams library.

Gently Down the stream

Before we examine how to accomplish this goal, though, we'll have to go into some detail about how the preexisting output functions behave. Let's start with a simple case using a version of operator << supplied by the iostream.h header file. The simplest possible use of ostream's operator <<, of course, uses only one occurrence of the operator. Here's an example where the value is a char:

cout << 'a';

As you may remember, using an operator such as << on an object is always equivalent to a "normal" function call. This particular example is equivalent to the following:

cout.operator << ('a');

Problem
Algorithms
C++
Executable
Hardware

which calls ostream::operator << (char) (i.e.,the version of the operator << member function of the iostream class that takes a char as its input) for the predefined destination cout, which writes the char on the screen.

That takes care of the single occurrence of operator <<. However, as we've already seen, it's possible to string together any number of occurrences of operator <<, with the output of each successive occurrence following the output created by the one to its left. We want our string output function to behave just like the ones predefined in iostream.h, so let's look next at an example that illustrates multiple uses of operator <<, taking a char and a C string:

cout << 'a' << " string";

This is equivalent to

(cout.operator << ('a')).operator << (" string");

What does this mean? Well, since an expression in parentheses is evaluated before one outside the parentheses, the first thing that happens is that ostream::operator << (char) is called for the predefined destination cout, which writes the *a* to the screen. Now here's the tricky part: The return value from every version of ostream::operator << is a reference to the ostream that it operates on (cout, in this case). Therefore, after the *a* has been written on the screen, the former expression reduces to this:

cout.operator << (" string");

That is, the next output operation behaves exactly like the first one. In this case, ostream::operator << (char*) is the function called, because char* is the type of the argument to be written out. It too returns a reference to the ostream for which it was called, so that any further << calls can add their data to that same ostream. It should be fairly obvious how the same process can be extended to handle any number of items to be displayed.

Problem
Algorithms
C++
Executable
Hardware

Friends of Global Progress

That illustrates how the designers of ostream could create member functions that would behave in this convenient way. However, we can't use the same mechanism that they did. We can't modify the definition of the ostream class in the library because we didn't write it in the first place and don't have access to its source code. Does that mean that we can't give our strings convenient input and output facilities?

In fact, we can. To do this, we create a *global* function called operator << that accepts an ostream& (that is, a reference to an ostream), adds the contents of our string to the ostream, and then returns a reference to the same ostream. This will allow multiple occurrences of operator << to be chained together in one statement, just as with the operator << member functions from the iostreams library. We can see the implementation of this function in Figure 8.29.

As usual, we should first examine the function declaration; in this case, a couple of points are worth noting. We've already seen that the first argument is an ostream&, to which we will add the characters from the string that's the second argument. Also notice that the second argument is a const string&, that is, a reference to a constant string. This is the best way to declare this argument because we aren't going to change the argument, and there's no reason to make a copy of it.

```
ostream& operator << (ostream& s, const string& Str)
{
    short i;

    for (i=0; i < Str.m_Length-1; i ++)
        S << Str.m_Data[i];

    return S;
}
```

Figure 8.29: An operator << function to output a string (from code\string5.cc)

But possibly the most important point about the function declaration is that this operator << is *not* a member function of the string class, which explains why it isn't called string::operator <<. It's a global function that can be called anywhere in a program that needs to use it, so long as that program has included the header file that defines it. This operator << function isn't at all complicated in its operation; it merely calls ostream::operator << (char) to write out each character from the array called m_Data that we use to store the data for our string. Since there is no ostream function to write out a specified number of characters from a char array, we have to call ostream::operator << (char) for each character in the array.[9] After all the characters have been written to the ostream, we return it so that the next operator << call in the line can continue producing output.

Problem
Algorithms
C++
Executable
Hardware

However, there's a loose end here. How can a global function, which by definition isn't a member function of class string, get at the internal workings of a string? We declared that m_Length and m_Data were private, so that they wouldn't be accessible to just any old function that wandered along to look at them. Is nothing sacred?

Members and Friends Only

In fact, private variables aren't accessible to just any function. However, operator << (ostream&, const string&) isn't just any function. Take a look at string5.h in Figure 8.17 to see why. The line we're interested in is this one:

```
friend ostream& operator << (ostream& s, const string& Str);
```

---

9. In case it's not obvious that we're calling ostream::operator <<(char) here, it's because s is an ostream&, which is just another name for the ostream that is the first argument to this function.

The key word here is friend. We're telling the compiler that a function with the signature ostream& operator << (ostream&, const string&) is permitted to access the information normally reserved for member functions of the string class; that is, anything that isn't marked public. It's possible to make an entire class a friend to another class; here, we're specifying one function that is a friend to this class. The signature of the function is important here, as elsewhere in C++. This friend declaration would not permit a function with the same name and a different signature, for example ostream& operator << (ostream&, int), to access non-public members of string.

That explains why this global function can access our non-public data. But why did we have to create a global function in the first place, rather than just adding a member function to our string class? Because a member function of a class has to be called for an object of that class, whose address then becomes the this pointer. In the case of the << operator, the class of the object is ostream, not string. Figure 8.30 is an example.

string x = "this is it";

cout << x;

Problem
Algorithms
C++
Executable
Hardware

Figure 8.30: Why we need a global function for operator <<

The line cout << x; is the same as cout.operator << (x);. Notice that the object to which the operator << call is applied is cout, not x. Since cout is an ostream, not a string, we can't use a member function of string to do our output, but a global function is perfectly suitable.

Before we move on to our next topic, it wouldn't hurt to take a bit more time to answer one question in the implementation of operator << for strings: Why is the loop continuation expression i < Str.m_Length–1? The reason is that the stored length of the string (m_Length) includes the added null byte at the end of the string. Thus, if we write out all the bytes indicated by the length, we'll include the null byte as well. This would work all right if we were writing the data out to the screen, because we can't read the data back from the screen. However, it would cause trouble if we wrote the data to a file and then tried to reread the data later, as we did in the StockItem class (see the discussion starting in the section titled "Vectoring In" in Chapter 6). Therefore, we have to be careful to avoid writing the null byte.

Of course, if we had a way to make a string that had null bytes inside it rather than just at the end, then we'd really have to deal with the problem of handling null bytes during input and output. However, in that case we would presumably have to deal with all the other ramifications of such strings, and this would be just another detail to handle. For now, it's best to avoid it in the interest of simplicity.

Reader and Advisor

Now that we have an output function that will write our string variables out to an ostream like cout, it would be very handy to have an input function that could read a string in from an istream like cin. You might expect that this would be pretty simple now that we've worked through the previous exercise, and you'd be mostly right. As usual, though, there are a few twists in the path.

Let's start by looking at the code in Figure 8.31.

```
istream& operator >> (istream& s, string& Str)
{
        const short BUFLEN = 256;

        char Buf[BUFLEN];
        memset(Buf,0,BUFLEN);

        if (S.peek() == '\n')
                S.ignore();
        S.getline(Buf,BUFLEN,'\n');
        Str = Buf;

        return S;
}
```

Problem
Algorithms
C++
Executable
Hardware

Figure 8.31: An operator >> function to input a string (from code\string5.cc)

The header is pretty similar to the one from the operator << function, which is reasonable since they're complementary functions. In this case, we're defining a global function with the signature istream& operator >> (istream& s, string& Str). In other words, this function, called operator >>, has a first argument that is a reference to an istream, which is just like an ostream except that we read data from it rather than writing data to it. One significant difference between this function signature and the one for operator << is that the second argument is a non-const reference, rather than a const reference, to the string into which we want to read the data from the istream. That's because the whole purpose of this function is to modify the string passed in as the second argument. To be exact, we're going to fill it in with the characters taken out of the istream.

Continuing with the analysis of the function declaration, the return value is another istream reference, which is passed to the next operator >> function to the right, if there is one. Otherwise, it will just be discarded.

After decoding the header, let's move to the first line in the function body, const short BUFLEN = 256;. While we've encountered const before, specifying that we aren't going to change an argument passed to us, that can't be the meaning here. What does const mean in this context?

Here, it specifies that the item being defined, which in this case is short BUFLEN, isn't a variable, but a constant, or const value.[10] That is, its value can't be changed. Of course, a logical question is how we can use a const if we can't set its value.

Initial Here

Problem
Algorithms
C++
Executable
Hardware

This is another of the places where it's important to differentiate between *initialization* and *assignment*. We can't assign a value to a const, but we can initialize it. In fact, because an uninitialized const is useless, the attempt to define a const without specifying its initial value is a compile time error. In this case, we're initializing it to the value 256; if we just wrote const short BUFLEN;, we'd get an error something like the one in Figure 8.32 when we tried to compile it.

```
gcc -c -I. -g uniconst.cc
uniconst.cc: In function 'int main()':
uniconst.cc:3: uninitialized const 'short int const BUFLEN'
```

Figure 8.32: Error from an uninitialized const (code\uniconst.out)

Now that we've disposed of that detail, let's continue with our examination of the implementation of operator >>. The next nonblank line is char Buf[BUFLEN];. This is a little different from any variable definition we've seen before; however, you might be able to guess something about it from its appearance. It seems to be defining a

---

10. In case you were wondering how I came up with the name BUFLEN, it's short for "buffer length". Also, I should mention the reason that it is all caps rather than mixed case or all lowercase: An old C convention (carried over into C++) specifies that named constants should be named in all caps to enable the reader to distinguish them from variables at a glance.

variable called Buf[11] whose type is related in some way to char. But what about the [BUFLEN] part?

This is a definition of a variable of that dreaded type, the *array*. Specifically, we're defining an array called Buf, which contains BUFLEN chars. As you may recall, this is somewhat like the vector type that we've used before, except that it has absolutely no error checking. If we try to access a char that is past the end of the array, something will happen, but not anything good.[12] In this case, as in our previous use of pointers, we'll use this dangerous construct only in a very small part of our code, under controlled circumstances; the user of our string class won't be exposed to the array. We'll see how it's used in this function.

Constant Comment

First, I should point out that C++ has a rule that the number of elements of an array must be known at compile time. That is, the program in Figure 8.33 isn't legal C++.

```
int main()
{
    short BUFLEN = 256;
    char ch;

    char Buf[BUFLEN];

    ch = Buf[0];
}
```

Problem
Algorithms
C++
Executable
Hardware

Figure 8.33: Use of a non-const array size (code\string5y.cc)

I'll admit that I don't understand exactly why using a non-const array size is illegal; a C++ compiler has enough information to create and access an array whose length is known at run time.[13] In fact, the DJGPP compiler supplied with this book by default does accept this construct: You have to set a special *warning option* (*pedantic-errors*)

---

11. This is another common C practice; using "buf" as shorthand for "buffer", or "place to store stuff while we're working on it".

12. This is covered in the discussion that starts in the section called "A Character Study".

13. According to Eric Raymond, a well-known historian of programming and the author of *The New Hacker's Dictionary*, there is no good reason for this limitation; it's a historical artifact.

to treat this as an error. I've added this option to the batch file mknorm.bat, which you can use to compile your programs. Figure 8.34 shows the output that you would get if you used that batch file to compile the program in Figure 8.33.

```
string5y.cc: In function 'int main()':
string5y.cc:6: ANSI C++ forbids variable-size array 'Buf'
```

Figure 8.34: Trying to compile a program with a non-const array size
(code\string5y.out)

Although the ability to declare an array whose size isn't known until run time is sometimes very convenient and is provided by the DJGPP compiler, you should avoid it. No other compiler I'm familiar with will accept this construct. It also won't be part of the C++ standard, so when such compilers are available, they won't accept it either. Therefore, we'll use the const value BUFLEN to specify the number of chars in the array Buf in the statement char Buf[BUFLEN];.

Pointers and Setters

Problem
Algorithms
C++
Executable
Hardware

Now we're up to the first line of the executable part of the operator >> function in Figure 8.31: memset(Buf,0,BUFLEN);. This is a call to a function called memset, which is in the standard C library. You may be able to guess from its name that it is related to the function memcmp that we used to compare two arrays of chars. If so, your guess would be correct; memset is C-talk for "set all the bytes in an area of memory to the same value". The first argument is the address of the area of memory to be set to the value, the second argument is the char value to be used, and the third argument is the number of characters to be set to that value, starting at the address given in the first argument. In other words, we're setting all of the characters in the array called Buf to 0. This is important because we're going to treat that array as a C string later. As you may recall, a C string is terminated by a null byte, so we want to make sure that no junk is lying around in the array Buf, which would be misinterpreted as part of the data we're reading in from the istream.

Next, we have an if statement:

```
if (S.peek() == '\n')
    S.ignore();
```

What exactly does this do? It solves a problem with reading C string data from a file; namely, where do we stop reading? With a numeric variable, that's easy. The answer is "whenever we see a character that doesn't look like part of a number". However, with a data type that can take just about any characters as part of its value, this is more difficult. The solution I've adopted is to stop reading when we get to a newline ('\n') character; that is, an end-of-line character. This is no problem when reading from the keyboard, as long as each data item is on its own line. But what about reading from a file?

When we read a C string from a file, the newline at the end of the line is discarded, so the next C string to be read in starts at the beginning of the next line of the file, as we wish. This approach to handling newline characters works well as long as all of the variables being read in are strings. However, in the case of the StockItem class, we needed to be able to mix shorts and strings in the file. In that case, reading a value for a short stops at the newline, because that character isn't a valid part of a numeric value. This is OK as long as the next variable to be read is also a short, because spaces and newlines at the beginning of a line are ignored when we're reading a numeric value. However, when the next variable to be read is a string, the leftover newline from the previous read is interpreted as the beginning of the data for the string, which messes up everything. Therefore, we have to check whether the next available char in the input stream is a newline, in which case we have to skip it. On the other hand, if the next character to be read in is something other than a newline, we want to keep it as the first character of our string. That's what the if statement does: First, the S.peek() function call returns the next character in the input stream without removing it from the stream; then, if it turns out to be a newline, we tell the input stream to ignore it, so it won't mess up our reading of the actual data in the next line.

Problem
Algorithms
C++
Executable
Hardware

Now that we've dealt with that detail, we're ready to read the data for our string. That's the job of the next line in the function: S.getline(Buf,BUFLEN,'\n');. Since s is an istream, this is a member function of istream. To be precise, it's the member function that reads a number of characters into a char array. The arguments are as follows:

1.   The array into which to read characters.
2.   The number of characters that the array can contain.
3.   The "terminating character", where getline should stop reading characters.

This function will read characters into the array (in this case Buf) until one of two events occurs:

1.   The size of the array is reached.
2.   The "terminating character" is the next character to be read.

Note that the terminating character is not read into the array.

Before continuing with the rest of the code for operator >>, let's take a closer look at the following two lines, so we can see why it's a bad idea to use the C string and memory manipulation library any more than we have to. The lines in question are

```
memset(Buf,0,BUFLEN);
S.getline(Buf,BUFLEN,'\n');
```

The problem is that we have to specify the length of the array Buf explicitly (as BUFLEN, in this case). In this small function, we can keep track of that length without much effort, but in a large program with many references to Buf, it would be all too easy to make a mistake in specifying its length. As we've already seen, the result of specifying a length that is greater than the actual length of the array would be a serious error in the functioning of the program. Namely, some memory belonging to some other variable would be overwritten. Whenever we use the mem functions in the C library, we're liable to run into such problems. That's an excellent reason to avoid them except in strictly controlled situations such as the present one, where the definition of the array is in the same small function as the uses of the array. By no coincidence, this is the same problem caused by the indiscriminate use of pointers. The difficulty with the C memory manipulation functions is that they use pointers (or arrays, which are essentially interchangeable with pointers) with all of the hazards that such use entails.

Now that I've nagged you sufficiently about the dangers of arrays, let's look at the rest of the operator >> code. The next statement is Str = Buf;, which sets the argument Str to the contents of the array Buf. Buf is the address of the first char in an array of chars, so its type is char*; Str, on the other hand, is a string. Therefore, this seemingly innocent assignment statement calls string::string(char*) to make a temporary string, and then calls string::operator=(const string&) to copy that temporary string to Str.[14]

Finally, we have the statement return S;. This simply returns the same istream that we got as an argument, so that the next input operator in the same statement can continue reading from the istream where we left off.

Problem
Algorithms
C++
Executable
Hardware

---

14. The details of this sequence can be found starting in the section titled "Running Out the String".

Now our strings can be read in from an input stream (such as cin) and written out to an output stream (such as cout), so our program that sorts strings can do some useful work.[15]

Assuming that you've installed the software from the CD-ROM in the back of this book, you can try out the program that sorts strings. First, you have to compile it by changing to the normal subdirectory under the main directory where you installed the software and typing mk strsort1. Then type strsort1 to run the program normally. To run it under gdb, make sure you are in the normal subdirectory, then type trace strsort1. The program will start up and ask you for the strings to be sorted. Once you've typed in all of the strings, it will allow you to step through the sorting process, displaying all of the relevant variables as it goes. When you get to the end of the program (or when you're tired of tracing), type q (for *quit*) and hit ENTER to exit from the debugger.

Now that we've finished our improvements to the string class, it's time to look back at what we've covered in this chapter.

Review

After finishing most of the requirements to make the string class a concrete data type in the previous chapter, we went back to look at why operator = needs a *reference argument* rather than a *value argument*. When we use a value argument a copy of the argument is made. In the case of a user-defined data type, this copy is made via the copy constructor defined for that type. If we don't define our own copy constructor, the compiler will generate one for us, which will use *memberwise copy*; that is, simply copying all of the member variables in the object. While a memberwise copy is fine for simple objects whose data is wholly contained within themselves, it isn't sufficient for objects that contain pointers to data stored in other places because copying a pointer from one object to another results in the two objects sharing the same actual data. Since our string class

Problem
Algorithms
C++
Executable
Hardware

---

15. The implementation of operator << will also work for any other output destination, such as a file; however, our current implementation of operator >> isn't really suitable for reading a string in from an arbitrary input source. The reason is that we're counting on the input data being able to fit into the Buf array, which is 256 bytes in length. This is fine for input from the keyboard, at least under DOS, because the maximum line length in that situation is 128 characters. It will also work for our inventory file, because the lines in that file are shorter than 256 bytes. However, there's no way to limit the length of lines in any old data file we might want to read from, so this won't do as a general solution.

Of course, increasing the size of the Buf array wouldn't solve the problem; no matter how large we make it, we couldn't be sure that a line from a file wouldn't be too long. The solution would be to handle long lines in sections; unfortunately, we don't have all of the infrastructure needed to implement that version of operator>>.

does contain such a pointer, the result of this simple(minded) copy is that the newly created string points to the same data as the caller's string. Therefore, when the newly created local string expires at the end of the operator = function, the destructor for that string frees the memory that the caller's string was using to store its data.

This problem is very similar to the reason why we had to write our own operator = in the first place; the compiler-generated operator = just copies the member variables from the source to the destination object, which causes similar havoc when one of the two "twinned" strings is changed. In the case of our operator =, we can solve the twinning problem by using a reference argument rather than a value argument. A reference argument is actually another name for the caller's variable rather than a copy of the value in that variable, so no destructor is called for a reference argument when the function exits. Therefore, the caller's variable is left unmolested.

Next, we examined how it was possible to assign a C string to one of our string variables. This didn't require us to write any more code because we already had a constructor that could create a string from a C string and an operator = that could assign one string to another one. The compiler helps us out here by employing a rule that can be translated roughly as follows: If we need an object of type A (string, in this case) and we have an object of type B (char*, in this case), and there is a constructor that constructs an A and requires exactly one argument, which is of type B, then invoke that constructor automatically. The example code is as follows:

Problem
Algorithms
C++
Executable
Hardware

```
n = "My name is: ";
```

where n is a string, and "My name is" is a C string (whose type is char*). We have an operator = with the declaration:

```
string& string::operator = (const string& Str);
```

which takes a string reference argument, and we have a constructor of the form

```
string::string(char* p);
```

which takes a char* argument and creates a new string. So we have a char*, "My name is: ", and we need a string. Since we have a constructor string::string(char*), the compiler will use that constructor to make a temporary string with the same value as the char* and then use the assignment operator string::operator = (const string& Str) to assign the value of that temporary string to the string n. The fact that the temporary is created also provides the clue as to why the argument to string::operator = (const string& Str) should be a const reference, rather than just a (non-const) reference, to a string. The temporary string having the value "My name is: " created during the execution of the statement n = "My name is: "; disappears after operator = is executed, taking with it any changes that operator = might have wanted to apply to the original value. With a const reference, the compiler knows that operator = doesn't wish to change that argument and therefore doesn't give us a warning that we might be changing a temporary value.

At that point, we'd taken care of operator =. However, to create a concrete data type, we have to allow our string variables to be passed as value arguments. Unfortunately, the compiler-generated copy constructor suffers from the same drawback as the compiler-generated operator =; namely, it copies the pointer to the actual data of the string, rather than the data itself. Logically, therefore, the solution to this problem is quite similar to the solution for operator =: We write our own copy constructor that allocates space for the character data to be stored in the newly created string and then copies the data from the old string to the new string.

However, we still can't use a value argument to our copy constructor, because a value argument needs a copy constructor to make the copy. This obviously won't work (and will be caught by the compiler). Therefore, as in the case of operator =, we have to use a reference argument. Since this is actually just another name for the caller's variable rather than a copy of it, no destructor for the reference argument is called at exit from our copy constructor. Because we are not going to change the caller's argument, we specify a constant reference argument of type string — in C++ terms, a const string&.

Problem
Algorithms
C++
Executable
Hardware

At that point we had met the requirements for a concrete data type, but such a type is of limited usefulness as long as we can't get the values displayed on the screen. Therefore, the next order of business was to add a Display member function that takes care of this task. This function isn't particularly complicated, but it does require us to deal with the notion of a C legacy type, the *array*. Since the compiler treats an array in almost the same way as a pointer, we can use array notation to extract each character that needs to be sent out to the screen. Continuing with our example of the Display function's use, the next topic was a discussion of how chars can be treated as numeric variables.

Then we saw a demonstration of how easy it is to misuse an array to destroy data that belongs to some other variable. This is an important warning of the dangers of uncontrolled use of pointers and arrays; these are the most error prone constructs in both C and C++, when not kept under tight rein.

We continued by revisiting the topic of access control and why it is advantageous to keep member variables out of the public section of the class definition. The reasons are similar to those for avoiding global variables; it's too hard to keep track of where the value of a public member variable is being referenced and to update all the affected areas of the code when changing the class definition. However, it is sometimes useful to allow external functions access to some information about a class object. We saw how to do this by adding a GetLength member function to our string class.

After finishing up the requirements to make the string class a concrete data type, we continued to add more facilities to the string class; to be precise, we wanted to make it possible to modify the sorting program of Chapter 4 to handle strings rather than shorts. To do this, we had to be able to compare two strings to determine which of the two would come first in the dictionary and to read strings from an input stream (like cin) and write them to an output stream (like cout). Although the Display function provided a primitive mechanism for

```
Problem
Algorithms
C++
Executable
Hardware
```

writing a string to cout, it's much nicer to be able to use the standard >> and << operators that can handle all of the native types, so we resolved to make those available for strings as well.

The changes to the actual application program turned out not to be very significant compared to those needed in the string class. Although it might not seem so, that's actually a good sign because changes to the string class have to be done only once, whereas changes to the application program would have to be done for every application program that needed to use the new features.

We started out by implementing the < operator so that we could compare two strings x and y to see which would come before the other in the dictionary, simply by writing if (x < y). The implementation of this function turned out to be a bit complicated because of the possibility of "running off the end" of one of the strings when the strings are of different lengths.

Once we worked out the appropriate handling for this situation, we examined one implementation of the algorithm for operator <. In the course of this examination, we ran across another logical operator, && (logical AND). This operator makes it possible to write an if statement that is true only when both the first *and* second of two expressions are true.

The next thing we did was to look at a much shorter, simpler implementation of the same algorithm. This one uses memcmp, a C function that compares two sets of bytes and returns a different value depending on whether the first one is "less than", "equal to", or "greater than" the second one, using dictionary ordering to make this determination.

Then we developed an implementation of operator == for strings. Interestingly enough, this function was considerably simpler than the second version of operator <, even though both functions used memcmp to do most of the work. The reason is that if two strings are of different lengths, then they're already not equal, so the comparison of the actual contents of the strings for equality is necessary only for two strings whose length is the same. This eliminates the complexities resulting from trying to compare the contents of two arrays that are of different lengths.

Next, we saw that it's possible to declare a function without actually implementing it (so long as you don't try to use it), as when we included string5.h in string5a.cc.

Then we started looking beneath the covers of the output functions <<, starting with the predefined versions of << that handle char and C string arguments. The simplest case of using this operator, of course, is to display one expression on the screen via cout. Next, we examined the mechanism by which several uses of this operator can be chained together to allow the displaying of a number of expressions with one statement.

Problem
Algorithms
C++
Executable
Hardware

The next question was: How could we provide these handy facilities for the users of our string class? Would we have to modify the ostream classes to add support for strings? Luckily, the designers of the stream classes were foresightful enough to enable us to add support for our own data types without having to modify their code. The key is to create a *global* function that can add the contents of our string to an existing ostream variable and pass that ostream variable on to the next possible user, just as in the chaining mentioned previously for native types.

The implementation of this function wasn't terribly complicated; it merely wrote each char of the string's data to the output stream. The unusual part of this function was that it wasn't a member function of string, but a global function, as noted. This is needed to maintain the same syntax as the output of native types. However, there was one point that needed further explanation: How can a global function get access to non-public members of string such as m_Length and m_Data?

The answer is that we have allowed this access by specifying that a version of operator << that takes a string argument is a friend of the string class. Making a function a friend of a class means that it is allowed access to non-public data of that class, as though it were a member function.

After we finished the examination of our version of operator << for sending strings to an ostream, we went through the parallel exercise of creating a version of operator >> to read strings from an istream. This turned out to be a bit more complicated, since we had to make room for the incoming data, which limited the maximum length of strings that we could read in. In the process of defining this maximum length, we also encountered a new construct, the const value. This is a data item that is declared just like a variable, except that its value is initialized once and cannot be changed. This makes it ideal for specifying a constant size for an array, a constant loop limit, or other value that doesn't change from one execution of the program to the next.

Next, we used this const value to declare an *array* of chars to hold the input data to be stored in the string, and we filled the array with null bytes by calling the C function memset. We followed this by using some member functions of the istream class to eliminate any newline ('\n') character that might have been left over from a previous input operation.

Problem
Algorithms
C++
Executable
Hardware

Finally, we were ready to read the data into the array of chars, in preparation for assigning it to our string. After doing that assignment, we returned the original istream to the caller, to allow chaining of operations as is standard with operator << and operator >>.

That completes the review of this chapter. Now let's do some exercises to help it all sink in.

Exercises

1. We have already implemented operator < and operator ==. However, a concrete data type that allows for ordered comparisons such as < should really implement all six of the comparison operators. The other four of these operators are !=, >, >=, and <= ("not equal to", "greater than", "greater than or equal to", and "less than or equal to", respectively). Add the declarations of these operators to the string interface definition.

2. Implement the four comparison operators that you have added to the interface of the string class in Exercise 2.

3. Write a test program to verify that all of the comparison operators work. This program should test that each of the operators returns the value true when its condition is true;

equally important, it should test that each of the operators
returns the value false when the condition is *not* true.

4.   Is the program in Figure 8.35 legal? Explain.

```
class string
{
public:
     string();
     string& operator = (const string& Str);
private:
     string(char* p);
     short m_Length;
     char* m_Data;
};
int main()
{
     string n;
     n = "My name is: ";
     return 0;
}
```

Figure 8.35: Exercise 4 (code\strex6.cc)

Answers to the preceding exercises can be found at the end of the
chapter.

Problem
Algorithms
C++
Executable
Hardware

5.   Add a constructor to the string class. The arguments to this
     constructor are the address of an array of bytes (i.e., a char*) and
     a short indicating the length of the array of bytes. The data of the
     resulting string should consist of a copy of all the bytes from the
     array followed by a null byte, and the length of the string should
     be the length specified by the second argument (+1 for the
     added null byte, of course).

6.   Write a test program to ensure that strings constructed via your
     new constructor will be properly compared to other strings even
     if the byte arrays from which either or both of the strings
     contained null bytes.

7.   Write an essay explaining, in your own words, exactly why the
     compiler-generated copy constructor is acceptable for the
     StockItem class but not for the string class.

8.   What would happen if we compiled the following program,
     which attempts to compare a C string to a string in two different
     ways? Why? How would you fix this?

```
#include <iostream.h>
#include "string6.h"

int main()
{
    string x = "x";

    if (x < "xx")
        cout << "x is less than xx" << endl;
    else if ("xx" < x)
        cout << "xx is less than x" << endl;

    return 0;
}
```

Figure 8.36: Exercise 8 (code\strcmp1.cc)

Conclusion

Problem
Algorithms
C++
Executable
Hardware

In this chapter, we have significantly improved the string class, learning some generally useful techniques and lessons in the process. Of course, there are many more features that we could add to this class to make it more suitable for general programming purposes. However, that will have to wait for another day (and another book). Right now it's time to return to our inventory control example, so turn to Chapter 9, where we'll see how to improve the flexibility and power of our classes by means of some new C++ ideas and constructs that are central to object-oriented programming.

Answers to Selected Exercises

1. These are the declarations, which can be found in string6.h.

```
bool operator != (const string& Str);
bool operator > (const string& Str);
bool operator >= (const string& Str);
bool operator <= (const string& Str);
```

Figure 8.37: The added string class declarations (from code\string6.h)

2. The implementations of the comparison operators are shown in Figure 8.38 through Figure 8.42. The implementation for the completed string class, including these functions, is in string6.cc.

```
bool string::operator != (const string& Str)
{
    short Result;

    if (m_Length != Str.m_Length)
        return true;

    Result = memcmp(m_Data,Str.m_Data,m_Length);

    if (Result == 0)
        return false;

    return true;
}
```

Figure 8.38: The string class implementation of operator != (from code\string6.cc)

```
bool string::operator > (const string& Str)
{
    short Result;
    short CompareLength;

    if (Str.m_Length < m_Length)
        CompareLength = Str.m_Length;
    else
        CompareLength = m_Length;

    Result = memcmp(m_Data,Str.m_Data,CompareLength);

    if (Result > 0)
        return true;

    if (Result < 0)
        return false;

    if (m_Length > Str.m_Length)
        return true;

    return false;
}
```

Problem
Algorithms
C++
Executable
Hardware

Figure 8.39: The string class implementation of operator > (from code\string6.cc)

```
bool string::operator >= (const string& Str)
{
    short Result;
    short CompareLength;

    if (Str.m_Length < m_Length)
        CompareLength = Str.m_Length;
    else
        CompareLength = m_Length;

    Result = memcmp(m_Data,Str.m_Data,CompareLength);

    if (Result > 0)
        return true;

    if (Result < 0)
        return false;

    if (m_Length >= Str.m_Length)
        return true;

    return false;
}
```

Figure 8.40: The string class implementation of operator >= (from code\string6.cc)

Problem
Algorithms
C++
Executable
Hardware

```
bool string::operator <= (const string& Str)
{
    short Result;
    short CompareLength;

    if (Str.m_Length < m_Length)
        CompareLength = Str.m_Length;
    else
        CompareLength = m_Length;

    Result = memcmp(m_Data,Str.m_Data,CompareLength);

    if (Result < 0)
        return true;

    if (Result > 0)
        return false;

    if (m_Length <= Str.m_Length)
        return true;

    return false;
}
```

Figure 8.41: The string class implementation of operator <= (from code\string6.cc)

3. The output of the compiler should look something like Figure 8.42.

```
strex6.cc: In function 'int main()':
strex6.cc:7: constructor 'string::string(char *)' is private
strex6.cc:16: within this context
strex6.cc:5: in passing argument 1 of 'string::operator =(const string &)'
```

Figure 8.42: Exercise 1 (code\strex6.cc)

If the string::string(char*) constructor is available, the compiler will use it to build a temporary string from a char* argument on the right side of an =, then feed that temporary string to string::operator = (const string&) to modify the string on the left of the =. However, making the constructor string::string(char*) private prevents automatic conversion from char* to string and thus makes this program illegal.

4. The test program appears in Figure 8.43.

```
#include <iostream.h>
#include "string6.h"
                                                    Problem
int main()                                          Algorithms
{                                                   C++
    string x = "x";                                 Executable
    string xx = "xx";                               Hardware
    string y = "y";
    string yy = "yy";

// testing <
    if (x < x)
        cout << "ERROR: x < x" << endl;
    else
        cout << "OKAY: x NOT < x" << endl;
    if (x < xx)
        cout << "OKAY: x < xx" << endl;
    else
        cout << "ERROR: x NOT < xx" << endl;
    if (x < y)
        cout << "OKAY: x < y" << endl;
    else
        cout << "ERROR: x NOT < y" << endl;
```

Figure 8.43: Testing the string class comparison operators (code\strcmp.cc)

```
// testing <=
    if (x <= x)
        cout << "OKAY: x <= x" << endl;
    else
        cout << "ERROR: x NOT <= x" << endl;
    if (x <= xx)
        cout << "OKAY: x <= xx" << endl;
    else
        cout << "ERROR: x NOT <= xx" << endl;
    if (x <= y)
        cout << "OKAY: x <= y" << endl;
    else
        cout << "ERROR: x NOT <= y" << endl;

// testing >
    if (y > y)
        cout << "ERROR: y > y" << endl;
    else
        cout << "OKAY: y NOT > y" << endl;
    if (yy > y)
        cout << "OKAY: yy > y" << endl;
    else
        cout << "ERROR: yy NOT > y" << endl;
    if (y > x)
        cout << "OKAY: y > x" << endl;
    else
        cout << "ERROR: y NOT > x" << endl;

// testing >=
    if (y >= y)
        cout << "OKAY: y >= y" << endl;
    else
        cout << "ERROR: y NOT >= y" << endl;
    if (yy >= y)
        cout << "OKAY: yy >= y" << endl;
    else
        cout << "ERROR: yy NOT >= y" << endl;
    if (y >= x)
        cout << "OKAY: y >= x" << endl;
    else
        cout << "ERROR: y NOT >= x" << endl;
```

```
Problem
Algorithms
C++
Executable
Hardware
```

Figure 8.43 continued

```
// testing ==
    if (x == x)
        cout << "OKAY: x == x" << endl;
    else
        cout << "ERROR: x NOT == x" << endl;
    if (x == xx)
        cout << "ERROR: x == xx" << endl;
    else
        cout << "OKAY: x NOT == xx" << endl;
    if (x == y)
        cout << "ERROR: x == y" << endl;
    else
        cout << "OKAY: x NOT == y" << endl;

// testing !=
    if (x != x)
        cout << "ERROR: x != x" << endl;
    else
        cout << "OKAY: x NOT != x" << endl;
    if (x != xx)
        cout << "OKAY: x != xx" << endl;
    else
        cout << "ERROR: x NOT != xx" << endl;
    if (x != y)
        cout << "OKAY: x != y" << endl;
    else
        cout << "ERROR: x NOT != y" << endl;

    return 0;
}
```

Problem
Algorithms
C++
Executable
Hardware

Figure 8.43 continued

Chapter 9

Stocking Up

Now it's time to return to our inventory control example. In this chapter we'll start to build on our previous StockItem class by using another of the primary organizing principles of C++: **inheritance**. First, let's define this new term and a few others that we'll be using in this chapter, then we'll take a look at the objectives.

Definitions

Inheritance is the definition of one class as a more specific version of another class that has been previously defined. The newly defined class is called the **derived** (or sometimes the **child**) class, and the previously defined class is called the **base** (or sometimes the **parent**) class. In this book, we will use the terms *base* and *derived*. The derived class inherits all of the member variables and regular member functions from the base class. Inheritance is one of the primary organizing principles of object-oriented programming.

A **regular member function** is one that is *not* in any of the following categories:

1. Constructor
2. Destructor
3. Assignment operator (operator =).

A member function in a derived class is said to **override** a base class member function if the derived class function has the same *signature* (name and argument types) as the base class member function. The derived class member function will be called instead of the base class

323

member function when the member function is referred to via an object of the derived class. A member function in a derived class with the same name but a different signature from a member function in the base class does *not* override the base class member function. Instead, it "hides" that base class member function, which is no longer accessible as a member function in the derived class.

For example, the function Reorder(istream &) may be defined in a base class (StockItem) and in a derived class (DatedStockItem). When Reorder is called via an object of the base class StockItem, the base class version of Reorder will be called, and when Reorder is called via an object of the derived class DatedStockItem, the derived class version of Reorder will be called. This behavior of C++ allows a derived class to supply the same functionality as a base class but implement that functionality in a different way.

A **manipulator** is a member function of one of the iostreams classes that controls how output will be formatted without itself producing any output.

```
Problem
Algorithms
C++
Executable
Hardware
```

The keyword protected is an access specifier. When present in a base class definition, it allows derived class functions access to members in the base class part of a derived class object while preventing access by other functions outside the base class.

The **base** class **part** of a *derived* class object is an unnamed component of the derived class object whose member variables and functions are accessible as though they were defined in the derived class, so long as they are either public or protected.

A static **member function** is a member function of a class that can be called without reference to an object of that class. Such a function has no this pointer passed to it on entry, and therefore cannot refer to member variables of the class.

Objectives of This Chapter

By the end of this chapter, you should

1. Understand how we can use *inheritance* to create a new class by extending an existing class.
2. Understand how to use *manipulators* to control the format of iostreams output.

Under Control

Before we get to the details of our extensions to the inventory control (StockItem) class, let's expand a bit on the first objective as it applies to this particular case.

There are two reasons to use *inheritance*. The first is to create a new class that has all of the capabilities of an existing class, adding capabilities that are unique to the new class. In such a case, objects of the new class are clearly not equivalent to objects of the preexisting class, which means that the user of these classes has to know which class any given object belongs to so that he or she can tell which operations that object can perform.[1] Therefore, it does not make sense to be able to substitute objects of the derived class for objects of the base class. We could call this "inheritance for extension"; it's illustrated by one of the Employee class exercises in this chapter.

In the current case, however, we'll be using inheritance to create a new class called DatedStockItem that will be exactly like the StockItem class except that its items will have expiration dates. As a result, the user of this class will be able to use it in exactly the same way as the StockItem class. Of course, to create an object of this class, the expiration date for the object must be provided, but once such an object exists its user can view it in exactly the same way as one of the base class, which makes this an example of "inheritance for re-implementation". In such a case, it is reasonable to be able to substitute objects of the derived class for those of the base class, and we will see how to do that in the next chapter.

Problem
Algorithms
C++
Executable
Hardware

First, though, we'll need to learn how to create a new class by derivation from an existing class, in this case the StockItem class. To refresh your memory, in Chapter 6 we had developed that class for a simplistic but not completely unrealistic inventory management program for a small grocery store.

There are a few minor changes between the final version of the StockItem header file from Chapter 6 and the first one in this chapter (code\item20.h) that we should get out of the way before moving on. The first of these changes is the addition of global functions operator << and operator >> to display and read a StockItem (respectively), as we did with our string class; this replaces the use of Read and Write functions in Chapter 6. I've also renamed the member function Display to FormattedDisplay (which is more descriptive) and added a new

---

1. As elsewhere in this book, the user of a class means the application programmer who is using objects of the class to perform work in his or her program, not the "end user" who is using the finished program.

member function called Reorder and a couple of new member variables called m_MinimumStock and m_MinimumReorder, whose purpose we'll see shortly. Of course, the arguments to the "normal" constructor have been updated to reflect these two new member variables. Figure 9.1 shows the new header file.

```
class StockItem
{
friend ostream& operator << (ostream& s, const StockItem& Item);
friend istream& operator >> (istream& s, StockItem& Item);

public:
        StockItem();

        StockItem(string Name, short InStock,
        short Price, short MinimumStock,
        short MinimumReorder, string Distributor, string UPC);

        void FormattedDisplay(ostream& s);
        bool CheckUPC(string ItemUPC);
        void DeductSaleFromInventory(short QuantitySold);
        short GetInventory();
        string GetName();
        string GetUPC();
        bool IsNull();
        short GetPrice();

        void Reorder(ostream& s);

private:
        short m_InStock;
        short m_Price;
        short m_MinimumStock;
        short m_MinimumReorder;
        string m_Name;
        string m_Distributor;
        string m_UPC;
};
```

Problem
Algorithms
C++
Executable
Hardware

Figure 9.1: The updated interface for the StockItem class (code\item20.h)

Figure 9.2 shows the implementations of the new I/O functions.

```
ostream& operator << (ostream& s, const StockItem& Item)
{
    s << Item.m_Name << endl;
    s << Item.m_InStock << endl;
    s << Item.m_Price << endl;
    s << Item.m_MinimumStock << endl;
    s << Item.m_MinimumReorder << endl;
    s << Item.m_Distributor << endl;
    s << Item.m_UPC << endl;

    return s;
}

istream& operator >> (istream& s, StockItem& Item)
{
    s >> Item.m_Name;
    s >> Item.m_InStock;
    s >> Item.m_Price;
    s >> Item.m_MinimumStock;
    s >> Item.m_MinimumReorder;
    s >> Item.m_Distributor;
    s >> Item.m_UPC;

    return s;
}
```

Problem
Algorithms
C++
Executable
Hardware

Figure 9.2: The implementations of operator << and operator >> (from code\item20.cc)

As you can see, there's nothing mysterious about these functions. They simply use the preexisting operator << and operator >> functions for the short and string variable types to read or write the member variables of a StockItem from or to the stream variable s.

Claiming an Inheritance

Now let's work out the details of a particular extension to this inventory control program: calculating how much of each item has to be ordered to refill the stock. I've chosen the imaginative name ReorderItems for the member function in the Inventory class that will perform this operation. Figure 9.3 shows the updated header file for the Inventory class.

```
class Inventory
{
public:
    Inventory();

    short LoadInventory(ifstream& InputStream);

    void StoreInventory(ofstream& OutputStream);

    StockItem FindItem(string UPC);
    short UpdateItem(StockItem Item);
    void ReorderItems(ofstream &OutputStream);

private:
    vector<StockItem> m_Stock;
    short m_StockCount;
};
```

Figure 9.3: The new header file for the Inventory class (code\invent20.h)

The new ReorderItems function is pretty simple. Its behavior can be described as follows:

```
Problem
Algorithms
C++
Executable
Hardware
```

"For each element in the StockItem vector in the Inventory object, call its member function Reorder to generate an order if that StockItem object needs to be reordered."

Of course, this analysis neglects a number of considerations that would be relevant in a real program. However, it has some resemblance to the real algorithm, which is good enough for our purposes.

Figure 9.4 shows the implementation of the ReorderItems member function in the Inventory class.

```
void Inventory::ReorderItems(ofstream& OutputStream)
{
    short i;

    for (i = 0; i < m_StockCount; i ++)
        m_Stock[i].Reorder(OutputStream);
}
```

Figure 9.4: The ReorderItems function for the Inventory class (from code\invent20.cc)

That could hardly be much simpler: as you can see, it merely tells each StockItem element in the m_Stock vector to execute its Reorder function. Now, let's see what that function, whose full name is void StockItem::Reorder(ofstream&), needs to do:

1. Check to see if the current stock of that item is less than the desired minimum.
2. If we are below the desired stock minimum, then order the amount needed to bring us back to the stock minimum, unless that order amount is less than the minimum allowable quantity from the distributor. In the latter case, order the minimum allowable reorder quantity.
3. If we are not below the desired stock minimum, do nothing.

To support this new Reorder function, we'll use the new data items m_MinimumStock and m_MinimumReorder, which I added to the first version of the StockItem header file in this chapter. As I've already mentioned, the normal constructor for a StockItem has two additional arguments to initialize these two new member variables.

Figure 9.5 shows the code for the Reorder function.

```
void StockItem::Reorder(ostream& s)
{
        short ActualReorderQuantity;

        if (m_InStock < m_MinimumStock)
                {
                ActualReorderQuantity = m_MinimumStock - m_InStock;
                if (m_MinimumReorder > ActualReorderQuantity)
                        ActualReorderQuantity = m_MinimumReorder;
                s << "Reorder " << ActualReorderQuantity;
                s << " units of " << m_Name;
                s << " with UPC " << m_UPC;
                s << " from " << m_Distributor << endl;
                }
}
```

Problem
Algorithms
C++
Executable
Hardware

Figure 9.5: The Reorder function for the StockItem class (from code\item20.cc)

Here's the translation of the code.

1. If the number of units in stock is less than the minimum number desired, we calculate the number needed to bring the inventory back to the minimum.

2. However, the number we want to order may be less than the minimum number that we are allowed to order; the latter quantity is specified by the variable m_MinimumReorder.
3. If the value of m_MinimumReorder is more than the number we actually needed, then we have to substitute the minimum quantity for that previously calculated number.
4. Finally, we display the order for the item. Of course, if we already have enough units in stock, we don't have to reorder anything, so we don't display anything.

A Dated Approach

Now we want to add one wrinkle to this algorithm: handling items that have expiration dates. This actually applies to a fair number of items in a typical grocery store, including dairy products, meats, and even dry cereals. To keep things as simple as possible, we'll assume that whenever we buy a batch of some item with an expiration date, all of the items of that type have the same date. When we get to the expiration date of a given StockItem, we send back all of the items and reorder as though we had no items in stock.

Problem
Algorithms
C++
Executable
Hardware

The first question to answer is how to store the expiration date. My first inclination was to use our old friend, the short, to store each date as a number representing the number of days from (for example) January 1, 1990 to the date in question. Since there are approximately 365.25 days in a year, the range of -32768 to 32767 should hold us till roughly the year 2080, which is good enough for our purposes. (Perhaps by that year, we'll all be eating food pills that don't spoil.)

However, storing a date as a number of days since a *base date* such as January 1, 1990 does require a means of translating from a "normal" date format like "September 4, 1995" into a number of days from the base date and vice versa. Owing to the peculiarities of our Gregorian calendar (primarily the different numbers of days in different months and the complication of leap years), this is not a trivial matter and is a distraction from our goal here.

However, there is a simpler way to store and use dates that still allows us to determine whether a given date is before or after another date. If we represent a date as a string of the form YYYYMMDD,[2]

---

2. In case you're wondering why I allocated 4 digits for the year, it was to ensure that the program will still work after 1999. Unfortunately, not all programmers have been so considerate. Many programs use a 2-digit number to represent the year portion of a date in the form "YYMMDD" and as a result will fail by the year 2000. For a number of perspectives on this "Year 2000" problem, see the February '96 issue of *American Programmer* magazine.

where YYYY is the year, MM is the month number, and DD is the day number within the month, then we can use the string comparison functions to tell us which of two dates is later than the other one. Here's the analysis:

1. Of two dates with different year numbers, whichever has the higher year number is a later date.
2. Of two dates with the same year number but different month numbers, whichever has the higher month number is a later date.
3. Of two dates having the same year and month numbers, whichever has the higher day number is a later date.

Since we know that the string comparison operators compare bytes from left to right and stop when a mismatch is detected, as is needed for alphabetical sorting, it should be clear that dates using the representation YYYYMMDD will have their year numbers compared first, followed by the month numbers if needed, followed by the day numbers if needed. Thus, string::operator > will produce the result true if the "date string" on the left represents a date later than the "date string" on the right, exactly as we would wish.

Now that we've figured out that we can store the expiration date as a string, how do we arrange for it to be included in the StockItem object? One obvious solution is to make up a new class called, say, DatedStockItem by copying the interface and implementation from StockItem, adding a new member variable m_Expires, and modifying the copied Reorder member function to take the expiration date into account. However, doing this would create a maintenance problem when we had to make a change that would affect both of these classes; we'd have to make such a change in two places. Just multiply this nuisance by ten or twenty times, and you'll get a pretty good idea of how program maintenance has acquired its reputation as difficult and tedious work. Since one of the purposes of object-oriented programming is to reduce the difficulty of maintenance, surely there must be a better way to create a new class "just like" StockItem but with an added member variable and a modified member function to use it.

Problem
Algorithms
C++
Executable
Hardware

Ancestor Worship

Yes, there is; it's called **inheritance**. We can define our new class called DatedStockItem with a notation that it inherits (or *derives*) from StockItem. This makes StockItem the *base* class (sometimes referred to as the *parent* class) and our new class DatedStockItem the *derived* class (sometimes referred to as the *child* class). By doing this, we are specifying that a DatedStockItem includes every data member and regular member function that a StockItem has. Since DatedStockItem is a separate class from StockItem, we can also add whatever other functions and data we need to handle the differences between StockItem and DatedStockItem.

I think a picture might help here. Let's start with a simplified version of the StockItem and DatedStockItem classes; Figure 9.6 shows the interface for these simplified classes. I strongly recommend that you print out the header and implementation files (code\itema.h and code\itema.cc, respectively), for reference as you are going through this section of the chapter.

```
#include "string6.h"

class StockItem
{
public:
        StockItem(string Name, short InStock, short MinimumStock);
        void Reorder(ostream& s);

protected:
        string m_Name;
        short m_InStock;
        short m_MinimumStock;
};

class DatedStockItem: public StockItem // deriving a new class
{
public:
        DatedStockItem(string Name, short InStock, short MinimumStock,
        string Expires);

        void Reorder(ostream& s);

protected:
static string Today();

protected:
        string m_Expires;
};
```

`Problem`
`Algorithms`
`C++`
`Executable`
`Hardware`

Figure 9.6: Simplified interface for StockItem and DatedStockItem classes
(code\itema.h)

Given these definitions, a StockItem object might look as depicted in Figure 9.7.[3]

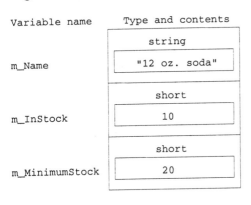

Figure 9.7: A StockItem object

And a DatedStockItem object might look as depicted in Figure 9.8.

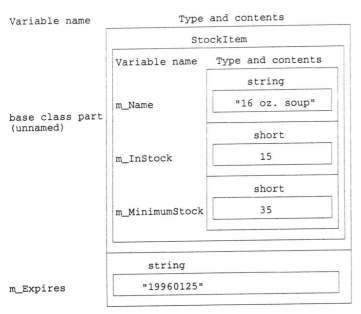

Problem
Algorithms
C++
Executable
Hardware

Figure 9.8: A DatedStockItem object

---

3. I'm simplifying by leaving out the internal structure of a string, which would change the actual layout of the object; this detail isn't relevant here.

As you can see, an object of the new DatedStockItem class contains a StockItem as part of its data. In this case, that base class part accounts for most of the data of a DatedStockItem; all we've added is a data member called m_Expires.

In fact, a derived class object always contains all of the variables and "regular" member functions in the base class because the derived class object has an object of the base class embedded in it, as indicated in Figure 9.8. We can access those member variables and functions that are part of the base class part of our derived class object exactly as though they were defined in the derived class object, so long as their access specifiers are either public or protected. Although the public and private access specifiers have been part of our arsenal of tools for some time, we haven't used protected before. We'll see shortly that the sole purpose of the protected access specifier is to allow member functions of a derived class unfettered access to member functions and variables of the base class part of an object of that derived class, while protecting those member functions and variables from use by unrelated classes.

Of course, as noted above, we don't have to rely solely on the facilities we inherit from our base class; we can also add whatever new functions or variables we need to provide the new functionality of the new class. As you will see, we don't want or need to add any public member functions in the present case, because our eventual goal is to allow the application programmer to treat objects of the new DatedStockItem class as being equivalent to objects of the StockItem class. To reach this goal, these two classes must have the same class *interface*, i.e., the same public member functions.

Instead of adding new public member functions, we will *override* the base class version of Reorder by writing a new version of Reorder for our DatedStockItem class. Our new function, which has the same signature as the base class function Reorder, will use the new data member m_Expires. Since the base class version of Reorder has been overridden by DatedStockItem::Reorder, the latter function will be called whenever the user's program calls the Reorder function of a DatedStockItem.

Why do we want to override the base class function Reorder rather than writing an entirely new function with a new name? Precisely because our eventual goal is to allow the user to be able to use stock items with and without dates interchangeably. If StockItem and DatedStockItem had different names for their reordering function, then the user would have to call a different function depending on which type the object really was, which would defeat our attempt to make them interchangeable.

Problem
Algorithms
C++
Executable
Hardware

Before we get into the details of the Reorder function in the DatedStockItem class, I should explain what I mean by "regular member function". A regular member function is one that is *not* in any of the following categories:

1. Constructor
2. Destructor
3. Assignment operator (operator =).

In other words, when we write a derived class (in this case, DatedStockItem), it does not inherit the constructor, destructor, or operator = functions from the base class (in this case, StockItem). Instead, we have to write these functions explicitly for the derived class if we don't want to rely on the compiler-generated versions in the derived class. Why is this?

It's because the base class versions of these functions are called automatically to construct, destroy, and assign the base class part of the derived class object. Therefore, all we have to worry about in our derived class is handling the newly added parts of that class. We'll see exactly how and when these base class functions are called as we go through the corresponding derived class functions.

For the moment, we won't have to define any of these derived class functions except two new constructors. Since the member variables and the base class part of DatedStockItem are all concrete data types, the compiler-generated versions of the destructor and assignment operator, which call the destructors and assignment operators for those member variables (and the base class part), will work perfectly well.

However, there is one change that we have to make to our previous definition of StockItem to make it a suitable base class; we have to change the *access specifier* for its member variables from private to protected. By this point, you should be familiar with the meaning of private: Any member variables or member functions that are marked as private can be referred to only by member functions of the same class, while all other functions are prohibited from accessing those private member variables or member functions. On the other hand, marking member functions or member data as public means that any function, whether a member or a nonmember function, can access those public member functions or data. That seems to take care of all the possibilities, so what is protected good for?

Problem
Algorithms
C++
Executable
Hardware

Protection Racket

Member variables and member functions that are listed in a protected section of the interface definition are treated the same as though they were private, with one important exception: Member functions of derived classes can access these member variables and member functions when they occur as the base class part of a derived class object.

In the current case, we've seen that a DatedStockItem is "just like" a StockItem with one additional member variable and some other additions and changes that aren't relevant here. The important point is that every DatedStockItem contains everything that a StockItem contains. For example, every DatedStockItem has a m_MinimumStock member variable included in it because the StockItem class has a m_MinimumStock member variable, and we're defining a DatedStockItem as being derived from StockItem. Logically, therefore, we should be able to access the value of the m_MinimumStock member variable in our DatedStockItem. However, if that member variable is declared as private, we can't. The private access specifier doesn't care about inheritance; since DatedStockItem is a different class from StockItem, private member variables and functions of StockItem wouldn't be accessible to member functions of DatedStockItem, even though the member variables of StockItem are actually present in every DatedStockItem! That's why we have to make those variables protected rather than private.[4]

Now that we've cleared up that point (I hope), we have to consider the question of when to use protected vs. private variables. Because private member variables of the base class cannot be accessed directly by derived class member functions, we have to decide whether we want any derived classes to be able to access member variables of the base class part of the derived object when we define the base class. If we do, we have to use the protected access specifier for those member variables. If we don't do that and later discover that we need access to those variables in a derived class, we will then have to change the definition of the base class so that the variables are protected rather than private. Such changes are not too much trouble when we have written all of the classes involved, but they can be extremely difficult or even impossible when we are trying to derive new classes from previously existing classes written by someone else.

Problem
Algorithms
C++
Executable
Hardware

---

4. Now that I've explained why we need a protected access specifier in the StockItem class, you may wonder why I have *two* protected access specifiers in the DatedStockItem class: the reason is that I like to specify the access specifiers for functions and for data separately to clarify what I'm doing. This duplication doesn't mean anything to the compiler, but it makes my intention more explicit to the next programmer.

However, protected variables and functions have some of the drawbacks of public variables and functions, because anyone can derive a new class that uses those variables or functions. Once they have done that, any changes to those variables or functions will cause their code to break. Hence, making everything protected isn't an unalloyed blessing.

Another possibility is to use protected member functions to allow access to private member variables in the base class part, rather than using protected member variables for the same purpose. I haven't investigated this approach enough to render a definitive opinion, but at first glance it appears to provide the advantages of protected variables while being less likely to cause maintenance problems down the road.

The moral of the story is that it's easier to design classes for our own use and derivation than for the use of others. Even though we could go back and change our class definitions to make them more flexible, that alternative may not be available to others. The result may be that our classes will not meet others' needs.

Stock Footage

Problem
Algorithms
C++
Executable
Hardware

After that excursion into the use of the protected access specifier, let's look at the revised header file containing the interface definitions of StockItem and DatedStockItem, Figure 9.9, as well as the implementation in Figure 9.10. I strongly recommend that you print out the files that contain this interface and its implementation, for reference as you are going through this section of the chapter; those files are code\item21.h and code\item21.cc, respectively.

Before we get to the interface definition for DatedStockItem, I should explain the new header file #included in the implementation file item21.cc. This file, dos.h, defines a data type needed by the Today function, which we'll get to in a little while.

In case you're writing programs to run under another operating system, such as Unix™, I should warn you that dos.h, as its name suggests, is specific to MS-DOS. Therefore, this program won't compile in its current form under other operating systems. While this problem is soluble, its solution is outside the scope of this book.

```
class StockItem
{
friend ostream& operator << (ostream& s, const StockItem& Item);
friend istream& operator >> (istream& s, StockItem& Item);

public:
        StockItem();
        StockItem(string Name, short InStock,
        short Price, short MinimumStock,
        short MinimumReorder, string Distributor, string UPC);
        short CheckUPC(string ItemUPC);
        void DeductSaleFromInventory(short QuantitySold);
        short GetInventory();
        string GetName();
        string GetUPC();
        short IsNull();
        short GetPrice();
        void Reorder(ostream& s);
        void FormattedDisplay(ostream& s);

protected:
        short m_InStock;
        short m_Price;
        short m_MinimumStock;
        short m_MinimumReorder;
        string m_Name;
        string m_Distributor;
        string m_UPC;
};

class DatedStockItem: public StockItem
{
friend ostream& operator << (ostream& s, const DatedStockItem& Item);
friend istream& operator >> (istream& s, DatedStockItem& Item);

public:
        DatedStockItem();
        DatedStockItem(string Name, short InStock, short Price,
        short MinimumStock, short MinimumReorder,
        string Distributor, string UPC, string Expires);
        void FormattedDisplay(ostream& s);
        void Reorder(ostream& s);

protected:
static string Today();

protected:
        string m_Expires;
};
```

Problem
Algorithms
C++
Executable
Hardware

Figure 9.9: Full interface for StockItem and DatedStockItem (code\item21.h)

```
#include <iostream.h>
#include <iomanip.h>
#include <strstream.h>
#include <string.h>
#include "string6.h"
#include "item21.h"
#include <dos.h>

StockItem::StockItem()
: m_InStock(0), m_Price(0), m_MinimumStock(0),
  m_MinimumReorder(0), m_Name(), m_Distributor(),
  m_UPC()
{
}

StockItem::StockItem(string Name, short InStock,
short Price, short MinimumStock,
short MinimumReorder, string Distributor, string UPC)
: m_InStock(InStock), m_Price(Price),
  m_MinimumStock(MinimumStock),
  m_MinimumReorder(MinimumReorder), m_Name(Name),
  m_Distributor(Distributor), m_UPC(UPC)
{
}

void StockItem::FormattedDisplay(ostream& s)
{
    s << "Name: ";
    s << m_Name << endl;
    s << "Number in stock: ";
    s << m_InStock << endl;
    s << "Price: ";
    s << m_Price << endl;
    s << "Minimum stock: ";
    s << m_MinimumStock << endl;
    s << "Minimum Reorder quantity: ";
    s << m_MinimumReorder << endl;
    s << "Distributor: ";
    s << m_Distributor << endl;
    s << "UPC: ";
    s << m_UPC << endl;
}
```

Problem
Algorithms
C++
Executable
Hardware

Figure 9.10: Implementation for StockItem and DatedStockItem
(code\item21.cc)

```
ostream& operator << (ostream& s, const StockItem& Item)
{
    s << Item.m_Name << endl;
    s << Item.m_InStock << endl;
    s << Item.m_Price << endl;
    s << Item.m_MinimumStock << endl;
    s << Item.m_MinimumReorder << endl;
    s << Item.m_Distributor << endl;
    s << Item.m_UPC << endl;

    return s;
}

istream& operator >> (istream& s, StockItem& Item)
{
    s >> Item.m_Name;
    s >> Item.m_InStock;
    s >> Item.m_Price;
    s >> Item.m_MinimumStock;
    s >> Item.m_MinimumReorder;
    s >> Item.m_Distributor;
    s >> Item.m_UPC;

    return s;
}

short StockItem::CheckUPC(string ItemUPC)
{
    if (m_UPC == ItemUPC)
        return 1;

    return 0;
}

void StockItem::DeductSaleFromInventory(short QuantitySold)
{
    m_InStock -= QuantitySold;
}

short StockItem::GetInventory()
{
    return m_InStock;
}
```

Problem
Algorithms
C++
Executable
Hardware

Figure 9.10 continued

```
string StockItem::GetName()
{
      return m_Name;
}

string StockItem::GetUPC()
{
      return m_UPC;
}

short StockItem::IsNull()
{
      if (m_UPC == "")
            return 1;

      return 0;
}

short StockItem::GetPrice()
{
      return m_Price;
}

void StockItem::Reorder(ostream& s)
{
      short ActualReorderQuantity;

      if (m_InStock < m_MinimumStock)
            {
            ActualReorderQuantity = m_MinimumStock - m_InStock;
            if (m_MinimumReorder > ActualReorderQuantity)
                  ActualReorderQuantity = m_MinimumReorder;
            s << "Reorder " << ActualReorderQuantity << " units of " << m_Name;
            s << " with UPC " << m_UPC << " from " << m_Distributor << endl;
            }
}

DatedStockItem::DatedStockItem()
: m_Expires()
{
}
```

Problem
Algorithms
C++
Executable
Hardware

Figure 9.10 continued

```
string DatedStockItem::Today()
{
      date d;
      short year;
      char day;
      char month;
      string TodaysDate;
      strstream FormatStream;

      getdate(&d);
      year = d.da_year;
      day = d.da_day;
      month = d.da_mon;

      FormatStream << setfill('0') << setw(4) << year <<
            setw(2) << month << setw(2) << day;
      FormatStream >> TodaysDate;

      return TodaysDate;
}

DatedStockItem::DatedStockItem(string Name, short InStock,
short Price, short MinimumStock,
short MinimumReorder, string Distributor, string UPC,
string Expires)
: StockItem(Name,InStock,Price,MinimumStock,MinimumReorder,
   Distributor,UPC),
   m_Expires(Expires)
{
}

void DatedStockItem::Reorder(ostream& s)
{
      if (m_Expires < Today())
            {
            s << "Return " << m_InStock << " units of " << m_Name;
            s << " with UPC " << m_UPC << " to " << m_Distributor << endl;
            m_InStock = 0;
            }

      StockItem::Reorder(s);
}
```

Problem
Algorithms
C++
Executable
Hardware

Figure 9.10 continued

```
void DatedStockItem::FormattedDisplay(ostream& s)
{
    s << "Expiration Date: ";
    s << m_Expires << endl;
    StockItem::FormattedDisplay(s);
}

ostream& operator << (ostream& s, const DatedStockItem& Item)
{
    s << Item.m_Expires << endl;
    s << Item.m_Name << endl;
    s << Item.m_InStock << endl;
    s << Item.m_Price << endl;
    s << Item.m_MinimumStock << endl;
    s << Item.m_MinimumReorder << endl;
    s << Item.m_Distributor << endl;
    s << Item.m_UPC << endl;

    return s;
}

istream& operator >> (istream& s, DatedStockItem& Item)
{
    s >> Item.m_Expires;
    s >> Item.m_Name;
    s >> Item.m_InStock;
    s >> Item.m_Price;
    s >> Item.m_MinimumStock;
    s >> Item.m_MinimumReorder;
    s >> Item.m_Distributor;
    s >> Item.m_UPC;

    return s;
}
```

```
Problem
Algorithms
C++
Executable
Hardware
```

Figure 9.10 continued

Now let's get to the interface definition for DatedStockItem. Most of this should be pretty simple to follow by now. We have to declare new versions of operator << and operator >>, which will allow us to write and read objects of the DatedStockItem class, as we have already arranged for the normal StockItem; as before, the friend specifiers are needed to allow these global input and output functions to access the internal variables of our class. Then we have the default constructor, DatedStockItem(), and the "normal" constructor that supplies values for

all of the member variables. We also have to declare the Reorder
function that we are writing for this class.

However, there are a couple of constructs here that we haven't
seen before. The first one is in the class header: DatedStockItem: public
StockItem. I'm referring specifically to the expression : public StockItem,
which states that this class, DatedStockItem, is publicly derived from
StockItem. We have already discussed the fact that deriving a new class
from an old one means that the new class has everything in it that the
old class had in it. But what does the public keyword mean here?

class **Interests**

It means that we are going to allow a DatedStockItem to be treated as a
StockItem; that is, any function that takes a StockItem as a parameter will
accept a DatedStockItem in its place. All of the public member functions
and public data items (if there were any) in StockItem are publicly
accessible in a DatedStockItem object as well. This is called,
imaginatively enough, public *inheritance*, and a class that is derived
from a base class via public inheritance is said to have an "**isA**"
relationship with its base class.[5]

Problem
Algorithms
C++
Executable
Hardware

This substitutability of an object of a publicly derived class for an
object of its base class extends to areas where its value is somewhat
questionable. In particular, a derived class object can be assigned to a
base class object. The result will be that any member variables that
exist in the derived class object but not in the base class object will be
ignored in the assignment. This "partial assignment" is called **slicing**,
and it can be a serious annoyance because the compiler won't warn
you that it's taking place. After all, since a DatedStockItem "isA"
StockItem, it's perfectly legal to assign an object of the former class to
an object of the latter class, even if that isn't what you had in mind.
However, you shouldn't worry about this problem too much; as we'll
see in the next chapter, we can solve it by using more advanced
techniques.

---

5. You might be wondering whether there are any other types of inheritance. The answer is that
there is one other type that is sometimes useful: private inheritance. If we specified "; private
StockItem" rather than ": public StockItem" when we stated the base class for DatedStockItem, then
DatedStockItem member functions would be able to use the protected and public member variables
and member functions of StockItem in their implementation, just as with public inheritance.
However, the fact that DatedStockItem is derived from StockItem would not be apparent to any
outside program. That is, if we had specified private inheritance rather than public, a
DatedStockItem would *not* be an acceptable substitute for a StockItem; alternatively we could say
that DatedStockItem would not have an "isA" relationship with StockItem. There aren't very many
applications for private inheritance, and we won't be seeing any in this book.

Before we get into the implementation of the DatedStockItem class, let's take a look at the other new construct in its interface; namely, the notion of a static member function. I'll give you a hint as to its meaning: In the grand old C/C++ tradition of keyword abuse, the meaning of static here is almost but not quite entirely unlike its meaning either for local variables or for global variables.

Getting static

Give up? Okay. It means that we don't have to specify an object for the member function to apply to. Thus, we can refer to the static member function called Today by just its name. Within DatedStockItem member functions, that means writing "Today();" is sufficient. Of course, if Today() were public, and we wanted to call it from a nonmember function, we would have to refer to it by its full name: DatedStockItem::Today(). Either of these calls differs from the normal use of a member function, where we specify the function along with the object to which it applies; for example, "soup.GetInventory();". What is the advantage of a static member function?

The advantage is precisely that we can call it without needing an object to call it for. In this case, the value of today's date is not dependent on any DatedStockItem object; therefore, it's quite handy to be able to call Today() without referring to any object of the DatedStockItem class.

Of course, if we made Today() a global function rather than a static member function, we also wouldn't have to supply an object when we called it. However, the advantages of using a static protected member function over a global function are much the same as the advantages of using private member variables rather than public ones. First, we can change the interface of this function more easily than that of a global function, as we know that it can be accessed only by member functions of DatedStockItem and any possible derived classes of that class, rather than by any function anywhere. Second, we don't have to worry that someone else might want to define a different function with the same signature, which could be a problem with a global function. The full name of this function, DatedStockItem::Today(), is sufficient to distinguish it from any other Today() functions that belong to other classes, or even from a global function of that name, should another programmer be so inconsiderate as to write such a function!

There's one other thing here that we haven't seen before: Today() is a protected member function, which means that it is accessible only to

Problem
Algorithms
C++
Executable
Hardware

member functions of DatedStockItem and descendants of DatedStockItem, just as a protected member variable is. We want to keep this function from being called by application programs for the same reason that we protect member variables by restricting access: to reserve the right to change its name, return value, or argument types. Since application code can't access this function, they can't depend on its interface.

Figure 9.11 is the implementation of the protected static member function DatedStockItem::Today().

```
string DatedStockItem::Today()
{
    date d;
    short year;
    char day;
    char month;
    string TodaysDate;
    strstream FormatStream;

    getdate(&d);
    year = d.da_year;
    day = d.da_day;
    month = d.da_mon;

    FormatStream << setfill('0') << setw(4) << year <<
        setw(2) << month << setw(2) << day;
    FormatStream >> TodaysDate;

    return TodaysDate;
}
```

Problem
Algorithms
C++
Executable
Hardware

Figure 9.11: DatedStockItem::Today (from code\item21.cc)

Here's where we're using the date type defined in #include dos.h. As its name suggests, a date is used to store the components of a date (i.e., its month, day, and year). Now that we've gotten that detail out of the way, let's look at this Today function. First, we have to call the getdate function (whose declaration is also in dos.h) to ascertain the current date; getdate handles this request by filling in the member variables in a variable of type date. Note that the argument to the getdate function is the address of the date variable (i.e., &date) rather than the variable itself. This is necessary because the getdate function is left over from C, which doesn't have reference variables. Since all C arguments are value arguments, a C function can't change any of its arguments. This limitation is handled in C by passing the **address** of the variable to be modified so that the function can use that address as a pointer to the actual variable. Happily, we don't have to concern ourselves about this in any more detail than what I've just mentioned.

By the way, this is a good example of the difference between calling a member function and calling a nonmember function: We have to specify the date variable when calling getdate because getdate isn't a member function of the date type. As getdate is a leftover from C, which doesn't have member functions, we have to supply the address of the variable on which the function should operate. Of course, with a member function, the compiler automatically supplies the this pointer to every (non-static) member function as a hidden argument, so we don't have to worry about it.

After we call getdate, the current year is left in the da_year member variable, and the current day and month are left in the other two member variables da_day and da_mon. Now that we have the current year, month, and day, the next step is to produce a string that has all of these data items in the correct order and format. To do this, we're going to use some functions from the iostreams library that we haven't seen before. However, to use any functions from that library, we need a stream of some sort to apply them to. So far, we've used istream and ostream objects, but neither of those will do the job here. We don't really want to do any input or output at all, we just want to use the formatting functions that ostreams provide. Since this is a fairly common requirement, the inventors of the iostreams library have anticipated it by supplying the strstream class.

Problem
Algorithms
C++
Executable
Hardware

A strstream is a stream that exists entirely in memory rather than as a conduit to read or write data. In this case, we've declared a strstream called FormatStream, to which we'll write our data. When we get done, we'll read the formatted data back from FormatStream.

This discussion assumes that you're completely comfortable with the notion of a stream, which may not be true. At this point, you have enough background for us to take a closer look at that concept, so let's proceed.

stream **of Consciousness**

A stream is a facility that allows us to use various input and output devices in a more-or-less uniform fashion. There are a number of variants of this data type, which are related by inheritance so that we can substitute a more highly specialized variant for a more basic variety. So far we've encountered istream, ostream, ifstream, and ofstream, and of course most recently strstream. The best place to start a further investigation of this family of classes is with one of the simplest types, an ostream. We've already used a predefined object of this type quite a few times: of course, I'm referring to cout. Take a look at the program in Figure 9.12.

```
#include <iostream.h>

int main()
{
    short x;
    char y;

    x = 1;
    y = 'A';

    cout << "Test " << x;
    cout << " grade: " << y;
    cout << endl;

    return 0;
}
```

Problem
Algorithms
C++
Executable
Hardware

Figure 9.12: A simple stream example (code\stream1.cc)

At the beginning of the program, cout would look something like Figure 9.13.

buffer

Figure 9.13: An empty ostream object

What is the purpose of the put pointer and the **buffer**? Here's a breakdown:

1. The put pointer holds the address of the next byte in the output area of the stream; i.e., where the next byte will be stored if we use << to write data into the stream. Please note that the type of this pointer is irrelevant to us, as we cannot ever access it directly. However, you won't go far wrong if you think of it as the address of the next byte.
2. The stream *buffer* is the area of memory where the characters put into the stream are stored.

At this point, we haven't put anything into the stream yet, so the put pointer is pointing to the beginning of the buffer. Now, let's execute the line

cout << "Test " << x;

After that line is executed, the contents of the stream will look something like Figure 9.14.

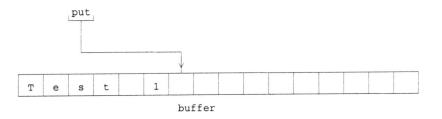

```
Problem
Algorithms
C++
Executable
Hardware
```

Figure 9.14: A stream object with some data

As you can see, the data from the first output line has been put into the stream buffer. Now let's look at the next statement, which is

cout << " grade: " << y;

After this statement is executed, the stream looks like Figure 9.15.

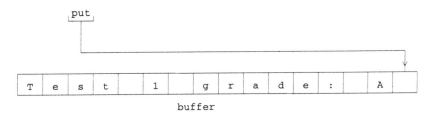

Figure 9.15: A stream object with some more data

Now we're ready for the final output statement, which is

cout << endl;

Once this statement has been executed, the stream looks like Figure 9.16.

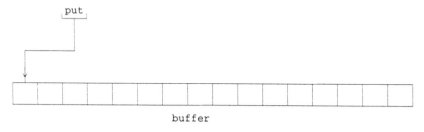

Figure 9.16: An empty stream object

At this point, you're probably wondering what happened to all the data we stored in the stream. The answer is that it went out to the screen, because that's what endl does (after sticking a newline character on the end of the buffer). After the data has been sent to the screen, we can't access it anymore in our program, so the space that it took up in the buffer is made available for further use.

Problem
Algorithms
C++
Executable
Hardware

We All stream **for** strstream

Now it's time to get back to our discussion of strstream. A strstream allows us to write data to its buffer and then read the resulting data back into a variable. For example, the program shown in Figure 9.17 uses a strstream object to combine a year, month, and day number to make one string containing all of those values.

A strstream is very similar to an ostream, except that once we have written data to a strstream, we can read the data from the strstream into a variable just as though we were reading from a file or the keyboard. Figure 9.18 shows what an empty strstream looks like.

```
#include <iostream.h>
#include <strstream.h>
#include "string6.h"

int main()
{
    strstream FormatStream;
    string date;

    short year = 1996;
    short month = 7;
    short day = 28;

    FormatStream << year;
    FormatStream << month;
    FormatStream << day;

    FormatStream >> date;

    cout << "date: " << date << endl;

    return 0;
}
```

Figure 9.17: A strstream formatting example (code\stream2.cc)

Problem
Algorithms
C++
Executable
Hardware

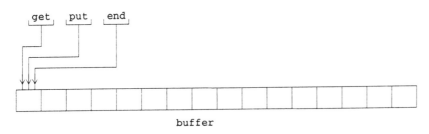

Figure 9.18: An empty strstream object

We've already discussed the put pointer and the buffer, but what about the get and end pointers? Here's what they're for:

1.   The get pointer holds the address of the next byte in the input area of the stream; i.e., the next byte that we would get if we used >> to read data from the stream.

2.   The end pointer indicates the end of the stream. Attempting to read anything at or after this position will cause the read to fail, because there isn't anything else to read.

After the statement

FormatStream << year;

the strstream might look like Figure 9.19.

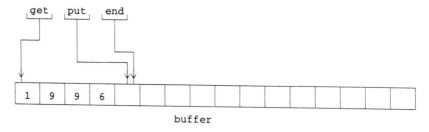

Figure 9.19: A strstream object with some contents

Problem
Algorithms
C++
Executable
Hardware

While the put pointer has moved to the next free byte in the strstream, the get pointer hasn't moved because we haven't gotten anything from the strstream. The next statement is

FormatStream << month;

which leaves the strstream looking like Figure 9.20.

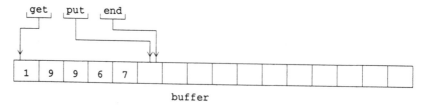

Figure 9.20: A strstream object with some more contents

After we have executed the statement

FormatStream << day;

the strstream looks like Figure 9.21.

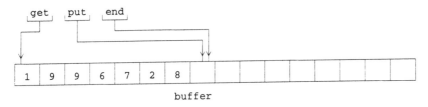

Figure 9.21: A strstream object with even more contents

Now it's time to get back what we've put into the strstream. That's the job of the next statement,

FormatStream >> date;

after which, the variable date has the value "1996728", and the strstream looks like Figure 9.22.

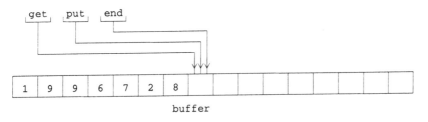

Figure 9.22: A strstream object after reading its contents

Problem
Algorithms
C++
Executable
Hardware

In other words, we've read to the end of the strstream, so we can't read from this strstream again until we "reset" it. This shouldn't seem too strange, as it is exactly analogous to the situation in Chapter 6 where we read all of the data in a file through an ifstream and the next read "fails" (see the section titled "References Required").

In these diagrams, the end and put pointers always point to the same place, so why do we need both? Because we can reset the put pointer to any place in the strstream before the current end pointer and write over the data we have already written. We don't make use of that facility in this book, but it's there when needed.

Use It or Lose It

Now let's get back to the problem of converting a date to a string so that we can compare it with another date. You might think that all we have to do is to write each data item out to the strstream, then read the resulting formatted data back in, as in the program in Figure 9.17. However, it's a bit more complicated than that because if we're going to be able to compare two of these values, we need to control the exact format in which the data will be written. To see why this is necessary, consider the program shown in Figure 9.23.

```
#include <iostream.h>
#include <strstream.h>
#include "string6.h"

int main()
{
    strstream FormatStream1;
    strstream FormatStream2;
    string date1;
    string date2;

    short year1 = 1996;
    short month1 = 12;
    short day1 = 28;

    short year2 = 1996;
    short month2 = 7;
    short day2 = 28;

    FormatStream1 << year1 << month1 << day1;
    FormatStream1 >> date1;

    FormatStream2 << year2 << month2 << day2;
    FormatStream2 >> date2;

    cout << "date1: " << date1 << ", date2: " << date2 << endl;
    if (date1 < date2)
        cout << "date1 is less than date2" << endl;
    else if (date1 == date2)
        cout << "date1 is the same as date2" << endl;
    else
        cout << "date1 is greater than date2" << endl;

    return 0;
}
```

Problem
Algorithms
C++
Executable
Hardware

Figure 9.23: Default formatting example (code\coutdef1.cc)

The output of that program is shown in Figure 9.24.

date1: 19961228, date2: 1996728
date1 is less than date2

Figure 9.24: Output of default formatting example (code\coutdef1.out)

What's wrong with this picture? Well, the string comparison of the first value with the second shows that the first one is less than the second one. Clearly, this is wrong, since the date that the first string represents is later than the date represented by the second string. The problem is that we're not formatting the output correctly; what we have to do is make month numbers less than 10 come out with a leading 0 (e.g., July would be 07 rather than 7). The same consideration applies to the day number; we want it to be two digits in every case. Of course, if we knew that a particular number was only one digit, then we could just add a leading 0 to it explicitly, but that wouldn't work correctly if the month or day number already had two digits. To make sure the output is correct without worrying about how many digits the value has, we can use iostreams member functions called **manipulators**, which are defined not in iostream.h but in another header file called iomanip.h. This header file defines setfill, setw, and a number of other manipulators that we don't need to worry about at the moment. These manipulators operate on **fields**; a field could be defined as the result of one << operator. In this case, we use the setw manipulator to specify the width of each field to be formatted and the setfill manipulator to set the character to be used to fill in the otherwise empty places in each field.

Problem
Algorithms
C++
Executable
Hardware

Let's change our example program to produce the output we want, as shown in Figure 9.25.

date1: 19961228, date2: 19960728
date1 is greater than date2

Figure 9.25: Output of controlled formatting example (code\coutdef2.out)

Manipulative Behavior

The new program is shown in Figure 9.26. Let's go over how this works in detail. To start with, setfill takes an argument specifying the char that will be used to fill in any otherwise unused positions in an output field. We want those unused positions to be filled with 0 characters, so that our output strings will consist entirely of numeric digits. (Actually, our comparison functions would work correctly even if we left the fill character at its default value of "space", but the date strings look silly that way!)

```
#include <iostream.h>
#include <strstream.h>
#include <iomanip.h>
#include "string6.h"

int main()
{
    strstream FormatStream1;
    strstream FormatStream2;
    string date1;
    string date2;

    short year1 = 1996;
    short month1 = 12;
    short day1 = 28;

    short year2 = 1996;
    short month2 = 7;
    short day2 = 28;

    FormatStream1 << setfill('0') << setw(4) <<
    year1 << setw(2) << month1 << setw(2) << day1;

    FormatStream1 >> date1;

    FormatStream2 << setfill('0') << setw(4) <<
    year2 << setw(2) << month2 << setw(2) << day2;

    FormatStream2 >> date2;

    cout << "date1: " << date1 << ", date2: " << date2 << endl;
    if (date1 < date2)
        cout << "date1 is less than date2" << endl;
    else if (date1 == date2)
        cout << "date1 is the same as date2" << endl;
    else
        cout << "date1 is greater than date2" << endl;

    return 0;
}
```

Problem
Algorithms
C++
Executable
Hardware

Figure 9.26: Controlled formatting example (code\coutdef2.cc)

The setfill manipulator is "sticky"; that is, it applies to all the following fields in the same output statement. However, this is not true of the other manipulator we're using, setw; that manipulator sets the field width only for the next field. Hence, we need three of those manipulators, one for each field in the output. The year field is four digits, while the month and day fields are two digits each.

Now let's get back to our DatedStockItem::Today function. It should be obvious how we can produce a formatted value on our strstream, but how do we get it back?

That turns out to be easy. Since the get pointer is still pointing to the beginning of the strstream, all we need is the statement FormatStream >> TodaysDate;, which reads data from the strstream into a string called TodaysDate, just as if we were reading data from cin or a file.

Baseless Accusations?

Now that we've taken care of the new function Today, let's take a look at the other functions of the DatedStockItem class that differ significantly from their counterparts in the base class StockItem; these are the constructors and the Reorder function.[6]

Let's start with the default constructor, which of course is called DatedStockItem::DatedStockItem() (Figure 9.27). It's a very short function, but there's a bit more here than meets the eye.

Problem
Algorithms
C++
Executable
Hardware

```
DatedStockItem::DatedStockItem()
: m_Expires()
{
}
```

Figure 9.27: Default constructor for DatedStockItem (from code\item21.cc)

A very good question here is "what happens to the base class part of the object?" This is taken care of by the default constructor of the StockItem class, which will be invoked by default to initialize that part of this object. The following is a general rule: Any base class part of a derived class object will automatically be initialized when the derived object is created at run time, by calling a base class constructor. By default, the default base class constructor will be called when we don't specify which base class constructor we want to execute. In

---

6. Besides these functions, there are some others that whose implementation in DatedStockItem is different from the versions in StockItem, but we'll wait until later to discuss them. These are the input and output functions FormattedDisplay, operator >>, and operator <<.

other words, the code in Figure 9.27 is translated by the compiler as though it were the code in Figure 9.28.

```
DatedStockItem::DatedStockItem()
: StockItem(),
  m_Expires()
{
}
```

Figure 9.28: Default constructor for DatedStockItem (from code\item21.cc)

The line

```
: StockItem(),
```

specifies which base class constructor we want to use to initialize the base class part of the DatedStockItem object. This is a construct called a **base** class **initializer**, which is the only permissible type of expression in a member initialization list other than a member initialization expression. In this case, we're calling the default constructor for the base class, StockItem.

Problem
Algorithms
C++
Executable
Hardware

Whether we allow the compiler to call the default base class constructor automatically, as in Figure 9.27, or explicitly specify that it's the one we want, as in Figure 9.28, the path of execution for the default DatedStockItem constructor is illustrated in Figure 9.29.

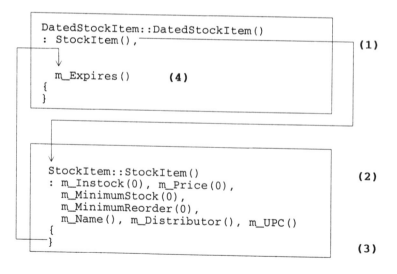

Figure 9.29: Constructing a default DatedStockItem object

At step **(1)**, the DatedStockItem calls the default constructor for StockItem, which starts in step **(2)** by initializing all the variables in the StockItem class to their default values. Once the default constructor for StockItem is finished, in step **(3)**, it returns to the DatedStockItem constructor. In step **(4)**, that constructor finishes the initialization of the DatedStockItem object by initializing m_Expires to the default string value.

This is fine as long as the base class default constructor does the job for us. However, if that constructor doesn't do what we want, we can specify which base constructor we wish to call, as shown in the "normal" constructor for the DatedStockItem class (Figure 9.30).

```
DatedStockItem::DatedStockItem(string Name, short InStock,
short Price, short MinimumStock,
short MinimumReorder, string Distributor, string UPC,
string Expires)
: StockItem(Name,InStock,Price,MinimumStock,MinimumReorder,
Distributor,UPC),
    m_Expires(Expires)
{
}
```

Figure 9.30: Normal constructor for DatedStockItem (from code\item21.cc)

As before, the line

```
: StockItem(Name, InStock, Price, MinimumStock, MinimumReorder, Distributor,
UPC),
```

is how we specify which base class constructor we want to use to initialize the base class part of the DatedStockItem object. In this case, the base class initializer specifies that we want to call the "normal" constructor for the base class, StockItem. This means that the StockItem part of the DatedStockItem object will be initialized exactly as though it were being created by the corresponding constructor for StockItem. Figure 9.31 illustrates how this works.

At step **(1)**, the DatedStockItem "normal" constructor is entered. In step **(2)**, that constructor calls the "normal" constructor for StockItem, which constructs the base class part of a DatedStockItem exactly as though it had been created by calling the StockItem constructor with the arguments Name, InStock, Price, MinimumStock, MinimumReorder, Distributor, and UPC. These arguments, of course, are the corresponding arguments of the DatedStockItem constructor, so in effect we are just passing them through to the base class constructor. Once the "normal"

Problem
Algorithms
C++
Executable
Hardware

constructor for StockItem is finished, in step **(3)**, it returns to the DatedStockItem constructor. In step **(4)**, that constructor finishes the initialization of the DatedStockItem object by initializing m_Expires to the value of the argument Expires.

```
DatedStockItem::DatedStockItem(
  string Name,
  short InStock,
  short Price,
  short MinimumStock,
  short MinimumReorder,
  string Distributor,
  string UPC,
  string Expires)
  : StockItem(Name,InStock,Price,
    MinimumStock,MinimumReorder,
    Distributor,UPC),                    (1)

    m_Expires(Expires)        (4)
  {
  }
```

Problem
Algorithms
C++
Executable
Hardware

```
StockItem::StockItem(
string Name,
short InStock,
short Price,
short MinimumStock,
short MinimumReorder,
string Distributor,
string UPC)                              (2)
: m_InStock(InStock), m_Price(Price),
  m_MinimumStock(MinimumStock),
  m_MinimumReorder(MinimumReorder),
  m_Name(Name),
  m_Distributor(Distributor),m_UPC(UPC)

  {
  }                                      (3)
```

Figure 9.31: Constructing a DatedStockItem object

As you can see by these examples, using a base class initializer allows us to use the base class constructor to initialize the base class object, which in turn means that our derived class constructor won't have to keep track of the details of the base class. This is an example of one of the main benefits claimed for object-oriented programming: We can confine the details of a class to the internals of that class, which simplifies maintenance efforts. In this case, after specifying the base class initializer, all we have to do in the DatedStockItem constructor is to initialize the member variable m_Expires.

There's another reason that we should use a base class initializer rather than trying to initialize the member variables of the base class part of our object directly: It's much safer. If we initialized the base class variables ourselves, and if the base class definition were later changed to include some new variables initialized according to arguments to the normal constructor, we might very well neglect to modify our derived class code to initialize the new variables. On the other hand, if we use a base class initializer, and its arguments changed (as they presumably would if new variables needed to be initialized), a derived class constructor that called that initializer would no longer compile. That would alert us to the change that we'd have to make.

Reordering Priorities

Now that we have dealt with the constructors, let's take a look at the Reorder function (Figure 9.32).

Problem
Algorithms
C++
Executable
Hardware

```
void DatedStockItem::Reorder(ostream& s)
{
    if (m_Expires < Today())
        {
        s << "Return " << m_InStock << " units of " << m_Name;
        s << " with UPC " << m_UPC << " to " << m_Distributor << endl;
        m_InStock = 0;
        }

    StockItem::Reorder(s);
}
```

Figure 9.32: Reorder function for DatedStockItem (from code\item21.cc)

We have added a new piece of code that checks whether the expiration date on the current batch of product is before today's date; if that is the case, we create an output line indicating the product to be returned. But what about the "normal" case handled by the base class Reorder function? That's handled by the line StockItem::Reorder(s);, which calls the StockItem::Reorder function, using the class name with the membership operator :: to specify the exact Reorder function that we want to use. If we just wrote Reorder(s), that would call the function that we're in again, a process known as *recursion*. Recursion has its uses in certain complex programming situations, but in this case, of course, it would not do what we wanted, as we have already handled the possibility of expired items. We need to deal with the "normal" case of running low on stock, which is handled very nicely by the base class Reorder function.

We should not pass by this function without noting one more point: The only reason that we can access m_InStock and the other member variables of the StockItem base class part of our object is that those member variables of StockItem were declared protected rather than private. Had they been declared private, we wouldn't be able to access them in our DatedStockItem functions, even though every DatedStockItem object would still have such member variables.

Now we have a good solution to the creation of stock items with dates. Unfortunately, it's not possible to have a vector of dissimilar types; that is, our current solution can't handle a combination of StockItem and DatedStockItem objects. On the other hand, it *is* possible to have a vector of *pointers* that can refer to either StockItem or DatedStockItem objects, by making use of the characteristic of C++ that a pointer to a base class object can point to a derived class object.

However, using a vector of StockItem*s to point to a mixture of StockItem and DatedStockItem objects won't give us the results we want with the current definitions of these classes; to be precise, the correct version of Reorder won't be called for DatedStockItem objects. To help explain why this is so, I've drawn a number of diagrams that show how C++ determines which function is called for a given type of pointer.

Before we get to the first diagram, there's one new construct that I should explain: the use of operator new for an object of a class type. The first example of this usage is the statement

```
SIPtr = new StockItem("beans",40,110);
```

In this statement, we're creating a StockItem via the expression new StockItem("beans",40,110)[7] and then assigning the address returned by new to the variable SIPtr (whose name is supposed to represent

---

7. The examples in this section use simplified versions of the StockItem and DatedStockItem classes to make the diagrams smaller; the principles are the same as with the full versions of these classes.

Problem
Algorithms
C++
Executable
Hardware

"StockItem pointer"). It should be fairly obvious why we have to use operator new here: to allocate memory for the newly constructed object, just as we did when we used new to allocate memory for an array of chars in our string class. The only difference from that previous usage is that with a class object, we have to choose which constructor we want to use to create the object. Here we're specifying the arguments for the name, price, and number in stock, so the constructor that accepts arguments of the correct type will be called. On the other hand, if we hadn't supplied any arguments, e.g., SIPtr = new StockItem;, we'd get the default constructor.

Now that I've explained this use of new, let's look at Figure 9.33, which shows how a normal function call works when Reorder is called for a StockItem object through a StockItem pointer.

```
main()

{

   StockItem* SIPtr;

   SIPtr = new StockItem("beans",40,110);

   SIPtr->Reorder(cout);                          (1)

}



   StockItem::Reorder(ostream& s)

   {

      //code to reorder a StockItem

   }                                              (2)
```

Problem
Algorithms
C++
Executable
Hardware

Figure 9.33: Calling the Reorder function through a StockItem pointer, part 1

Step **(1)** calls StockItem::Reorder via the StockItem* variable named SIPtr. Then at the end of that function, it returns to the next statement in the main program (step **(2)**). So far, so good. Now let's see what happens when we call Reorder for a DatedStockItem object through a DatedStockItem pointer (Figure 9.34).

```
main()

{

  DatedStockItem* SIPtr;

  SIPtr = new DatedStockItem("milk",
    2,5,"19960629");

  SIPtr->Reorder(cout);

}
```
(1)

```
DatedStockItem::Reorder(ostream& s)

{

  //code to reorder a DatedStockItem

}
```
(2)

Problem
Algorithms
C++
Executable
Hardware

Figure 9.34: Calling the Reorder function through a DatedStockItem pointer

In Figure 9.34, step **(1)** calls StockItem::Reorder via the DatedStockItem* variable named SIPtr. Then at the end of that function, it returns to the next statement in the main program (step **(2)**). That looks okay too. But what happens if we call Reorder for a DatedStockItem object through a StockItem pointer, as in Figure 9.35?

Unfortunately, step **(1)** in Figure 9.35 is incorrect, because line SIPtr->Reorder(cout) calls StockItem::Reorder, not DatedStockItem::Reorder as we want it to. This is because when we call a normal member function through a pointer, the compiler uses the declared type of the pointer to decide which actual function will be called. In this case, we've declared SIPtr to be a pointer to a StockItem, so even though the actual data type of the object it points to is DatedStockItem, the compiler thinks it's a StockItem. Therefore, the line SIPtr->Reorder(cout) results in a call to StockItem::Reorder.

```
main()

{

   StockItem* SIPtr;

   SIPtr = new DatedStockItem("milk",
     2,5,"19960629");

   SIPtr->Reorder(cout);                              (1)

}
```

```
StockItem::Reorder(ostream& s)

{

   //code to reorder a StockItem

}                                                     (2)
```

Figure 9.35: Calling the Reorder function through a StockItem pointer, part 2

```
Problem
Algorithms
C++
Executable
Hardware
```

Before we see how to fix this problem, let's look at a test program that actually uses these versions of the Reorder functions with a simplified version of our StockItem and DatedStockItem classes. Figure 9.36 shows the test program, Figure 9.37 shows the output of the test program, Figure 9.38 shows the interface for these simplified classes, and Figure 9.39 shows the implementation of the classes. (You may very well want to print out the files that contain this interface and its implementation, as well as the test program. Those files are code\itema.h, code\itema.cc, and code\nvirtual.cc, respectively).

```
#include <iostream.h>
#include "itema.h"

int main()
{
    StockItem StockItemObject("soup",32,100);
    StockItem* StockItemPointer;
    DatedStockItem DatedStockItemObject("milk",10,15,"19950110");
    DatedStockItem* DatedStockItemPointer;

    StockItemObject.Reorder(cout);
    cout << endl;
    DatedStockItemObject.Reorder(cout);
    cout << endl;

    StockItemPointer = new StockItem("beans",40,110);
    StockItemPointer->Reorder(cout);
    cout << endl;

    DatedStockItemPointer = new DatedStockItem("ham",22,30,"19970110");
    DatedStockItemPointer->Reorder(cout);
    cout << endl;

    StockItemPointer = new DatedStockItem("steak",90,95,"19960110");
    StockItemPointer->Reorder(cout);
    cout << endl;
}
```

Problem
Algorithms
C++
Executable
Hardware

Figure 9.36: Function call example (code\nvirtual.cc)

```
StockItem::Reorder says:
Reorder 68 units of soup

DatedStockItem::Reorder says:
Return 10 units of milk
StockItem::Reorder says:
Reorder 15 units of milk

StockItem::Reorder says:
Reorder 70 units of beans

StockItem::Reorder says:
Reorder 8 units of ham

StockItem::Reorder says:
Reorder 5 units of steak
```

Figure 9.37: Function call example output (code\nvirtual.out)

```
#include "string6.h"

class StockItem
{
public:
      StockItem(string Name, short InStock, short MinimumStock);
      void Reorder(ostream& s);

protected:
      string m_Name;
      short m_InStock;
      short m_MinimumStock;
};

class DatedStockItem: public StockItem // deriving a new class
{
public:
      DatedStockItem(string Name, short InStock, short MinimumStock,
      string Expires);

      void Reorder(ostream& s);

protected:
static string Today();

protected:
      string m_Expires;
};
```

Problem
Algorithms
C++
Executable
Hardware

Figure 9.38: Simplified interface for StockItem and DatedStockItem classes
(code\itema.h)

```
#include <iostream.h>
#include <iomanip.h>
#include <strstream.h>
#include <string.h>
#include "itema.h"
#include <dos.h>

StockItem::StockItem(string Name, short InStock,
short MinimumStock)
: m_InStock(InStock), m_Name(Name),
  m_MinimumStock(MinimumStock)
{
}
```

Figure 9.39: Simplified implementation for StockItem and DatedStockItem
classes (code\itema.cc)

```
void StockItem::Reorder(ostream& s)
{
      short ActualReorderQuantity;

      if (m_InStock < m_MinimumStock)
            {
            ActualReorderQuantity = m_MinimumStock - m_InStock;
            s << "StockItem::Reorder says:" << endl;
            s << "Reorder " << ActualReorderQuantity << " units of ";
            s <<  m_Name << endl;
            }
}

string DatedStockItem::Today()
{
   struct date d;
   unsigned short year;
   unsigned short day;
   unsigned short month;
   string TodaysDate;
   strstream FormatStream;

   getdate(&d);
   year = d.da_year;
   day = d.da_day;
   month = d.da_mon;

   FormatStream << setfill('0') << setw(4) << year <<
      setw(2) << month << setw(2) << day;
   FormatStream >> TodaysDate;

   return TodaysDate;
}

void DatedStockItem::Reorder(ostream& s)
{
      short ReturnQuantity = 0;

      if (m_Expires < Today())
            {
            s << "DatedStockItem::Reorder says:" << endl;
            ReturnQuantity = m_InStock;
            m_InStock = 0;
            s << "Return " << ReturnQuantity <<  " units of ";
            s << m_Name << endl;
            }

      StockItem::Reorder(s);
}
```

Problem
Algorithms
C++
Executable
Hardware

Figure 9.39 continued

```
DatedStockItem::DatedStockItem(string Name, short InStock,
short MinimumStock, string Expires)
: StockItem(Name, InStock,MinimumStock),
   m_Expires(Expires)
{
}
```

Figure 9.39 continued

There shouldn't be anything too surprising in this program; when we call the Reorder function for an object, we get the function for that type of object, and when we call the Reorder function through a pointer to an object, we get the function for that type of pointer. However, what we really want is to have the DatedStockItem version of Reorder called if the object in question is a DatedStockItem, even if the pointer is of type StockItem*. We'll see how to solve that problem in the next chapter.

Review

We started the chapter by adding some new functions to the StockItem class and the Inventory class that were missing from the final versions of these classes in Chapter 6, including a function called ReorderItem that can be called for an Inventory object to produce a reordering report. This function calls a Reorder function for each StockItem in its StockItem vector to calculate how many items of that StockItem need to be ordered, based on the desired stock and the current stock.

Then we built on the previous StockItem class by adding an expiration date. Rather than copying all of the old code and class definitions, we made use of a concept that is essential to the full use of C++ for object-oriented programming, namely, *inheritance*. Inheritance is a method of constructing one class (the *derived* class) by specifying how it differs from another class (the *base* class) rather than writing it from scratch. We used inheritance to create a new DatedStockItem class that had all of the capabilities of the StockItem class and added the ability to handle items with expiration dates.

In the process, we wrote a new Reorder function with the same signature as the base class function of the same name. This is called *overriding* the base class function. When the function with that signature is called via an object of the base class, the base class function will be called. On the other hand, when the function with that signature is called via an object of the derived class, the derived class function will be called. This allows a derived class to supply the

Problem
Algorithms
C++
Executable
Hardware

same functionality as a base class but implement that functionality in a different way.

The reason a derived class object can do anything that a base class object can do is that a derived class object actually contains an object of the base class, called the *base* class *part* of the derived class object. This base class part is very similar to a member variable in the derived class, but it is not the same, for two reasons:

1.   A member variable always has a name, whereas the base class part does not.
2.   The base class definition can give derived class member functions privileged access to some member variables and functions of the base class part of an object of the derived class, by marking those member variables and functions protected.

Problem
Algorithms
C++
Executable
Hardware

In the process of writing the new Reorder function for the DatedStockItem class, we saw how we could store a date as a string that allowed comparison of two dates to see which was later. This required us to create a formatted string representing the date as YYYYMMDD; that is, a four-digit year number, a two-digit month number, and a two-digit day number. This led to a discussion of specifying the formatting of data rather than accepting the default formatting as we have done previously.

After wading into streams a bit deeper, we returned to the notion of a strstream, which is a stream that exists only in memory as a formatting aid. We can use the << operator to write formatted output to the strstream, then use the >> operator to read the formatted data back into a variable such as a string.

Once that was out of the way, we investigated how to use setw to specify the minimum number of digits of a number to be displayed via the << operator, as well as how to use setfill to specify the fill character to be used to pad the output. We also used the date variable type along with its associated getdate function to retrieve the year, month, and day of the current date. Then we used the << operator to write the date out to a strstream in the required YYYYMMDD format and used >> to read it back into a string for comparison with the expiration date stored in a DatedStockItem object (see Figures 9.25 and 9.26).

After the discussion of the formatting of the date string, we continued by examining the default constructor of the DatedStockItem class. While this is an extremely short function, having only one member initialization expression and no code in the constructor proper, there is more to it than meets the eye. The default constructor deals only with the newly added member variable m_Expires, but behind the scenes, the base class part of the DatedStockItem object is being initialized by the default constructor of the base class, i.e., StockItem::StockItem(). The rule here is that a base class constructor will *always* be called for the base class part of a derived class object. If we don't specify which base class constructor we want to use, the default constructor for the base class will be used. If we do want to select the constructor for the base class part, we can use a construct known as a base class initializer, which is an expression that can be used in a member initializer list. In our "normal" constructor for DatedStockItem, we used this construct to call the corresponding constructor for the base class (see Figures 9.30 and 9.31).

Then we looked at the Reorder function for the DatedStockItem class, which included code to request the return of any items that were past their expiration date and called the base class Reorder function to handle the rest of the job.

At that point, we had a working DatedStockItem class, but we still couldn't mix StockItem and DatedStockItem objects in the same vector. However, it was possible to have a vector of pointers to StockItems and use the C++ feature that a pointer to a base class can also point to an object of a derived class. After seeing how to use operator new to allocate StockItem and DatedStockItem variables, we discovered that using a base class pointer wouldn't really do what we wanted. The version of the Reorder function that would be called through that pointer would always be the base class version, rather than the appropriate version for the actual type of the object the pointer was referring to.

```
Problem
Algorithms
C++
Executable
Hardware
```

Exercises

1. Rewrite the DrugStockItem class that you wrote in Chapter 6, using derivation from the StockItem class.
2. Rewrite the Employee class that you wrote in Chapter 6 as two classes, the base Manager class and a Hourly class derived from the base class. The CalculatePay member function for each of these classes should use the appropriate method of calculating the pay for each class; in particular, this member function doesn't need an argument specifying the number of hours worked for the Manager class, while the corresponding member function in the Hourly class does need such an argument.
3. Rewrite the Employee class that you wrote in Chapter 6 as two classes, the base Manager class and a Hourly class derived from the

base class. However, to maintain the same interface for these two classes, the CalculatePay member function in both classes should have an argument specifying the number of hours worked. The implementation of the Manager class will ignore this argument, while the Hourly implementation will use the argument.

4. Write an essay comparing the advantages and disadvantages of the two approaches to inheritance in the previous two exercises.

Conclusion

In this chapter, we have extended the functionality provided in the StockItem class by deriving a new class called DatedStockItem, based on StockItem. However, we have not yet seen how to allow objects of these two classes to be used interchangeably. Although we could use base class pointers to point to objects of both base and derived types, we couldn't arrange for the correct function to be called based on the actual type of the object to which the pointer referred. In Chapter 10, we will see how to overcome this barrier.

```
Problem
Algorithms
C++
Executable
Hardware
```

Chapter 10

Pretty Poly

At the end of the previous chapter, we had created a DatedStockItem class by *inheritance* from the StockItem class, adding an expiration date field. This was a fine solution to the problem of creating a new class based on the existing StockItem class without rewriting all of the already functioning code in that class. Unfortunately, however, it didn't allow us to mix objects of the original StockItem class in the same vector with those of the new DatedStockItem class and still have the correct Reorder function called for the derived class object. To do that, we need to use the third and final major organizing principle that characterizes object-oriented programming: **polymorphism**. Once we have defined some terms, we'll get right to using polymorphism to solve our problem of freely interchanging StockItems and DatedStockItems in our application programs.

Definitions

Static typing means determining the exact type of a variable when the program is compiled. It is the default typing mechanism in C++. Note that this has no particular relation to the keyword static.

Dynamic typing means delaying the determination of the exact type of a variable until run time rather than fixing that type at compile time as in *static typing*.

Polymorphism is the major organizing principle in C++ that allows us to implement several classes with the same interface and treat objects of all these classes as though they were of the same class. *Dynamic typing* in C++ uses polymorphism. The word *polymorphism* is derived from the Greek words *poly*, meaning "many", and *morph*, meaning "form". In other words, the same behavior is implemented in different forms.

Declaring a function to be virtual means that it is a member of a set of functions having the same signatures and belonging to classes related by inheritance. The actual function to be executed as the result of a given function call is selected from this set of functions dynamically (i.e., at run time) based on the actual type of an object referred to via a base class pointer (or base class reference). This is the C++ mechanism used to implement *dynamic typing*, in contrast to the *static typing* used for nonvirtual functions, which are selected at compile time.

Objectives of This Chapter

By the end of this chapter, you should

```
Problem
Algorithms
C++
Executable
Hardware
```

1. Understand how we can use *polymorphism* to allow objects of different classes to be treated interchangeably by the user of these classes.
2. Understand how to create a **polymorphic object** that allows polymorphism to be used safely in application programs, without exposing the class user to the hazards of pointers.
3. Understand how to use **reference-counting** to allow one data item to be safely shared among several users.

Polymorphism

To select the correct function to be called based on the actual type of an object at run time, we have to use **polymorphism**. Polymorphic behavior of our StockItem and DatedStockItem classes means that we will be able to (for example) mix StockItem and DatedStockItem objects in a vector and have the right Reorder function be executed for each object in the vector.

Why would we want to do this? Because the objects of these two classes perform the same operation, although in a slightly different way. In our example, a DatedStockItem acts just like a StockItem, except that it has an additional data field and produces different reordering information. Ideally, we would like to be able to mix these two types in the application program without having to worry about which class each object belongs to except when creating an individual item (at which time we have to know whether the item has an expiration date).

However, there is a serious complication in using polymorphism; we have to refer to the objects via a pointer, rather than directly.[1] This exposes us to all the dangers of pointers, both those that we've already discussed and others that we'll get to later in this chapter. As we did with the string class, it would be ideal to confine pointers to the interior of classes we design; that way, we can keep track of them and let the application programmer worry about getting the job done.

As it happens, we can obtain the benefits of polymorphism without exposing the application programmer (as opposed to the class designers; i.e., us) to the hazards of pointers, and we'll see how to do that later in this chapter. But before investigating that more sophisticated method of providing polymorphism, we'll need to understand the workings of the native polymorphism mechanism in C++. As we've already seen, the address of a derived class object can be assigned to a pointer of its base class. While this does not by itself solve the problem of calling the correct function in these circumstances, there is a way to get the behavior we want. If we define a special kind of function called a virtual **function** and we refer to that function through a pointer (or a reference) to an object, the version of that function to be executed will be determined by the actual type of the object to which the pointer (or reference) refers, rather than being based on the declared type of the pointer (or reference). This implies that declaring a function to be virtual means that when that function is called via a base class pointer, the selection of the function to be called is postponed to run time rather than being determined at compile time as with nonvirtual functions. Clearly, if the actual run time type of the object determines which version of the function is called, the compiler can't select the function at compile time.

Problem
Algorithms
C++
Executable
Hardware

virtual **Certainty**

But exactly how does this help us with our Reorder function? Let's see how a virtual function affects the behavior of our final example program from the previous chapter (Figure 9.36). Figure 10.1 shows

---

1. We could also use a reference, as we'll see in the implementation of the << and >> operators. However, that still doesn't provide the flexibility of using real objects.

the same interface as before, except that StockItem::Reorder is declared to be a virtual function.[2] Because the current test program (virtual.cc) and implementation file (itemb.cc) are almost identical to the final test program (nvirtual.cc) and implementation file (itema.cc, Figure 9.39) from the previous chapter, differing only in that the new ones #include itemb.h rather than itema.h, I haven't reproduced the new versions here.

If you've printed out the corresponding files from the previous chapter, you might just want to mark them up to indicate these changes. Otherwise, I strongly recommend that you print out the files that contain this interface and its implementation, as well as the test program, for reference as you are going through this section of the chapter; those files are itemb.h, itemb.cc, and virtual.cc, respectively.

```
#include "string6.h"

class StockItem
{
public:
        StockItem(string Name, short InStock, short MinimumStock);
virtual void Reorder(ostream& s);

protected:
        string m_Name;
        short m_InStock;
        short m_MinimumStock;
};

class DatedStockItem: public StockItem // deriving a new class
{
public:
        DatedStockItem(string Name, short InStock, short MinimumStock,
        string Expires);

        void Reorder(ostream& s);

protected:
static string Today();

protected:
        string m_Expires;
};
```

Problem
Algorithms
C++
Executable
Hardware

Figure 10.1: Interface of StockItem with virtual function (code\itemb.h)

---

2. You will notice that the virtual declaration for Reorder isn't repeated in DatedStockItem. You can write virtual again in the derived class declaration of Reorder if you want to, but it's not necessary: it's still a virtual function in that class. The rule is "once virtual, always virtual".

Figure 10.2 shows the output of the new test program.

StockItem::Reorder says:
Reorder 68 units of soup

DatedStockItem::Reorder says:
Return 10 units of milk
StockItem::Reorder says:
Reorder 15 units of milk

StockItem::Reorder says:
Reorder 70 units of beans

StockItem::Reorder says:
Reorder 8 units of ham

DatedStockItem::Reorder says:
Return 90 units of steak
StockItem::Reorder says:
Reorder 95 units of steak

Figure 10.2: virtual function example (code\virtual.out)

You'll notice that the output of this program is exactly the same as the output of the previous test program except for the last entry. With the nonvirtual Reorder function in the previous program, we got the following output:

```
Problem
Algorithms
C++
Executable
Hardware
```

StockItem::Reorder says:
Reorder 5 units of steak

whereas with our virtual Reorder function, we get the following output:

DatedStockItem::Reorder says:
Return 90 units of steak
StockItem::Reorder says:
Reorder 95 units of steak

According to our rules, the correct answer is 95 units of steak, because the previous stock has expired. Why does the current program work correctly when the previous one didn't? Because when we call a virtual function through a base class pointer, the function that will be executed will be the one defined in the class of the actual object to which the pointer points, not the one defined in the class of the pointer.

To see how this works, let's start by looking at the way in which the layout of an object with virtual functions differs from a "normal" object. First, Figure 10.3 shows a possible memory representation of a simplified StockItem having only nonvirtual functions.

```
                        StockItem soup

Address     Name

12340000   m_InStock                    |      0005      |

12340002   m_MinimumStock               |      0008      |
```

```
                  StockItem member functions

Address     Name

12350000   StockItem(short,short)
12351000   Reorder(ostream&)
```

Figure 10.3: A simplified StockItem object without virtual functions

Problem
Algorithms
C++
Executable
Hardware

One of the interesting points about this figure is that there is no connection at run time between the StockItem object and its functions. Such a connection is unnecessary because the compiler can tell exactly which function will be called whenever a function is referenced for this object, whether directly or through a pointer. Therefore, the object itself doesn't need to know anything about its functions, and in fact it does not.

However, the situation is different if we have virtual functions. In that case, the compiler can't decide exactly which functions will be called for an object pointed to by a StockItem*, because the actual object may be a descendant of StockItem rather than an actual StockItem. In that case, we will want the function defined in the derived class (e.g., DatedStockItem) to be called even though the pointer is declared to point to an object of the base class (e.g., StockItem).

Since the actual type of the object for which we want to call the function isn't available at compile time, another way must be found to determine which function should be called. The most logical place to store this information is in the object itself, because after all we need to know where the object is located in order to call the function for it. In fact, an object of a class for which any virtual functions are declared does have an extra data item in it for exactly this purpose. So whenever a call to a virtual function is compiled, the compiler translates that call into instructions that use the information in the object to determine at run time which version of the virtual function will be called.

If every object needed to contain the addresses of all its virtual functions, that might make objects a lot larger than they would otherwise have to be. However, this is not necessary because all objects of the same class have the same virtual functions. Therefore, the addresses of all of the virtual functions for a given class are stored in a virtual function address table, or vtable for short, and every object of that class contains the address of the vtable for that class. Thus, if we make the Reorder function virtual, for example, then a StockItem object would look more like Figure 10.4.

```
                    StockItem soup

Address     Name

12340000   (vtable address)      12350000

12340004   m_InStock               0005

12340006   m_MinimumStock          0008                  Problem
                                                         Algorithms
                                                         C++
                                                         Executable
                    StockItem vtable                     Hardware


12350000   Reorder address        12351000



              StockItem member functions

Address     Name

12350000   StockItem(short, short)

12351000   Reorder(ostream&)
```

Figure 10.4: A simplified StockItem object with a virtual function

On the other hand, a DatedStockItem object might look like Figure 10.5.

```
                        DatedStockItem milk

        Address    Name

        12330000   (vtable address)        ┌──────────────┐
                                           │   12360000   │──┐
        12330004   m_InStock               ├──────────────┤  │
                                           │     0002     │  │
        12330006   m_MinimumStock          ├──────────────┤  │
                                           │     0005     │  │
        12330008   m_Expires               ├──────────────┤  │
                                           │ "19960629"   │  │
                                           └──────────────┘  │
                                                             │
                                                             │
                        DatedStockItem vtable                │
                                                             │
                                                             │
                                                             │
                                                             ▼
Problem                                    ┌──────────────┐
Algorithms    12360000  Reorder address    │   12361000   │──┐
C++                                        └──────────────┘  │
Executable                                                   │
Hardware                                                     │
                                                             │
                                                             │
                    DatedStockItem member functions          │
                                                             │
        Address    Name                                      │
                                                             │
        12360000   DatedStockItem(short, short, string)      │
                                                             │
        12361000   Reorder(ostream&)  ◄──────────────────────┘
```

Figure 10.5: A simplified DatedStockItem object with a virtual function

Now that we have declared Reorder as a virtual function, let's see how the previous function call examples behave. First, Figure 10.6 shows how a virtual (i.e., dynamically determined) function call works when Reorder is called for a StockItem object through a StockItem pointer such as SIPtr.

```
main()

{

   StockItem* SIPtr;

   SIPtr = new StockItem("soup",5,8);

   SIPtr->Reorder(cout);

}
```

StockItem

Name

(vtable address) | 12350000

m_InStock | 0005

m_MinimumStock | 0008

StockItem vtable

Reorder address | 12351000

```
StockItem::Reorder(ostream& s)

{

   //code to reorder a StockItem

}
```

Problem
Algorithms
C++
Executable
Hardware

Figure 10.6: Calling a virtual Reorder function through a StockItem pointer to a StockItem object

The net result of the call illustrated in Figure 10.6 is the same as the call illustrated in Figure 9.33, which is what we want in this situation.

Next, Figure 10.7 shows how a virtual (i.e., dynamically determined) function call works when Reorder is called for a DatedStockItem object through a DatedStockItem pointer.

```
main()

{

  DatedStockItem* SIPtr;

  SIPtr = new DatedStockItem("milk",
    2,5,"19960629");

  SIPtr->Reorder(cout);

}
```

DatedStockItem

Name

(vtable address) | 12360000 |

m_InStock | 0002 |

m_MinimumStock | 0005 |

m_Expires | "19960629" |

DatedStockItem vtable

Reorder address | 12361000 |

Problem
Algorithms
C++
Executable
Hardware

```
DatedStockItem::Reorder(ostream& s)

{

   //code to reorder a DatedStockItem

}
```

Figure 10.7: Calling a virtual Reorder function through a DatedStockItem pointer

The net result of the call illustrated in Figure 10.7 is the same as the call illustrated in Figure 9.34, which is correct in this situation.

Finally, Figure 10.8 shows how a virtual (i.e., dynamically determined) function call works when Reorder is called for a DatedStockItem object through a StockItem pointer.

```
main()

{

  StockItem* SIPtr;

  SIPtr = new DatedStockItem("milk",
    2,5,"19960629");

  SIPtr->Reorder(cout);

}
```

DatedStockItem

Name

(vtable address)	12360000
m_InStock	0002
m_MinimumStock	0005
m_Expires	"19960629"

DatedStockItem vtable

| Reorder address | 12361000 |

```
DatedStockItem::Reorder(ostream& s)

{

  //code to reorder a DatedStockItem

}
```

```
Problem
Algorithms
C++
Executable
Hardware
```

Figure 10.8: Calling the virtual Reorder function of a DatedStockItem object
through a StockItem pointer

Figure 10.8 is where the virtual function pays off. The correct function, DatedStockItem::Reorder, is called even though the type of the pointer through which it is called is StockItem*. This is in contrast to the result of that same call with the nonvirtual function, illustrated in Figure 9.35. In that case, StockItem::Reorder was called rather than DatedStockItem::Reorder.

To translate this into what I hope is understandable English, a call to the virtual function Reorder might be expressed as follows:

1.   Get the vtable address from the object whose address is in SIPtr.
2.   Since Reorder is the first defined virtual function, retrieve its address from the first function address slot in the vtable.
3.   Execute the function at that address.

By following this sequence, you can see that while both versions of Reorder are referred to via the same relative position in both the StockItem and DatedStockItem vtables, the particular version of Reorder that is executed will depend on which vtable the object refers to. Since all objects of the same class have the same member functions, all StockItem objects will point to the same StockItem vtable, and all DatedStockItem objects will point to the same DatedStockItem vtable.

What happens if we add another virtual function, say Write, to the StockItem class, after the Reorder function? The new virtual function will be added to the vtables for both the StockItem and DatedStockItem classes. The situation for a StockItem object might look like Figure 10.9.

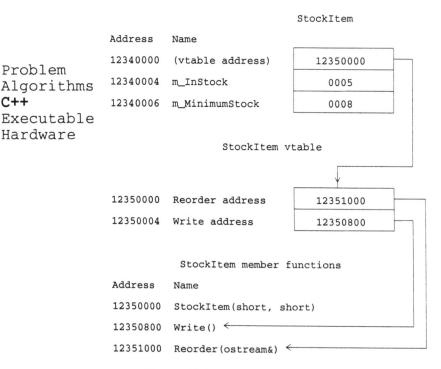

```
Problem
Algorithms
C++
Executable
Hardware
```

Figure 10.9: A simplified StockItem object with two virtual functions

The situation for a DatedStockItem object might look like Figure 10.10.

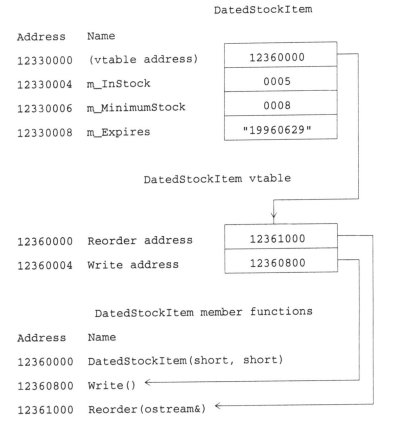

DatedStockItem

Address	Name	
12330000	(vtable address)	12360000
12330004	m_InStock	0005
12330006	m_MinimumStock	0008
12330008	m_Expires	"19960629"

DatedStockItem vtable

Address	Name	
12360000	Reorder address	12361000
12360004	Write address	12360800

DatedStockItem member functions

Address	Name
12360000	DatedStockItem(short, short)
12360800	Write()
12361000	Reorder(ostream&)

Problem
Algorithms
C++
Executable
Hardware

Figure 10.10: A simplified DatedStockItem object with two virtual functions

As you can see, the new function has been added to both vtables, so that a call to Write through a base class pointer will call the correct function.

A Pointed Reminder

Unfortunately, it's not quite as simple to make polymorphism work for us as this might suggest. As is so often the case, the culprit is the use of pointers. To see how pointers cause trouble with polymorphism, let's start by adding the standard I/O functions, operator << and operator >>, to our simplified interface for the StockItem and DatedStockItem classes, resulting in the header file itemc.h (Figure 10.11). I strongly recommend that you print out that header file, as

well as its implementation and the test program, for reference as you
are going through this section of the chapter; the latter two files are
itemc.cc (Figure 10.12) and polyioa.cc (Figure 10.13), respectively.[3]

```
#include "string6.h"

class StockItem
{
friend ostream& operator << (ostream& s, StockItem* Item);
friend istream& operator >> (istream& s, StockItem*& Item);

public:
      StockItem(string Name, short InStock, short MinimumStock);
virtual ~StockItem();

virtual void Reorder(ostream& s);
virtual void Write(ostream& s);

protected:
      string m_Name;
      short m_InStock;
      short m_MinimumStock;
};

class DatedStockItem: public StockItem
{
public:
      DatedStockItem(string Name, short InStock, short MinimumStock,
      string Expires);

      void Reorder(ostream& s);
      void Write(ostream& s);

static string Today();

protected:
      string m_Expires;
};
```

Problem
Algorithms
C++
Executable
Hardware

Figure 10.11: StockItem interface with operator << and operator >>
(code\itemc.h)

---

3. Note that we've had to specify a destructor for this class, which we haven't had to do with
   previous incarnations of StockItem, and that this destructor is declared as virtual. We'll see
   exactly why this function needs to be specified here, and why it needs to be virtual, later in the
   chapter.

```
#include <iostream.h>
#include <iomanip.h>
#include <strstream.h>
#include <string.h>
#include "itemc.h"
#include <dos.h>

StockItem::StockItem(string Name, short InStock,
short MinimumStock)
: m_InStock(InStock), m_Name(Name),
  m_MinimumStock(MinimumStock)
{
}

StockItem::~StockItem()
{
}

void StockItem::Reorder(ostream& s)
{
    short ReorderAmount;

    if (m_InStock < m_MinimumStock)
        {
        ReorderAmount = m_MinimumStock-m_InStock;
        s << "Reorder " << ReorderAmount << " units of " << m_Name;
        }
}

ostream& operator << (ostream& s, StockItem* Item)
{
    Item->Write(s);
    return s;
}
```

Problem
Algorithms
C++
Executable
Hardware

Figure 10.12: StockItem implementation with operator << and operator >>
(code\itemc.cc)

```
void StockItem::Write(ostream& s)
{
    s << 0 << endl;
    s << m_Name << endl;
    s << m_InStock << endl;
    s << m_MinimumStock << endl;
}

istream& operator >> (istream& s, StockItem*& Item)
{
    string Expires;
    short InStock;
    short MinimumStock;
    string Name;

    s >> Expires;
    s >> Name;
    s >> InStock;
    s >> MinimumStock;

    if (Expires == "0")
        Item = new StockItem(Name,InStock,MinimumStock);
    else
        Item = new DatedStockItem(Name,InStock,
        MinimumStock,Expires);

    return s;
}

void DatedStockItem::Reorder(ostream& s)
{
    if (m_Expires < Today())
        {
        s << "DatedStockItem::Reorder says:" << endl;
        s << "Return " << m_InStock <<  " units of ";
        s << m_Name << endl;
        m_InStock = 0;
        }

    StockItem::Reorder(s);
}
```

Problem
Algorithms
C++
Executable
Hardware

Figure 10.12 continued

```
string DatedStockItem::Today()
{
    struct date d;
    unsigned short year;
    unsigned short day;
    unsigned short month;
    string TodaysDate;
    strstream FormatStream;

    getdate(&d);
    year = d.da_year;
    day = d.da_day;
    month = d.da_mon;

    FormatStream << setfill('0') << setw(4) << year <<
        setw(2) << month << setw(2) << day;
    FormatStream >> TodaysDate;

    return TodaysDate;
}

DatedStockItem::DatedStockItem(string Name, short InStock,
short MinimumStock, string Expires)
: StockItem(Name, InStock,MinimumStock),
    m_Expires(Expires)
{
}

void DatedStockItem::Write(ostream& s)
{
    s << m_Expires << endl;
    s << m_Name << endl;
    s << m_InStock << endl;
    s << m_MinimumStock << endl;
}
```

Problem
Algorithms
C++
Executable
Hardware

Figure 10.12 continued

Let's start with the declaration of operator <<. Its second argument is a StockItem* rather than a StockItem, because we have to refer to our StockItem and DatedStockItem objects through a base class pointer (i.e., a StockItem*) to get the benefits of polymorphism. Although operator << isn't a virtual function (since it's not a member function at all), we will see that it still makes use of polymorphism to do its work. First, though, let's see how we would use this new function (Figure 10.13).

```
#include <iostream.h>
#include <vector.h>
#include "itemc.h"

int main()
{
    vector <StockItem*> x(2);

    x[0] = new StockItem("3-ounce cups",71,78);

    x[1] = new DatedStockItem("milk",76,87,"19970719");

    cout << "A StockItem: " << endl;
    cout << x[0];

    cout << endl;

    cout << "A DatedStockItem: " << endl;
    cout << x[1];

    delete x[0];
    delete x[1];
}
```

Problem
Algorithms
C++
Executable
Hardware

Figure 10.13: Using operator << with a StockItem* (code\polyioa.cc)

Before we get to the analysis of this program, Figure 10.14 shows its output.

```
A StockItem:
0
3-ounce cups
71
78

A DatedStockItem:
19970719
milk
76
87
```

Figure 10.14: Result of using operator << with a StockItem* (code\polyioa.out)

The first item of note in this program is that we can create a vector of StockItem*s to hold the addresses of any mixture of StockItems and DatedStockItems, because we can assign the addresses of variables of either of those types to a base class pointer (i.e., a StockItem*). Once we have the vector of StockItem*s, we use operator new to acquire the memory for whichever type of object we're creating. This allows us to access these objects via pointers rather than directly and thus to use polymorphism. Once we have finished using the objects, we have to free the memory for these objects explicitly by calling operator delete at the end of the program; otherwise, a *memory leak* would result.[4]

The other point worthy of discussion here is that we can use the same operator << to display both a StockItem and a DatedStockItem, even though the display functions for those two types are actually different. Let's look at the implementation of this version of operator <<, shown in Figure 10.15.

```
ostream& operator << (ostream& s, StockItem* Item)
{
    Item->Write(s);
    return s;
}
```

Figure 10.15: The implementation of operator << with a StockItem* (from code\itemc.cc)

This looks pretty simple, as it merely calls the previously mentioned Write function. In fact, it looks too simple: How does it decide whether to display a StockItem or a DatedStockItem?

```
Problem
Algorithms
C++
Executable
Hardware
```

The Old Switcheroo

This is an application of polymorphism: operator << doesn't have to decide whether to call the version of Write in the StockItem class or the one in the DatedStockItem class because that decision is made automatically at run time. Write is a virtual function declared in the StockItem class; therefore, the exact version of Write that is called through a StockItem* is determined by the run time type of the object that the StockItem* actually points to.

To complete the explanation of how operator << works, we'll need to examine Write. Let's look at the implementation of Write for StockItem (Figure 10.16) and for DatedStockItem (Figure 10.17).

---

4. Technically, in this case we don't actually have to use operator delete, because the end of the main function is also the end of the program. However, the general rule is that if you allocate memory with operator new, you have to free it with operator delete.

```
void StockItem::Write(ostream& s)
{
    s << 0 << endl;
    s << m_Name << endl;
    s << m_InStock << endl;
    s << m_MinimumStock << endl;
}
```

Figure 10.16: StockItem::Write (from code\itemc.cc)

```
void DatedStockItem::Write(ostream& s)
{
    s << m_Expires << endl;
    s << m_Name << endl;
    s << m_InStock << endl;
    s << m_MinimumStock << endl;
}
```

Figure 10.17: DatedStockItem::Write (from code\itemc.cc)

Problem
Algorithms
C++
Executable
Hardware

The only thing that might not be obvious about these functions is why StockItem::Write writes the "0" out as its first action. We know that there's no date for a StockItem, so why not just write out the data that it does have? The reason is that if we want to read the data back in, we'll need some way to distinguish between a StockItem and a DatedStockItem. Since "0" is not a valid date, we can use it as an indicator meaning "the following data belongs to a StockItem, not a DatedStockItem". In other words, when we read data from the inventory file to create our StockItem and DatedStockItem objects, any set of data that starts with a "0" will end up as a StockItem, while any set of data that starts with a valid date will end up as DatedStockItem.

If this still isn't perfectly clear, don't worry. The next section, which covers operator >>, should clear it up.

It's Not Polite to Point

First, let's examine the declaration of the operator >> function:

friend istream& operator >> (istream& s, StockItem*& Item);

Most of this should be familiar by now, but there is one oddity: The declaration of the second argument to this function is StockItem*&. What could that mean?

It's a reference to a pointer. Now, before you "go postal", recall that we use a reference when we need to modify a variable in the calling function. In this case, that variable is a StockItem* (a pointer to a StockItem or one of its derived classes), and we are going to have to change it by assigning the address of a newly created StockItem or DatedStockItem to it. Hence, our argument has to be a reference to the variable in the calling function, and since that variable is a StockItem*, our argument has to be declared as a reference to a StockItem*, or a StockItem*&.

After clearing up that point, let's look at how we would use this new function (Figure 10.18). In case you want to print out the file containing this code, it is polyiob.cc.

```
#include <iostream.h>
#include <vector.h>
#include <fstream.h>
#include "itemc.h"

int main()
{
    StockItem* x;
    StockItem* y;

    ifstream ShopInfo("polyiob.in");

    ShopInfo >> x;

    ShopInfo >> y;

    cout << "A StockItem: " << endl;
    cout << x;

    cout << endl;

    cout << "A DatedStockItem: " << endl;
    cout << y;

    delete x;
    delete y;
}
```

Problem
Algorithms
C++
Executable
Hardware

Figure 10.18: Using operator >> and operator << with a StockItem*
(code\polyiob.cc)

Before we continue, Figure 10.19 shows the output that this program produces.

A StockItem:
0
3-ounce cups
71
78

A DatedStockItem:
19970719
Ajax-substitute
76
87

Figure 10.19: The results of using operator >> and operator << with a StockItem*
(code\polyiob.out)

Now let's get back to the code. The alert reader will have noticed something odd here: How can we assign a value to a variable such as x or y without allocating any memory for it? For that matter, how can we call operator delete for a variable that hasn't had memory assigned to it? These aren't errors, but consequences of the way that we have to implement operator >>. To see why this is so, let's take a look at that implementation, as shown in Figure 10.20.

Problem
Algorithms
C++
Executable
Hardware

We start out reasonably enough by declaring variables to hold the expiration date (Expires), number in stock (InStock), minimum number desired in stock (MinimumStock), and name of the item (Name). Then we read values for these variables in from the istream supplied as the left-hand argument in the operator >> call, which in the case of our example program is ShopInfo. Then we test the variable Expires, which was the first variable to be read in from the istream. If the value of Expires is "0", meaning "not a date", then we create a new StockItem by calling the normal constructor for that class and assigning memory to that new object via operator new. If the Expires value isn't "0", we assume it's a date and create a new DatedStockItem by calling the constructor for DatedStockItem and assigning memory for it via operator new. Finally, we return the istream that we started with, so it can be used in further operator >> calls.

The fact that we have to create a different type of object in these two cases is the key to why we have to allocate the memory here rather than in the calling program. The actual type of the object isn't known until we read the data in from the file, so we can't allocate memory for the object until that time. This isn't necessarily a bad thing in itself; after all, we allocated a variable amount of memory in our string class without causing any grief for the application programmer. However, in this case we can't free the memory in our destructor as we did with our string class because the application programmer is in charge of the vector of StockItem* pointers and therefore has to remember to free the memory allocated to those pointers when the calling program is finished with the objects.

```
istream& operator >> (istream& s, StockItem*& Item)
{
    string Expires;
    short InStock;
    short MinimumStock;
    string Name;

    s >> Expires;
    s >> Name;
    s >> InStock;
    s >> MinimumStock;

    if (Expires == "0")
        Item = new StockItem(Name,InStock,MinimumStock);
    else
        Item = new DatedStockItem(Name,InStock,
        MinimumStock,Expires);

    return s;
}
```

Problem
Algorithms
C++
Executable
Hardware

Figure 10.20: The implementation of operator >> (istream&, StockItem*&) (from code\itemc.cc)

While it is legal (and even very common) to write programs in which memory is allocated and freed in this way, it isn't a very good idea. The likelihood of error in any large program that uses this method of memory management is approximately 100%. Even if the original programmers get it right, the first time someone tries to maintain the program they are very likely to mess up the memory management in one way or another. Besides the problem of forgetting to free memory or using memory that has already been freed, we also have the problem that copying pointers leaves two pointers pointing to the same data, as we found when we dealt with copying strings using the compiler-generated copy constructor and assignment operators. We'll begin to solve these problems right after the following exercises.

Exercises, First Set

1. Rewrite the DrugStockItem class that you wrote in Chapter 6 as a derived class of DatedStockItem, using virtual functions to allow DrugStockItem objects to be used in place of StockItem objects or DatedStockItem objects, just as you can use DatedStockItem objects in place of StockItem objects.

2. Rewrite the Employee class that you wrote in Chapter 6 as three classes: the base Employee class, a Manager class and an Hourly class. The latter two classes will be derived from the base class. The virtual CalculatePay member function for each of these derived classes should use the appropriate method of calculating the pay for each class, so that a Manager object or a Hourly object can be substituted for a Employee class object. The Employee class CalculatePay object should display an error message, as that class does not have a method of calculating pay. Note that unlike the first Employee exercise in the previous chapter, you *must* maintain the same interface for the CalculatePay function in these classes because you are using a base class pointer to access derived class objects.

```
Problem
Algorithms
C++
Executable
Hardware
```

Pretty Polly Morphic

As we have just seen, the "standard" method of adding polymorphism to our programs is, to use a technical term, *ugly*; that is, error prone and virtually impossible to maintain. As soon as we get some more definitions out of the way, we're going to see how to fix these problems by using an advanced technique that I refer to as the *polymorphic object* idiom.[5]

More Definitions

A **polymorphic object** is a C++ object that presents the appearance of a simple object that behaves polymorphically without the hazards of exposing pointers to the user of the polymorphic object. The user

---

5. This idiom is a specific application of what I refer to as the *manager/worker* idiom. This is my name for what James Coplien calls the *envelope/letter* idiom in his book *Advanced C++: Programming Styles and Idioms* (Addison-Wesley Publishing Company, Reading, Massachusetts, 1992). Warning: as its title indicates, his is *not* an easy book; however, it does merit study by those who have a solid grasp of C++ fundamentals.

does not have to know about any of the details of the implementation, but merely instantiates an object of the single visible class (the *manager* class). That object does what the user wants with the help of an object of a *worker* class, which is derived from the *manager* class.

The **manager/worker** idiom is a mechanism that allows the effective type of an object to be determined at run time without requiring the user of the object to be concerned with pointers.

The **reference-counting** idiom is a mechanism that allows one object (the *reference-counted object*) to be shared by several other objects (the *client objects*) rather than requiring a copy to be made for each of the client objects.

Paging Miss Management

You may be wondering what an "idiom" is in programming. Well, in English or any other natural language, an idiom is a phrase whose meaning can't be derived directly from the meanings of the individual words that make it up. An example would be "to make good time", which actually means "to proceed rapidly". Similarly, the polymorphic object idiom has effects that aren't at all obvious from a casual inspection of its components.

Problem
Algorithms
C++
Executable
Hardware

I should tell you that many, if not most, professional C++ programmers don't know about this idiom and therefore don't have the tools necessary to make polymorphism safe and easy to use for the application programmer. Why then am I including it in a book for beginning programmers?

Because I believe it is the best solution to the very serious problems caused by dynamic memory allocation when using polymorphism. As such, every serious C++ programmer should know this idiom and how to apply it to real-life problems.

Now that I hope I have impressed the importance of this technique on you, how does it work? The high-level answer is that it involves creating a set of classes that work together as a team to present the appearance of a simple object that has the desired polymorphic behavior. The user (i.e., the application programmer) doesn't have to know about any of the details of this idiom; the user merely defines an object of the single visible class and that object does what the user wants with the help of an object of another class. James Coplien calls these two kinds of classes **envelope** and **letter** classes, respectively, but I'm going to call them **manager** and **worker** classes instead. I think these names are easier to remember because the outside world sees only objects of the manager class, which take credit for everything done by the polymorphic object, even though most of the work is actually done by objects of the **worker** classes.

As usual, all of the intricacies of the implementation are the responsibility of the class designers (that's us). However, before we get into the details of how a polymorphic object works, let's see how it would affect the way we use the StockItem class. For reference, Figure 10.21 shows the way we used the old StockItem class in Chapter 9, whereas Figure 10.22 shows how we will use the new StockItem class; note the lack of the deletes and the fact that the variables are StockItems rather than StockItem*s.

```
#include <iostream.h>
#include <vector.h>
#include <fstream.h>
#include "itemc.h"

int main()
{
    StockItem* x;
    StockItem* y;

    ifstream ShopInfo("polyiob.in");

    ShopInfo >> x;

    ShopInfo >> y;

    cout << "A StockItem: " << endl;
    cout << x;

    cout << endl;

    cout << "A DatedStockItem: " << endl;
    cout << y;

    delete x;
    delete y;
}
```

Problem
Algorithms
C++
Executable
Hardware

Figure 10.21: Using operator >> and operator << with a StockItem*
(code\polyiob.cc)

```
#include <iostream.h>
#include <vector.h>
#include <fstream.h>
#include "itemp.h"

int main()
{
    StockItem x;
    StockItem y;

    ifstream ShopInfo("shop22.in");

    ShopInfo >> x;

    ShopInfo >> y;

    cout << "A StockItem: " << endl;
    cout << x;

    cout << endl;

    cout << "A DatedStockItem: " << endl;
    cout << y;
}
```

Figure 10.22: Using operator >> and operator << with a polymorphic StockItem
(code\polyioc.cc)

```
Problem
Algorithms
C++
Executable
Hardware
```

I strongly recommend that you print out the files that contain the interface and the implementation of the polymorphic object version of StockItem, as well as the test program, for reference as you are going through this section of the chapter; those files are itemp.h (StockItem interface, in Figure 10.23), itempi.h (UndatedStockItem and DatedStockItem interfaces, in Figure 10.24), itemp.cc (UndatedStockItem and DatedStockItem implementation, in Figure 10.25), and polyioc.cc (test program, in Figure 10.22). By the way, the line class string; at the beginning of itemp.h merely tells the compiler that string is the name of a class, so that it won't complain when we try to use it as an argument type in our function declarations in StockItem.

I'm sure you're happy to see that we've eliminated the visible pointers in the new version of the example program, but how does it work? Let's start by looking at Figure 10.23, which shows the interface for the *manager* class StockItem. As we've just seen, this is the class of the objects that are visible to the user of the polymorphic object.

```
class string;

class StockItem
{
friend ostream& operator << (ostream& s, const StockItem& Item);
friend istream& operator >> (istream& s, StockItem& Item);

public:
      StockItem();
      StockItem(const StockItem& Item);
      StockItem& operator = (const StockItem& Item);
virtual ~StockItem();

      StockItem(string Name, short InStock,
      short Price, short MinimumStock,
      short MinimumReorder, string Distributor, string UPC);

      StockItem(string Name, short InStock,
      short Price, short MinimumStock,
      short MinimumReorder, string Distributor, string UPC,
      string Expires);

virtual bool CheckUPC(string UPC);
virtual void DeductSaleFromInventory(short QuantitySold);
virtual short GetInventory();
virtual string GetName();

virtual void Reorder(ostream& s);
virtual void FormattedDisplay(ostream& s);

protected:
      StockItem(int);
virtual ostream& Write(ostream& s);

protected:
      StockItem* m_Worker;
      short m_Count;
};
```

Problem
Algorithms
C++
Executable
Hardware

Figure 10.23: The polymorphic object version of the StockItem interface
(code\itemp.h)

```
class UndatedStockItem : public StockItem
{
public:
      UndatedStockItem();
      UndatedStockItem(const UndatedStockItem& Item);
      UndatedStockItem& operator = (const UndatedStockItem& Item);
      ~UndatedStockItem();

      UndatedStockItem(string Name, short InStock,
      short Price, short MinimumStock,
      short ReorderQuantity, string Distributor, string UPC);

void Reorder(ostream& s);
void FormattedDisplay(ostream& s);

bool CheckUPC(string UPC);
void DeductSaleFromInventory(short QuantitySold);
short GetInventory();
string GetName();

protected:
ostream& Write(ostream& s);

protected:
      short m_InStock;
      short m_Price;
      short m_MinimumStock;
      short m_MinimumReorder;
      string m_Name;
      string m_Distributor;
      string m_UPC;
};

class DatedStockItem : public UndatedStockItem
{
public:
      DatedStockItem();
      DatedStockItem(const DatedStockItem& Item);
      DatedStockItem& operator = (const DatedStockItem& Item);
      ~DatedStockItem();
```

Problem
Algorithms
C++
Executable
Hardware

Figure 10.24: The UndatedStockItem and DatedStockItem interfaces for the
          polymorphic version of StockItem (code\itempi.h)

```
DatedStockItem(string Name, short InStock,
short Price, short MinimumStock,
short MinimumReorder, string Distributor, string UPC,
string Expires);

void Reorder(ostream& s);
void FormattedDisplay(ostream& s);
static string Today();

protected:
ostream& Write(ostream& s);

protected:
    string m_Expires;
};
```

Figure 10.24 continued

Problem
Algorithms
C++
Executable
Hardware

```
#include <iostream.h>
#include <iomanip.h>
#include <strstrea.h>
#include <string.h>
#include "string6.h"
#include "itemp.h"
#include "itempi.h"
#include <dos.h>

//friend functions of StockItem

ostream& operator << (ostream& s, const StockItem& Item)
{
        return Item.m_Worker->Write(s);
}
```

Figure 10.25: The implementation of the UndatedStockItem and DatedStockItem classes (code\itemp.cc)

```
istream& operator >> (istream& s, StockItem& Item)
{
      string Expires;
      string Name;
      short InStock;
      short Price;
      short MinimumStock;
      short MinimumReorder;
      string Distributor;
      string UPC;

      s >> Expires;
      s >> Name;
      s >> InStock;
      s >> Price;
      s >> MinimumStock;
      s >> MinimumReorder;
      s >> Distributor;
      s >> UPC;

      if (Expires == "0")
            {
            Item = StockItem(Name, InStock, Price, MinimumStock,
            MinimumReorder, Distributor, UPC);
            }
      else
            {
            Item = StockItem(Name, InStock, Price, MinimumStock,
            MinimumReorder, Distributor, UPC, Expires);
            }

      return s;

}


// StockItem member functions

StockItem::StockItem()
: m_Count(0), m_Worker(new UndatedStockItem)
{
      m_Worker->m_Count = 1;
}
```

Problem
Algorithms
C++
Executable
Hardware

Figure 10.25 continued

```
StockItem::StockItem(const StockItem& Item)
: m_Count(0), m_Worker(Item.m_Worker)
{
     m_Worker->m_Count ++;
}

StockItem& StockItem::operator = (const StockItem& Item)
{
     if (&Item != this)
          {
          m_Worker->m_Count --;
          if (m_Worker->m_Count <= 0)
               delete m_Worker;
          m_Worker = Item.m_Worker;
          m_Worker->m_Count ++;
          }
     return *this;
}

StockItem::~StockItem()
{
     if (m_Worker == 0)
          return;

     m_Worker->m_Count --;
     if (m_Worker->m_Count <= 0)
          delete m_Worker;
}
```

Problem
Algorithms
C++
Executable
Hardware

```
StockItem::StockItem(string Name, short InStock,
short Price, short MinimumStock,
short MinimumReorder, string Distributor, string UPC)
: m_Count(0),
  m_Worker(new UndatedStockItem(Name, InStock, Price,
  MinimumStock, MinimumReorder, Distributor, UPC))
{
     m_Worker->m_Count = 1;
}

StockItem::StockItem(int)
: m_Worker(0)
{
}
```

Figure 10.25 continued

```
StockItem::StockItem(string Name, short InStock,
short Price, short MinimumStock,
short MinimumReorder, string Distributor, string UPC,
string Expires)
: m_Count(0),
    m_Worker(new DatedStockItem(Name, InStock, Price,
    MinimumStock, MinimumReorder, Distributor, UPC, Expires))
{
      m_Worker->m_Count = 1;
}

bool StockItem::CheckUPC(string UPC)
{
      return m_Worker->CheckUPC(UPC);
}

short StockItem::GetInventory()
{
      return m_Worker->GetInventory();
}

void StockItem::DeductSaleFromInventory(short QuantitySold)
{
      m_Worker->DeductSaleFromInventory(QuantitySold);
}

string StockItem::GetName()
{
      return m_Worker->GetName();
}

ostream& StockItem::Write(ostream& s)
{
      return s; // dummy
}

void StockItem::Reorder(ostream& s)
{
      m_Worker->Reorder(s);
}
```

```
Problem
Algorithms
C++
Executable
Hardware
```

Figure 10.25 continued

```
void StockItem::FormattedDisplay(ostream& s)
{
    m_Worker->FormattedDisplay(s);
}


// UndatedStockItem member functions

UndatedStockItem::UndatedStockItem()
: StockItem(1),
  m_InStock(0),
  m_Price(0),
  m_MinimumStock(0),
  m_MinimumReorder(0),
  m_Name(),
  m_Distributor(),
  m_UPC()
{
}

UndatedStockItem::UndatedStockItem(const UndatedStockItem& Item)
: m_InStock(Item.m_InStock),
  m_Price(Item.m_Price),
  m_MinimumStock(Item.m_MinimumStock),
  m_MinimumReorder(Item.m_MinimumReorder),
  m_Name(Item.m_Name),
  m_Distributor(Item.m_Distributor),
  m_UPC(Item.m_UPC)
{
}

UndatedStockItem& UndatedStockItem::operator = (const UndatedStockItem& Item)
{
    if (&Item != this)
        {
        m_InStock = Item.m_InStock;
        m_Price = Item.m_Price;
        m_MinimumStock = Item.m_MinimumStock;
        m_MinimumReorder = Item.m_MinimumReorder;
        m_Name = Item.m_Name;
        m_Distributor = Item.m_Distributor;
        m_UPC = Item.m_UPC;
        }
    return *this;
}
```

Problem
Algorithms
C++
Executable
Hardware

Figure 10.25 continued

```
UndatedStockItem::UndatedStockItem(string Name, short InStock,
short Price, short MinimumStock,
short MinimumReorder, string Distributor, string UPC)
: StockItem(1),
   m_InStock(InStock),
   m_Price(Price),
   m_MinimumStock(MinimumStock),
   m_MinimumReorder(MinimumReorder),
   m_Name(Name),
   m_Distributor(Distributor),
   m_UPC(UPC)
{
}

void UndatedStockItem::FormattedDisplay(ostream& s)
{
     s << "Name: ";
     s << m_Name << endl;
     s << "Number in stock: ";
     s << m_InStock << endl;
     s << "Price: ";
     s << m_Price << endl;
     s << "Minimum stock: ";
     s << m_MinimumStock << endl;
     s << "Reorder quantity: ";
     s << m_MinimumReorder << endl;
     s << "Distributor: ";
     s << m_Distributor << endl;
     s << "UPC: ";
     s << m_UPC << endl;
     s << endl;
}

ostream& UndatedStockItem::Write(ostream& s)
{
     s << 0 << endl;
     s << m_Name << endl;
     s << m_InStock << endl;
     s << m_Price << endl;
     s << m_MinimumStock << endl;
     s << m_MinimumReorder << endl;
     s << m_Distributor << endl;
     s << m_UPC << endl;

     return s;
}
```

```
Problem
Algorithms
C++
Executable
Hardware
```

Figure 10.25 continued

```
UndatedStockItem::~UndatedStockItem()
{
}

void UndatedStockItem::Reorder(ostream& s)
{
    short ReorderAmount;

    if (m_InStock < m_MinimumStock)
        {
        ReorderAmount = m_MinimumStock-m_InStock;
        if (ReorderAmount < m_MinimumReorder)
            ReorderAmount = m_MinimumReorder;
        s << "Reorder " << ReorderAmount << " units of " << m_Name;
        s << " with UPC " << m_UPC << " from " << m_Distributor << endl;
        }
}

bool UndatedStockItem::CheckUPC(string UPC)
{
    return (UPC == m_UPC);
}

short UndatedStockItem::GetInventory()
{
    return m_InStock;
}

void UndatedStockItem::DeductSaleFromInventory(short QuantitySold)
{
    m_InStock -= QuantitySold;
}

string UndatedStockItem::GetName()
{
    return m_Name;
}


// DatedStockItem member functions

DatedStockItem::DatedStockItem()
: m_Expires()
{
}
```

Problem
Algorithms
C++
Executable
Hardware

Figure 10.25 continued

```
DatedStockItem::DatedStockItem(const DatedStockItem& Item)
: m_Expires(Item.m_Expires)
{
}

DatedStockItem& DatedStockItem::operator = (const DatedStockItem& Item)
{
     if (&Item != this)
            m_Expires = Item.m_Expires;
     return *this;
}

DatedStockItem::~DatedStockItem()
{
}

DatedStockItem::DatedStockItem(string Name, short InStock,
short Price, short MinimumStock, short MinimumReorder,
string Distributor, string UPC, string Expires)
: UndatedStockItem(Name,InStock,Price,MinimumStock,
   MinimumReorder,Distributor,UPC),
   m_Expires(Expires)
{
}

ostream& DatedStockItem::Write(ostream& s)
{
     s << m_Expires << endl;
     s << m_Name << endl;
     s << m_InStock << endl;
     s << m_Price << endl;
     s << m_MinimumStock << endl;
     s << m_MinimumReorder << endl;
     s << m_Distributor << endl;
     s << m_UPC << endl;

     return s;
}
```

Problem
Algorithms
C++
Executable
Hardware

Figure 10.25 continued

```
void DatedStockItem::FormattedDisplay(ostream& s)
{
    s << "Expiration date: ";
    s << m_Expires << endl;
    s << "Name: ";
    s << m_Name << endl;
    s << "Number in stock: ";
    s << m_InStock << endl;
    s << "Price: ";
    s << m_Price << endl;
    s << "Minimum stock: ";
    s << m_MinimumStock << endl;
    s << "Reorder quantity: ";
    s << m_MinimumReorder << endl;
    s << "Distributor: ";
    s << m_Distributor << endl;
    s << "UPC: ";
    s << m_UPC << endl;
    s << endl;
}
```

```
string DatedStockItem::Today()
{
    struct date d;
    unsigned short year;
    unsigned short day;
    unsigned short month;
    string TodaysDate;
    strstream FormatStream;

    getdate(&d);
    year = d.da_year;
    day = d.da_day;
    month = d.da_mon;

    FormatStream << setfill('0') << setw(4) << year <<
       setw(2) << month << setw(2) << day;
    FormatStream.seekg(0);
    FormatStream >> TodaysDate;

    return TodaysDate;
}
```

Problem
Algorithms
C++
Executable
Hardware

Figure 10.25 continued

```
void DatedStockItem::Reorder(ostream& s)
{
    if (m_Expires < Today())
        {
        s << "Return " << m_InStock << " units of " << m_Name;
        s << " with UPC " << m_UPC << " to " << m_Distributor << endl;
        m_InStock = 0;
        }

    StockItem::Reorder(s);
}
```

Figure 10.25 continued

Unlike the classes we've dealt with before, where the member functions deserve most of our attention, possibly the most interesting point about this new version of the StockItem class is its member variables, especially the variable named m_Worker. It's a pointer, which isn't all that strange; we've seen pointer member variables before in our string class. But what type of pointer is it?

It's a pointer to a StockItem; that is, a pointer to the same type of object that we're defining! Even if that were useful, is it even legal?

Problem
Algorithms
C++
Executable
Hardware

We'll Manage Somehow

Yes, it is legal, because the compiler can figure out how to allocate storage for a pointer to any type, whether it knows the full definition of that type or not. However, this doesn't answer the question of why we want a pointer to a StockItem in our StockItem class in the first place. The answer is that, as we saw in the discussion of polymorphism earlier in this chapter, a pointer to a StockItem can actually point to an object of any class derived from StockItem via public inheritance. We're going to make use of this fact to implement the bulk of the functionality of our StockItem objects in the derived classes UndatedStockItem and DatedStockItem, which are derived from StockItem.

In essence, we're renaming the old StockItem class to UndatedStockItem and creating a new StockItem class that will handle the interaction with the application programmer. Objects of this new StockItem class will pass the actual class-specific operations to an object of either the UndatedStockItem or DatedStockItem classes, as appropriate.

Let's start our examination of this new StockItem class by looking at the implementation of operator << in Figure 10.26.

```
ostream& operator << (ostream& s, const StockItem& Item)
{
      return Item.m_Worker->Write(s);
}
```

Figure 10.26: The implementation of operator << for a polymorphic StockItem
(from code\itemp.cc)

At first glance, this isn't particularly complicated. It just calls a function named Write via the StockItem* member variable m_Worker. But what does that pointer point to?

This is the key to the polymorphic object idiom: The pointer m_Worker points to either an UndatedStockItem or a DatedStockItem, depending on whether the object was created with or without an expiration date. Since the type of object that m_Worker points to is determined when the StockItem object is created, rather than when the program is compiled, the actual function that is called by operator << will vary accordingly, as it does with any type of polymorphism. The difference between this version of StockItem and the one earlier in this chapter is that the pointer is used only in the implementation of StockItem rather than being accessible to the user of the class. This allows us to prevent the plague of memory allocation errors associated with pointer manipulation in the application program.

Problem
Algorithms
C++
Executable
Hardware

Before we get into the details of how we can create an object of this new version of StockItem, let's look at a couple of diagrams of the StockItem variables from the example program in Figure 10.22, so we can see exactly how this "internal polymorphism" works. First, Figure 10.27 shows a possible layout of the StockItem object x that is the argument to operator << in the statement cout << x;.

Let's trace the execution of the line return Item.m_Worker->Write(s); from operator << (Figure 10.26) when it is executed to display the value of the StockItem x (i.e., as a result of the statement cout << x; in the example program). In step **(1)**, the pointer m_Worker is followed to location 12341000, the worker object that will handle the operations of the StockItem manager class object. This location contains the address of the vtable for the worker object. In this case, the worker object is an UndatedStockItem object, so the vtable is the one for the UndatedStockItem class. In our diagram, that vtable is at location 12360000, so in step **(2)**, we follow the vtable pointer to find the address of the Write function. The diagram makes the assumption that the Write function is the second virtual function defined in the StockItem class, so in step **(3)** we fetch the contents of the second entry in the vtable, which is 12370900.

That is the address of the *Write* function that will be executed in this case.

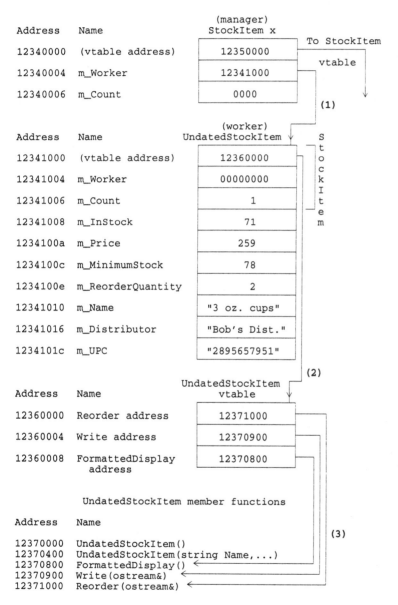

Figure 10.27: A polymorphic StockItem object with no date

Figure 10.28 shows a possible layout of the StockItem object y that is the argument to operator << in the statement cout << y;.

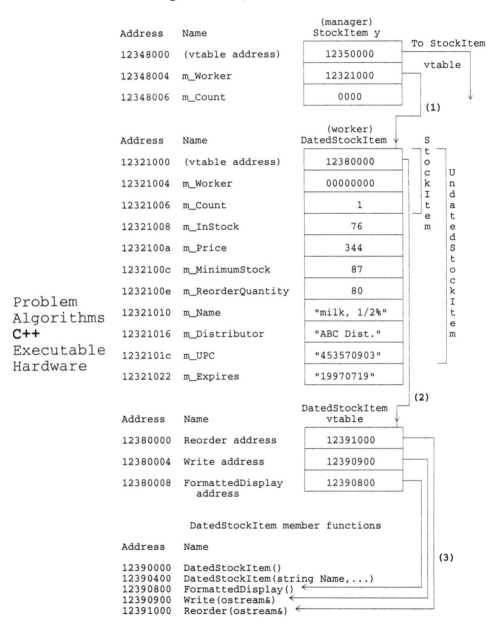

Figure 10.28: A polymorphic StockItem object with a date

Now let's trace how the line return Item.m_Worker->Write(s); is executed to display the value of the StockItem y (i.e., as a result of the statement cout << y in the example program). In step **(1)**, the pointer m_Worker is followed to location 12321000, the worker object that will handle the operations of the StockItem manager class object. This location contains the address of the vtable for the worker object. In this case, the worker object is a DatedStockItem object, so the vtable is the one for the DatedStockItem class. In our diagram, that vtable is at location 12380000, so in step **(2)**, we follow the vtable pointer to find the address of the Write function. As before, the diagram makes the assumption that the Write function is the second virtual function defined in the StockItem class, so in step **(3)** we fetch the contents of the second entry in the vtable, which is 12390900. That is the address of the Write function that will be executed in this case.

Setting the Standard

Now that we have seen how a polymorphic object works once it is set up, let's continue our examination of the StockItem class by looking at the "standard" member functions; that is, the ones that are necessary to make it a concrete data type. As you may remember, these are the default constructor, the copy constructor, the assignment operator, and the destructor.

Problem
Algorithms
C++
Executable
Hardware

It may occur to you to wonder why we have to rewrite all these functions; what's wrong with the ones we've already written for StockItem? The answer is that these functions create, copy, and destroy objects of a given class. Now that we have changed the way we want to use the StockItem class and the way it works, we have to rewrite these functions to do the right thing in the new situation. So let's start with the default constructor, shown in Figure 10.29.

```
StockItem::StockItem()
: m_Count(0), m_Worker(new UndatedStockItem)
{
        m_Worker->m_Count = 1;
}
```

Figure 10.29: The default constructor for the polymorphic StockItem class (from code\itemp.cc)

The first member initialization expression in this function merely initializes m_Count to 0. We won't actually be using this variable in a

StockItem object, but I don't like leaving uninitialized variables around.

The second member initialization expression, however, is already a bit odd-looking; why are we creating an UndatedStockItem object here when we have no data to put in it? Because we need *some* worker object to perform the work of a default-constructed StockItem. For example, if the user asks for the contents of the StockItem to be displayed on the screen with labels (by calling FormattedDisplay), we would like to have the default values displayed with the appropriate labels, which can only be done by an object that has a working FormattedDisplay function. The StockItem class itself doesn't have any data except for the StockItem* and the m_Count variable, which we'll get to later. Therefore, all of the functionality of a StockItem has to be handed off to the worker object, which in this case is the newly created UndatedStockItem.

But what does the member initialization expression m_Worker(new UndatedStockItem) actually do? It creates a new object of type UndatedStockItem via the default constructor of that class and uses the address of the resulting object to initialize m_Worker. However, there are some tricks in the implementation of the constructor of a worker class, and now is the time to see how such a constructor actually

Problem
Algorithms
C++
Executable
Hardware

works. Figure 10.30 shows the code for that constructor.

```
UndatedStockItem::UndatedStockItem()
: StockItem(1),
    m_InStock(0),
    m_Price(0),
    m_MinimumStock(0),
    m_MinimumReorder(0),
    m_Name(),
    m_Distributor(),
    m_UPC()
{
}
```

Figure 10.30: The default constructor for the UndatedStockItem class (from code\itemp.cc)

Figure 10.31 shows what a default-constructed StockItem might look like.[6]

---

6. As before, I'm simplifying the layout of the string member variables, as their internal data isn't of interest to us here.

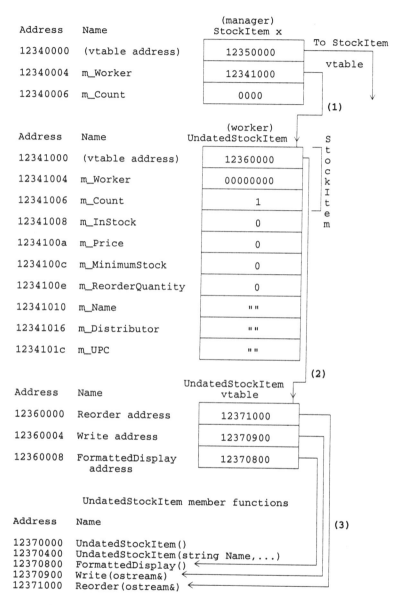

Figure 10.31: A default-constructed polymorphic StockItem object

Most of this is pretty conventional: all we're doing is initializing the values of the member variables to reasonable default values. But there's something a bit unusual about that base class initializer, StockItem(1). Before we get into exactly what the argument 1 means, it's important to understand why we *must* specify a base class initializer here.

As we saw in Chapter 9 in the discussion of Figure 9.30, a base class initializer is used when we want to specify which base class constructor will be used to initialize the base class part of a derived class object. If we don't specify any particular base class initializer, then the base class part will be initialized using the default constructor for that base class. In the example in Chapter 9, we needed to call a specific base class constructor to fill in the fields in the base class part of the UndatedStockItem object. That should seem reasonable enough, but we don't need to do that here because the StockItem object doesn't have any data fields that we need to initialize in our UndatedStockItem object constructor. So why can't we just let the compiler use the default constructor for the base class part of an UndatedStockItem?

Base Instincts

Problem
Algorithms
C++
Executable
Hardware

We can't do that because the default constructor for StockItem calls the default constructor for UndatedStockItem; that is, the function that we're examining right now. Therefore, if we allow the StockItem default constructor to be used to initialize the StockItem part of an UndatedStockItem, that default constructor will call our UndatedStockItem default constructor again, which will call the StockItem default constructor again, and the program will eventually use up all the stack space and die.

To avoid this problem, we have to make a special constructor for StockItem that doesn't call a constructor for UndatedStockItem and therefore prevents an indefinite chain of constructor calls. As no one outside the implementation of the StockItem polymorphic object knows anything about classes in this idiom other than StockItem, they don't need to call this constructor. As a result, we can make it protected.

Okay, so how do we declare a special constructor for this purpose? As was shown in Figure 10.23, all we have to do is to put the line StockItem(int); in a protected section of the class definition. The implementation of this function is shown in Figure 10.32.

How could a function that doesn't even have any code inside its {} be complicated? In fact, this apparently simple function raises three questions. First, why do we need an argument when the function isn't going to use it? Second, why don't we have a name specified for the argument, as we have had in the past? And third, why are we initializing m_Worker to the value 0? We'll examine the first two of these questions now and defer the answer to the third until we discuss the destructor for the StockItem class.

```
StockItem::StockItem(int)
: m_Worker(0)
{
}
```

Figure 10.32: Implementing a special protected constructor for StockItem (from code\itemp.cc)

The answers to the first two questions are related: The reason we don't need to specify a name for the argument is that we aren't going to use the argument. The only reason for this function to take an argument is to distinguish it from the other constructors via the function overloading mechanism. Remember that the compiler can tell functions with the same names (such as the constructors for a given class) apart so long as they have different argument types, so we're supplying an argument we don't need to allow the compiler to pick this function when we want to use it. In this case, when we call the function from the worker object's constructor, we'll supply the value 1, which will be ignored in the function itself but will tell the compiler that we want to call this constructor rather than any of the other constructors.

Of course, there's nothing to stop us from giving the argument a name even though we aren't going to use it in the constructor, but it's better not to, to avoid confusing both the compiler and the next programmer to look at this function. The compiler may give us a warning message if we don't use an argument that we've declared, while the next programmer to look at this function may think we've forgotten to use the argument. We can solve both of these problems by not giving it a name, which makes it clear that we weren't planning to use it in the first place.

So now we've followed the chain of events down to the initialization of the base class part of the UndatedStockItem object that was created as the worker object inside the default constructor for StockItem. The rest of Figure 10.30 is pretty simple; it simply initializes the data for the UndatedStockItem class itself. When that's done, we're ready to execute the lone statement inside the {} in Figure 10.29, which is m_Worker->m_Count = 1;. Clearly, this sets the value of m_Count in the newly created UndatedStockItem object to 1, but what might not be as clear is *why* we need to do this.

Problem
Algorithms
C++
Executable
Hardware

References Count

The reason we have to set m_Count to 1 in the UndatedStockItem variable pointed to by m_Worker is that we're going to keep track of the number of StockItems that are using that UndatedStockItem rather than copying it every time we copy a StockItem that points to it. If you recall, we encountered a similar situation with the implementation of our string class. In that case, we decided to copy the data for the string whenever we copied the string. However, this time we're going to avoid that inefficient method of sharing data and instead will use an idiom called **reference-counting**.

The general idea of reference-counting is fairly simple, as most great ideas are (after you understand them, at least). It's inefficient to copy a lot of data whenever we set one variable to the same value as another; on the other hand, copying a pointer to the data is much easier. However, we have to consider how we will know when we can delete the data being pointed to, which will be when no one needs the data anymore. If we don't take care of this requirement, we'll have the same problem as with the compiler-generated copy constructor and the compiler-generated assignment operator for the string class. (In case you've mercifully forgotten that problem, the discussion is in Chapter 8, starting in the section titled "For Reference Only".)

In a nutshell, the problem that we saw there was that the compiler-generated functions merely copy the pointer to the string's data without keeping track of the number of users of the data. Hence, when one of the strings that refers to the data goes out of scope and is destroyed, the destructor can do either of the following, neither of which is correct:

1. Free the memory where the data is kept, via delete.
2. Fail to free the memory.

The first of these is incorrect because there may be other strings that still want to use the data in question, and those other strings will now be referring to memory that is no longer allocated to that data. Therefore, at any time the data in that area of memory may be overwritten by new data. The second is also incorrect because when the last string that was using the shared data goes away, a *memory leak* results. That is, although the data used by the string can no longer be accessed, the memory it occupies cannot be used for other purposes because it has not been released back to the system via operator delete.

Problem
Algorithms
C++
Executable
Hardware

The correct way to share data in such a situation is to change the constructor(s), destructor, and assignment operator to keep track of the number of objects that are using a particular set of data, and when there are no more users of that set of data, to free the memory used by the data. Let's see how this notion of reference-counting works with our StockItem class.

Starring Sharon Sharalike

Suppose that we have the example program in Figure 10.33 (which is contained in the file refcnt1.cc, if you want to print it out).

This program doesn't do anything very useful. However, it does illustrate the constructors and assignment operator, as follows. First, it creates two StockItems, item1 and item2, with specified contents (via the "normal" constructors for undated and dated items, respectively). Then it creates another StockItem, item3, with the same value as item1 via the copy constructor. Then it assigns the value of item2 to item1, using the assignment operator.

The line StockItem item1("3 oz. cups",32,129,10,5,"Bob's Dist.","2895657951"); calls the constructor illustrated in Figure 10.34 to create a StockItem whose m_Worker points to an UndatedStockItem.

Problem
Algorithms
C++
Executable
Hardware

```
#include <iostream.h>
#include "string6.h"
#include "itemp.h"

int main()
{
    StockItem item1("3 oz. cups",32,129,10,5,"Bob's Dist.",
        "2895657951"); // create an undated object

    StockItem item2("Hot Chicken",48,158,15,12,"Joe's Dist.",
        "987654321", "19960824"); // create a dated object

    StockItem item3 = item1; // copy constructor
    item1 = item2; // assignment operator

    item1.FormattedDisplay(cout); // display an object with labels

    return 0;
}
```

Figure 10.33: An example program for reference-counting with StockItems
(code\refcnt1.cc)

```
StockItem::StockItem(string Name, short InStock,
short Price, short MinimumStock,
short MinimumReorder, string Distributor, string UPC)
: m_Count(0),
    m_Worker(new UndatedStockItem(Name, InStock, Price,
    MinimumStock, MinimumReorder, Distributor, UPC))
{
        m_Worker->m_Count = 1;
}
```

Figure 10.34: A normal constructor for StockItem (from code\itemp.cc)

Immediately after the execution of the line StockItem item1("3 oz. cups",32,129,10,5,"Bob's Dist.","2895657951");, the newly constructed StockItem object and its UndatedStockItem worker object look something like the diagram in Figure 10.35.[7]

Problem
Algorithms
C++
Executable
Hardware

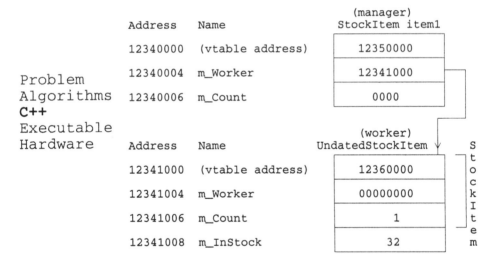

Figure 10.35: A polymorphic StockItem object

The next line, StockItem item2("Hot Chicken", 48, 158, 15, 12, "Joe's Dist.", "987654321", "19960824"); calls the constructor illustrated in Figure 10.36, which creates a StockItem whose m_Worker member variable points to a DatedStockItem. As you can see, this is almost identical to the previous constructor, except of course that it creates a DatedStockItem as the worker object rather than an UndatedStockItem.

---

7. In this and the following diagrams, I've omitted a number of the data elements to make the figure fit on the page.

After the statement StockItem item2("Hot Chicken", 48, 158, 15, 12, "Joe's Dist.", "987654321", "19960824"); is executed, the newly constructed StockItem object and its DatedStockItem worker object look something like the diagram in Figure 10.37.

```
StockItem::StockItem(string Name, short InStock,
short Price, short MinimumStock,
short MinimumReorder, string Distributor, string UPC,
string Expires)
: m_Count(0),
    m_Worker(new DatedStockItem(Name, InStock, Price,
    MinimumStock, MinimumReorder, Distributor, UPC, Expires))
{
      m_Worker->m_Count = 1;
}
```

Figure 10.36: Another normal constructor for StockItem (from code\itemp.cc)

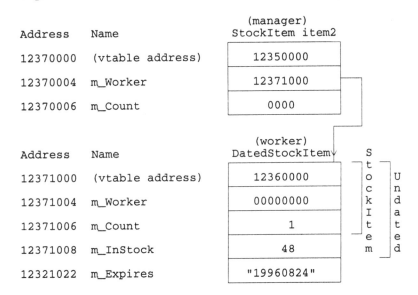

Figure 10.37: Another polymorphic StockItem object

Now let's take a look at what happens when we execute the next statement, StockItem item3 = item1;. Since we are creating a new StockItem with the same contents as an existing StockItem, this calls the copy constructor, shown in Figure 10.38.

```
StockItem::StockItem(const StockItem& Item)
: m_Count(0), m_Worker(Item.m_Worker)
{
      m_Worker->m_Count ++;
}
```

Figure 10.38: The copy constructor for StockItem (from code\itemp.cc)

This uses the pointer from the existing StockItem object (Item.m_Worker) to initialize the newly created StockItem object's pointer, m_Worker, which means that the new and existing StockItem objects will be sharing a worker object. Then we initialize the value of m_Count in the new object to 0 so that it has a known value. Finally, we increment the m_Count variable in the worker object because it has one more user than before the new StockItem was constructed.

After this operation, the variables item1 and item3, together with their shared worker object, look something like Figure 10.39.

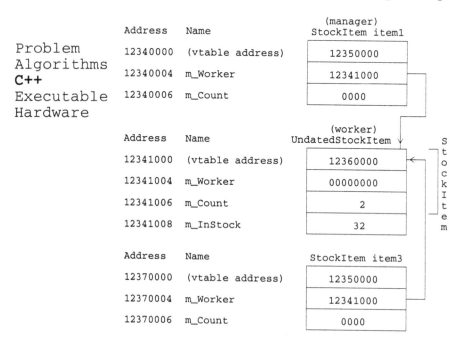

Figure 10.39: Two polymorphic StockItem objects sharing the same worker object

How does this differ from the situation we saw in the string class, where we discovered the problems with sharing data? Only in the fact that we have the m_Count variable to keep track of the number of users of the worker object, so our StockItem destructor will know when it is time to delete that object. This should be abundantly clear when we get to the end of the program and see what happens when the destructor is called for the StockItem variables.

Now let's continue by looking at the next statement in the test program, item1 = item2;. As you have probably figured out already, this is actually a call to the assignment operator (operator =) for the StockItem class. Let's take a look at the code for that operator, in Figure 10.40.

```
StockItem& StockItem::operator = (const StockItem& Item)
{
    if (&Item != this)
        {
        m_Worker->m_Count --;
        if (m_Worker->m_Count <= 0)
            delete m_Worker;
        m_Worker = Item.m_Worker;
        m_Worker->m_Count ++;
        }
    return *this;
}
```

Problem
Algorithms
C++
Executable
Hardware

Figure 10.40: The assignment operator (operator =) for StockItem (from code\itemp.cc)

This function starts out with the line if (&Item != this), which implements the standard test to see if the object being copied from and the object being copied to are actually the same object, in which case it doesn't have to (and doesn't) do anything. In the example program, the object being copied from is item2 and the object being copied to is item1, which are in fact different objects. So we continue with the next statement in the code for operator =, m_Worker->m_Count --;, which decrements the count in the worker object pointed to by the object being copied to (item1). If you look at Figure 10.39, you'll see that the previous value of that variable was 2, so it is now 1, meaning that there is one StockItem that is still using that worker object. Therefore, the condition in the next line, if (m_Worker->m_Count <= 0), is false, which means that the controlled statement of the if statement, namely, delete m_Worker;, is not executed. Because there is still at least one user of the worker object, it cannot be deleted.

The next statement in the code for operator = is m_Worker = Item.m_Worker;, which sets the worker object pointer in the object being copied to (item1) equal to the pointer in the object being copied from (item2), which was the main point of the whole operation in the first place. Now item1 and item2 are sharing a worker object, so they are effectively the same StockItem. Then the statement m_Worker->m_Count ++; increments the count of users of the shared worker object (in this case, to 2). Again, this is necessary so that we'll know when it's safe and appropriate to delete the worker object and reclaim the memory it occupies. Finally, as is standard with assignment operators, we return the object that we have assigned to by the statement return *this;.

After all this has been done, item1 and item2 share a DatedStockItem, while item3 has its own UndatedStockItem. The manager variables item1 and item2, together with their shared worker object, look something like Figure 10.41.

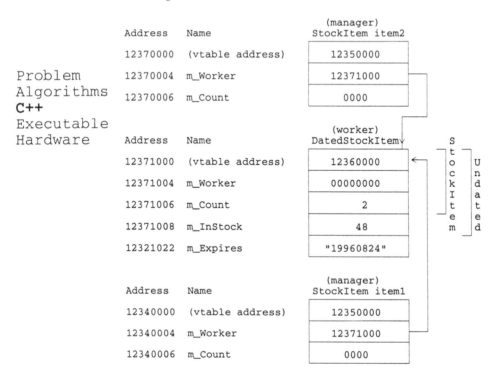

Figure 10.41: Two polymorphic StockItem objects sharing the same worker object

It's important to note that item1 has effectively changed its type from UndatedStockItem to DatedStockItem as a result of the assignment statement. This is one of the benefits of the polymorphic object idiom; the effective type of an object can vary not only when it is created but at any time thereafter. Hence, we don't have to be locked in to a particular type when we create an object, but can adjust the type as necessary according to circumstances. By the way, this ability to change the effective type of an object at run time also solves the slicing problem referred to in the previous chapter, where we assign an object of a derived class to a base class object with the result that the extra fields from the derived class object are lost.

Finally, item3 looks pretty much as shown in Figure 10.42.

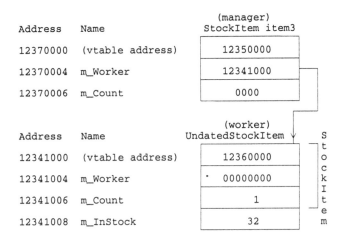

Problem
Algorithms
C++
Executable
Hardware

Figure 10.42: A polymorphic StockItem object

The Last Shall Be First

Now let's take a look at what happens when the StockItem objects are destroyed at the end of the main program, which will occur in reverse order of their creation as mandated for auto variables in the C++ language. So item3 will be destroyed first, followed by item2, and finally item1. Figure 10.43 shows the code for the destructor for StockItem.

```
StockItem::~StockItem()
{
    if (m_Worker == 0)
        return;

    m_Worker->m_Count --;
    if (m_Worker->m_Count <= 0)
        delete m_Worker;
}
```

Figure 10.43: The destructor for the StockItem class (from code\itemp.cc)

Before we get into the details of this code, I should mention that whenever any object is destroyed, all of its constituent elements that have destructors are automatically destroyed as well. In the case of StockItem, the string variables are automatically destroyed by calling their destructors during the destruction of the StockItem.

The first if statement in the destructor, if (m_Worker == 0), provides the clue as to why our special StockItem constructor (Figure 10.32) had to set the m_Worker variable to 0. We'll see exactly how that comes into play shortly. For now, we know that the value of m_Worker in item3 is not 0, as it points to an UndatedStockItem (see Figure 10.42), so the condition in the first if statement is false. Therefore, we move to the next statement, m_Worker->m_Count --;. Since according to Figure 10.42 the value of m_Count in the UndatedStockItem to which m_Worker points is 1, that will reduce the value of that variable to 0. Therefore, the condition in the next statement, if (m_Worker->m_Count <= 0) is true, which means that the controlled statement of the if, delete m_Worker;, is executed. Since the value of m_Count is 0, no other StockItem variables are currently using the UndatedStockItem pointed to by m_Worker. Therefore, we want that UndatedStockItem to go away so that its memory can be reclaimed, and we use the delete operator to accomplish that goal.

However, this is not quite as simple as it may seem, because before the memory used by a UndatedStockItem can be reclaimed, the destructor for that UndatedStockItem must be called to allow all of its constituent parts (especially the string variables it contains) to expire properly. Luckily, the delete operator, when applied to a variable that has a destructor, automatically calls the destructor for that variable. So the next function that is called is the destructor for the UndatedStockItem that is being deleted. Figure 10.44 shows the code for the destructor for UndatedStockItem.

Problem
Algorithms
C++
Executable
Hardware

UndatedStockItem::~UndatedStockItem()
{
}

Figure 10.44: The destructor for the UndatedStockItem class (from code\itemp.cc)

Before going into the details of this function, I should explain why it is called in the first place. Remember, the only pointers that are used to refer to either DatedStockItem or UndatedStockItem objects are StockItem*s. How does the compiler know to call the right destructor?

Just as it does with other functions in the same situation: We have to make the destructor virtual, so that the correct destructor will be called, no matter what the type of the pointer through which the object is accessed. This answers the earlier question of why we had to define a destructor and declare it to be virtual in Figure 10.11. As a general rule, destructors should be virtual if there are any other virtual functions in the class, as we have to make sure that the right destructor will be called via a base class pointer. Otherwise, data elements that are defined in the derived class won't be destroyed properly, possibly resulting in memory leaks or other undesirable effects.

Now that we know why this function is called, what does it do? Going solely by its appearance, it appears to do absolutely nothing. But, as is so often the case in C++, appearances are deceiving. In fact, just as the constructor for a derived class always calls a constructor for its embedded base class object, so a destructor for a derived class always calls the destructor for its embedded base class object. There are two differences between these situations, however. The first is that whereas the constructor for the base class object is called before any of the code in the derived class constructor is executed, the base class destructor is called after the code in the derived class destructor is executed. Here, of course, this distinction is irrelevant because there is no code in the derived class destructor.

However, we do have to consider the other distinction between constructors and destructors: There is only one destructor for a given class. This means that we can't use a trick similar to the "special base class constructor" trick that we used to prevent the base class constructor from calling the derived class constructor again. Instead, we have to arrange a way for the base class destructor to determine whether it's being asked to destroy a "real" base class object (a StockItem) or the embedded base class part of a derived class object (the StockItem base class part of an UndatedStockItem or DatedStockItem). In the

Problem
Algorithms
C++
Executable
Hardware

latter case, the destructor should exit immediately, since the base class part of either of those classes contains nothing that needs special handling by the destructor. The special constructor that is called by the UndatedStockItem constructor to initialize its StockItem part works together with the first if statement in the StockItem destructor (Figure 10.43) to solve this problem. The special StockItem constructor sets m_Worker to 0, which cannot be the address of any object, during the initialization of the base class part of an UndatedStockItem. When the destructor for StockItem is executed, a 0 value for m_Worker is the indicator of a StockItem that is the base class part of a derived class object. This allows the StockItem destructor to distinguish between a real StockItem and the base class part of an object of a class derived from StockItem by examining the value of m_Worker and bailing out immediately if it is the reserved value of 0.

Going, Going, Gone

Problem
Algorithms
C++
Executable
Hardware

Now that we've cleared up that point, it's time to return to what happens when item3, item2, and item1 are destroyed. They go away in that order because the last object to be constructed on the stack in a given scope is the first to be destroyed, as you might expect when dealing with stacks.

Figure 10.45 is another listing of the destructor for the StockItem class (StockItem::~StockItem()), for reference as we trace through it.

```
StockItem::~StockItem()
{
        if (m_Worker == 0)
            return;

        m_Worker->m_Count --;
        if (m_Worker->m_Count <= 0)
            delete m_Worker;
}
```

Figure 10.45: The destructor for the StockItem class (from code\itemp.cc)

First, item3 dies at the end of its scope. When it does, the StockItem destructor is automatically invoked to clean up. Since m_Worker isn't 0, the statement controlled by the first if statement isn't executed. Next, we execute the statement m_Worker->m_Count --;, which reduces the value of the variable m_Count in the UndatedStockItem pointed to by m_Worker to 0. Since this makes that variable 0, the condition in the second if statement is true, so its controlled statement delete m_Worker; is executed. We've already seen that this eliminates the object pointed to by m_Worker, calling the UndatedStockItem destructor in the process.

As before, calling this destructor does nothing other than destroying the member variable that has a destructor (namely, the m_Expires member variable, which is a string), followed by the mandatory call to the base class destructor.

At that point, the first if statement and its controlled statement,

```
if (m_Worker == 0)
    return;
```

comes into play. Remember the special base class constructor StockItem(int)? That constructor, which is called from our UndatedStockItem default and normal constructors, initializes m_Worker to 0. Therefore, we know that m_Worker will be 0 for any object that is actually an UndatedStockItem or a DatedStockItem because all of the constructors for DatedStockItem call one of those two constructors for UndatedStockItem to initialize their UndatedStockItem base class part. Therefore, the if statement will be true for the base class part of all UndatedStockItem and DatedStockItem objects. Since the current object being destroyed is in fact an UndatedStockItem object, the if is true. Therefore, the destructor exits immediately, ending the destruction of the UndatedStockItem object. Then the destructor for item3 finishes by freeing the storage associated with that object.

Next, the StockItem destructor is called for item2. Since m_Worker is not 0, the controlled statement of the first if is false. Therefore, we proceed to the next statement, m_Worker->m_Count --;. As you can see by looking back at Figure 10.41, the previous value of that variable was 2, so it is now 1. As a result, the condition in the next if statement, if (m_Worker->m_Count <= 0), is also false. Thus the controlled statement that uses delete to get rid of the DatedStockItem pointed to by m_Worker is not executed. Then the destructor for item2 finishes by freeing the storage associated with that object.

Finally, item1 dies at the end of its scope. When it does, the StockItem destructor is called to clean up its act. As before, m_Worker isn't 0, so the controlled statement of the first if statement isn't executed. Next, we execute the statement m_Worker->m_Count --;, which reduces the value of the variable m_Count in the DatedStockItem pointed to by m_Worker to 0. This time, the condition in the next if statement is true, so its controlled statement delete m_Worker; is executed. We've

Problem
Algorithms
C++
Executable
Hardware

already seen that this eliminates the object pointed to by m_Worker, calling the destructor for DatedStockItem (Figure 10.46).

DatedStockItem::~DatedStockItem()
{
}

Figure 10.46: The destructor for the DatedStockItem class (from code\itemp.cc)

Lastly, the call to the StockItem destructor occurs exactly as it did in the destruction of item3, except that there is an additional step because the base class of DatedStockItem is UndatedStockItem, and the destructor for that class in turn calls the destructor for *its* base class part, which is a StockItem. Once we get to the destructor for StockItem, the value of m_Worker is 0, so that destructor simply returns to the destructor for UndatedStockItem, which returns to the destructor for DatedStockItem. Then the destructor for item1 finishes by freeing the storage associated with that object.

For the Benefit of Posterity

Problem
Algorithms
C++
Executable
Hardware

Now it's time to clear up a point we've glossed over so far. We have already seen that the member initialization expression m_Count(0), present in the constructors for the StockItem object, is there just to make sure we don't have an uninitialized variable in the StockItem object, even though we actually won't be using the value in that type of variable. While this is true as far as it goes, it doesn't answer the question of why we need this variable at all, if we're not using it in the StockItem class. The clue to the answer is that we *are* using that variable in the object pointed to by m_Worker. However, why don't we just add the m_Count variable when we create the UndatedStockItem class rather than carrying along extra baggage in the StockItem class?

The answer is that the type of m_Worker is not UndatedStockItem, but StockItem. Remember, the compiler doesn't know the actual type of the object being pointed to at compile time; all it knows is the declared type of the pointer, which in this case is StockItem*. It must therefore use that declared type to determine what operations are permissible through that pointer. Hence, if there's no m_Count variable in a StockItem, the compiler won't let us refer to that variable through a StockItem*.

This also brings up another point that may or may not be obvious to you: The workings of the polymorphic StockItem object don't depend on the fact that DatedStockItem is derived from UndatedStockItem.

So long as both UndatedStockItem and DatedStockItem are derived directly or indirectly from StockItem, we can use a StockItem* to refer to an object of either of these classes, DatedStockItem, which is all that we need to make the idiom work.

Review

We started this chapter with a DatedStockItem class that was derived from the StockItem class, with the addition of an expiration date field. While this was a fine solution to the problem of creating a class based on the StockItem class without having to rewrite all the previously functioning code in the latter class, it didn't solve the bigger problem: how to create a vector of objects that might or might not have expiration dates. That is, we wanted to be able to mix StockItem objects with DatedStockItem objects in the same vector, which can't be done directly in C++.

Part of this difficulty was solved easily enough by making a vector of StockItem*'s rather than StockItems. Because C++ allows us to assign an object of a derived type to a pointer of its base class, creating such a vector allowed us to create both StockItems and DatedStockItems and assign them to various elements of the StockItem* vector. However, this didn't solve the problem completely, because when we called the Reorder function through a StockItem* pointer, the function that was executed was always StockItem:Reorder. This result may seem reasonable, but it doesn't meet our needs. We want a reference to the Reorder function to call the correct Reorder function for the *actual* type of the object the pointer is referring to, even though the pointer is declared as a StockItem*.

```
Problem
Algorithms
C++
Executable
Hardware
```

The reason the StockItem function is always called in this situation is precisely that when we use the ability to make a base class pointer (e.g., a StockItem*) refer to a derived class object (e.g., a DatedStockItem), the compiler doesn't know what the actual type of the object is at compile time. When we call a "normal" function, the compiler determines exactly which function will be called at compile time, and the only information the compiler has about the type of the object at compile time is that it's either a StockItem or an object of a class derived from StockItem. Hence, the compiler can't tell which function should be called at compile time, and it defaults to the base class function.

The solution to this problem is to make the Reorder function virtual. This means that when the compiler sees a call to the Reorder function, it will generate code that will call the appropriate version of that function for the actual type of the object being referred to. In this case, StockItem::Reorder will be called if the actual object being referred to through a StockItem* is a StockItem, and DatedStockItem::Reorder will be called if the actual object being referred to through a StockItem* is a DatedStockItem. This is exactly the behavior that we need to make our StockItem objects and DatedStockItem objects do the right thing when we call them through a StockItem*.

To make this run time determination of which function will be called, the compiler has to add something to every object that contains at least one virtual function. What it adds is a pointer to a vtable (virtual function table), which contains the addresses of all the virtual functions that are defined in the current class or any of its ancestors. The code that the compiler generates for a virtual function call uses this table to look up the actual address of the function to be called at run time.

After going over the use of virtual functions, we looked at the implementation of the usual I/O functions, operator << and operator >>. Even though these cannot be virtual functions, as they aren't member functions at all, that's fairly easy to fix by having them call virtual functions that provide the correct behavior for each different class. However, while this solves most of the problems with operator <<, the implementation of operator >> is still pretty tricky because it has to allocate the memory for the object that it is creating, since the actual type of that object isn't known until the data for the object has been read. The real problem here, though, is not that operator << has to allocate that memory, or even that it has to use a reference to a pointer to notify the calling function of the address of this memory. The big difficulty is that after the input operator allocates the memory, the calling function has to free the memory when it is done with the object. Getting a program written in this way to work properly is very difficult; keeping it working properly after later changes is virtually impossible. Unfortunately, there's no solution to this problem, so long as we require the user program to use a vector of StockItem*s to get the benefits of polymorphism.

As is often the case in C++, though, there is a way to remove that requirement. We can hide the pointers and the consequent memory allocation problems from the user, by using the *polymorphic object idiom*. With this idiom, the user sees only a base class object, while the pointers are hidden inside that base class object. This idiom is a particular use of the *manager/worker idiom*. The base class is the *manager* class, which "contains" an object of one of the *worker* classes.

```
Problem
Algorithms
C++
Executable
Hardware
```

Possibly the most unusual aspect of the manager/worker idiom is that the type of the pointer inside the manager object is the same as the type of the manager class. In the current case, each StockItem object contains a StockItem* called m_Worker as its main data member. While this may seem peculiar, it really makes sense; the actual type of the object being referred to is always one of the worker classes, which in this case means UndatedStockItem or DatedStockItem. Since we know that a StockItem* can refer to an object of any of the derived classes of StockItem, and because we want the interface of the StockItem class to be the same as any of its derived classes, declaring that pointer as a StockItem* is quite appropriate.

We started our examination of this new StockItem class with operator <<, whose header indicates one of the advantages of this new implementation of StockItem. Rather than taking a StockItem*, as the previous version of this function did, it takes a reference to a StockItem. The implementation of this function consists of a call to a protected virtual function called Write. Since Write is virtual, the version of Write that will be called here depends on the actual type of the object pointed to by m_Worker, which is exactly the behavior we want.

After going into more detail on how this "internal polymorphism" works, we continued by looking at how such a polymorphic object comes into existence in the first place, starting with the default constructor for StockItem. This constructor is a bit more complicated than it seems at first glance, because when it creates an empty UndatedStockItem to perform the duties of a default-constructed StockItem, that newly constructed UndatedStockItem has to initialize its base class part, as is required for all derived class objects. That may not seem too unusual, but you have to keep in mind that the base class for UndatedStockItem is StockItem; therefore, the constructor for UndatedStockItem will necessarily call a constructor for StockItem. We have to make sure that it doesn't call the default constructor for StockItem, as that is where the UndatedStockItem constructor was called from in the first place! Hence, the result of such a call would be a further call to the default constructor for UndatedStockItem, then to the default constructor for StockItem, and so on forever (or at least until we run out of stack space). The solution is simple enough: We have to create a special constructor for StockItem, StockItem::StockItem(int), that we call explicitly via a base class initializer in the default and normal constructors for UndatedStockItem; this special constructor doesn't do anything but initialize m_Worker to zero, for reasons we'll get to later, and then return to its caller. Since it doesn't call any other functions, we avoid the potential disaster of an infinite regress.

Problem
Algorithms
C++
Executable
Hardware

This simple function, StockItem::StockItem(int), however, does have a couple of other interesting features. First, we declared it protected, so that it couldn't be called by anyone other than our member functions and those of our derived classes. This is sensible, because after all we don't want anyone to be able to create a StockItem with just an int argument. In fact, we aren't using that argument for anything other than to allow the compiler to tell which constructor we mean; that is, to allow proper overloading of the constructor. This also means that we don't need to provide a name for that argument, since we're not using it. Therefore, we don't provide such a name. Leaving the name out tells both possible future programmers and the compiler that we didn't forget to use the argument accidentally, which means that we don't get "unused argument" warnings when we compile this code.

Then we started to examine the notion of using *reference-counting* to keep track of the number of users of a given DatedStockItem or UndatedStockItem object, rather than copying those objects whenever we copied their manager objects. As long as we keep track of how many users there are, we can safely delete the DatedStockItem or UndatedStockItem as soon as there aren't any more users left. To keep track of the number of users, we use the m_Count member variable in the StockItem class.

Problem
Algorithms
C++
Executable
Hardware

To see how this works in practice, we went through the steps that occur when StockItem objects were created, copied, and destroyed. This involved the implementation of the assignment operator, which, unlike the case with the string class, does copy the pointer to the worker object contained in the manager object. The reason that this approach works here is that we are keeping track of the number of users of each object, so memory is freed correctly when the objects are destroyed at the end of the program rather than being freed twice as would have happened with the implementation of the string class in the earlier chapters.

The destructor for the StockItem class has a number of new features. First, it is virtual. This is necessary because the derived class object pointed to by the StockItem object must be destroyed when it no longer has any users, but the type of the pointer through which it is accessed is StockItem*. Hence, to call the correct destructor, we must declare it virtual, as with all other functions that have to be resolved according to the run time type of the object for which they are called.

Second, the StockItem destructor has to check whether it has been called as the base class destructor for a derived class object. Just as in the case of the constructor for StockItem, we have to prevent an infinite regress in which the destructor for StockItem calls the destructor for DatedStockItem, which calls the destructor for StockItem, which calls the destructor for DatedStockItem again, and so on. In fact, in this case, we can't avoid the first "round-trip" because the destructor for DatedStockItem must call the destructor for StockItem; we don't have any control over that. However, the first if statement in the StockItem destructor cuts off the regress right there, as m_Worker will be 0 only in the base class part of a derived class object. That's why we initialized m_Worker to 0 in the special constructor for StockItem that was used to construct the base class part of an object of a class derived from StockItem.

We finished by examining the exact sequence of events that occurs when the objects in the example program are destroyed, as well as the reason that we had to include m_Count in the base class when it was never used there; the reason is that the type of the pointer we use to access it is StockItem*. If there were no m_Count variable in a StockItem, we wouldn't be able to access it through such a pointer.

Exercises, Second Set

3. Rewrite the DrugStockItem class that you wrote earlier in this chapter as an derived class of DatedStockItem, adding the new class to the polymorphic object implementation that we've already created with the base class StockItem. The Reorder member function of the DrugStockItem class will be inherited from DatedStockItem, and the DeductSaleFromInventory member function will have to be made a virtual function in StockItem so that the correct version will be called via the StockItem* in the StockItem class. The resulting set of classes will allow the effective type of a StockItem object to be any of UndatedStockItem, DatedStockItem, or DrugStockItem.

    `Problem`
    `Algorithms`
    `C++`
    `Executable`
    `Hardware`

4. Rewrite the Employee, Manager, and Hourly classes that you wrote earlier in this chapter as a set of classes implementing a polymorphic object type. The base class will be Employee, with a Manager class and an Hourly class derived from the base class. The resulting set of classes will allow the effective type of an Employee object to be either Manager or Hourly, with the CalculatePay function producing the correct result for either of these types. To distinguish between the different effective types, you will need to write two different versions of the constructor for the Employee class. To do this, add an additional argument of type float in the constructor that creates an Hourly worker object, specifying the multiplier used to calculate overtime pay. For example, a value of 1.5 would specify the standard "time-and-a-half for overtime"

multiplier. Note that unlike the first Employee exercise in the previous chapter, you *must* maintain the same interface for the CalculatePay function in these classes because you are using a base class pointer to access derived class objects.

5.   Rewrite the final version of the string class from Chapter 8, using the reference-counting idiom described in this chapter. *Hint*: you will want to introduce a separate class that contains the reference-count as well as the char* and the length of the string.

Conclusion

We have reached the end of this book. If you've made it this far, you can take comfort in knowing that you have a good grasp of the major organizing principles of C++. Congratulations!

```
Problem
Algorithms
C++
Executable
Hardware
```

Appendix

Tying Up Loose Ends

Where Am I, Anyway?

Now that you've reached the end of this book, there are some questions that have probably occurred to you. For example,

1. Am I a programmer now?
2. What am I qualified to do?
3. Where do I go from here?
4. Is that all there is to C++?

The answer to the first three of these questions, as usual with such open-ended topics, is "It all depends". Of course, I can give you some general answers; let's start with questions 1 and 2.

Yes, in the broadest sense, you are a programmer. You've read a fair amount of code and written some programs yourself. In fact, if you really understand the contents of Chapter 10, you know more about polymorphism than a lot of people who are professional C++ programmers. But, of course, this doesn't mean that you *are* a professional programmer. As I said way back at the beginning, no book can turn a novice into a professional programmer. Being a professional in any field takes a lot of hard work, and although you've undoubtedly worked hard in understanding this book, you've just begun the exploration of programming.

Questions 3 and 4 are also closely related. You now have enough background that you should be able to get some benefit from a well-written book about C++ that assumes you are already somewhat acquainted with programming in C++. That would be a good way to continue. As for whether we've covered everything about C++, the answer is unequivocal: absolutely not. I would estimate that we have examined less than 10% of the very large, complicated, and powerful C++ language, but that relatively small fraction of the language is the foundation for the rest of your learning in this subject. Most books try to cover every aspect of the language and, as a result, cannot provide deep coverage of fundamentals, whereas I've concentrated on making sure that you have the correct tools to continue your learning.

Tying Up Loose Ends

I've skipped over some topics because they weren't essential to the discussion. However, since they are likely to be covered in any other book that you might read on programming in C++, I'll discuss them here briefly. This will ensure that they won't be completely foreign to you when you encounter them in your future reading.

Operator Precedence

```
Problem
Algorithms
C++
Executable
Hardware
```

You may recall from high school arithmetic that an expression like 5 + 3 * 9 is calculated as though it were written 5 + (3 * 9), not (5 + 3) * 9. That is, you have to do the * before the +, so that the correct result is 32, not 72, as it would be under the latter interpretation. The reason for performing the operations in the former order is that multiplication has a higher *precedence* than addition. Well, every operator in C++ also has a precedence that determines the order of application of each operator in an expression with more than one operator. This seems like a good idea at first glance, since after all, arithmetic does follow precedence rules like the one we just saw. Unfortunately, C++ is just a little more complicated than arithmetic, and so its precedence rules are not as simple and easy to remember as those of arithmetic. In fact, there are 17 different levels of precedence, which no one can remember. Therefore, everyone who is sensible uses parentheses in any complex expression to specify what order was meant when the expression was written. Of course, if we're going to have to use parentheses, then why do we need the precedence rules in the first place?[1]

---

1. In the event that you're worried about using redundant parentheses, you might want to check with the Department of Redundancy Department.

Other Native Data Types

We've confined our use of native data types to short, unsigned short, char, bool, float (in the Employee exercises), and int (for the return type of main only). As I mentioned in Chapter 6, there are a couple of other native types that we haven't used because they weren't necessary to the task at hand, which was teaching you how to program (in C++). Now that we have made significant progress toward that task, you might as well add them to your arsenal of tools.

These other native types are double and long, the latter of which is available in either signed or unsigned varieties. The double data type has properties similar to float, but with greater accuracy and range. As briefly mentioned before, float and double variables can contain fractional parts, (so-called *floating-point* numbers), rather than being restricted to whole numbers as in the case of short and the other integral types. Of course, this raises two questions: First, why don't we use these types all the time, if they're more flexible? Second, why are there two of these types rather than only one? These questions are related, because the main difference between float and double is that a float is 4 bytes long and a double is 8 bytes long. Therefore, a double can store larger values and maintain higher accuracy. However, it also uses twice the amount of memory of a float, which may not be important when we're dealing with a few values but is quite important if we have a vector or array of thousands or tens of thousands of elements.

Problem
Algorithms
C++
Executable
Hardware

So that explains why we'd use a float rather than a double, but not why we would use a long rather than a float; after all, they both take up 4 bytes. The reason that we would use a long is that it can store larger whole values than a float while retaining exact accuracy in results. Also, on a machine that doesn't have a built-in numeric processor, longs can be processed much more rapidly than floats.

Glossary

Special Characters

& has a number of distinct meanings. When it precedes the name of a *variable* without following a *type* name, it means "the address of the following variable". For example, &Str means "the address of the variable Str". When & follows a type name and precedes a variable name, it means that the variable which is being declared is a *reference*; that is, another name for a preexisting variable. In this book, references are used only in argument lists, where they indicate that the variable being defined is a new name for the caller's variable rather than a new local variable.

< is the "less than" operator, which returns the value true if the expression on its left has a lower value than the expression on its right; otherwise, it returns the value false. Also see operator < in the index.

= is the *assignment* operator, which assigns the value on its right to the *variable* on its left. Also see operator = in the index.

> is the "greater than" operator, which returns the value true if the expression on its left has a greater value than the expression on its right; otherwise, it returns the value false. Also see operator > in the index.

[is the left square bracket; see *square brackets* for usage.

] is the right square bracket; see *square brackets* for usage.

{ is the left curly brace; see *curly braces* for usage.

} is the right curly brace; see *curly braces* for usage.

!= is the "not equals" operator, which returns the value true if the expression on its left has a value different from the expression on its right; otherwise, it returns the value false. Also see operator != in the index.

&& is the "logical AND" operator. It produces the result true if both of the expressions on its right and left are true; if either of those expressions is false, it produces the result false. However, this isn't the whole story. There is a special rule in C++ governing the execution of the && operator: If the expression on the left is false, then the answer must be false and the expression on the right is not executed at all. The reason for this *short-circuit evaluation* rule is that in some cases you may want to write a right-hand expression that will only be legal if the left-hand expression is false.

++ is the *increment* operator, which adds 1 to the variable to which it is affixed.

+= is the *add to variable* operator, which adds the value on its right to the variable on its left.

-= is the *subtract from variable* operator, which subtracts the value on its right from the variable on its left.

// is the comment operator; see *comment* for usage.

<< is the "stream output" operator, used to write data to an ostream. Also see operator << in the index.

<= is the "less than or equal to" operator, which returns the value true if the expression on its left has the same value or a lower value than the expression on its right; otherwise, it returns the value false. Also see operator <= in the index.

== is the "equals" operator, which returns the value true if the expression on its left has the same value as the expression on its right; otherwise, it returns the value false. Also see operator == in the index.

>= is the "greater than or equal to" operator, which returns the value true if the expression on its left has the same value or a greater value than the expression on its right; otherwise, it returns the value false. Also see operator >= in the index.

>> is the "stream input" operator, used to read data from an istream. Also see operator >> in the index.

[ ] is used after the delete operator to tell the compiler that the *pointer* for which delete was called refers to a group of elements rather than just one data item. This is one of the few times when we have to make that distinction explicitly, rather than leaving it to context.

|| is the "logical OR" operator. It produces the result true if at least one of the two expressions on its right and left is true; if both of those expressions are false, it produces the result false. However, this isn't the whole story. There is a special rule in C++ governing the execution of the || operator: If the expression on the left is true, then the answer must be true and the expression on the right is not executed at all. The reason for this *short-circuit evaluation* rule is that in some cases you may want to write a right-hand expression that will only be legal if the left-hand expression is true.

A **#include statement** has the same effect as copying all of the code from a specified file into another file at the point where the #include statement is written. For example, if we wanted to use definitions contained in a file called iostream.h in the implementation file test.cc, we could insert the include statement #include <iostream.h> in test.cc rather than physically copying the lines from the file iostream.h into test.cc.

A

An **access specifier** controls the access of nonmember functions to the member functions and variables of a class. The C++ access specifiers are public, private, and protected. See public, private, and protected for details. Also see friend.

Access time is a measure of how long it takes to retrieve data from a storage device, such as a hard disk or *RAM*.

Address; see *memory address*.

An **algorithm** is a set of precisely defined steps guaranteed to arrive at an answer to a problem or set of problems. As this implies, a set of steps that might never end is *not* an algorithm.

An **application program** is a program that actually accomplishes some useful or interesting task. Examples include inventory control, payroll, and game programs.

An **application programmer** (or *user*) is a programmer who uses native and class variables to write an application program. Also see *library designer*.

An **argument** is a value that is supplied by one function (the *calling function*) that wishes to make use of the services of another function (the *called function*). There are two main types of *arguments*: *value arguments*, which are copies of the values from the *calling function*, and *reference arguments*, which are not copies but actually refer to *variables* in the calling function.

An **argument list** is a set of *argument* definitions specified in a *function declaration*. The argument list describes the types and names of all the *variables* that the *function* receives when it is called by a *calling function*.

An **array** is a group of *elements* of the same type; for example, we can create an array of chars. The array name corresponds to the address of the first of these elements; the other elements follow the first one immediately in memory. As with a vector, we can refer to the individual elements by their indexes. Thus, if we have an array of chars called m_Data, m_Data[i] refers to the ith char in the array. Also see *pointer*.

The **ASCII code** is a standardized representation of characters by binary or hexadecimal values. For example, the letter *A* is represented as a char with the *hexadecimal* value 41, and the digit *0* is represented as a char with the *hexadecimal* value 30. All other printable characters also have representations in the ASCII code.

An **assembler** is a program that translates *assembly language* instructions into *machine instructions*.

An **assembly language** instruction is the human-readable representation of a *machine instruction*.

Assignment is the operation of setting a *variable* to a value. The operator that indicates assignment is the equal sign, =.

An **assignment operator** is a function that sets a preexisting variable to a value of the same type. There are three varieties of assignment operators:

1. For a variable of a native type, the compiler supplies a native assignment operator.
2. For a variable of a class type, the compiler will generate its own version of an assignment operator (a *compiler-generated* assignment operator), if the class writer does not write one.
3. The class writer can write a *member function* to do the assignment; see operator = in the index.

An **assignment statement** such as x = 5; is *not* an algebraic equality, no matter how much it may resemble one. It is a command telling the compiler to assign a value to a variable. In the example, the variable is x and the value is 5.

The **auto storage class** is the default storage class for *variables* declared within C++ *functions*. When we define a variable of the auto storage class, its *memory address* is assigned *auto*matically upon entry to the function where it is defined; the memory address is valid for the duration of that function.

B

Base class: see *inheritance*.

A **base class initializer** specifies which base class constructor we want to use to initialize the base class part of a *derived* class object. It is one of the two types of expressions allowed in a *member initialization list*. Also see *inheritance*.

The **base class part** of a *derived* class object is an unnamed component of the derived class object whose member variables and functions are accessible as though they were defined in the derived class, so long as they are either public or protected.

A **binary** number system uses only two digits, 0 and 1.

A **bit** is the fundamental unit of storage in a modern computer; the word *bit* is derived from the phrase *bi*nary digi*t*. Each bit, as this suggests, can have one of two states: 0 and 1.

A **block** is a group of *statements* that are considered one logical statement. A block is delimited by the "curly braces", { and }. The first of these symbols starts a block, and the second one ends the block. A block can be used anywhere that a statement can be used and is treated in exactly the same way as if it were one statement. For example, if a block is the *controlled block* of an if statement, then all of the statements in the block are executed if the condition in the if is true and none is executed if the condition in the if is false.

A **bool** (short for *Boolean*) is a type of variable whose range of values is limited to true or false. This is the most appropriate return type for a function that uses its return value to report whether some condition exists, such as operator <. In that particular case, the return value true indicates that the first argument is less than the second, while false indicates that the first argument is not less than the second.

Brace; see *curly brace*s.

A **break statement** is a loop control device that interrupts processing of a *loop* whenever it is executed within the *controlled block* of a *loop control statement*. When a break statement is executed, the flow of control passes to the next statement after the end of the *controlled block*.

A **byte** is the unit in which data capacities are stated, whether in *RAM* or on a disk. In modern computers, a byte consists of eight *bits*.

C

A **C string** is a literal value representing a variable number of characters. An example is "This is a test.". C strings are surrounded by double quotes ("). Please note that this is *not* the same as a C++ string.

A **cache** is a small amount of fast memory where frequently used data is stored temporarily.

Call; see *function call* or call *instruction*.

A **call instruction** is an *assembly language* instruction that is used to implement a *function call*. It saves the *program counter* on the *stack*, and then transfers execution from the *calling function* to the *called function*.

A **called function** is a *function* that starts execution as the result of a *function call*. Normally, it will return to the *calling function* via a return *statement* when finished.

A **calling function** is a *function* that suspends execution as a result of a *function call*; the *called function* begins execution at the point of the function call.

A **char** is an *integer variable* type that can represent either one character of text or a small whole number. Both signed and unsigned chars are available for use as "really short" integer variables; a signed char can represent a number from −128 to +127, whereas an unsigned char can represent a number from 0 to 255.

 (In case you were wondering how to pronounce this term, the most common pronunciation has an *a* like the *a* in "married", while the *ch* sounds like *k*. Other pronunciations include the standard English pronunciation of "char", as in overcooking meat, and even "car", as in "automobile".)

A **char*** (pronounced "char star") is a *pointer* to (i.e., the *memory address* of) a char or the first of a group of chars.

Child class: see *inheritance*.

cin (pronounced "see in") is a predefined istream; it gets its characters from the keyboard.

A **class** is a user-defined type; for example, string is a class.

A **class implementation** tells the compiler how to implement the facilities defined in the class interface. A class implementation is usually found in a *implementation file*, which the compiler on the CD-ROM in the back of this book assumes has the extension .cc.

A **class interface** tells the user of the class what facilities the class provides by specifying the public member functions of the class. It also tells the compiler what data elements are included in objects of the class, but this is not logically part of the interface. A class interface is usually found in a *header file*; that is, one with the extension .h.

The **class membership** operator, ::, indicates which class a function belongs to. For example, the full name of the default constructor for the string class is string::string().

class scope describes the visibility of *member variables*; that is, those that are defined within a class. These *variables* can be accessed by any *member function* of that class; their accessibility to other *functions* is controlled by the *access specifier* in effect when they were defined in the class *interface*.

A **comment** is a note to yourself or another programmer; it is ignored by the compiler. The symbol // marks the beginning of a comment; the comment continues until the end of the line containing the //. For those of you with BASIC experience, this is just like REM (the "remark" keyword); anything after it on a line is ignored by the compiler.

Compilation is the process of translating *source code* into an *object program*, which is composed of *machine instructions* along with the data needed by those instructions. Virtually all of the *software* on your computer was created by this process.

A **compiler** is a program that performs the process of compilation.

A **compiler-generated** function is supplied by the compiler because the existence of that function is fundamental to the notion of a concrete data type. The compiler will automatically generate its own version of any of the following functions if they are not provided by the creator of the class: the *assignment operator*, the *copy constructor*, the *default constructor*, and the *destructor*.

Compile time means "while the compiler is compiling the source code of a program".

A **concrete data type** is a class whose objects behave like variables of native data types. That is, the class gives the compiler enough information that *objects* of that class can be created, copied, assigned, and automatically destroyed just as native variables are.

The keyword **const** has two distinct meanings as employed in this book. The first is as a modifier to an *argument* of a function. In this context, it means that we are promising not to modify the value of that argument in the function. An example of this use might be the function declaration string& operator = (const string& Str);.

The second use of const in this book is to define a data item similar to a *variable*, except that its value cannot be changed once it has been initialized. For this reason, it is mandatory to supply an initial value when creating a const. An example of this use is const short x = 5;.

A **constructor** is a *member function* that creates new *objects* of a (particular) class type. All constructors have the same name as the class for which they are constructors; for example, the constructors for the string class have the name string.

A **continuation expression** is the part of a for statement computed before every execution of the *controlled block*. The block controlled by the for will be executed if the result of the computation is true, but not if it is false. See for *statement* for an example.

A **controlled block** is a *block* under the control of a *loop control statement* or an if or else statement. The controlled block of a loop control statement can be executed a variable number of times, whereas the controlled block of an if or else statement is executed either once or not at all.

Controlled statement; see *controlled block.*

A **copy constructor** makes a new *object* with the same contents as an existing object of the same type.

cout (pronounced "see out") is a predefined ostream; characters sent to it are displayed on the screen.

CPU is an abbreviation for Central Processing Unit. This is the "active" part of your computer, which executes all the *machine instructions* that make the computer do useful work.

The **curly braces** { and } are used to surround a *block*. The *compiler* treats the *statements* in the block as one statement.

D

Data are the pieces of information that are operated on by programs. Originally, "data" was the plural of "datum"; however, the form "data" is now commonly used as both singular and plural.

A **debugger** is a program that controls the execution of another program, so that you can see what the latter program is doing. The

CD-ROM in the back of this book contains the gdb debugger, which works with the DJGPP compiler on the CD-ROM.

A **dedicated register** is a *register* such as the *stack pointer* whose usage is predefined, rather than being determined by the programmer. Compare with *general registers* such as eax.

A **default constructor** is a *member function* that is used to create an *object* when no initial value is specified for that object. For example, string::string() is the default constructor for the string class.

The **delete** operator is used to free memory that was previously used for *variables* of the *dynamic storage class*. This allows the memory no longer needed for those variables to be reused for other variables.

Derived class: see *inheritance*.

A **destructor** is a *member function* that cleans up when an *object* expires; for an object of the auto *storage class*, the destructor is called automatically at the end of the *function* where that object is defined.

A **digit** is one of the characters used in any positional numbering system to represent all numbers starting at 0 and ending at one less than the base of the numbering system. In the decimal system, there are ten digits, 0 through 9, and in the hexadecimal system there are sixteen digits, 0 through 9 and a through f.

A **double** is a type of *floating-point variable* that can represent a range of positive and negative numbers including fractional values. With most current C++ compilers including DJGPP, these numbers can vary from approximately 4.940656e−324 to approximately 1.79769e+308 (and 0), with approximately 16 digits of precision.

The **dynamic storage class** is used for *variables* whose size is not known until *run time*. Variables of this storage class are assigned *memory addresses* at the programmer's explicit request.

Dynamic type checking refers to the practice of checking the correct usage of *variables* of different types during execution of a program rather than during *compilation*; see *type system* for further discussion.

Dynamic typing means delaying the determination of the exact type of a variable until run time rather than fixing that type at compile time as in *static typing*. Please note that dynamic typing is not the same as *dynamic type checking*; C++ has the former but not the latter. See *type system* for further discussion.

E

An **element** is one of the *variables* that makes up a vector or an array.

The keyword **else** causes its *controlled block* to be executed if the condition in its matching *if* statement turns out to be false at run time.

An **empty stack** is a *stack* that currently contains no values.

Encapsulation is the concept of hiding the details of a class inside the implementation of that class rather than exposing them in the interface. This is one of the primary organizing principles that characterize object-oriented programming.

An **end user** is the person who actually uses an *application program* to perform some useful or interesting task. Also see *application programmer*, *library designer*.

Envelope class; see *manager/worker idiom*.

Executable; see *executable program*.

An **executable program** is a program in a form suitable for running on a computer; it is composed of *machine instructions* along with data needed by those instructions.

F

The keyword **false** is a predefined value, representing the result of a conditional expression whose condition is not satisfied. For example, in the conditional expression x < y, if x is not less than y, the result of the expression will be false. Also see bool.

A **fencepost error** is a logical error that causes a loop to be executed one more or one less time than the correct count. A common cause of this error is confusing the number of *elements* in a vector or *array*

with the *index* of the last *element*. The derivation of this term is by
analogy with the problem of calculating the number of fence sections
and fenceposts that you need for a given fence. For example, if you
have to put up a fence 100 feet long and each section of the fence is
10 feet long, how many sections of fence do you need? Obviously,
the answer is 10. Now, how many fenceposts do you need? 11. The
confusion caused by counting fenceposts when you should be
counting segments of the fence (and vice-versa) is the cause of a
fencepost error.

To return to a programming example, if you have a vector with 11
elements, the index of the last element is 10, not 11. Thus, confusing
the number of elements with the highest index has much the same
effect as the fencepost problem.

This sort of problem is also known, less colorfully, as an *off-by-
one* error.

Field; see *manipulator*.

A **float** is a type of *floating-point variable* that can represent a range
of positive and negative numbers including fractional values. With
most current C++ compilers including DJGPP, these numbers can
vary from approximately 1.401298e–45 to approximately
3.40282e+38 (and 0), with approximately 6 digits of precision.

A **floating-point variable** is a C++ approximation of a mathematical
"real number". Unlike mathematical real numbers, C++ floating-
point variables have a limited range and precision, depending on their
types. See the individual types float and double for details.

A **for statement** is a *loop control statement* that causes its *controlled
block* to be executed while a specified logical expression (the
continuation expression) is true. It also provides for a *starting
expression* to be executed before the first execution of the controlled
block, and a *modification expression* to be executed after every
execution of the controlled block. For example, in the for statement for
(i = 0; i < 10; i ++), the initialization expression is i = 0, the continuation
expression is i < 10, and the modification expression is i ++.

The keyword **friend** allows access by a specified class or *function* to
private or protected members of a particular class.

A **function** is a section of code having a name, optional *arguments*,
and a *return type*. The name makes it possible for one function to

start execution of another one via a *function call*; the arguments are used to provide input for the function, and the return type allows the function to provide output to its *calling function* when the return *statement* causes the calling function to resume execution. See Figure 5.2 for a diagram illustrating a function call and return.

A **function call** (or *call* for short) causes execution to be transferred temporarily from the current *function* (the *calling function*) to the one named in the function call (the *called function*). Normally, when a called function is finished with its task, it will return to the calling function, which will pick up execution at the statement after the function call.

A **function declaration** tells the compiler some vital statistics of the function: its name, its *arguments*, and its *return type*. Before we can use a *function*, the compiler must have already seen its function declaration. The most common way to arrange for this is to use a #include *statement* to insert the function declaration from the header file where it exists into our implementation file.

Function header; see *function declaration*.

Function overloading is the C++ facility that allows us to create more than one *function* with the same name. So long as all such functions have different *signatures*, we can write as many of them as we wish and the compiler will be able to figure out which one we mean.

G

A **general register** is a *register* whose usage is determined by the programmer, rather than being predefined as with *dedicated registers* such as the *stack pointer*. On an Intel CPU such as the 486 or Pentium, the 16-bit general registers are ax, bx, cx, dx, si, di, and bp; the 32-bit general registers are eax, ebx, ecx, edx, esi, edi, and ebp.

Global scope describes the visibility of *variables* that are defined outside any *function*; such variables can be accessed by code in any function. It also describes the visibility of *functions* that are defined outside any class.

H

Hardware refers to the physical components of a computer, the ones you can touch. Examples include the keyboard, the monitor, and the printer.

A **header file** is a file that contains class *interface* definitions and/or global *function declarations*. By convention, header files have the extension .h.

The **heap** is the area of memory where *variables* of the *dynamic storage class* store their data.

Hex is an abbreviation for *hexadecimal*.

A **hexadecimal** number system has 16 digits, 0–9 and a–f.

I

An **identifier** is a user-defined name; both *function* names and *variable* names are identifiers. Identifiers must not conflict with *keywords* such as if and for; for example, you cannot create a function or a variable with the name for.

An **if statement** is a *statement* that causes its *controlled block* to be executed if the *logical expression* specified in the if statement is true.

An **ifstream** (pronounced "i f stream") is a stream used for input from a file.

Implementation; see class *implementation*.

An **implementation file** contains source code statements that are turned into executable code by a compiler. In this book, implementation files have the extension *.cc*.

Include; see #include statement.

Inheritance is the definition of one class as a more specific version of another class that has been previously defined. The newly defined class is called the *derived* (or sometimes the *child*) class, while the previously defined class is called the *base* (or sometimes the *parent*) class. In this book, we use the terms *base* and *derived*. The derived class inherits all of the *member variables* and *regular member functions* from the base class. Inheritance is one of the primary organizing principles of object-oriented programming.

To **increment a variable** means to add 1 to its value. This can be done in C++ by using the increment operator, ++.

An **index** is an expression used to select one of a number of *elements* of a vector or an *array*. It is enclosed in *square brackets* ([ ]). For example, in the expression a[i+1], the index is the expression i+1.

An **index variable** is a *variable* used to hold an index into a vector or an *array*.

Initialization is the process of setting the initial value of a *variable* or const. It is very similar to *assignment* but is not identical. Initialization is done only when a variable or const is created, whereas a variable can be assigned to as many times as desired. A const, however, cannot be assigned to at all, so it must be initialized when it is created.

Input is the process of reading data into the computer from the outside world. A very commonly used source of input for simple programs is the keyboard.

Instruction; see *machine instruction*.

An **int** (short for *integer*) is a type of *integer variable*. While the C++ language definition requires only that an int be at least as long as a short and no longer than a long, with most current C++ compilers this type is usually equivalent to either a short or a long, depending on the compiler you are using. A 16-bit compiler such as Borland C++ 3.1 has 16-bit ints that are the same size as shorts. A 32-bit compiler such as DJGPP (the compiler on the CD-ROM that comes with this book) has 32-bit ints that are the same size as longs.

An **integer variable** is a C++ representation of a whole number. Unlike mathematical integers, C++ integers have a limited range, which varies depending on their types. See the individual types char, short, int, and long for details. The type bool is sometimes also considered an integer variable type.

Interface; see class *interface*.

I/O is an abbreviation for "input/output". This refers to the process of getting information into and out of the computer. See *input* and *output* for more details.

iostream.h is the name of the *header file* that tells the *compiler* how to compile code that uses predefined stream *variables* like cout and operators like <<.

An **istream** is a stream used for input. For example, cin is a predefined istream that reads characters from the keyboard.

K

A **keyword** is a word defined in the C++ language, such as if and for. It is illegal to define an *identifier* such as a *variable* or *function* name that conflicts with a keyword; for example, you cannot create a function or a variable with the name for.

L

Letter class; see *manager/worker idiom*.

A **library** (or library module) contains the *object code* generated from several *implementation files*, in a form that the *linker* can search when it needs to find general-purpose functions.

A **library designer** is a programmer who creates classes for *application programmers* to use in writing *application programs*.

The **linker** is a program that combines information from all of the *object files* for our program, along with some previously prepared files called *libraries*, to produce an *executable program*.

Linking is the process of creating an *executable program* from *object files* and *libraries*.

A **literal** value doesn't have a name, but represents itself in a literal manner. Some examples are 'x' (a char literal having the ASCII value that represents the letter *x*) and 5 (a numeric literal with the value 5).

Local scope describes the visibility of *variables* that are defined within a *function*; such variables can be accessed only by code in that function.[1]

A **logical expression** is an expression that takes on the value true or false, rather than a numeric value. Some examples of such expressions are x > y (which will be true if x has a greater value than y and false otherwise) and a == b (which will be true if a has the same value as b, and false otherwise). Also see bool.

A **long** is a type of *integer variable* that can represent a whole number. With most current C++ compilers, including DJGPP, a long occupies 4 bytes of storage and therefore can represent a number in either the range -2147483648 to 2147483647 (if signed) or the range 0 to 4294967295 (if unsigned).

A **loop** is a means of executing a *controlled block* a variable number of times, depending on some condition. The statement that controls the controlled block is called a *loop control statement*. This book covers the while and for loop control statements. See while and for for details.

A **loop control statement** is a *statement* that controls the *controlled block* in a *loop*.

M

Machine address; see *memory address*.

Machine code is the combination of *machine instructions* with the data used by those instructions. A synonym is *object code*.

---

1. In fact, a variable can be declared in any *block*, not just in a *function*. In that case, its scope is from the point where it is declared until the end of the block where it is defined. However, in this book all local variables have function scope, so this distinction is not critical here and omitting it simplifies the discussion.

A **machine instruction** is one of the fundamental operations that a *CPU* can perform. Some examples of these operations are addition, subtraction, or other arithmetic operations; other possibilities include operations that control what instruction will be executed next. All C++ programs must be converted into machine instructions before they can be executed by the *CPU*.

A **machine language** program is a program composed of *machine instructions*.

A **manipulator** is a member function of one of the iostreams classes that controls how output will be formatted without necessarily producing any output of its own. Manipulators operate on *fields*; a field could be defined as the result of one << operator.

The **manager/worker** idiom (also known as the envelope/letter idiom) is a mechanism that allows the effective type of an object to be determined at run-time without requiring the user of the object to be concerned with pointers. It is used to implement *polymorphic objects* in C++.

A **member function** is a *function* defined in a class interface. It is viewed as "belonging" to the class, which is the reason for the adjective *member*.

A **member initialization expression** is the preferred method of specifies how a member variable is to be initialized in a constructor. Also see *inheritance*.

A **member initialization list** specifies how member variables are to be initialized in a constructor. It includes two types of expressions: *base class initializers* and *member initialization expressions*. Also see *inheritance*.

A **member variable** is a *variable* defined in a class interface. It is viewed as "belonging" to the class, which is the reason for the adjective *member*.

Memberwise copy means to copy every *member variable* from the source *object* to the destination object. If we don't define our own *copy constructor* or *assignment operator* for a particular class, the *compiler-generated* versions will use memberwise copy.

A **memory address** is a unique number identifying a particular *byte* of *RAM*.

A **memory hierarchy** is the particular arrangement of the different kinds of storage devices in a given computer. The purpose of using various kinds of storage devices having different performance characteristics is to provide the best overall performance at the lowest cost. See Figure 2.2 for a sample memory hierarchy.

A **memory leak** is a programming error in which the programmer forgot to delete something that had been dynamically allocated. Such an error is very insidious, because the program appears to work correctly when tested casually. The usual way to find these errors is to notice that the program runs apparently correctly for a (possibly long) time and then fails due to running out of available memory.

A **modification expression** is the part of a for statement executed after every execution of the *controlled block*. It is often used to *increment* an *index variable* to refer to the next *element* of an *array* or a vector; see for *statement* for an example.

N

A **nanosecond** is one-billionth of a second.

A **native** data type is one that is defined in the C++ language, as opposed to a *user-defined* data type (class).

The **new** operator is used to allocate memory for *variables* of the *dynamic storage class*; these are usually variables whose storage requirements may not be known until the program is executing.

Nondisplay character; see *nonprinting* character.

A **nonmember function** is one that is not a member of a particular class being discussed, although it may be a *member function* of another class.

A **nonnumeric variable** is a *variable* that is not used in calculations like adding, multiplying, or subtracting. Such variables might represent names, addresses, telephone numbers, Social Security numbers, bank account numbers, or drivers license numbers. Note that just because something is called a *number* or even is composed entirely of the digits 0–9, does not make it a *numeric variable* by our standards; the question is how the item is used. No one adds, multiplies, or subtracts drivers license numbers, for example; they serve solely as identifiers and could just as easily have letters in them, as indeed some of them do.

A **nonprinting character** is used to control the format of our displayed or printed information, rather than to represent a particular letter, digit, or other special character. The *space* ( ) is one of the more important nonprinting characters.

A **null byte** is a byte with the value 0, commonly used to indicate the end of a *C string*. Note that this is not the same as the character '0', which is a normal printable character having the *ASCII* code 48.

A **null object** is an *object* of some (specified) class whose purpose is to indicate that a "real" object of that class does not exist, analogously to a *null pointer*. One common use for a null object is as a *return value* from a *member function* that is supposed to return an object with some specified properties but cannot find such an object. For example, a null StockItem object might be used to indicate that an item with a specified UPC cannot be found in the inventory of a store.

A **null pointer** is a *pointer* with the value 0. This value is particularly suited to indicate that a pointer isn't pointing to anything at the moment, due to some special treatment of zero-valued pointers built into the C++ language.

A **numeric variable** is a *variable* representing a quantity that can be expressed as a number, whether a whole number (an *integer variable*) or a number with a fractional part (a *floating-point variable*), and that can be used in calculations such as addition, subtraction, multiplication, or division. The integer variable types in C++ are char, short, int, and long. Each of these integer types can be further subdivided into signed and unsigned versions. The former of these can represent both negative and positive values (and 0), whereas the latter can represent only positive values (and 0) but provides a greater range of positive values than the corresponding signed version does.

The floating-point variable types are float and double, which differ in their range and precision. Unlike the integer variable types, the floating-point types are not divided into signed and unsigned versions;

all floating-point variables can represent either positive or negative numbers as well as 0. See float and double for details on range and precision.

O

An **object** is a *variable* of a class type, as distinct from a *variable* of a *native* type. The behavior of an object is defined by the code that implements the class to which the object belongs. For example, a variable of type string is an object whose behavior is controlled by the definition of the string class.

Object code; see *machine code*. This term is unrelated to C++ *objects*.

An **object code module** is the result of compiling a *implementation file* into *object code*. A number of object code modules are combined to form an *executable program*. This term is unrelated to C++ *objects*.

Object file; see *object code module*. This term is unrelated to C++ *objects*.

Object-oriented programming is an approach to solving programming problems by creating *objects* to represent the entities being handled by the program, rather than relying solely on *native* data types. This approach has the advantage that you can match the language to the needs of the problem you're trying to solve. For example, if you were writing a nurse's station program in C++, you would want to have objects that represented nurses, doctors, patients, various sorts of equipment, and so on. Each of these objects would display the behavior appropriate to the thing or person it was representing.

Off-by-one error; see *fencepost error*.

An **ofstream** (pronounced "o f stream") is a stream used for output to a file.

An **op code** is the part of a *machine instruction* that tells the *CPU* what kind of instruction it is and sometimes also specifies a *register* to be operated on.

An **operating system** is a program that deals with the actual hardware of your computer. It supplies the lowest level of the software infrastructure needed to run a program. By far the most common operating system for Intel CPUs, at present, is MS-DOS (which is also the basis for Windows 95), followed by OS/2 and Windows NT.

The keyword **operator** is used to indicate that the following symbol is the name of a C++ operator that we are redefining, either globally or for a particular class. For example, to redefine =, we have to specify operator = as the name of the function we are writing, rather than just =, so that the *compiler* does not object to seeing an operator when it expects an *identifier*.

An **ostream** is a stream used for output. For example, cout is a predefined ostream that displays characters on the screen.

Output is the process of sending data from the computer to the outside world. The most commonly used source of output for most programs is the screen.

A member function in a derived class is said to **override** the base class member function if the derived class function has the same *signature* (name and argument types) as the base class member function. The derived class member function will be called instead of the base class member function when the member function is referred to via an object of the derived class.

A member function in a derived class with the same name but a different signature from a member function in the base class does *not* override the base class member function. Instead, it "hides" that base class member function, which is no longer accessible as a member function in the derived class.

P

Parent class; see *inheritance*.

A **pointer** is essentially the same as a *memory address*. The main difference between these two concepts is that a memory address is "untyped" (i.e., it can refer to any sort of *variable*), but a pointer always has an associated data type. For example, char* (pronounced "char star") means "pointer to a char".

To say "a variable points to a memory location" is almost exactly the same as saying "a variable's value is the address of a memory location". In the specific case of a variable of type char*, to say "the char* x points to a C string" is equivalent to saying "x contains the address of the first byte of the C string". Also see *array*.

A **polymorphic object** is a C++ object that presents the appearance of a simple object that behaves polymorphically without the hazards of exposing pointers to the user of the polymorphic object. The user does not have to know about any of the details of the implementation, but merely instantiates an object of the single visible class (the *manager* class). That object does what the user wants with the help of an object of a *worker* class, which is derived from the *manager* class. Also see *manager/worker idiom*.

Polymorphism is the major organizing principle in C++ that allows us to implement several classes with the same interface and treat objects of all these classes as though they were of the same class. This is the C++ mechanism for *dynamic typing*. The word *polymorphism* is derived from the Greek words *poly*, meaning "many", and *morph*, meaning "form". In other words, the same behavior is implemented in different forms.

Pop means to remove the top value from a *stack*.

The keyword **private** is an *access specifier* that denies *nonmember functions* access to *member functions* and *member variables* of its class.

A **program** is a set of instructions specifying the solution to a set of problems, along with the data used by those instructions.

The **program counter** is a *dedicated register* that holds the address of the next instruction to be executed. During a *function call*, a call *instruction* pushes the contents of the program counter on the *stack*. This enables the *called function* to return to the *calling function* when finished.

Programming is the art and science of solving problems by the following procedure:

1. Find or invent a general solution to a set of problems.
2. Express this solution as an *algorithm* or set of algorithms.

3. Translate the algorithm(s) into terms so simple that a stupid machine like a computer can follow them to calculate the specific answer for any specific problem in the set.

Warning: This definition may be somewhat misleading since it implies that the development of a program is straightforward and linear, with no revision. This is known as the "waterfall model" of programming, since water going over a waterfall follows a preordained course in one direction. However, real-life programming doesn't usually work this way; rather, most programs are written in an incremental process as assumptions are changed and errors are found and corrected.

The keyword **protected** is an *access specifier*. When present in a base class definition, it allows derived class functions access to member variables and functions in the base class part of a derived class object, while preventing access by other functions outside the base class.

The keyword **public** is an *access specifier* that allows *nonmember functions* access to *member functions* and *member variables* of its class.

Specifying **public inheritance** means that we are going to let outside functions treat an object of the derived class as an object of the base class. That is, any function that takes a base class object as a parameter will accept a derived class object in its place. All of the public member functions and public data items (if there are any) in the base class are accessible in a derived class object as well.

Push means to add another value to a *stack*.

A **put** pointer holds the address of the next byte in the output area of an ostream; i.e., where the next byte will be stored if we use << to write data into the stream.

R

RAM is an acronym for Random Access Memory. This is the working storage of a computer, where data and programs are stored while we're using them.

A **reference argument** is another name for a *variable* from a *calling function*, rather than an independent variable in the *called function*. Changing a reference argument therefore affects the corresponding *variable* in the calling function. Compare with *value argument*.

The **reference-counting** idiom is a mechanism that allows one object (the "reference-counted object") to be shared by several other objects (the "client objects") rather than requiring a copy to be made for each of the client objects.

A **register** is a storage area that is on the same chip as the *CPU* itself. Programs use registers to hold data items that are actively in use; data in registers can be accessed within the time allocated to instruction execution, rather than the much longer times needed to access data in *RAM*.

A **regular member function** is any *member function* that is not in any of the following categories:
1. *Constructor*
2. *Destructor*
3. The *assignment operator*, operator =.
   A *derived* class inherits all regular member functions from its *base* class.

A **retrieval function** is a *function* that retrieves data, which may have been previously stored by a *storage function* or may be generated when needed by some other method such as calculation according to a formula.

A **return address** is the *memory address* of the next *machine instruction* in a *calling function*. It is used during execution of a return *statement* in a *called function* to transfer execution back to the correct place in the calling function.

A **return statement** is used by a *called function* to transfer execution back to the *calling function*. The return statement can also specify a value of the correct *return type* for the called function. This value is made available to the calling function to be used for further calculation. An example of a return statement is return 0;, which returns the value 0 to the calling function.

A **return type** tells the *compiler* what sort of data a *called function* returns to the *calling function* when the called function finishes executing. The *return value* from main is a special case; it can be used to determine what action a batch file should take next.

ROM is an abbreviation for Read-Only Memory. This is the permanent internal storage of a computer, where the programs needed to start up the computer are stored. As this suggests, ROM does not lose its contents when the power is turned off, as contrasted with *RAM*.

Run time means "while a (previously compiled) program is being executed".

S

A **scalar variable** has a single value (at any one time); this is contrasted with a vector or an *array*, which contains a number of values each of which is referred to by its *index*.

The **scope** of a *variable* is the part of the program in which the variable can be accessed. The scopes with which we are concerned are *local*, *global*, and class; see *local scope*, *global scope*, and class *scope* for more details.

A **selection sort** is a sorting algorithm that selects the highest (or lowest) *element* from a set of elements (the "input list") and moves that selected element to another set of elements (the "output list"). The next highest (or lowest) element is then treated in the same manner; this operation is repeated until as many elements as desired have been moved to the output list.

A **short** is a type of *integer variable* that can represent a whole number. With most current C++ compilers including DJGPP, a short occupies 2 bytes of storage and therefore can represent a number in either the range -32768 to 32767 (if signed) or the range 0 to 65535 (if unsigned).

The **short-circuit evaluation rule** governs the execution of the || and the && operators. See || and && for details.

A **side effect** is any result of calling a *function* that persists beyond the execution of that function, other than its returning a *return value*. For example, writing data to a file is a side effect.

The **signature** of a *function* consists of its name and the types of its *arguments*. In the case of a *member function*, the class to which the function belongs is also part of its signature. Every function is uniquely identified by its signature, which is what makes it possible to have more than one function with the same name; this is called *function overloading*.

A **signed char** is a type of *integer variable*. See char for details.

A **signed int** is a type of *integer variable*. See int for details.

A **signed long** is a type of *integer variable*. See long for details.

A **signed short** is a type of *integer variable*. See short for details.

A **signed variable** can represent either negative or positive values. See char, short, int, or long for details.

Software refers to the nonphysical components of a computer, the ones you cannot touch. If you can install it on your hard disk, it's software. Examples include a spreadsheet, a word processor, and a database program.

Source code is a program in a form suitable for reading and writing by a human being.

Source code file; see *implementation file*.

Source code module; see *implementation file*.

The **space** character ( ) is one of the *nonprinting characters* (or *nondisplay characters*) that controls the format of displayed or printed information.

The **square brackets**, [and], are used to enclose an *array* or vector *index*, which selects an individual *element* of the *array* or vector. Also see [].

A **stack** is a data structure with characteristics similar to a spring-loaded plate holder such as you might see in a cafeteria. The last plate deposited on the stack of plates will be the first one to be removed when a customer needs a fresh plate; similarly, the last value deposited (*pushed*) onto a stack is the first value retrieved (*popped*).

The **stack pointer** is a *dedicated register*. The stack pointer is used to keep track of the address of the most recently *pushed* value on the *stack*.

A **starting expression** is the part of a for statement that is executed once before the *controlled block* of the for statement is first executed. It is often used to initialize an *index variable* to 0, so that the index variable can be used to refer to the first element of an *array* or vector. See for *statement* for an example.

A **statement** is a complete operation understood by the C++ compiler. Each statement is ended with a semicolon (;).

A **static member function** is a member function of a class that can be called without reference to an object of that class. Such a function has no this pointer passed to it on entry, and therefore cannot refer to member variables of the class.

The **static storage class** is the simplest of the three *storage classes* in C++; *variables* of this storage class are assigned *memory addresses* in the *executable program* when the program is *linked*.

Static type checking refers to the practice of checking the correct usage of variables of different types during compilation of a program rather than during execution. C++ uses static type checking. See *type system* for further discussion. Note that this has no particular relation to the keyword static.

Static typing means determining the exact type of a variable when the program is compiled. It is the default typing mechanism in C++. Note that this has no particular relation to the keyword static, nor is it exactly the same as *static type checking*. See *type system* for further discussion.

Stepwise refinement is the process of developing an *algorithm* by starting out with a "coarse" solution and "refining" it until the steps are within the capability of the C++ language.

Storage; synonym for *memory*.

A **storage class** is the characteristic of a *variable* that determines how and when a *memory address* is assigned to that variable. C++ has three different storage classes: static, auto, and *dynamic*. Please note that the term *storage class* has nothing to do with the C++ term class. See static storage class, auto storage class, and *dynamic* storage class for more details.

A **storage function** is a *function* that stores data for later retrieval by a *retrieval function*.

A **stream** is a place to put (in the case of an ostream) or get (in the case of an istream) characters. Some predefined streams are cin and cout.

A **stream buffer** is the area of memory where the characters put into the stream are stored.

The **string class** defines a type of *object* that contains a group of chars; the chars in a string can be treated as one unit for purposes of *assignment*, *I/O*, and comparison.

T

Temporary; see *temporary variable*.

A **temporary variable** is automatically created by the *compiler* for use during a particular operation, such as a *function call* with an *argument* that has to be converted to a different type.

The keyword **this** represents a hidden *argument* automatically supplied by the compiler in every *member function* call. Its value during the execution of any member function is the address of the class object for which the member function call was made.

A **token** is a part of a program that the *compiler* treats as a separate unit. It's analogous to a word in English; a *statement* is more like a sentence. For example, string is a token, as are :: and (. On the other hand, x = 5; is a statement.

The keyword **true** is a predefined value representing the result of a conditional expression whose condition is satisfied. For example, in the conditional expression x < y, if x is less than y the result of the expression will be true.

The **type** of an *object* is the class to which it belongs. The type of a native *variable* is one of the predefined variable types in C++. See *integer variable*, *floating-point variable*, and bool for details on the native types.

The **type system** refers to the set of rules that the compiler uses to decide how a variable of a given *type* may legally be employed. In C++, these determinations are made by the compiler (*static type checking*). This makes it easier to prevent type errors than it is in languages where type checking is done during execution of the program (*dynamic type checking*).

Please note that C++ has both *static type checking* and *dynamic typing*. This is possible because the set of types that is acceptable in any given situation can be determined at compile time, even though the exact type of a given variable may not be known until run time.

U

An **uninitialized variable** is one that has never been set to a known value. Attempting to use such a *variable* is a logical error that can cause a program to act very oddly.

An **unqualified name** is a reference to a *member variable* that doesn't specify which *object* the member variable belongs to. When we use an unqualified name in a *member function*, the compiler assumes that the object we are referring to is the object for which that member function has been called.

An **unsigned char** is a type of *integer variable*. See char for details.

An **unsigned int** is a type of *integer variable*. See int for details.

An **unsigned long** is a type of *integer variable*. See long for details.

An **unsigned short** is a type of *integer variable*. See short for details.

An **unsigned variable** is an *integer variable* that represents only positive values (and 0). See char, short, int, and long for details.

The term **user** has several meanings in programming. The primary usage in this book is *application programmer*. However, it can also mean *library designer* (in the phrase *user-defined data type*) or even *end user*.

A **user-defined** data type is one that is defined by the user. In this context, *user* means "someone using language facilities to extend the range of variable types in the language", i.e., *library designer*. The primary mechanism used to define a user-defined type is the class.

V

A **value argument** is a *variable* of *local scope* created when a *function* begins execution. Its initial value is set to the value of the corresponding *argument* in the *calling function*. Changing a value argument does not affect any variable in the calling function. Compare with *reference argument*.

A **variable** is a programming construct that uses a certain part of *RAM* to represent a specific item of data that we wish to keep track of in a program. Some examples are the weight of a pumpkin or the number of cartons of milk in the inventory of a store.

A **vector** is a group of *variables* that can be addressed by their position in the group; each of these variables is called an *element*. A vector has a name, just as a regular variable does, but the elements do not. Instead, each element has an *index* which represents its position in the vector.

Declaring a function to be **virtual** means that it is a member of a set of *functions* having the same *signatures* and belonging to classes related by *inheritance*. The actual function to be executed as the result of a given *function call* is selected from the set dynamically (i.e., at run time) based on the actual type of an *object* referred to via a base class pointer (or base class reference). This is the C++ mechanism used to implement *dynamic typing*, in contrast to the *static typing* used for non-virtual functions.

A **void** return type specifier in a *function* declaration indicates that the function in question does not return any value when it finishes executing.

The term **vtable** is an abbreviation for "virtual *function* address table". This is the table where the addresses of all of the virtual *functions* for a given class are stored; every object of that class contains the address of the vtable for that class.

W

A **while statement** is a *loop control statement* that causes its *controlled block* to be executed while a specified logical expression is true.

Z

Zero-based indexing refers to the practice of numbering the *elements* of an *array* or vector starting at 0 rather than 1.

Index

About the CD-ROM

Compiler setup instructions

Here are the instructions on setting up the DJGPP compiler from the CD-ROM in the back of this book. They will work DOS, as well as for DOS sessions under Windows 3.1 and Windows 95, but haven't been tested with other operating syste such as OS/2. If you don't have a printed copy of these instructions, you should print them out first.

If you want to copy the compiler from the CD-ROM to your hard disk (recommended, if you have at least 20 MB free), st with step 1. You can also install the compiler so that it will run from the CD-ROM without copying it to your hard di However, if you set up the compiler to run from the CD-ROM, the CD-ROM drive will be in your path. That means t you'll get "invalid path" messages any time that drive does not have a CD-ROM in it. If you still want to do this, start w step 2.

1. To copy the compiler from the CD-ROM to your hard disk: (Warning: the compiler requires approximately 20 MB of d space!)

a. Make a directory on your hard disk, say c:\djgpp

b. Use XCOPY to copy all the files in the CD-ROM directory \djgpp and below to your hard disk. If your CD-ROM drive drive d: and you want to install to c:\djgpp, then you can type:

xcopy d:\djgpp c:\djgpp /s

Make sure that the letter of your CD-ROM is the same as the first drive letter in the xcopy line (d: in the example), and letter of the drive where you want to install the files is the same as the second drive letter in the xcopy line (c: in example).

c. Add the following lines to the end of your "autoexec.bat" file, (but before the "win" line if you are running Windows 3. These lines assume that you want to use c: to hold temporary files, and that you have installed the compiler on drive C. M: sure that the drive letter in the line "setdjgpprun=c:" matches the drive letter where you have installed the compiler in step (To save typing, you might want to cut and paste them from this file, which is \readme.txt on the CD-ROM).

set djgpptmp=c:
set djgpprun=c:
set DJGPP=%djgpprun%\DJGPP\DJGPP.ENV
set PATH=%djgpprun%\DJGPP\BIN;%PATH%
call setdjgpp %djgpprun%\djgpp %djgpprun%/djgpp

If you are running Windows 95 and don't have an autoexec.bat, you can create one and put the above lines in it. Alternative you can create a batch file that you can call "setdos.bat" (for example), containing the entries from the "readme.txt" file t would go into autoexec.bat if you were running DOS and put it in whatever directory you like, like "c:\util". Then right-cl on your "MS-DOS Prompt" icon, and select "Properties" and then the "Program" tab. Type the full name of that batch ("c:\util\setdos.bat") into the "Batch file" entry in that dialog box, and it will be executed whenever you start an MS-D session through that icon.

d. Under Windows 95, skip to step 3. Otherwise, make sure that your "config.sys" file contains lines that look like following:

DEVICE=C:\DOS\HIMEM.SYS
DOS=HIGH
FILES=30
lastdrive=z

1. To copy the sample files to your hard disk, change to the root directory on the CD-ROM and run the batch file "copysamp", supplying a parameter to indicate where you want the sample files to go. For example, if you want the sample files to be placed under the directory "c:\introcpp", type:

```
d:
cd\
copysamp c:\introcpp
```

2. Now you can compile any of the sample programs by changing to the directory "c:\introcpp\normal" and running the batch file "mk.bat", giving the name of the sample program as a parameter. For example, to compile "itemtst1", type

```
mk itemtst1
```

The compiled version will be placed in the "\introcpp\normal" directory. You can execute it by typing its name at the DOS prompt. For example, to run "itemtst1", type

```
itemtst1
```

The results of running itemtst1 should look like this:

```
Name: Chunky Chicken
Number in stock: 32
Price: 129
Distributor: Bob's Distribution
UPC: 123456789
```

Writing and compiling your own programs

Change to the "\introcpp\code" directory on the drive where you installed the compiler.

Use EDIT or Notepad to create a text file containing the source code for your program, giving it the extension ".cc". In other words, if you want your program to be called "party", then name this file "party.cc".

To compile your program, switch to the "\introcpp\normal" directory and type "mk party", substituting the name of your file for "party". Note: do *not* add the ".cc" to the end of the file name.

To run your program normally, make sure you are in the "\introcpp\normal" directory, and then type the name of the program, without the extension. In this case, you would just type "party".

To run your program under the debugger, make sure you are in the "\introcpp\normal" directory, and then type "trace party" (substituting the name of your program for "party"). Again, do *not* add the ".cc" to the end of the file name. Instructions for using the debugger can be found in the text.

Other assistance

If you have any problems setting up the compiler or compiling the sample code, or have any other questions, you might want to check my web page for updates to the instructions or sample code. That address is:

http://ourworld.compuserve.com/homepages/steve_heller

If "config.sys" already has lines in it containing "himem.sys", "dos=high", "files=nn" (when nn is at least 30) and "lastdrive=z", don't add the lines above. Also note that "himem.sys" may be in a different directory than "c:\dos"; if so, make sure that line refers to the directory where "himem.sys" actually is.

e. Go to step 3

2. If you prefer to run the compiler from the CD-ROM instead of copying it to your hard disk, assuming that your CD-ROM is drive d: and that you want to use c: to hold temporary files:

a. Add the following lines to the end of your "autoexec.bat" file (but before the "win" line if you are running Windows 3.1). If you are running Windows 95 and don't have an autoexec.bat, you can create one and put these lines in it, or you can follow the procedure under 1c above to create a startup batch file for use when running a DOS session. (To save typing, you might want to cut and paste them from this file, which is \readme.txt on the CD-ROM).

```
set djgpptmp=c:
set djgpprun=d:
set DJGPP=%djgpprun%\DJGPP\DJGPP.ENV
set PATH=%djgpprun%\DJGPP\BIN;%PATH%
call setdjgpp %djgpprun%\djgpp %djgpprun%/djgpp
```

Make sure to set the drive letter in the line "set djgpprun=d:" to the letter of your CD-ROM drive.

b. Under Windows 95, skip to step 3. Otherwise, make sure that your "config.sys" file contains lines that look like the following:

```
DEVICE=C:\DOS\HIMEM.SYS
DOS=HIGH
FILES=30
lastdrive=z
```

If "config.sys" already has lines in it containing "himem.sys", "dos=high", "files=nn" (when nn is at least 30) an "lastdrive=z", don't add the lines above. Also note that "himem.sys" may be in a different directory than "c:\dos"; if so, mak sure that line refers to the directory where "himem.sys" actually is.

3. After making either of the above sets of changes, reboot so that they will take effect.

4. To check whether the compiler has been set up correctly, run the go32-v2.exe program by typing the following comma at a DOS prompt:

go32-v2

The last two lines of its output should report how much DPMI memory and swap space DJGPP can use on your system, li this:

```
DPMI memory available: 8020 Kb
DPMI swap space available: 240 Kb
```

If you don't get output that looks like this, with the exception of different numbers, check that you've followed instructions exactly.

Copying and compiling the sample programs

After you have set up the compiler as shown above, you should copy the sample programs to your hard disk. They are in directory d:\introcpp\code (assuming that your CD-ROM is drive d:).